WILLIAM Z. FOSTER AND THE
TRAGEDY OF AMERICAN RADICALISM

The Working Class in American History

Editorial Advisors
David Brody
Alice Kessler-Harris
David Montgomery
Sean Wilentz

A list of books in the series appears at the end of this book.

William Z. Foster and the Tragedy of American Radicalism

JAMES R. BARRETT

UNIVERSITY OF ILLINOIS PRESS
URBANA AND CHICAGO

Publication of this work was supported by a grant from the Oliver
M. Dickerson Fund. The fund was established by Mr. Dickerson
(Ph.D., Illinois, 1906) to enable the University of Illinois Press to
publish selected works in American history, designated by the
executive committee of the Department of History.

Library of Congress Cataloging-in-Publication Data
Barrett, James R., 1950–
William Z. Foster and the tragedy of American radicalism /
James R. Barrett.
p. cm.—(The working class in American history)
Includes bibliographical references and index.
ISBN 0-252-02046-4 (cloth : alk. paper)
1. Foster, William Z., 1881–1961.
2. Communists—United States—Biography.
3. Labor leaders—United States—Biography.
4. Radicalism—United States—History—20th century.
5. Trade-unions—United States—History—20th century.
6. Communism—United States—History—20th century.
7. Working class—United States—History—20th century.
I. Title. II. Series.
HX84.F6 B37   1999
331.88'092—dc21   99-6192
[B]   CIP

C   5   4   3   2   1

For Jenny and Sean

Contents

Preface

I ENCOUNTERED William Z. Foster early in my historical ramblings. It was his organizing among immigrant and African American workers during World War I that first captured my attention. The working class had its own geniuses, though they are seldom celebrated. Rather than orchestrate symphonies or corporate mergers, they worked their organizational miracles in the form of industrial unions, cooperatives, and political organizations. Foster seemed to be one of these rare individuals. Reared in the worst slum conditions and with little formal education, he demonstrated a real brilliance for organizing and strike strategy in what appeared to be hopeless situations. In his own sphere, Foster was every bit as cosmopolitan and sophisticated as the corporate strategists he loved to battle. As I surveyed the scope of twentieth-century labor history, particularly its radical dimensions, he seemed to be everywhere.

Quite apart from my interest in Foster as a person, I also believed that biography represented a curious gap in the renaissance of labor history scholarship that had mushroomed over the past two decades. Social historians may not agree with Frank Sulloway's argument that "history is biography writ large," but we have been turning to biography and the study of auto-biography and personal narrative in the past decade because the earlier methods of workplace and community studies failed to plumb the depths of workers' experiences. The right sort of biography, I thought, might allow us to integrate the classic problem of individual experience and development—the subjective dimension of history—with the usual concerns of social his-tory—social movements, communities, work, culture, and everyday life that have transformed our understanding of history. I was inspired by Nick Sal-vatore's brilliant biography of the American socialist Eugene V. Debs, and I hoped to write a comparable study of Foster.

I was convinced that Foster's story could tell us a great deal about Ameri-can labor radicalism in general and the Communist Party in the United States in particular. The history of American communism has become a growth industry recently. I hoped that Foster, arguably the key figure in the Party's rise and decline, might serve as a focal point for reinterpreting its history in the wake of numerous monographs, interpretive studies, and personal narra-tives. The questions raised and the important archival sources opened as a result of Glasnost and the political transformation of the former Soviet Union in the early 1990s encouraged me along these lines.

Two problems emerged amidst all of this dreaming, one practical, the other a deeper one deriving from Foster's own personality. In the first place, there was a severe shortage of sources on Foster's personal life. After a long search, I located his papers at the Russian Center for the Preservation and Study of Documents of Recent History (the old Central Party Archive) in Moscow, and I was able to flesh out some aspects of Foster's personal life with his scattered correspondence and other material from this collection. But even these sources, composed largely of book, article, and pamphlet manu-scripts and political ephemera, helped little in unlocking what Foster was like as a person. I have had to piece that part of the story together from inter-views, material in other archival collections, Foster's own autobiographical writing, and research relating to those movements he helped create.

As I worked on Foster's story and came to understand him a bit better, I recognized that the trouble with grasping his personal identity was part of a deeper problem. It would be difficult to analyze Foster's own development as distinct from that of the Communist Party and the other organizations he helped shape because his identity had *merged* with these movements. To put the matter another way, the paucity of personal material in what fol-lows reflects Foster's personality as much as a dearth of sources. He was a su-premely political person for whom personal details seemed to matter little.

He lacked the introspective quality that might have permitted a more intimate sort of biography. For Foster, life was politics, and politics was the class struggle. This characteristic led me in the direction of what might be termed a social and political biography, a study of the person in relation to the development of the movements and organizations he created and led. His personality became fused with his politics. It would be misleading to disengage the two, and I have not tried to do so.

As it happens, I have written this book at a very turbulent moment in the history of political radicalism and in the midst of a great deal of contention over the history of communism and the Communist Party in the United States in particular. This is not a coincidence. From the beginning, I hoped to say as much about American communism—its roots, development, and decline—as about Foster, and the recent collapse of world communism simply sharpens many of the questions I already had in mind about the relationship between American labor radicalism and international politics. Foster's own story has a great deal of significance for anyone interested in this relationship. While I continue to believe that it is impossible to understand such radicals as Foster without carefully reconstructing the indigenous roots of their politics, I am also convinced that some of the more recent histories of American communism have failed to gauge the significance of the international movement in shaping the lives of these radicals.

I started research on this project in the mid-1980s. Its publication has been slowed for a number of professional and personal reasons. In the meantime, Ed Johanningsmeier's excellent biography of Foster has appeared, drawing on many of the same sources with which I have worked for more than a decade. I have tried to indicate in my introduction some of the ways in which our interpretations differ, but I have chosen not to frame my own story of Foster as a rebuttal to Johanningsmeier. Any thoughtful reader of the two works will see important differences in method as well as interpretation.

Whatever the delays, this work might not have appeared at all without the support of many people. It is a pleasure to acknowledge some of them and to offer my thanks to all of them collectively.

Early in the research, I made a conscious decision not to rely heavily on oral testimony, but I am very grateful to those who did take the time to speak or correspond with me. A number of veterans of the Communist movement, some still in and others now outside its ranks, were kind enough to share with me their memories of Foster and the Party and to offer advice. In particular, I would like to acknowledge Sam Darcy, Arthur Zipser, Fritz Jennings, Martha Stone Asher, Carl Dorfman, and the late Steve Nelson. The late Gil Green was especially open and helpful. Sandra Epstein, whose father, Harry Epstein, served as Foster's personal physician, allowed me to use copies of her father's personal papers.

For reading all or parts of the manuscript in its various incarnations and offering many helpful comments and suggestions, I am grateful to Jenny Barrett; David Roediger; David Montgomery; Diane Koenker; Fraser Ottanelli and Bryan Palmer, both readers for the press; and the members of the University of Illinois Social History Group. David Brody offered encouragement toward the end of the writing. I especially thank Mark Leff for his generous support and friendship as well as his careful reading of the manuscript. Malcolm Sylvers and Kerby Miller shared some of their unpublished work with me.

Diane Koenker, Ed Johanningsmeier, John Haynes, and Harvey Klehr provided practical advice regarding the Russian archives. Dasha Lotoreva of the Historical Institute, Russian Academy of Sciences was extremely important to my work in Moscow, and I thank her heartily for all of her advice and good cheer.

For their research assistance, ideas, and inspiration, I gratefully acknowledge the efforts of my splendid students at the University of Illinois—Brian Garrett, Dan Soloff, Youn-jin Kim, Toby Higbie, Kathy Mapes, Caroline Waldron, Adam Stephanides, Val Littlefield, Ruth Fairbanks, Nicole Ranganath, Randi Storch, Adam Hodges, and Steve Hageman. Randi, Kathy, Caroline, and Nicole were especially helpful to me in checking and correcting endnote references. Adam Hodges helped with proofs and the index.

A University Scholar Award from the Chancellor's Office at the University of Illinois and grants from the National Endowment for the Humanities, the University of Illinois at Urbana-Champaign Research Board, and the International Research and Exchange Program helped a great deal with travel and expenses. I am particularly grateful for a fellowship at the University of Illinois Center for Advanced Study, which allowed me to begin the project, and for a Lloyd Lewis Fellowship at the Newberry Library, which allowed me to complete much of the writing. My colleagues at the Newberry Library, particularly Jan Reiff and Jim Grossman, made that a happy and productive year, as did Ciara Ottaviano by mail from Italy. Back at Illinois, Aprel Orwick organized my work life, and Kim Holland helped with some of the final typing of the manuscript. Joseph Kolko helped by supplying a photograph and also granted me permission to work with the William Z. Foster Papers in Moscow. My colleagues in the Department of History at the University of Illinois at Urbana-Champaign helped in numerous small ways, especially by leaving me alone on Thursdays, and provided a stimulating place to work.

My parents, Catherine and the late Tom Barrett; my parents in-law, Shew and Mary Wong; and my brothers and sisters and their spouses, Pat Fabsits, Tom Barrett and Janine Goldstein, Jack and Bonnie Barrett, and Mike and Teri Barrett; and Ed and Diana Wong hosted me on trips to Chicago, while Larry and Cathy Bussetti and colleagues at the Russian State Humanities University did the same during extended stays in New York City and Moscow.

Many professional librarians helped me locate and work with sources vital to my research. Those at the following institutions were particularly helpful: University of Illinois at Urbana-Champaign, Tamiment Library at New York University, Chicago Historical Society, New York Public Library, State Historical Society of Wisconsin, Woodruff Library of Emory University, Newberry Library, Hoover Institution at Stanford University, Columbia University Library, and the Russian Center for the Preservation and Study of Documents of Recent History in Moscow.

Early advice from David Montgomery and David Howell saved me from some publication mistakes. Dick Wentworth of the University of Illinois Press provided encouragement and stuck with the project. Jane Mohraz did a brilliant job editing the manuscript, saving me from countless errors.

As always, I owe the most to Jenny and Sean. Thanks to them for their understanding and sacrifices during my absences in Chicago and Moscow and for their love and support, humor and ideas. I am fortunate to have them in my life.

WILLIAM Z. FOSTER AND THE
TRAGEDY OF AMERICAN RADICALISM

Introduction

WILLIAM Z. FOSTER was the real article. A wage earner, native-born of immigrant stock, raised in the slums of a large industrial city, self-educated, toughened in the life of an unskilled transient laborer, he was what one historian has called "the archetypal proletarian of a Diego Rivera mural." As Theodore Draper has written, "He personified the American proletariat as few radical leaders have ever done."[1] If a revolutionary labor movement were to develop in the United States, people like Foster would build it. Whatever his failings as a politician or theorist, he shared a personal background and common experiences with the great mass of American workers. More than most historians have realized, his politics were shaped as much by these experiences and the character of class relations in the United States as by any particular organization or theory.

This is not to suggest that Foster was in any sense a "typical" American worker. Rather, he was a member of what he and other labor radicals often called the "militant minority," men and women who endeavored, as David Montgomery has written, "to weld their work mates and neighbors into a self-aware and purposeful working class." In the United States, as elsewhere, "class consciousness was more than the unmediated product of daily experience. It was also a project."[2] The key figures in this enterprise were people like Foster, indigenous worker radicals determined to build a revolutionary movement and to transform their society. Part of the attraction of Foster's story is that he was very much a product of American working-class life. A worker who became a revolutionary, he was in his element as he organized and agitated in industrial cities and towns and in mining and logging camps throughout the United States.

Yet when Foster's life ended in 1961, it was not at the head of a powerful American socialist movement but in a Moscow hospital, far from the urban slums, railroad yards, and steel mill towns where he had earned his reputation. Having helped create a radical labor movement in the years leading up to the Great Depression, Foster died in the shadow of the Kremlin, which symbolized his own isolation and that of American labor radicalism in the postwar era. He is central to the story of American radicalism in part, then, because his life and experiences encapsulate and exemplify the movement's social basis, its rise and ideological transformation during the early twentieth century and depression years, and its ultimate destruction in the era after World War II. We can follow the ebb and flow of various radical influences—socialism, syndicalism, and communism—through Foster's own ideological development and analyze them not in the abstract but in terms of how they were conceived of and practiced in the life of an American worker.

Foster's life reads like a chronicle of class conflict in the United States during the twentieth century. He grew up amidst labor's crushing defeats in the late nineteenth century. Active in the movement to build the American Federation of Labor (AFL) in the early years of this century, he was also central in the efforts to create a radical alternative to its conservative leadership. He joined first the Socialist Party and then the Industrial Workers of the World (IWW), finally making his way in a series of his own syndicalist movements. During the first great round of organizing in American basic industry during World War I, Foster proved himself a brilliant organizer and strike strategist, leading historic movements of unskilled workers in the meat-packing and steel industries. Won over to revolutionary communism through his experiences in the United States and by the spectacle of the world's first successful working-class revolution in Russia, Foster remained at the center of labor politics throughout the 1920s, organizing the Trade Union Educational League (TUEL) as a radical opposition group within the AFL.

Even Foster's increasing isolation from the mainstream of American working-class life from the late 1920s on can tell us a great deal about labor radicalism in the United States. In terms of appointments to the top leadership and longevity there, he was easily the most important of the Party's cadre up to his death.[3] Drawn into the factionalism of the American Communist movement, he focused increasingly on the ideological twists and turns of the Communist International. Foster's impact was greatly reduced after he suffered a major physical and personal crisis in the early thirties and the Comintern's decisions bolstered his rival Earl Browder. He regained his stature only when Browder's Popular Front line was decisively rejected at the end of World War II at the behest of the international movement rather than for domestic reasons. The subsequent decline of the Communist Party can be explained largely by government repression and the conservative political climate of the McCarthy period. But there is little doubt that the organization's own policies played a vital role in its disintegration or that Foster's voice was dominant in these years. With deep roots in the American labor movement, Foster nevertheless symbolized the triumph of dogmatism on the American left. Ever the disciplined revolutionary, he cut himself and his organization off from American working-class life. In this sense, his story is a left-wing tragedy.

That Foster was always at the center of American radicalism's history, shaping both its rise and decline, underscores the significance of his story for our understanding the broader phenomenon. It also raises important questions. What brought Foster and his generation of radicals to the Communist movement? In his excellent biography of the American socialist Eugene V. Debs, Nick Salvatore locates the roots of Debs's socialist commitment in a particular set of values and experiences common to many American skilled male workers during the late nineteenth century: radical republicanism, notions of self-help, manliness, and craft pride. Their world seemed threatened on all sides by the advance of industrial capitalism, and this crisis brought some of them to a new, more radical conception of American democracy.[4] Foster's attraction to socialism and his later adherence to syndicalism and then to revolutionary communism drew on very different values, reflecting the experiences of a generation of unskilled, often itinerant workers who came of age politically during World War I and the Russian Revolution. By exploring Foster's experiences in particular American work contexts and probing his political commitment as a worker and organizer in the American West and Midwest, we can begin to understand the basis for radicalism among twentieth-century American workers.

Foster's commitment evolved in the course of the early twentieth century. What can his journey from socialism, through syndicalism, to communism tell us about the relationships between these ideologies and the movements that promoted them? Perhaps because of the bitter sectarian conflicts among various elements of the American Left and the very real ideological divisions separating them, historians have tended to analyze the stories of American socialism, anarcho-syndicalism, and communism as distinct organizational histories.[5] One advantage of a biographical approach is that it suggests the ideological and experiential *links* between these movements and allows us to trace the evolution of radical thought over the course of an individual's lifetime. Such ideological development is seldom linear, and it certainly was not in Foster's case. Yet it is possible to discern relationships between his own personal experiences over time and particular political concepts as well as between the ideas and strategies of the different movements he helped build.

In *Forging American Communism: The Life of William Z. Foster,* Edward Johanningsmeier emphasizes the continuing influence of Foster's particular brand of syndicalism on his later career in the Communist Party. Perhaps even more than Johanningsmeier suggests, Foster's embrace of communism may be explained by the peculiar "fit" between his own belief that revolutionary prospects depended on the efforts of a radical elite "boring from within" the mainstream unions and Lenin's formulation of the united front strategy. This occurred in 1921 at the very moment Foster was searching for a new organizational vehicle for radicalizing the American labor movement. Much of Foster's subsequent behavior, certainly through the 1920s and to some extent even after that, can be understood in terms of these syndicalist tendencies. This emphasis on Foster's persistent syndicalism is not new, but Johanningsmeier certainly is correct that it is "impossible to understand Foster's career in the Communist party in isolation from his earlier radicalism."[6]

In emphasizing the roots of Foster's radicalism in a particular American working-class experience, I embrace the arguments of recent historians of American communism regarding the continuity between American communism and earlier forms of radicalism. In accounting for the failure of Foster's politics and by extension the failure of American communism, however, I emphasize more than some of these historians the significance of the international dimension, a significance that must be understood in broad social-historical terms as well as within the context of the Party's relationship with the Communist International and the Soviet Union.

In this regard, I differ from Johanningsmeier, who argues, "Once Foster's Communism is grounded in the history of modern American radicalism, the influence of the Comintern becomes less important in explaining his motivations. . . ."[7] On the contrary, the essence of Foster's radical experience lies precisely at the juncture between these two great influences in his life. Over and over, his own instincts and ideas were constrained and often distorted by the exigencies of international Communist politics, particularly from the mid-1920s on, as these became increasingly dominated by Soviet Party politics and Soviet policy considerations. As Foster's power waned and he became more detached from the mass movements of the late 1930s and 1940s, he seemed to become more fixed on the Soviet line and more rigid in his understanding and application of Marxism-Leninism.

It is this dimension of Foster's story, his embrace of what Johannings-meier calls "a logic of decline, isolation, and helplessness during the Cold War," that receives least attention in *Forging American Communism*.[8] To be fair, this is partially because the sources for the period following World War II were weaker. But Foster's distinctive role in the Party's decline is an element I emphasize here.

It is hardly surprising that part of the impulse for Foster's politics was international. Imperialism, the heterogeneous mass migrations of the early twentieth century, and the worldwide revolutionary ferment of the World War I era provided the economic, social, and political background for Foster's politics and gave his generation of radicals a perspective that was even more international than the old Socialist Party's. Foster's path from socialism and syndicalism to communism was one he shared with thousands of revolutionaries around the world. His ideas were not simply products of his experiences in the Pacific Northwest, Chicago, and Pittsburgh but also lessons drawn from the French, German, and British labor movements. This international dimension was all the more compelling, of course, in the case of the American Communist Party, which was so deeply influenced by the Comintern and the Soviet Communist Party.

These international relationships raise one of the most pressing questions facing historians of American communism. In what sense was this an *American* movement at all? How did foreign ideas, strategies, and personalities shape it? How did Stalinism and even the original formulation of Leninism shape Foster and the American Communist Party in ways that made it difficult for indigenous radicals to create a movement capable of transforming their society?

An older historiography, reflecting the preoccupations of the cold war, emphasized the crucial significance of international Marxism-Leninism and the decisive intervention of the Soviet Union in shaping American communism. "Whatever has changed from time to time, one thing has never changed," Theodore Draper wrote, "—the relationship of American Communism to Soviet Russia. This relation has expressed itself in different ways, sometimes glaring and strident, sometimes masked and muted. But it has always been the determining factor, the vital element." Given this conception of the movement, the approach in the older and in some of the newer, more conservative writing has naturally been political and institutional. Until recently, the focus has been on the Party's national leadership, particularly its relationship with the Comintern and the Communist Party of the Soviet Union. "Even when the party's tracks are clear and seemingly autonomous," Harvey Klehr wrote, "one must search for their Soviet sources." "Within the limits of their knowledge, American Communists always strove to provide what the Comintern wanted," Klehr concluded, "nothing more, nothing less." Individual American Communists and even human initiative and agency have virtually no role in these histories. Like other Communists around the world, the Americans functioned as cogs in the great Soviet machine. As Irving Howe and Lewis Coser concluded, the Party "reduced its members to the level of malleable objects."[9]

More recent works have invested American Communists with a good deal more agency. The new histories embrace social history's emphases on gender, ethnic, and racial difference and employ community and workplace case studies. Focusing primarily, and not coincidentally, on the Popular Front and World War II years when the Party's line was more flexible and its social and political base much broader, they aim to rewrite the movement's history from a very different perspective. The vision that has emerged, while often critical of particular policies, is at once fundamentally different and more sympathetic. Many of these studies describe a grass-roots movement shaped by local conditions and the ideas and actions of indigenous radicals more than by Moscow masters. Using the memoirs and personal narratives of Party leaders and more or less typical Communist activists, these historians have stressed the significance of local conditions and have portrayed a party rooted in the experiences of real people, an organization that could be quite flexible and even creative, one that had great potential for organizing mass democratic struggles and achieving important reforms.[10]

I have tried to keep both the indigenous domestic and the international perspectives in mind while reconstructing and interpreting William Z. Foster's career and what it can tell us about the history of American radicalism. We ignore either at the risk of misunderstanding Foster's worldview and the constraints within which he and other Communists thought and worked. Those activists associated most closely with Foster were proletarian veterans of countless free speech fights, organizing campaigns, and strikes. Many of them emerged from the IWW or the industrially oriented left wing of the Socialist Party. Like Foster's political experience, theirs was firmly rooted in the world of work and trade unions. Their commitment to such "practical" organizing shaped the Party, which was in this sense more the product of social conflict in the United States than most of the more conservative historians of American communism have been prepared to acknowledge.

There was, of course, another dimension of American communism and Foster's own political persona. From the day the Bolsheviks seized power through the final collapse of international communism, radicals throughout the world have set their eyes on Russia. It is difficult to understand *why* without first grasping the explosive departure that the Russian Revolution represented in the lives of working-class revolutionaries throughout the world. "For those whose political memories go back no farther than Khrushchev's denunciation of Stalin, or the Sino-Soviet split," Eric Hobsbawm wrote in the late 1960s, "it is almost impossible to conceive what the October revolution meant to those who are now middle-aged and old. It was the first proletarian revolution, . . . the proof both of the profundity of the contradictions of capitalism . . . and of the possibility—the *certainty*—that socialist revolution would succeed. It was the beginning of world revolution. It was the beginning of the new world."[11]

William Z. Foster put the matter rather more simply. "Once in awhile," he wrote from Russia in the summer of 1921, "one has an experience that can never be forgotten as long as life lasts. . . . It seemed as though I saw the soul of the revolution."[12] This vision was one that Foster carried with him throughout his life, constantly shaping and reshaping his experiences in situations and places throughout the United States. For those of us who have never experienced such a transformation, it is difficult to understand such people as Foster. They were won over not simply to Soviet authority but also to the Soviet ideal and to a model of disciplined Bolshevik politics they believed was the key to human liberation. For Foster and others, adhering to this discipline often meant suppressing more creative and flexible forms of politics based on personal experience and instincts. They were not naïve. They understood that in surrendering to Party discipline, they were surrendering a degree of individual initiative and that in deferring to the Soviets, they were often subverting their own better judgments. Such discipline often made Communists much more effective than they might otherwise have been—often toward good ends. But the makings of their ultimate failure also lay in this model of politics.

Both the domestic and international dimensions of communism are vital to sorting out its history. "Each communist party was the child of two ill-assorted partners," Hobsbawm wrote, "a national left and the October revolution." Historians of Communist movements, he argued, must

> separate the national elements within communist parties from the international, including those currents within the national movements which carried out the international line not because they had to, but because they were

in genuine agreement with it. They must separate genuinely international elements in Comintern policy from those that reflected only the state interests of the USSR or the tactical or other preoccupations of Soviet internal politics. . . . They must, above all, make up their minds which policies were successful and sensible and which were neither, resisting the temptation to dismiss the Comintern *en bloc* as a failure or a Russian puppet show.[13]

To these problems of writing Communist history, one might add the biographer's special burden of considering the individual's character and personality. While this is always a challenge—to try to enter the mind, the soul of another person—it seems to be particularly difficult in the case of Communist veterans who have tended to privilege the political and ignore the personal.[14] Foster was even more taciturn than most. The fact that he so seldom showed himself and his feelings to others and so seldom reflected on his personal position in the movement makes this last, most intimate dimension of the analysis very difficult. There are undoubtedly elements of his personality and even his political thinking that we will never understand.

Yet the recurrent tension between Foster's own political experience and instinct and his adherence to Marxism-Leninism created a series of crises that were as much personal as political. As Johanningsmeier has suggested, there was a strong *continuity* between Foster's syndicalist ideas and his experiences as a Communist, particularly during his early years in the Party. But a series of *disjunctures* are crucial to explaining a key question raised by Foster's life: how did this outstanding organizer with his almost instinctive understanding of American workers conform to a type of politics that has come to be called Stalinist? Foster's adherence to an increasingly rigid form of Marxism-Leninism was conditioned both by his political experiences in the Communist Party and by the emotional and psychological ways in which he handled these crises. Wherever possible, I have tried to relate his personal characteristics and his experience of these crises to the political story of which he was such an important part.

Confronting these tensions in the life of an individual makes it more difficult to explain them in simple terms. The real tragedy of Foster's life and the story of American communism was not that talented, dedicated people were duped or even that these American radicals never really had a chance. American communism's complex history was shaped by local factors, personal experiences, and contingencies as well as by global events and international politics. The tragedy in Foster's story and that of American communism lies in the convergence of all these factors and the destruction of radical initiative in the United States.

1 *Skittereen and the Open Road, 1881–1904*

THE IRISH CALLED IT "Skittereen"—a squalid stretch of Philadelphia's West End from Sixteenth Street to Seventeenth Street, between South Street and Fitzwater. When the Foster family moved there from Taunton, Massachusetts, in the winter of 1887, Skittereen was already an aging slum in the city's old working-class neighborhood of Moyamensing. Just when the handloom industry was declining in the mid-nineteenth century, thousands of Irish immigrants had poured into Moyamensing, Kensington, and other Philadelphia neighborhoods in headlong flight from the potato famine or the queen's troops. This heavy mid-nineteenth-century Irish influx brought discrimination and nativist violence in its wake. Unable to gain a foothold in the remaining skilled trades, by the 1880s most Irish workers had settled into laboring jobs, raising large families on low wages, walking to their work in building construction, on the docks, and in the remaining textile plants that crowded in on such densely populated neighborhoods as Skittereen. By the time the Foster family arrived, the neighborhood was more mixed, containing Germans, Eastern European Jews, and other immigrants, but the immediate area was still dominated by Irish street gangs. Some of these dated back to midcentury volunteer fire companies that had provided a social and political base for the city's Irish immigrants.[1]

James Foster was one of these immigrants. Born into a County Carlow peasant family, he was a Fenian who had fled to the United States in 1868, settling first in Boston and later in the small town of Taunton. In Ireland, James had enlisted in the British army and had agitated among the Irish soldiers for an insurrection, but the plan was betrayed, and he fled to the New World. Queen Victoria's jubilee year brought an amnesty, but James chose to remain in the United States. After trying his hand briefly as a storekeeper and failing, he worked most of his life, until his death at age sixty, as a carriage washer and stableman. Nominally a Catholic and a Democrat, he took little interest in either church or party and devoted his energies instead to Irish republicanism, amateur athletics, and street fighting. He was physically powerful, a "rough and tumble scrapper of local renown," his son later recalled, "and his special predilection was to fight Irish policemen." The Fosters' Philadelphia home, which was located, in his son's words, on a "noisome, narrow side street, made up of several stables, a wood yard, a carpet cleaning works, a few whorehouses, and many ramshackle dwellings," was a rallying point in Philadelphia for ball players, boxers, and cockfighters as well as Irish patriots and Molly Maguires.[2]

Philadelphia had long been a hotbed of Irish nationalism when the Fosters arrived in the late 1880s, by which point the Irish Land League and its successor, the Irish National League, had at least twenty-four branches based in the city's various Irish neighborhoods. The league fused nationalist aspirations with American labor reform and antimonopoly traditions to emerge as the focal point for Irish American radicalism in the late nineteenth century. Such a militant Irish nationalism was the "meat and drink" of James Foster and his children and undoubtedly was William Foster's first taste of politics.[3]

Elizabeth McLaughlin Foster was a weaver by trade, born in Carlisle, England, to a family of textile operatives of English and Scottish ancestry. Reared in poverty, Elizabeth had lived through the decline of the handloom trade and the deprivation that followed. She was a devout Catholic and passed this devotion on to her children. Of the twenty-three she bore, however, most died in infancy and only five or six survived to maturity. Infant mortality was quite high among the foreign-born working class in the late nineteenth century, but it seems that the Foster family had more than its share of tragedy. Her son remembered Elizabeth as a victim—of slender build and frail health and "quite intelligent," despite having very little formal schooling. Her life, he recalled, "was one long struggle against the sea of poverty in which we nearly always lived."[4]

Of all her children, Elizabeth held out the greatest hope for William Edward, born in 1881. She encouraged him to get as much education as possible and to use the Philadelphia Free Library; she grieved when the family's poverty forced the boy to leave school for work at the age of ten. But the promise that Elizabeth recognized in William did not die easily. The ideas that shaped his early life most profoundly were his father's Irish nationalism and his mother's Catholicism, each encouraging a sense of commitment in otherwise dismal surroundings. When the boy took a copy of *Irish Martyrs and Patriots* to the neighborhood priest, Father Joseph O'Connor took an interest in the lad and encouraged the family to send William to the same Jesuit college the priest had attended. William Foster was destined for a very different sort of schooling, though. Poverty was probably one obstacle to the priest's plan, but soon there were more, for other intellectual influences besides Catholicism vied for the boy's attention.[5]

Hawking newspapers on the city streets, young Foster often settled down on a curb to make some sense of his world. With little background in reading, he spelled out the words for himself and in the process tried to understand the events swirling around him. What he found most exciting were the news stories describing the labor conflicts of the era and Jacob Coxey's "petition in boots," a march of thousands of unemployed on the nation's capital in 1894. He began to follow politics closely, and during William Jennings Bryan's 1896 presidential campaign on a radical Free Silver platform, the fifteen-year-old Foster marched in torchlight parades and absorbed the campaign's propaganda against the giant trusts. When Bryan arrived in Philadelphia, William was in the crowd that heard his stirring speech. Bryan's defeat "came as a heavy blow," although the campaign had "a big educational effect," according to Foster.[6]

Some immigrant workers, through a combination of hard work, talent, and luck, achieved a stable life—cohesive family, union organization, steady work at decent wages, perhaps even a home of their own. By the late nineteenth century, wage rates were generally rising, and a second generation of Irish American workers was beginning to enter the city's more skilled and better paid occupations. Home ownership was fairly common in Philadelphia, even among working-class families, and the average population density was low by the standards of contemporary industrial cities.[7] But the lives of James Foster and his children represented a different sort of experience. A large number of Philadelphia's Irish remained in the ranks of the laboring poor, unskilled workers who faced extremely precarious employment situations, low wages, and often dangerous working conditions. A comparison of the Commissioner of Labor Statistics' estimate for a minimum adequate budget and wage data for Philadelphia laborers in the 1880s suggests that James Foster's income probably fell well below the level required to support his family. Like most working-class housewives in this era, Elizabeth Foster apparently did not work outside the home, though it was surely her work in the home, together with pregnancies and the burdens of childrearing, that sent her to an early grave. James may have made up some of the difference by selling dogs and game cocks and by wagering on the disreputable dog and cock fighting in his neighborhood, but the family clearly spent most of its time in desperate straits. Certainly this was William Foster's recollection.

Late-nineteenth-century Philadelphia was characterized by peculiarly uneven economic development. Such huge establishments as Cramp's Shipyard and the Baldwin Locomotive Works, among the largest industrial plants in the country, drew thousands of workers, providing them with fairly stable employment and higher wages. But the industrial landscape was still dotted with hundreds of small sweatshops and was still heavily dependent on various sorts of unskilled jobs in transportation and construction. James Foster's Philadelphia was made up of these sweatshops and stables, where employment remained precarious and wages low. Even the Fosters' extremely high number of infant deaths fits into a more general pattern. The city had the second highest infant mortality rate in the country—one of every four babies died before the age of two—a rate that was undoubtedly much higher among the city's immigrant working-class households. For all of its growth and diversification in the course of the nineteenth century, Philadelphia, with its complicated matrix of labor markets, remained a difficult place for people like the Fosters to make a living.[8]

But Philadelphia was changing in the late nineteenth century. As housing construction caught up with the growth of population, streetcar lines extended out from the central city, dispersing much of the middle-class population into outlying neighborhoods. Population density fell accordingly. Compared with the old "walking city," in which rich and poor lived in close proximity, Philadelphia was becoming increasingly segregated along class lines. Skittereen was surely affected by all this, yet in many respects, the place was more typical of the city in an earlier time. It had always been and still was a preserve of the laboring poor and still housed its dense population in substandard buildings. Streetcars ran through the district, but since most people could not afford to ride them on a daily basis, they still walked to work and labored not in large factories but in sweatshops or on the docks.

Compared with many American cities at the end of the nineteenth century, Philadelphia had a remarkably stable racial and ethnic population. With 43 percent of its population native-born of native parents, turn-of-the-century Philadelphia was the most "American" of the nation's great cities.

The Irish remained the city's largest foreign-born group well into the twentieth century and continued to dominate life in several neighborhoods, though Italian, Jewish, and African American migrants were entering South Philadelphia in large numbers by the end of the nineteenth century.[9]

In the immediate area around Skittereen, such changes were reflected in the gradual racial transformation of the neighborhood from the end of the nineteenth century through the early years of the twentieth. Although the city's black population was never large in the nineteenth century and did not grow substantially in the 1890s, Foster's own community adjoined an area with the largest concentration of African Americans in Philadelphia—the Seventh Ward, just north of Skittereen. In 1896 and 1897, when the teenage Foster was roaming the streets and working a variety of jobs in his own neighborhood, the black scholar W. E. B. Du Bois, who eventually followed Foster into the Communist Party, wandered other streets just a few blocks away interviewing the residents of the Seventh Ward. Those parts of the Seventh Ward closest to Skittereen showed two very different faces of the black community, according to Du Bois. "From Sixteenth to Eighteenth, intermingled with some estimable families," Du Bois wrote, "is a dangerous criminal class . . . shrewd and sleek politicians, gamblers and confidence men, with a class of well-dressed and practically undetected prostitutes." Within a block was "one of the best Negro residence sections of the city." Although almost one-third of the Seventh Ward's black residents were born and reared in Philadelphia, more than one-half were migrants from neighboring southern and mid-Atlantic states, most of whom were young, unmarried men and women working as domestics or laborers. In the years following Foster's departure, Skittereen itself was transformed from a white, largely Irish neighborhood into a black ghetto. At the time of the 1900 census, Foster's home, a three-story brick row house on Seventeenth Street, was inhabited by three black families, but Foster himself was gone by then.[10]

The proximity of the Seventh Ward to Foster's home meant that the discrimination against the city's African American population in housing, employment, schooling, and other domains, documented so forcefully in Du Bois's study, was a reality in Foster's daily life. Eventually, he developed a special interest in the problems of black workers and wrote extensively on the subject. Yet it is difficult to say what he made of this racism at the time, since he drew no direct connection between his earliest experiences with race and his later views on the subject. Certainly, he was aware of racial difference from an early age and may have been one of those rare white working-class youths who somehow grasped an alternative perspective to the racism he encountered all about him.

The streets in Skittereen and many other nineteenth-century urban slums were ruled by street gangs, such as Foster's own Bulldogs. Later, he held gangs responsible for all sorts of problems in and around the neighborhood, but his own narratives suggest the important social and political functions the Bulldogs served, providing, as the economist Paul Douglas observed, "whatever youthful social cohesion [that] existed in the neighborhoods." The predominantly Irish Catholic gang, perhaps five hundred strong, was organized into three distinct age groups and sponsored various sports teams, a social club, and even a fife and drum band of some renown. The Bulldogs also organized the slum vote and served as the military arm for the local political machine. But it seems that the Bulldogs and similar groups spent much of their time drinking, stealing, and fighting rival gangs. This fusion of sociability, crime, physical violence, and politics was an old tradition among Irish street gangs that had often emerged from mid-nineteenth-century fire companies in Moyamensing and elsewhere in the city. Like others, Foster's gang operated as "an efficient school" for crime as well as religious, ethnic, and racial prejudice: Catholics fought Protestants and launched what Foster called "pogroms in miniature" against the area's Jewish small businesspeople. "With the Negroes it was still worse," Foster recalled. Black-Irish riots were old news in Philadelphia, having occurred regularly more than a generation earlier, in 1832, 1842, and at Sixth Street and Lombard, not far from Foster's own neighborhood, in 1849. In the course of these confrontations, a Black-Irish antagonism developed, marked by street fighting and a persistent tension between the two communities. By the time of Foster's childhood, racial lines were sharply drawn. He recalled that blacks were "deadlined at Lombard Street, one square north, and at Broad Street, two squares east, and strictly forbidden to cross over into white, Bulldog territory. The Negro man or boy who ventured across these rigid deadlines was unmercifully slugged." It was the Bulldogs who enforced the invisible line between Skittereen and the Seventh Ward that Du Bois observed at this time.[11]

While we can re-create the historical context for Foster's childhood with some confidence, the subjective side of this atmosphere and his experiences there—that is, the precise effects of the place on his development—is much more difficult to judge. His recollections of the place and time were framed long after and clearly were shaped by his adherence to various forms of working-class radicalism. As Mary Jo Maynes noted in her study of European workers' autobiographies, later political allegiances surely influence radicals' recollections of their childhoods.[12]

William Foster's vivid memories of life in Skittereen suggest that this environment had a profound impact on him, even if its precise nature remains obscure. Far from romanticizing his origins, Foster's memoirs are rather moralistic in tone and almost lurid in their descriptions of Skittereen and its denizens. If his childhood molded his image of working-class people, his later politics shaped his own childhood, or at least his recollections of it, and it was not a flattering portrait that emerged. This was a place where "indolence, ignorance, thuggery, crime, disease, drunkenness and social degeneration flourished," and its inhabitants were "half-starved, diseased, hopeless." It is unlikely that he thought about the place in these terms at the time, but in retrospect at least, he was repulsed by much of what he recalled. The rhetoric he employed to describe the neighborhood and its residents was reminiscent of the language and tone he frequently used later in his career to describe the unorganized rank and file of the working class, those beyond the reach of the militant minority with whom he eventually identified. The language suggests that this was a world Foster disapproved of and found difficult to accept. With all of his travels after he left Skittereen, it took Foster thirty years to return for a visit, as if this neighborhood, which he called a "fine flower of capitalist civilization," harbored images he would just as soon forget.[13]

Like many poor children before him, Foster escaped from this world and discovered another through books. In his early teens, he began reading histories of the American and French revolutions, which he compared with the struggle of the Irish people for independence. In the mid-1890s, he went on to Tom Paine's *Age of Reason,* William Lecky's *History of European Morals,* John William Draper's *History of the Conflict between Science and Religion,* and Edward Gibbon's *Decline and Fall of the Roman Empire,* "the total effect of which," he said, "was to knock religion out of my head," to destroy his adherence to Catholicism once and for all. In its place came a staunch rationalism that left little room for sentiment of any kind. His attitude toward religious faith hardened to the point of condescension or even intolerance. "During the course of my life," Foster later wrote,

> I have never failed to marvel at how intelligent people can believe, for example, in the idea of a human-like Deity, who rules over the immense universe. . . . For my part, I'll take natural laws as the explanation. Likewise with the question of immortality . . . I see no necessity whatever for this self-deception. . . . In my judgment the only way modern people can accept such ideas as a Deity and immortality (not to mention various other religious beliefs), totally unsupported as they are by any reasonable weighing of facts or logic, is by accepting them blindly on faith. . . . Were people really to weigh them thoughtfully, as they do other matters in their lives, they could do nothing else but reject them. The days of heaven and hell are past for men and women who actually think about such matters.[14]

By his late teens Foster had also acquired his lifelong interest in the social and biological sciences and a tendency to view social development in evolutionary terms. He began his reading with Charles Darwin's *Origin of the Species* and the *Descent of Man,* going on to Herbert Spencer and the American sociologist Lester Frank Ward.

Years later, when congressional investigators asked him to name the most important influence on his own thinking, Foster mentioned Ward, whom he judged "perhaps the greatest scholar ever born in the western hemisphere." Given Foster's personal deprivation, the misery he saw about him, and his frustrated desires for an education, it is not difficult to see the appeal of Ward's ideas. Ward, the son of a self-educated engineer, was reared in Illinois while it was still frontier country, served in the Union Army during the Civil War, and earned degrees in law and medicine, but he made his living as a government clerk. All the while, he studied the sciences and languages, becoming what Henry Steele Commager called "perhaps the most variously learned man in the country." "A master of half a dozen fields of science," Commager wrote, "he was a master, too, of social science—in a sense he may be said to have created it." A strong proponent of social as well as biological evolution, Ward argued that education and freedom from economic deprivation were essential prerequisites for social progress. The progressive society, he argued, was one characterized by systematic planning for human welfare. It was not only possible but essential to control nature and the process of social evolution. Ward attacked the rationalized conventional wisdom of laissez faire, which was frequently employed to justify poverty and racism, and he embraced government regulation and social and political reforms.[15]

In the squalid and chaotic atmosphere in which he matured, Foster was strongly attracted to Ward's vision of a society rationally organized on the basis of human needs. Ward provided Foster with his first notion that the rampaging market and the social carnage that he saw about him might somehow be brought under control. Long before he confronted the ideas of socialism, he found in Ward a critical assessment of capitalism and some notion of a way out, an alternative social vision. In much of his own writing, Foster showed a strong commitment to the notion of social evolution and a fascination with the sort of systematic planning Ward advocated. Like Ward, he frequently resorted to biological metaphors in explaining the mechanics of social development. It was through Ward and his other reading, then, that Foster made sense of the world in which he lived and began to envision a different one. In the depths of the slums, he became what he later called an "omnivorous reader" with an "insatiable spirit of observation," and he found a love for learning that never left him.[16]

There were lessons to be learned in the streets and shops of the city as well, more important lessons perhaps than those learned in the Philadelphia

Free Library. In 1891, Foster began an apprenticeship with an old sculptor who worked in stone, wood, and clay and who encouraged the boy to become a craftsman. William never took to the work, however, and later claimed that he consciously chose to become an industrial worker. A more likely explanation for his abandoning the sculptor in 1894 was his father's and older brother's unemployment. William Foster came of age in the throes of the great depression of 1893–97 that threw millions out of work. For a poor family already living on the margins, the depression represented a genuine crisis, which clearly left its mark on William. Decades later he recalled that the family made it only with handouts at a nearby soup line and the younger children's wages. With the family struggling in the midst of such poverty, Foster's future seemed determined by distant, impersonal forces. He felt the obligation to earn more.[17]

After leaving his apprenticeship, Foster spent three years at a neighboring foundry, the first of several dangerous jobs he faced during his young manhood. At the Harrison White Lead plant, workers joked that if you labored diligently and saved your money, you might have enough for a coffin by the time the inevitable lead poisoning killed you. The details of Foster's life in these years are particularly sketchy, but it seems that they brought together the world of rationalist thought, represented by such writers as Darwin and Ward, and the unskilled worker's world of long hours, dangerous work, and low pay. As it turned out, this was a politically volatile mix.

Whatever personal cohesion Foster's family might have provided him in the midst of these experiences evaporated by his late teens, between 1898 and 1901. The three eldest children, including William, left the city in 1898. James and Elizabeth Foster probably died within a year of one another; certainly they were both gone by 1901, Elizabeth at the age of fifty-three, James at about fifty-six.[18] By the turn of the century, the family had largely disintegrated. It is difficult to judge the precise effect all this had on Foster, but it certainly left him a rootless young man. This and his problems finding steady work help explain his itinerant lifestyle over the next two decades; there was simply little to hold him in any one spot. Such a lifestyle is important in understanding a generation of American workers. Social historians undoubtedly have been right to emphasize the importance of family and community, ethnic cohesion, and a sense of stability as hallmarks in the worldview of many American workers in the late nineteenth century and early twentieth. But the ubiquity of hobos and tramps in this era and the importance of itinerant labor throughout the country, particularly in the Midwest and Far West, suggest that Foster's experience, characterized much more by uncertainty, mobility, and alienation, was very common.

When he left Philadelphia, Foster went first to live with his older sister, Anna, and her husband, George McVey, in Wyomissing near Reading, Pennsylvania, where he found work in the fertilizer plants. What little contact Foster maintained with his family over the years was with the McVeys, with whom he stayed periodically in the course of his drifting.

In the fertilizer industry, Foster worked as a laborer, steamfitter, fireman, engineer, and mixer. His own description of the American Reduction Company in West Reading, Pennsylvania, conveys the conditions that helped shape his impressions of work during his late teens:

> The plant was indescribably filthy, a menace to the health of its own workers and the community. Within the place garbage was indiscriminately littered about and allowed to decompose, and I often saw whole sections of the dumping floor a living, creeping carpet of maggots. In summer, when garbage collections were heaviest, the plant was swamped, and hundreds of tons of rotting swill, besprinkled decaying cats, [and] dogs . . . was left to fester outside in the blazing sun. With the stench, flies and maggots it was a sickening mess.

The fertilizer plants were filled with a fine dust from ground bones, so that even with lantern light the places were quite dark in the middle of the day. Tuberculosis was common, and years later court-appointed physicians and doctors in Moscow discovered on X-rays of Foster's lungs scar tissue that he had apparently developed during this period of his life.[19]

Such conditions fueled many workers' sullen resentment toward the giant corporations that increasingly controlled the nation's economy in this era. During the last two decades of the nineteenth century, strike waves periodically engulfed American industry, and people on both sides of the class divide worried about what they often called the "labor problem." Precisely what one meant by the term varied greatly, depending on one's vantage point in the wage labor system. From an employer's perspective, the expression was often intended to describe the spread of trade unions and the threat strikes posed to the developing system of industrial capitalism. Employers were also troubled about the increasing agitation against the wage system carried on by such labor reform groups as the Knights of Labor, late-nineteenth-century America's premier labor organization, and by those in the nascent socialist movement, notably the Socialist Labor Party.[20]

In the labor movement of such a city as Philadelphia, where the Knights of Labor had been secretly established in 1869, the term often meant something very different. Skilled, highly literate unionists in particular were troubled not only by low wages, long hours, and dangerous conditions but also by the general degradation of labor in American society and the implications of massive concentrations of wealth and power in a democratic republic. For these activists, the "labor problem" signified a general onslaught on the status and standards of American labor and the burning question of what workers must do to protect not only their economic interests but also their rights as citizens.

Philadelphia had been a focal point for labor agitation since the early years of the Republic. The first court cases involving craft societies as a conspiracy in constraint of trade were argued in the 1790s against the Philadelphia cordwainers. In the 1830s, the General Trades Union, led by early radicals and encompassing a broad spectrum of the city's laboring population, was perhaps the strongest of the many city organizations created in that decade. Workers published their own newspaper, ran their own political candidates, and supported one another in strikes. A general strike in 1837 helped establish a ten-hour day in many of the city's industries, but this impressive movement was destroyed in the course of the following decade by an economic depression, employer repression, and religious sectarian strife. During the 1850s and 1860s, strong craft unions were established once again, and by the mid-1880s, when the Fosters moved to Skittereen, the Knights of Labor was a powerful force among the area's factory workers.[21]

Although William Foster was only a child during the Knights' heyday, he often heard older workers recall the struggles of the 1880s, particularly the eight-hour movement of 1886. Foster's first personal experience with class conflict came in the midst of another strike wave during the depression of the mid-1890s. In his old age, he still remembered his father's outrage when the Philadelphia militia was employed to suppress the great Homestead strike outside Pittsburgh in 1892. He was greatly moved by the Pullman strike of 1894, which pitted the giant American Railway Union (ARU), an organization embracing railroad workers from all trades throughout the nation, against the General Managers' Association, a federation of the largest railroad corporations. The strike was defeated and the ARU destroyed amidst federal military intervention and considerable violence. While the Pullman strike was notable for its size and the extent of violence used to repress it, the general situation was familiar in cities and industrial towns throughout the country in the 1890s.[22] In 1895, not long after the Pullman strike had been crushed, this conflict came to the streets of Skittereen.

In December of that year Philadelphia streetcar workers struck against a wage cut, and the events that followed left a strong impression on the fourteen-year-old boy. The fare-paying public hated the streetcar companies almost as much as did the firms' employees, and the conflict galvanized working-class neighborhoods. Trouble spread throughout the city, but much

of the worst violence came in the southern sections of the city near Skittereen. Professional strikebreakers and mounted police were brought into the
neighborhoods to defeat the strike, while gangs, including Foster's own Bulldogs, mobilized to stop the cars. For all of their "social degeneration," the
Bulldogs also displayed what Foster called "real proletarian spirit." Foster's
neighbors barricaded the car tracks with lumber, boxes, and stones, and the
Irish gang wrecked every car that ventured past the corner of Seventeenth
and South streets, often in spite of the presence of armed police. Thousands
of men, women, and children poured into the streets, fighting with police
and attacking the cars with rocks, lumber, rotten fruit, and lumps of coal.[23]

Foster attended the car men's meetings and was impressed with their
fighting spirit. On December 17, a crowd of between six hundred and a thousand men and boys, led by a small group with wind instruments, set out for
city hall with flags and banners flying. Young William Foster was among
them. There was little sign of trouble until the marchers neared city hall,
where they were attacked by a phalanx of police riding at full gallop. Several
of the marchers were injured. Foster himself was slugged by a cop and was
narrowly pulled to safety by an office worker.[24]

"It was my baptism in the class struggle and it exerted a profound influence upon my general outlook," Foster later wrote. Writing thirty-seven years
later in the language of a Party leader, Foster saw these as his first steps on a
road that led him to communism: "I had learned the elementary lesson that
the individual worker is helpless against the employer and that only by com-
bining his forces with other workers can he exercise any influence in the vital
matter of his wages. From then on I followed the trade union manifestations
of the class struggle with an increasing ardor, and my interest in Ireland began to sink into a secondary position. My attention was now definitely cen-
tered upon the American class struggle."[25]

By his early teens, then, William Foster nurtured a strong sense of grievance over the conditions facing him and his neighbors, a class identity, and
an interest in the labor movement. He took away from his experiences a deep
resentment that remained with him throughout life: "In these years as a boy
worker, denied the opportunity for an education and living in a poverty-
stricken home, I early felt the iron of the class struggle sink into my heart." In
1949, as an old man, he said he could not remember "the time when I was not
imbued with that class hatred against employers which is almost instinctive
to workers." Perhaps more sensitive than most working-class boys his age, he
often reflected on what was happening to him and became embittered. "I, of
course, had no inkling of what was wrong," he recalled, "and who was my
real enemy, beyond a vague feeling that the rich were somehow at the bottom

of it all. But I deeply resented the poverty in which I had to live, for even my boyish eyes could see that there were many well-off people who apparently did no work, yet lived in luxury." Coping with this poverty, his parents had still conveyed to him a sense of idealism, though Foster located his own ideals in a very different realm. "A man must have principles and stick to them," he told Paul Douglas toward the end of his life. "He must recognize fundamentals." For Foster, the elementary lesson of his youth was the class struggle. His interest in labor news and his experiences in the streetcar strike awakened in him "a sense of solidarity with the workers." His voracious reading suggests as well an active intellect, a search for some way to make sense of the world around him, and, perhaps, the will to do something to improve it. By the turn of the century, he recalled, "forces were at work which were rapidly developing my native proletarian instinct into genuine class consciousness." Yet these forces were as much a product of Foster's later construction of his personal revolutionary narrative as of any situations during his early years in Philadelphia. There is little evidence of any ideological commitment to his ramblings until the turn of the century, when his worldview changed with what he termed a "dramatic suddenness."[26]

By Foster's account, he was back in Philadelphia, out for an evening walk in the early summer of 1900. He stopped near the corner of Broad and South streets to listen to a soapbox agitator, probably a member of Daniel DeLeon's Socialist Labor Party. The speaker distributed a crude leaflet that Foster could still describe in detail many years later. A small cartoon figure labeled "the Boss" cowered beneath a much larger one, "Labor," holding a whip. "It was my first actual contact with the revolutionary movement," Foster recalled. "I had never even encountered a Socialist book or pamphlet, despite my wide reading... His arguments and analysis seemed to give real meaning to all my experience in the class struggle. The speaker was a good one and I drank in his words earnestly. . . . I began to count myself, from that time on, a Socialist. That street meeting indeed marked a turning point in my life." The experience, which Foster described as a "conversion," is evoked in language common to radical working-class autobiographies, which usually identify a moment when the subject's feet found the proper path. In Maynes's words, "These moments signify the point when the plots of their life stories are revealed to their heroes or heroines." The conversion in this case may have been one of the heart, more than of the head, but certainly the seed was planted. In 1900, at the age nineteen, William Z. Foster embraced the cause. He joined the new Socialist Party of America the following year.[27]

Over the next decade, Foster would make his living as a migratory worker, tramping and riding the rails, often organizing as he moved from one place to another. Between 1900 and 1916, he would travel about 35,000 miles by rail, making seven coast-to-coast trips and at least two journeys between Chicago and the West Coast. He would log another 50,000 miles on four different British square-rigged sailing ships and had extended stays in Africa, Australia, and South America.

During the winter of 1900, Foster worked his way down from Philadelphia to Havana, but finding no work there, he returned to Florida. He worked briefly at an Armour and Company fertilizer plant in Jacksonville and landed a lower-level management job because of his previous experience in the industry. The plant superintendent promised Foster rapid promotion into an executive level position if he remained, but Foster later observed that he "simply could not become part of the employers' apparatus for exploiting the workers."[28] Instead, he moved on, discovering along the way that there were situations worse than wage labor. With labor scarce, unemployed workers were arrested as vagrants under the peonage system and then farmed out on chain gangs to work under armed guard in turpentine forests, phosphate mines, and other dirty and dangerous work. The guards often brutalized the predominantly black prisoners. Foster's vivid descriptions of all this in his memoirs suggest that it may have been only at this point that he became clearly aware of and interested in the problem of race relations, an issue that consumed much of his attention from this point onward.

Foster next hired on to a railroad construction gang, where conditions were little better. The mostly white laborers earned only eighty cents a day, from which various inflated living expenses were deducted. Troublemakers were threatened with the chain gang, and Foster concluded, "The line between 'free' and prison labor was a thin one in the Florida backwoods." When he discovered that most of the men on the gang were in debt to the contractor, Foster ran off and took work in a sawmill, where he labored from daylight to dark felling trees for a dollar a day, minus room and board. Here he found more trouble. Riders from a white supremacist organization arrived in the middle of the night to terrorize the mill's African American workers. When the blacks managed to escape into the woods, the riders lined up and questioned the whites, one warning Foster that a Yankee in southern Florida was "almost as good as a dog" if he minded his own business. When his boss refused to pay and threatened him with the chain gang, Foster waited for nightfall and hopped a northbound freight train.[29]

Landing in New York, young Foster worked for several months during 1901 as a motorman on the bustling Third Avenue line, "a man killing job" in his estimation. The car had neither seats nor air brakes, and no vestibule for the motorman. As the motorman inched his way through Manhattan's crowded streets jammed with other slow-moving vehicles and pedestrians, he stood on an open platform, exposed to all manner of weather, wrenching the stiff hand brake every few seconds. Foster helped organize groups in a number of car barns and made contact with the appropriate American Federation of Labor union. Before they could make much progress, however, all of the activists were sacked, and Foster was once again "on the bum," this time headed west.[30]

He was hired as a cook on another railroad construction gang in east Texas near the Louisiana border. The main difference Foster observed between the labor systems here and in Florida was simply that in Texas the peons were largely Mexican rather than black. He saved a small stake and once again hit the road.

The hobo subculture, in which Foster thrived throughout the early twentieth century, hopping freights and moving from one job to another, was an overwhelmingly male world, populated mainly by unmarried, native-born, unskilled, young whites. Aside from occasional liaisons with prostitutes, they rarely had contact with women, and homosexuality was not unusual. Characteristically, Foster's memoirs mention neither sort of relations, but it is clear from his travel recollections that he spent nearly all of his time with men.

Far fewer criminals lived among the hobos than their popular image as shiftless, dangerous characters might suggest. A small, aristocratic element of tough, hard-core tramps known as "Yeggs" was far more likely to prey on other isolated hobos for their few possessions than on people in the mainstream. Settled, respectable folk feared and despised them not because they were criminals but because they were outsiders.[31]

Some of these itinerants were genuinely stricken with wanderlust. Foster himself sometimes showed an affinity for the mobility: it was a big, open country with plenty to see and do. Others swore that this was a healthier and more honorable life than settled workers lived. Most, however, were simply looking for work. As John C. Schneider observed, "Men had to go where the jobs were." And so they moved—across the Midwest with the wheat harvest, into the Rockies for metal mining or railroad maintenance work, out to the Far West to pick fruit or work in the canneries, up to the Pacific Northwest to live in lumber or mining camps. For many young men, the experience probably represented a mixture of necessity and an alternative lifestyle that brought them not only work but also companionship and occasional excitement.[32]

Yet the hobo's life could be grim. Nearly 25,000 railroad "trespassers" were killed on trains between 1901 and 1905. Foster himself saw several men killed—bones "crushed like pipe-stems" by shifting freight or between boxcars; frozen and starved in empty cars; thrown from fast moving trains; or "dragged under the wheels and cut to pieces." While a sort of solidarity developed among the hobos themselves, their relations with railroad workers were often less cordial. Brakemen extorted money from the itinerants in exchange for rides, and armed railroad detectives threw them from trains. Foster came within inches of his own death more than once. He was nearly killed while trying to jump one freight, and on another he rode for many miles clinging to the roof of a boxcar, dangling a few feet from certain death under the train's wheels. On an organizing trip during the severe winter of 1911–12, Foster traveled all the way from Chicago to the West Coast in temperatures reaching thirty degrees below zero and very nearly froze to death on a stretch between McCook, Nebraska, and Akron, Colorado.[33]

Even when hobos arrived at their destinations, they were without money or a place to sleep, and the choices were few. Some pennies could buy a spot in a flophouse, but otherwise they slept in a jail, a religious mission, or outside. The difficulties of the hobo life are significant in the light of Foster's harsh view of the system with which he contended. The hobo subculture was, however, characterized by a rather active intellectual and cultural life. A variety of radical literature circulated among the floating laborers. The "mainstems" or casual labor markets of cities along the various lines were frequented by soapbox speakers representing a wide variety of revolutionary and reform perspectives. Transient workers did not remain on the road for long without encountering what one historian has called "the radicalism of the dispossessed."[34]

For more than a decade before World War I, Foster haunted the railroads as a worker as well as a hobo, serving as a fireman, brakeman, freight handler, construction laborer, camp cook, and car repairman and inspector. Here, too, he saw men killed, usually crushed under or between coupling cars. Even more than most industrial workers, railroaders were killed and maimed with alarming regularity. Seeing daily evidence of such industrial carnage undoubtedly strengthened Foster's resentments. Yet he also had a real fascination for this work and a strong affinity for the men who did it. The railroad worker was a breed apart. "His sense of control over the long trains, his feeling that he occupies a strategic position in industry, his meeting with new scenes and people daily, his relative freedom on the road from the spying presence of the boss, his realization that he is a member of a strong labor union," Foster later wrote, "—all combine to give him a sense of sturdy independence."[35] Long after he had devoted his life to political agitation, the railroads held a special fascination for him and remained a focal point for his organizing.

Between 1901 and 1904, however, largely for health reasons, Foster spent much of his working time on the sea rather than the rail. After a few months working on the docks of Portland, Oregon, he shipped out in the winter of 1901 on an old square-rigged British bark, the *Pegasus*, bound with a load of wheat for Cape Town, South Africa. Over the next three years, Foster sailed almost twice around the world, with extended stays in Africa, Australia, Latin America, and ports of call along the way—"my most interesting and unforgettable experience as a worker," Foster recalled more than three decades later.[36]

This, too, was a hard life. A normal workday lasted twelve hours, with the crew divided into four-hour watches and able seamen taking two-hour turns each at the wheel and in the lookout. As they adjusted sails, repaired rigging, cleaned, and painted, the sailors sang sea chanteys to entertain themselves and to organize and regulate the pace of their labors. The type of work usually determined the character of the song. Lyrics might vary according to the crew's nationality, but many reflected the sailors' hard lot, often expressing grievances otherwise suppressed by the ship's harsh discipline. Decades later, Foster still remembered the songs. Climbing up masts and all around the ship on old and frayed ratlines to adjust sails, even during storms, early twentieth-century British merchant seamen were at least twice as likely to be killed in an accident as soldiers or sailors were. Foster himself was nearly washed overboard during a five-day storm off Cape Horn. Two men standing on either side of him during his watch were lost.[37]

These were "hungry ships." The hardtack might be filled with weevils and the drinking water, when it was available at all, with worms. What little meat the crew received was likely to be rotten, and the lack of fresh water and proper soap meant that the men themselves were usually filthy, covered with the grease and tar used to maintain the ship. Few vessels had lavatory accommodations, washbasins, or baths. As a result, health conditions on board were generally dismal. A Glasgow medical officer testified that most vessels suffered from "inadequate crew-space, interrupted ventilation, and a moist atmosphere." Toilets, of a sort, were "generally speaking, abominations." As late as 1913, British merchant ships had disease rates much higher than those for either the army or navy. Pneumonia, dysentery, and malaria were all fairly common. The fact that alcoholism and suicide rates were also high among seamen suggests psychological stresses as well. The reason for such poor conditions was simple, a former Royal Navy fleet surgeon concluded: "The truth was that ship owners took no interest in their men."[38]

In spite of all this, Foster clearly enjoyed his life at sea. Part of the attraction, of course, was the wonder that the sea itself must have held for a young man from the slums of Philadelphia. Recalling later its effects on him and his mates, Foster wrote, "Spending many months at a time on its broad bosom in a small ship and rarely sighting land, they became literally saturated with its magic influence. In spite of all the bitter hardships of their life, they grew insensibly to love the sea, which profoundly shaped their psychology and their whole outlook on life."[39] Foster's interest in science and the natural world was stimulated by the sea creatures and natural phenomena he saw about him, and his health, damaged by his earlier jobs, improved markedly.

Finally, there were the sailors themselves and the comradery that life aboard a ship engendered. They took what Foster called a "craftsman's pride" in their ship, and they often developed "the warmest relationships." "No group of men, unless it be war veterans," Foster recalled, "know the degree of intimacy expressed by the term 'shipmate.'"[40] The sailors spent much of their free time playing cribbage, telling stories, singing, and occasionally swimming and boxing. Foster's reflections on the sailor's life convey an affinity he held throughout his life for all-male work cultures and the masculine bonding that often occurred in such environments. In his early years and even long after he joined the Communist Party, he sought the company of men who had enjoyed similar experiences. Still, he insisted that on his ships he saw none of the homosexual relationships that had made the British navy notorious. The need Foster felt to reject vigorously such characterizations is suggestive of his own gender norms and those that dominated the Communist Party as well as the society and system it sought to end.[41]

That Foster was rather well read by this point in his life was not unusual, for the sailors also spent a good part of their time in this solitary pursuit. Foster read constantly aboard ship, but apparently he stuck largely to fiction and did not delve much into socialist theory. Since access to books was limited, he read what he found aboard the ship. Foster was deeply moved by the French proletarian writer Eugene Sue's novel *Wandering Jew,* and he recalled finishing *Les Miserables* while circumnavigating the Cape of Good Hope.[42]

The good fellowship among the sailors seldom extended to the ships' officers, so Foster once again found himself in a situation where class lines were very sharply drawn. Strikes aboard ship were classed as mutinies and strictly illegal, yet refusals to "turn to" were not unusual. Sailors were routinely imprisoned for their part in these affairs, and Foster's leadership of such a strike aboard the Welsh ship *County of Cardigan* in the port of Talcuhano, Chile, is significant because it suggests that he was already acknowledged as a leader and willing to take the responsibility. When the ship reached port, Foster was chosen as a spokesman by his shipmates, who demanded that they be paid off and allowed to transfer to other ships. Instead, they were all jailed for several days under rather brutal conditions until a compromise could be worked out.[43]

Despite all this, Foster seriously considered a career at sea. He planned to study navigation during a three-year voyage to China but eventually abandoned the sailor's life. He later claimed that he gave up the sea because "it took me too far from the acute phases of the class struggle," and perhaps this was true.[44] But Foster clearly had ambivalent feelings about the life itself. He was affected by the plight of aging sailors he encountered aboard ship and in the various ports of call. Wedded to the sea after years of sailing, they could not keep up with the vigorous work and often ended their days in miserable poverty. Writing to his remaining family from Queenstown, South Africa, in November 1904, he mentioned the shipmates that had been washed overboard and observed that as a sailor "you have no home, no friends, and are the prey of all kinds land sharks and are liable to unsteady employment and other ill conditions too numerous to mention . . . your letter has set me to thinking seriously again as I had just about adopted the sea as my means of livelihood." Foster's ambivalence about the life is captured in a poem he enclosed in this letter home.

> A British ship comes sailing with the wind going free
> With all sails drawing a noble sight to see
> But again that old saying, it seems always true
> That distance its enchantment lends to the view
> Like a frightened bird as she goes rushing past
> With foam covered bows and spray flying past
> And while she goes pitching into the billows high
> Her masts are writing hunger all over the sky.[45]

Soon after writing this letter, Foster collected his pay in North Shields, England, and boarded a tramp steamer for Philadelphia. From there, he hoboed across the country to Portland, Oregon, probably arriving around the end of 1904.

At this point, Foster veered in a direction that seems an abrupt departure but was in many respects consistent with his restless frame of mind. Taking advantage of the old federal homesteading laws, he settled in 1905 on a 160-acre tract and an adjacent 160-acre forest on the eastern slope of Oregon's beautiful Cascade Mountains, twelve miles south of the Columbia River. With magnificent Mount Hood in the distance, Foster spent his springs and summers clearing some of the land, building a log cabin, and growing potatoes. He earned his living during the rest of the year working on the railroad, herding sheep, laboring as a construction worker and hard-rock miner, and toiling in nearby lumber camps and sawmills. He was, he later recalled, "a pretty typical Western floating worker," with "no idea of ceasing to be an industrial worker."[46]

Foster loved the mountains, canyons, and streams but was never an enthusiastic property owner. He sold the homestead after only three years and never again owned any property. The homesteads never realized their potential as viable farms, and most were abandoned as large lumber firms grabbed the most valuable timber areas. As usual, Foster drew a political lesson from the experience. "The Mosier homesteads," he concluded, "were enterprises of rugged individualism wrecked on the rocks of inhospitable economic conditions."[47]

What were the effects of this sort of life on Foster? Having rejected the ideologies and value systems his parents had to offer, Foster soon lost contact with whatever home he had found in Skittereen. Long after leaving Philadelphia, his livelihood remained precarious at best, yet he seemed to be looking for more than work in his travels. Filled with hard times but also comradery, his early years on the open road and the high seas broadened his perspective considerably. His life as a floating proletarian was an experience that Foster shared with a generation of labor radicals and with thousands of other western and midwestern workers with no pretensions to radicalism. At the very least, Foster and people like him became cosmopolitans of a sort, with wide experience and knowledge of the world about them, active intellects, and expansive worldviews. Their hands were callused and their necks sunburned from vigorous physical work, but their minds were active, and they were sophisticated in their own world of work and politics.

The range of jobs Foster held and the breadth of locales he came to know made him a sensitive and effective working-class leader. The conditions under which he worked, traveled, and lived in these years provided a rich variety of experiences that eventually helped make him a talented working-class organizer and strategist. "He had learned economic geography by travel, studied sociology as a hobo," Paul Douglas observed. "He had taken his introduction to rail-and-water transportation by stepping the mast and riding the hods. . . . He had become acquainted with books in the public library, on board ship, and from the reading of socialist literature."[48]

Such experiences constituted the raw material from which Foster fashioned his worldview and the beginnings of a political perspective. "I am one who was raised in the slums," Foster told Senate investigators in 1919 when they asked about the radicalism he had embraced while still a youth. "I am one who has had a hard experience in life. I have probably seen some of the worst sides of it, and I have knocked around in the industries, and I have seen many things that I did not agree with."[49]

But Foster's life in these years, relived over and over again in speeches, in pamphlets, and later in two autobiographical works, also provided him with a firm pedigree, an identity as a proletarian radical. He was, by his late twenties, a weathered veteran, one who knew the working class and had paid his dues, someone with whom workers might identify and who would be capable of leading them where intellectuals and professional revolutionaries had so often failed.

2 *From Socialism to Syndicalism, 1904–12*

MUCH OF WILLIAM Z. FOSTER'S early thought and his early career as a revolutionary were shaped by his life as an itinerant worker, tramping and riding the rails in search of work, organizing as he went along in the period before World War I. This experience, which he shared with millions of western and midwestern wage earners, placed him at the center of a distinctive brand of working-class radicalism, one that continued to affect his thinking long after he had become a prominent figure in the American labor movement and throughout his early years as a Communist.

In these same years, Foster's perspective expanded considerably. He traveled around Europe, studying social movements in England, France, and Germany. He read extensively and began to write regularly for the working-class press in the United States and abroad. Foster became a kind of blue-collar cosmopolitan, surveying the social problem more globally and beginning to develop his own prescription for its eradication.

Between 1904 and 1909, Foster immersed himself in local socialist movements for the first time, in Portland from 1904 to 1907 and then in Seattle from 1907 to 1909. As he searched for work in and around Portland, he settled into the city's radical movement and read widely in the socialist press. During these years, Foster read the Marxist classics for the first time—*The Communist Manifesto, Wage Labor and Capital,* and volume one of *Capital,* which had just been published in English in the United States. He also read pamphlets by Plekhanov, Bebel, Kautsky, and others, as well as Shakespeare, but it seems that Foster was most impressed by the works of Daniel DeLeon, the doctrinaire leader of the Socialist Labor Party. This might have been because of DeLeon's strong emphasis on industrial unionism, which meshed with Foster's own orientation to politics. Indeed, Foster later called DeLeon "the intellectual father of American syndicalism."[1] Foster might also have been attracted to the very dogmatism of DeLeon's works. Foster's tendencies in this direction emerged early in the course of factional conflicts in the socialist movements of the Pacific Northwest, where the Socialist Party's proletarian left wing thrived.

DeLeon's cerebral Socialist Labor Party, with its impossibilist rhetoric and its strong industrial orientation, continued to exert a strong intellectual influence well beyond Foster's circles in the early twentieth century, but the popular center of the mass socialist movement lay in the Socialist Party of America. Founded in 1901, just before Foster joined, the party represented a complex amalgam of Marxism and nineteenth-century American reform ideals. Its membership reflected this ideological diversity. The party had bases not only among native-born farmers and skilled workers in the immigrant slums of New York, Chicago, and other large cities but also among radical intellectuals, Christian socialists, and a wide range of middle-class reformers. This social and ideological breadth represented the party's great potential as an inclusive radical movement, but it also brought the danger of factional conflict over ethnic, class, and ideological lines. Foster joined the movement in its first great burst of activity and left before its high point on the eve of World War I.[2]

Within the Portland local of the Socialist Party, a conflict emerged in the course of 1904-7 between a reformist wing dominated by professionals looking toward a gradual social transformation through piecemeal reforms and a left wing led by Tom Sladden, who aimed to build a revolutionary proletarian party. Foster gravitated quickly to the latter group: "All my experience and reading in the class struggle had tended to make a militant of me. I had learned the elementary lesson that the class struggle is indeed a fight. . . . the ruthless capitalist class could never be talked, voted or bought out of power; but would yield only to the superior force of the toiling masses. So I joined definitely with the proletarian elements that wanted to make of the Socialist Party a revolutionary organization."[3]

Like those in some other industrial areas with large working-class constit-uencies, the Portland and Seattle locals were both colored by what the French called "ouvrierism," an influence that continued to shape Foster's thinking long after he had left Seattle.[4] Proletarian elements in the party demanded that it be reconstituted as a party of wage earners, since only workers them-selves could make the revolution. To allow middle-class and professional peo-ple a role was to invite reformism. "There is one thing and one thing only which makes the line of demarcation between the classes," Tom Sladden of the Portland party wrote, "and that one thing is the wage system." Farmers were not revolutionary. Employers of any kind could not be taken into social-ist organizations or trade unions, and even skilled workers were suspect be-cause of their privileged positions. According to Marx and Engels, Sladden concluded, only the unskilled worker, "the man who thinks with his stom-ach," was a true proletarian. "He has no shops, mills, mines, factories or farms. He has no profession, no trade and no property. He has no home—no country—no religion. He has little education, no manners and little care for what people think of him. His school has been the hard school of want. But upon his shoulders rests the problem of freeing society. The chains that bind him bind all. From his brain must come the plan of the new order." It was upon the unskilled worker that the Socialist Party was to build its movement. Here was a theory of social evolution that reflected the perspective of the unskilled, transient western worker.[5] Sladden's views and his tone were close to those that Foster assumed in his own early writing.

If Foster was swayed by ideas like Tom Sladden's, it was because they re-flected his own life experiences. He had known poverty and engaged in a seemingly endless search for work. He had few possessions and never ex-pected to have many. He had witnessed brutal conditions, violence, and death in a wide range of work environments. Any hope he had placed in the system had quickly evaporated. His plan to work his way up from locomotive firemen to engineer was frustrated by a serious recession that settled on the country in late 1907. The dramatic suddenness of this crisis, which demol-ished Foster's plans overnight, left a deep impression. His description of the experience accentuates the unpredictable and seemingly irrational quality of the system with which he contended. "A week before it hit," he recalled, "every industry was booming, workers were in great demand and wages were at record levels. But two weeks later the bottom had fallen out of everything; industry simply folded up and armies of unemployed appeared as if by magic. It was an economic hurricane, a graphic example of the insanity of the cap-italist system of production and distribution."[6]

This economic crisis uprooted Foster once again. This time he headed for

Seattle, where he worked as a building laborer and sawmill hand. In these years, Seattle was a town of fairly small workplaces and little manufacturing; it was a transportation hub, a processing center for the surrounding forests and farms, and a clearinghouse for the migratory labor of the Pacific Northwest. It was populated largely by native-born migrants from the East, like Foster, as well as British, Canadian, and Scandinavian immigrants. There were tiny pockets of Japanese and African American workers, who were relegated to the margins of society and excluded from most jobs. Because of the character of work and migration patterns in the area, the town was also disproportionately male. Although Seattle already had dozens of AFL locals by the time Foster arrived, both black and Asian workers were systematically excluded from virtually all of them. Aside from the waitresses' organization, the only women unionists were found among the musicians and in the less skilled jobs in the printing trades.[7] Foster mentions neither nonwhite workers nor women in any of his descriptions of life in the region. For Foster, as for most of the city's labor activists, Seattle was largely a white man's world.

Foster sought out the Socialist Party's left-wing, and it was in Seattle, which fostered a fascinating array of radical labor organizations in the early twentieth century, that he experienced his most sustained involvement with the Socialist Party. During the depression of 1907 and in 1908, the Seattle Socialists carried on a campaign for aid to the unemployed and a related free speech fight. Although composed largely of native-born workers, the Seattle party also had Polish, Lettish, and Scandinavian clubs, a strong Finnish local, and plans for an Italian club. Sunday evening meetings included musical entertainments, speeches, and debates that drew from eight hundred to a thousand. Middle-class reformers participated, but membership seems to have been largely proletarian. Even eight of ten identified candidates in the 1908 municipal elections, for example, were trade union members. As the movement grew in the years before World War I, it had considerable influence on the leaders of Seattle's labor movement.

Seattle became the battleground in the first major confrontation between the Socialist Party's left and right wings, and Foster entered into the thick of this fight. He later argued that the eventual split of the Washington party rose from "a long-developing opposition generally to petty-bourgeois domination of the S.P." by doctors, lawyers, and middle-class reformers, whom Foster dubbed "post-office socialists." As in Oregon and many other state organizations, the Washington party was badly divided between activists who emphasized electoral politics and municipal reform and those who focused primarily on industrial unionism. The right-wing group proposed to "fuse" the socialist organization with a Labor/Democratic Party ticket, while the left wing had strong syndicalist sentiments and held out for a revolutionary position. Foster was thus correct in emphasizing the social basis of this split. He identified staunchly with the proletarian elements. In the course of 1908, Seattle's left wing began to "cleanse" the local of many middle-class reformers by expelling the fusionists.[8]

Once in control, the left wing did away with salaried party officials but kept the entertainment. As Arthur Jensen explained, "Unless the serious business of the local be occasionally interrupted by a real good time, we will soon become tired and worn out." The new leadership celebrated its proletarian cast by changing the *Socialist* to the *Workingman's Paper.* The reconstituted paper harbored deep suspicions of intellectuals. "We hold no brief for 'the Intellectuals,' " an editorial announced. "The assumption of superiority to the manual workers, frequently observed among the college graduates in the Socialist movement, is intolerably caddish."[9]

The key figure in Seattle's left-wing faction was Hermon F. Titus, a remarkable character whom Foster described as "a brilliant speaker, a forceful writer, an energetic agitator and one of the outstanding Marxians then in the United States." Born in 1852 and college educated, Titus first became a Baptist theologian but quit after seven years, concluding that the church did not represent Christ. He graduated from Harvard Medical School at the age of thirty-eight, joined the Great Northern Railway as company doctor, and landed in Seattle on the eve of the great depression of 1893–97. Deeply influenced by the evolutionary socialist Lawrence Gronlund, Titus first joined Seattle's Fabian Society. He helped to establish the Citizens' Non-Partisan League in 1900, taking an active role in the municipal reform movement. While doing social work in Seattle's Skid Row, Titus read Marx's *Das Kapital,* which completely transformed his understanding of politics and society. He soon rejected all palliatives and embraced the revolutionary industrial socialism of Daniel DeLeon. Titus never joined DeLeon's Socialist Labor Party, however, probably because he rejected the party's strategy of establishing dual revolutionary unions to compete with the AFL. Instead, in 1900 he founded the *Seattle Socialist,* which served as a focal point for the city's burgeoning socialist movement, and he quickly became a theoretical spokesman for the left wing of the Socialist Party of America.[10]

Beyond his demands for a proletarian socialist movement, Titus's ideas may have appealed to Foster because of their emphasis on a *scientific* language and approach. "To the scientific man, facts are everything, theories nothing," Titus wrote. Like Foster's first mentor, Lester Frank Ward, Titus applied Darwinian principles and language to society. "Karl Marx scientifically investigated the facts of human society and formulated its laws of development," he argued, "as Charles Darwin did in the life history of animals other than man." Reflecting Daniel DeLeon's industrialism and the "worker-ism" common to many syndicalist theorists throughout the world, Titus demanded a party that was purely proletarian in base and steadfastly revolutionary in perspective.[11]

The main threat to socialism for Titus and Seattle's left wing came from the fusionists' plan to support labor and other reform electoral candidates who refused to embrace an explicitly socialist program. Although Socialists supported labor candidates in a number of cities during the early twentieth century, the opening for such a strategy was particularly wide in Seattle, where the city's progressive labor council and even many middle-class reformers cooperated with the party. Left-wing Socialists enjoyed strong support among the city's proletarian activists, but when an open break came in late 1909, the party's national executive committee sided with the right wing, which retained the official franchise. Titus and his followers, including Foster, founded the United Wage Workers Party, which "confined its membership solely to proletarians, specifically excluding lawyers, doctors, detectives, soldiers, policemen, and capitalists." The logical extension of tendencies that had been developing for years in Seattle and elsewhere in the Northwest, the party flourished briefly but soon went into decline. Titus changed the name of the *Seattle Socialist* to the *Workingman's Paper* and later published the *Wage Worker*. With what Foster called "a grim logic," Titus himself quit his profession to become an elevator operator and continued his search for the ultimate proletarian party until his death in 1931.[12] The strong syndicalist tendencies of the United Wage Workers Party's rank-and-file members, however, led some of them into that quintessentially American radical working-class organization, the Industrial Workers of the World (IWW).

Whatever his agreement with the dogmatism of DeLeon and Titus, Foster was driven by a desire to put such ideas to the test in the workplace and out in the streets. Throughout his career, his sense of doctrinal purity, clearly an influence even this early in his political development, was tempered by his instincts and his knowledge of workers' values. Like other radical workers of his generation, Foster had an affinity for anarcho-syndicalism that had less to do with any particular body of thought than with his accumulated experience—grievances on the job, the failure of the mainstream labor organizations to address the plight of the unskilled and migratory worker, and the strong middle-class reformist element in the Socialist Party. By 1909, he was ready to embrace a different sort of movement, one comprising unskilled workers and emphasizing industrial action over political action. He found such a movement, if only briefly, in the IWW.

With its distinctively western brand of anarcho-syndicalism so important in Foster's development, the IWW has mesmerized a generation of American labor historians. Yet such tendencies were rather widespread, if somewhat amorphous, throughout the American labor movement. Quite apart from the IWW as an organization, many American workers were experimenting with new forms of organization, such as workers' councils and systems federations, and with new tactics, such as sabotage and restriction of output. While the IWW popularized such activity and sometimes led these sorts of movements, the changes in working-class ideas, organizations, and strategies were as much the products of workers' daily experience in industry as of any particular group. Conceived as a more general phenomenon rather than a formal ideology, syndicalism was an important influence in the American labor movement as well as Foster's own long-term political development. Turned in this direction by his work and travels, Foster continued to be influenced by syndicalist thinking long after he had left the IWW and joined the Communist Party. Part of his success and even his personality as an organizer, leader, and working-class intellectual derived from his close identification with such tendencies.

In its theory and some of its tactics, the IWW resembled the French syndicalist organizations that emphasized organization at the point of production; "direct action" through slowdowns, work-to-rules, and sabotage as well as strikes; and the general strike as the ultimate weapon in the workers' arsenal. Like the Confederation Générale du Travail (French General Confederation of Labor—CGT) and other European syndicalist groups, the IWW argued that only the working class itself could make a revolution and create the new industrial commonwealth. Like Tom Sladden and Hermon Titus, the Wobblies had little use for intellectuals.

In several respects, however, the IWW's revolutionary industrial unionism differed significantly from European syndicalism. The Wobblies turned against political activity only gradually between 1905 and 1912. Early activists maintained strong ties to both the Socialist Party of America and the Socialist Labor Party. They emphasized industrial action, but some saw politics as an important instrument of working-class power. While the IWW talked, sang, and editorialized about sabotage, they seldom engaged in the practice that was common in many parts of Europe. The Wobblies were also unusual in their emphasis on the need for revolutionary industrial unions, and this part of their program led quite easily to the strategy of dual unionism. While French and eventually German and British syndicalists all worked within mainstream unions, calling for their amalgamation and pushing them in the direction of industrial organization, the Wobblies dismissed the AFL from the beginning. Indeed, their purpose in launching the IWW in the summer of 1905 was to establish a revolutionary alternative to the conservative AFL. From its inception, the IWW showed its greatest interest in those unskilled workers the labor movement tended to ignore, yet the organization also chartered alternative unions to compete with the AFL craft organizations wherever a potential for unionization surfaced.

Within the American context, the IWW was truly unique in several respects. In contrast to the typical AFL union, the IWW not only accepted but also enthusiastically organized among the most oppressed elements of the working-class population—recent immigrants, blacks and Asians, women operatives, and the unskilled transients of the Great Plains and western states. The IWW considered the unskilled transients "the leaven of the revolutionary movement." The Wobblies' homespun militancy "gave outlet, meaning, and dignity to a group of workers who roamed rootless and poverty-stricken in a land of plenty, despised and exploited by society and unwanted by any other labor organization."[13]

Never very large, the IWW aimed to spread its influence through a "militant minority," activists who would educate workers and win their support through direct action and example more than by theory and ideas. This educational effort was designed to create an alternative mass culture peculiarly suited to the realities of the unskilled itinerant worker's experiences. The IWW conveyed its message on street corners and on stickers and broadsides plastered to boxcars, factory walls, and shovel handles. To reach immigrant workers, the Wobblies published their leaflets and newspapers in French, Spanish, Polish, Lithuanian, Slovak, Swedish, Japanese, and other languages as well as in English. They also conveyed their message through such cartoons as "Mr. Block" and through the songs of Joe Hill. Block was the stereotypical loyal worker, a supporter of the mainstream political parties and the conservative AFL, a believer in the work ethic and the rags to riches myth, and, at his worst, a strikebreaker. He always did his best and always suffered as a result. Through the adventures of Mr. Block, the IWW taught the lessons of working-class solidarity, industrial unionism, and direct action. Joe Hill lampooned the wage labor system and organized religion and celebrated the accomplishments of working-class radicals and the IWW through his songs, published in a little red song book easily tucked into the pocket of overalls or work shirts. "There are 38 songs in the IWW song book," an old Wobbly recalled, "and out of that number 24 are educational. . . . every one of them is almost a lecture in itself."[14]

Far more inclusive in its industrial organizing than the AFL and far more tolerant in its ideology than the Socialist Party, the IWW embraced workers from diverse racial and ethnic backgrounds. Still, like the work settings in which it operated, it was primarily a male organization. Spurred by prominent women activists, the Wobblies launched impressive organizing drives among women mill workers in the years before World War I. "Rebel girls" also occupied an important symbolic position in the iconography and folk culture of the movement. Yet women activists stood out precisely because they were rare, and the successful organizing efforts among women, confined almost entirely to the eastern part of the United States, never lasted long or constituted an influential element in the movement's organizational life. The heart of the IWW lay in the Midwest and Far West, among lumber and harvest workers, metal miners, and migratory laborers of all kinds. The hobo jungles, lumber camps, and frontier mining towns that spawned and nurtured IWW activism were overwhelmingly male in composition and character. The raw and rather brutal quality of such work environments seemed to validate the IWW's class war language and worldview.[15]

But this masculine dimension of the IWW's persona derived from more than dangerous working conditions and physical exertion. The typical Wobbly was often rather distant from female contact even when he was not working. A big city factory hand, streetcar conductor, or construction worker might spend part of each evening with fellows in a saloon or club, but he eventually returned home—if not to his own family, then perhaps to the domain of his landlady. Increasingly in the course of the early twentieth century, he was apt to come into contact with women at work as well. By contrast, the migratory workers of the West not only spent enormous amounts of time in the company of only males—in lumber camps and mills, down in mines, and on box cars—but frequently lived and socialized in virtually all-male environments as well. Such experiences nourished a male bonding that shines through many of Foster's recollections. Nearly all his references to friends and companions from these years and well beyond evoke other men. This reality shaped his political and personal perspective even more than it did other labor radicals of his generation.[16]

The IWW also developed strategies uniquely suited to the situation of poor people that often resurfaced later in labor, civil rights, and other American social movements. In the "free speech fight," for example, Wobblies enforced the right by simply speaking publicly on street corners, often in defiance of local ordinances aimed at curbing radical activities. As the jails filled with free speech activists, local authorities faced a crisis and often relented. The tactic was peculiarly suited to migratory workers. It allowed Wobblies to recruit among the unemployed who gathered in large numbers in western cities during the winter season and provided a vehicle for carrying the IWW's message to the population at large. Most important, it created an atmosphere in which radicals could organize unmolested. "The issue for the IWW was clear," the labor historian Philip Foner concluded: "The right to speak meant the right to organize." Foster had seen the tactic used by Seattle socialists as early as 1907, and by 1908 such conflicts were being waged across the nation by various organizations, including the IWW. What was unusual about the IWW's free speech fights was their scope. When they were planning a fight, the Wobblies sent word out through hobo networks around the nation, and transients poured into the target city. As always with the Wobblies, there was a musical accompaniment:

There is one thing I can tell you,
And it makes the bosses sore.
As fast as they can pinch us,
We can always get some more.[17]

Between 1909 and 1916, the Wobblies waged free speech fights in more than two dozen cities, including Missoula, Montana; Fresno, San Diego, San Francisco, and Oakland, California; Aberdeen, South Dakota; Vancouver and Victoria, British Columbia; Kansas City, Kansas; Denver, Colorado; Cleveland, Ohio; Detroit, Michigan; and Hilo, Hawaii. One of the earliest fights, the one that drew Foster into the IWW orbit, surfaced in Spokane, Washington, in the winter of 1909.

As one of the largest centers for migratory labor in the Pacific Northwest, Spokane was a natural target. The city was the center for a regional labor market involving seasonal metal mining, lumbering, and agricultural work. In the winter, Spokane filled with unemployed harvest hands, railroad construction gangs, and others who were broke and desperate for work. Labor "sharks" working in collusion with employers preyed on the transients, charging exorbitant fees for placing them in low-wage jobs. Employers often fired the transients soon after hiring them, and the cycle started over again. Building on the resentment produced by such abuses, the organizer J. H. Walsh had created an impressive movement in the course of 1908. The IWW headquarters had a library and reading room as well as a meeting hall, where the organization held educational events and presented movies and musical programs. The local retained its own lawyer and even provided medical assistance. By 1909, Spokane claimed perhaps three thousand Wobblies, about half of them dues paying, and the IWW's influence was growing.[18]

Organizers called for street demonstrations and boycotts of labor agencies and demanded that all hiring be done through the union so that abuses could be rooted out. To combat the organizing drive, city authorities passed a local ordinance forbidding public gatherings. Since the Salvation Army and other religious groups were specifically exempted, the law appeared to be a transparent attempt to crush the IWW. When arrests started in November 1909, the Wobblies sent out a distress call: "Wanted—Men To Fill the Jails of Spokane."[19] Hobos and revolutionaries from around the country converged on the city.

The IWW was famous for its characters, but no one made a greater impression on the public or was considered a more dangerous agitator than Elizabeth Gurley Flynn, whose lifelong friendship with Foster was forged in the course of this fight. A strikingly beautiful redhead, the child of Irish immigrants, Flynn had already made a name for herself as a speaker at open-air socialist meetings on the streets of Harlem in New York. At the age of nineteen, she arrived in Spokane, pregnant, "frail, slender, pretty and graceful, with a resonant voice and an explosive eloquence that drew large crowds." The authorities clearly saw Flynn as the most dangerous of the IWW speakers, but they had trouble keeping her in jail. A jury declined "to send that pretty Irish girl to jail merely for bein' big-hearted and idealistic, to mix with all those whores and crooks down at the pen."[20]

Other Wobblies were not as lucky. Police arrested hundreds of soapboxers for violating the local ordinance, repeatedly raided the *Industrial Worker* office and IWW headquarters, and incarcerated the organization's local leaders and the paper's editorial staff. Even newsboys were pinched. Foster arrived in early November as a special correspondent for Titus's *Workingman's Paper* and quickly sent a flood of short dispatches back to Seattle. It was at this point that he took his distinctive middle initial to distinguish himself from another William E. Foster working in Spokane at the time. His short articles showed a new side of Foster's abilities. Earthy, witty, and full of colorful details and local characters, they suggest he not only could write well but also enjoyed his role of correspondent. In "Three Spokane Mushrooms," he roasted the town's mayor, judge, and police chief, and his enthusiasm helped him convey the IWW's own exuberant spirit: "To say that they will win is superfluous. There is no lay-down to this fighting bunch of revolutionaries. There can be but one outcome to this fight—Free Speech on the streets of Spokane."[21]

Watching a Wobbly soapboxer on the afternoon of December 16, Foster was plucked from the crowd and charged with disorderly conduct. He produced five witnesses who swore he was only listening, but he was "railroaded in the usual manner," charged $100 plus court costs, and sentenced to thirty days. Since the town's regular jail was filled to capacity, Foster was fitted with a ball and chain and confined to the unheated Franklin schoolhouse, along with hundreds of Wobblies. He spent his days shackled to the leg of another prisoner, swinging a hammer on the rock pile. Guards physically abused the inmates and denied them needed medical care. Foster later claimed that three of the imprisoned Wobblies died soon after as a result of such treatment.[22]

Foster helped organize a sort of convict union, which had regular business meetings, listened to grievances, and provided training in public speaking. When the political prisoners went on strike, they were reduced to a daily diet of water and a crust of bread and were confined to freezing cells. When they complained, the guards doused them with fire hoses. At one point, Foster was locked, along with burglars, a safe-cracker, and at least one accused murderer, in "the Strong Box," a steel cage normally reserved for the most serious criminals. He claimed to get along fairly well with all of them.

Foster maintained a stiff upper lip in his correspondence from jail, but there is little doubt that the experience shook him. A woman socialist from Seattle, who managed a short meeting with him several weeks after his imprisonment, reported that although he never complained, his hands were cut and he was in "bad shape." When Foster was finally released at the end of January 1910 after forty days in jail, he was reported to be "very sick." The main effect, however, seemed to be to strengthen Foster's resolve and perhaps also to further embitter him. He refused the assistance of Judge Richardson, a member of the Socialist Party, because it would appear that he was "deserting the rest of the boys." "I don't intend to get out until I can do so honorably . . . but when I get out (if ever) I'll give you some hot stuff," Foster wrote to the *Workingman's Paper.*[23]

While Foster already sympathized with the IWW because of his experiences in the Seattle Socialist Party, this jail time won him over to the organization. He was deeply impressed by the "customary IWW discipline." The Wobblies sang "The Red Flag" and other songs from their Little Red Songbook, held educational and business meetings, and adhered to very strict rules of decorum while imprisoned. Foster's respect for the IWW prisoners was clearly mutual. They elected him to a three-man committee to meet with the mayor. "I consider my experience in the Spokane City jail as almost invaluable," Foster wrote back to the Seattle paper. "Through it I have learned a few of the possibilities of organization and direct action, and more especially of the marvelous effectiveness of the passive resistance strike, in addition to learning new wrinkles about the law, police, etc." "It has convinced me," Foster concluded, "that it is possible to really organize the working class."[24]

Joining the IWW, Foster took part in the negotiations that resulted in some improvements in the local employment situation and a victory of sorts for the organization. The IWW had publicly called for a spirited renewal of the fight, focusing on March 1, 1910, as the day for an all-out offensive. As the day drew near, it was clear to organizers that they would not be able to turn out the necessary people. Most IWW members were jailed, and others had drifted away. City officials had also been worn down by the fight, however, and apparently took the threat at face value. When the IWW called for negotiations, the authorities made several key concessions. All prisoners were released, and street speeches were allowed. The hated ordinance was not actually repealed, but the mayor agreed to work for the implementation of a fairer law. The IWW hall reopened, and its suppressed *Industrial Worker* resumed publication. Although the local government revoked the licenses of nineteen employment agents and the state of Washington eventually instituted some regulation of such firms, casual labor problems persisted in the area.

The Wobblies claimed that the Spokane experience revitalized their movement, but the direct link between Spokane and the IWW's rebirth is questionable.[25] There is no doubt that the IWW's membership and activities flourished in the following decade, but their recovery and growth were part of a much broader mass strike wave. At the very moment of the Spokane fight, unskilled immigrant garment workers, most of them young women, launched a general strike in the industry at New York. A new union in the men's clothing industry was born in the midst of a big strike in Chicago the following year. Slavic mill laborers struck in McKees Rocks and other plants near Pittsburgh, and blast-furnace workers at the giant Bethlehem Steel works walked out in sympathy with machinists. In early 1910, Foster's own Philadelphia erupted. The city's Central Labor Union ordered a general strike, bringing thousands of workers out in support of the same streetcar men who had provided Foster with his first lesson in class conflict. The general strike ultimately disintegrated, but the show of solidarity impressed many labor radicals. This strike movement slowed perceptibly in late 1910 and in 1911 but then resumed, reaching its crest in the World War I era.

Several aspects of these mass strikes affected Foster's thinking. First, most strikes were launched by mainstream unions and supported by various elements of the labor movement. Second, numerous occupational groups participated, but unskilled immigrants, precisely those workers the AFL had tended to ignore, were important in the movement. Third, socialists and other radicals often played a role in organizing and leading the strikes, but they did so within the context of AFL unions. Finally, several of the large strikes, such as those in the garment industry, involved industrial unions embracing all the workers in a given industry or even broader-based bodies, such as the system federation on the Illinois Central Railroad. The federation coordinated the activities of motive trades, shop and maintenance, and right-of-way workers in the giant Illinois Central and Harriman Lines strike, which began in 1911.[26]

To Foster and some other labor radicals, all of this suggested the potential for organizing unskilled immigrant workers. It also showed the possibility, indeed the wisdom, of organizing within the heart of the labor movement instead of launching separate revolutionary unions on its periphery, as the IWW had done. Finally, it demonstrated the importance of a key group of experienced organizers, often radicals, within each of these industries. These lessons were just beginning to crystallize in Foster's thinking, though they were apparent in the experiences of workers all around him. Ironically, Foster realized the implications of these experiences not in the Northwest but on yet another sojourn, this one far beyond his familiar turf.

His experience in the struggle at Spokane had turned Foster firmly away from political activity and toward direct action at the point of production. He left Seattle in the late spring of 1910 with $100 in his pocket, hoboed across the country to New York, and set sail for Europe on a German ocean liner in early August. On board, Foster wrote a long letter to Hermon Titus that suggested his thinking on the eve of his European journey: "I don't profess to know a great deal about direct action at present writing. But I am on my way to a country where I should learn a little, namely France."[27]

As important as Foster's experiences in Portland, Seattle, and Spokane were to his thinking, his European travels in 1910–11 were decisive. His tendency toward syndicalism had been fueled by his disgust with Seattle's "slow-cialists" and his admiration for the IWW, and he grasped the significance of the 1909–10 upsurge. But he was particularly impressed with the explosive growth of the French CGT and was anxious to study its methods. No sooner had he joined the IWW than his European experiences pushed him away from the Wobblies' conception of revolutionary industrial unionism and toward a purer form of syndicalism.

Foster's year in Europe provided a classic mixture of theory and practice. He studied languages intensely, not only French but also German, Spanish, and Russian, with a view to traveling throughout the Continent. He devoured the writings of Fernand Pelloutier, an early syndicalist theorist; Victor Griffuelhes, leader of the CGT; and Emile Pouget and Georges Sorel, the movement's key intellectuals. The personal contacts Foster developed and his observations of the French movement during his stay appear to have been more important to his political development than the reading he did. He stayed with the families of militants and visited local unions. He attended and reported on the annual CGT conference at Toulouse, where the revolutionary syndicalists carried the day against a reformist opposition. Foster was in almost daily contact with the leading lights of the French movement—Leon Jouhaux, a CGT leader; Alphonse Merrheim, secretary of the metal workers' union and a member of the CGT's council; Pierre Monatte, editor of *La vie ouvrière;* and Georges Yvetot of the ultraradical *La guerre sociale.* He visited Gustave Hervé, editor of *La guerre sociale,* at La Santé Prison, where Hervé had been confined for his antimilitary agitation. Foster's visit occurred when anarchist influence was strong in the French movement.[28]

French syndicalism, which had assumed the proportions of what one historian has termed a "quasi-millenarian revolt" in the early years of the twentieth century, was already beginning its decline by the time Foster arrived. Having sustained an eight-year strike wave after the turn of the century, CGT membership was stagnating, more strikes were being lost, and a narrower craft consciousness was reemerging in some quarters. Nonetheless, the movement remained the "authentic voice" of French workers in the prewar years, and Foster saw it as a vibrant alternative to what he had left in the United States. He was perhaps most impressed by the French railway strike in the fall of 1910, which he reported on for *Solidarity* and the *Industrial Worker.* Inspired by what he saw, he emphasized two points in his dispatches. The first was the tremendous strength of organized working-class militancy and the effectiveness of sabotage—more than 2,400 acts reported in less than four months between October 1908 and January 1909. "Simply by studied clumsiness, carelessness, deliberate mistakes, and general cussedness they so confuse matters that it is impossible to transact business," he wrote. "The French slaves know what tactics hurt their masters," Foster concluded, "and they also know that the word 'sabotage' stands for the most revolutionary sentiments the working class can have, i.e., utter contempt for capitalist life and property."[29]

Foster also saw in the railroad strike a confirmation of what he viewed as the corrupting influence of socialist electoral politics. Until his experiences in Spokane, he seemingly shared the IWW view that politics was simply a waste of time. By the time he left for France, Foster already believed that workers' power lay in the economic sphere. "There is one kind of power recognized in the world today," Foster wrote to Titus, "and this is the ability to control industry. This is an economic power. . . . When the ineffectiveness of the ballot has finally been demonstrated so clearly that even the workers can see it, then they will repudiate it entirely, and adopt Working Class tactics, even as the tendency seems to be the vanguard of the labor movement of Europe. . . . Harry, I think you fellows should get next to the ballot—it's on the bum entirely."[30] The French government's behavior during the strike finally convinced Foster of the syndicalist argument that politics was actually an *impediment* to revolutionary change. Socialist government was an abstraction in the United States, except occasionally on the most local level, where its influence was often confined to such issues as sanitation and education. In France, however, the national coalition government included several politicians who considered themselves socialists. The prime minister, Aristide Briand, and other cabinet members were ex-members of the Socialist Party in France, and many delegates to the French Parlement were active Socialists. The party also controlled local administrations in several parts of the country.

When Socialists were elected to power, however, the long-awaited revolution never arrived. On the contrary, Foster observed, they "interpreted the class struggle as the collaboration of the classes" and actively cooperated with employers and union bureaucrats to stifle the railway strike. The entire strike leadership and hundreds of rank-and-file workers were arrested, thousands of troops were mobilized to protect property and keep the trains running, and the government appealed to its working-class constituents for calm. On the surface, Foster noted, the defeat of the strike was a victory for the ruling Socialists, but Foster believed the syndicalists achieved something more important than winning the strike. They demonstrated conclusively that the Socialists had betrayed the working class and that the electoral strategy was bankrupt. The behavior of Briand, the author of a well-known plan for the general strike, showed "how completely even a radical revolutionist can forget his principles when enmeshed in the dovetailing influence of political action."[31]

The practical implications for workers in the United States seemed obvious to Foster. Even such men as the Wobbly leader William D. Haywood and the Socialist Robert Rives La Monte, who argued for a kind of syndicalism in tandem with Socialist Party activity, were wrong. Eventually, Foster would view the French antipolitical perspective as the theory's greatest liability, but in the heat of the industrial battle he found it one of syndicalism's soundest arguments, one that reinforced his own experiences with reformist socialists in Seattle and elsewhere. For Foster, the social question did not break down into separate industrial and political spheres; rather, the class struggle was essentially economic. "The prevalent anarchistic theories of spontaneous action and decentralized organization of the workers appealed to me as a corrective to bureaucratic control of the trade unions by reactionaries," Foster later recalled. "In short, I became a thorough syndicalist."[32]

Yet Foster was not an uncritical admirer of syndicalist methods. He observed that the French militants viewed sabotage as "a general panacea for all their social ills" and that violence opened the door to government repression. Eventually, the French syndicalists themselves came to the same conclusion and altered their tactics accordingly.[33]

While bringing the French movement to the attention of American radicals, Foster interpreted the United States for the French. *La vie ouvrière,* Pierre Monatte's lively syndicalist paper, carried his articles on the Wobbly leader "Big Bill" Haywood and on the Spokane free speech fight, in which he argued at length for the effectiveness of revolutionary nonviolent mass action. Although Foster undoubtedly received some help with the smooth French the articles display, a careful textual analysis suggests that he had indeed mastered the basics of the language.[34]

After six months in France, Foster set off for Germany. Here, too, he quickly immersed himself in the life of the movement, but Foster found the German situation to be very different from what he had seen in France. He lived for six months with Fritz Kater, head of a German syndicalist union. Instead of working and socializing with the leading militants as he had in France, he spent a good deal of the time in his room, reading and studying German, which he found more difficult than French. He seems never to have settled in or made the sort of contacts he had in France.

This distance might be explained by his hostile reaction to the German labor movement and his withering public criticism of its leaders. The giant German trade union federation, the Frei Gewerkschaften, and the German Social Democratic Party (SPD) were far larger and more influential but were also far more bureaucratic and reformist than the French movement Foster had just observed at close range. At the time of Foster's visit, the socialist trade union federation had nearly 2.5 million members; the SPD, with its elaborate complex of choral and sports societies, hiking and cycling clubs, theatrical and educational groups—"the state within the state"—had nearly 1.0 million. The movement constituted an influential political presence in German society.[35] Yet the bureaucratic character of the German movement offended Foster's political sensibilities.

Foster conveyed this in a letter to Pierre Monatte soon after his arrival in Germany, describing the funeral and demonstration for the SPD leader Paul Singer. He heard no loud chants and saw no red flags or police, in spite of the huge size of the demonstration. They were simply not needed; the line of march was very orderly. What seemed to distress Foster most was the abundance of top hats. All the Socialists seemed to be wearing them. "To tell the truth," he confided, "I was completely disgusted." The letter, which Pierre Monatte published in *La vie ouvrière* without Foster's knowledge, brought a storm of protest from SPD leaders and could hardly have endeared Foster to his hosts.[36]

Foster met and interviewed Karl Liebknecht, who would go on to found the German Communist Party, and the Marxist theorist Karl Kautsky; both conversations disappointed him. He must have enraged Kautsky by explaining that he had read a good deal of the man's works, but he "could not find the revolution in them." Although Foster later carefully drew distinctions between right-wing SPD leaders, such as Kautsky or the trade union head Karl Legien, and revolutionaries, such as Liebknecht and Rosa Luxemburg, at the time he criticized them all with equal enthusiasm.[37]

Predictably disappointed with May Day in Berlin, where there was no general demonstration at all, Foster was repulsed by what he saw as the rampant militarism in the city and the Social Democratic Party's obsession with electoral politics. He found the German Socialist Union Congress at Dresden "the tamest affair I ever attended and almost a perfect model of what a union congress should not be." The guiding principle, Foster observed, seemed to be that the rank and file was incapable of making any important decisions. He found the German unions more like insurance societies than "combat organizations." "Not only was it destitute of even the suggestion of revolutionary spirit, but [it] was also run on a machine plan that Sammy [Gompers] and company could learn from."[38] The control of the German labor movement by the SPD's right wing convinced him of the need for an autonomous revolutionary syndicalist policy. At the same time, however, he rejected the German syndicalists' current policy of separation from the powerful mainline unions, a strategy that left them isolated from the great mass of German workers who remained within the SPD and its affiliated labor organizations.

The most important lessons Foster learned in Germany, then, were negative. Between his German and French experiences, he realized the baneful influence of electoral politics and the crucial importance of the French syndicalist strategy of "boring from within." Radicals must continue to organize and agitate *within* the mainstream unions, with a view to winning them over to revolutionary goals, forms of organization, and tactics. By withdrawing from the old unions, as the IWW had done, he reasoned, "they [the German syndicalists] were simply turning the mass trade unions over to [Karl] Legien's deadly control . . . good tactics required the use of boring-from-within methods. I was led to conclude that the policy of dual unionism was wrong not only in Germany, but also in the United States."[39] Foster was determined to follow the French syndicalist Leon Jouhaux's admonition that he "tell the IWW when you return to America to get into the labor movement."[40]

This could be accomplished, Foster reasoned, by maintaining a disciplined "militant minority"—the "most revolutionary elements among the masses, the natural leaders of the workers" who organized themselves into *noyaux,* or what the British syndicalists called "ginger groups," to win control over the old unions. "So I resolved to raise these two questions in the IWW when I returned to the United States," Foster later wrote, "and the sequel showed that they were to play a very large part in my future labor activities."[41] Indeed, a staunch resistance to dual unionism and a determination to develop disciplined groupings of revolutionaries *within* the old-line unions dominated "Fosterism" for most of the next two decades, long after he had joined the Communist Party.

Foster was not the only militant to draw inspiration from the French example. The British syndicalist Tom Mann, originally sympathetic to the IWW's dual industrial union model, had visited France just a few months before Foster and came away with the same lesson: the only way to build a revolutionary labor movement was by boring from within. Against strong opposition from the British IWW, he formed the Industrial Syndicalist Education League, which provided another model for Foster. The league set up "amalgamation committees" in the various industries, led organizing drives, and played a key role in the massive labor unrest of 1910 to 1914.[42] Mann's conversion to the boring-from-within creed had a profound effect on Foster, whose writing suggests he followed these events closely. Here was an internationally recognized labor activist for whom Foster had the greatest respect endorsing Foster's gut feelings.[43]

William D. "Big Bill" Haywood, however, came away from his 1910 travels with a very different lesson in mind. Haywood attended the 1910 Congress of the Second International as a delegate from the IWW and later traveled in Great Britain, Sweden, and France observing workers' movements, though certainly far less intimately than Foster did. He and Foster met at the CGT's Paris office. There was simply no comparison between the vigorous, progressive French unions and the moribund, conservative AFL, Haywood argued. For Haywood, who had had somewhat ambivalent feelings about the IWW up to this point, the French situation proved there was real potential for building a revolutionary labor movement. He dedicated himself to the IWW with renewed vigor. The contrast between Haywood's reaction to European events and Foster's foreshadowed Foster's looming conflict with IWW leaders.[44]

Foster's original plan of going on to spend six months each in Spain and Italy, studying the movements in those countries, was abruptly altered by a telegram from the IWW's Vincent St. John in July 1911. The cable provided

Foster with $10 and instructed him to attend the meeting of the International Trade Union Secretariat on August 10–12 in Budapest as a representative of the IWW. He traveled fourth class by rail from Berlin, then walked the 150 miles to Dresden. Arriving in Budapest with a great deal of confidence but very little money, Foster sparked a day-long debate by challenging the credentials of AFL vice president James Duncan, the American labor movement's official delegate. As a representative of the only revolutionary labor federation in the United States, Foster argued, he should be seated, not Duncan. He focused particularly on Duncan's membership in the National Civic Federation, where labor and business leaders came together to anticipate and resolve issues of conflict. Several important AFL officials, including Samuel Gompers, played active roles in the federation, and Foster held this as a clear example of class collaboration. The question of American representation may have been the most important issue at the conference. Foster received support from his two friends and comrades—Leon Jouhaux, CGT secretary, and Pierre Monatte, the official French delegate—but his argument impressed few beyond the CGT group. He was ruled out of order and expelled from the conference. These events, fully covered in the AFL's journal, brought Foster to the attention of the federation's leadership and undoubtedly soured his reputation in mainstream labor circles at the very moment he was poised to argue that radicals must immerse themselves in precisely this milieu.[45]

Without money now, Foster wandered out to the outskirts of Budapest and fell asleep in the back of a horse-drawn moving van amidst a pile of rags and machinery. Arrested for vagrancy and released to the custody of a Hungarian trade union official, he located Yvetot and Jouhaux, members of the French delegation, who found his predicament rather amusing but agreed to lend him enough money to live on. Remarkably, Foster seems to have lost none of his fire in the midst of these rather daunting circumstances. At this point, he received a second cable from Vincent St. John, enclosing $50 and asking Foster to return to Chicago for the IWW convention.[46]

St. John came to regret the invitation. Foster returned a man on a mission: to turn the IWW around and rebuild it on the French syndicalist model. Up to this point, Foster had largely evaded the critical issue of dual unionism in his dispatches to *Solidarity* and the *Industrial Worker*. Now he was determined to face it head-on. Although earlier socialist unions did not seem to use the expression "boring from within," they had certainly tried to operate in mainstream unions, and the Socialist Party itself had generally followed the practice of working within the AFL. Yet this strategy was always subordinated to the party's electoral activities, and it was in any case an anomaly. The concept of setting up alternative radical unions to compete with AFL unions was firmly entrenched in American radicalism. Socialists represented a strong presence in some AFL unions, such as the International Association of Machinists and the International Ladies Garment Workers Union, and a few industrial organizations, such as the Brewery Workers and the United Mine Workers. The AFL's record on the issues of industrial unionism and organizing the unorganized, however, was generally rather bleak.[47]

Nowhere did the distrust of the AFL go deeper than in the IWW. Big Bill Haywood once said he would cut off his right arm rather than join the federation and concluded that "the 28,000 local unions of the AF of L are 28,000 agencies of the capitalist class." Joe Ettor, the IWW's talented Italian mass organizer, declared that it was "the first duty of every revolutionist to destroy the AFL." Most Wobblies seemed to agree with Karl Rathje that the AFL was "a contemptible measly little job trust, and absolutely nothing else."[48] Clearly, Foster was swimming upstream.

Foster returned to the United States at the beginning of September 1911, helped organize the Wobbly contingent in New York City's Labor Day parade, and then headed out to Chicago for the IWW convention. Despite his efforts, the main issue at the convention was not dual unionism at all but centralization. The "decentralizers," particularly strong in the West, feared that the IWW was becoming overly bureaucratic, and they pushed for the weakening if not the total abolition of the organization's general executive board. This initiative lost, but the time and energy expended during the debate suggest the strong anarcho-syndicalist tendencies, especially among the western activists.

Foster persisted. He formulated a proposal that "the IWW shall give up its attempt to create a new labor movement, turn itself into a propaganda league, get into the labor movement and, by building better fighting machines within the old unions than those possessed by our reactionary enemies, revolutionize these unions." He lobbied delegates for his position but received only limited encouragement, notably from Earl Ford of Seattle and Jack Johnstone of British Columbia. Fearful that a formal proposal would be overwhelmingly defeated, Foster retreated, determined to take the fight directly to the membership.[49]

When the western decentralizer faction nominated him for editor of the *Industrial Worker,* Foster opened his offensive with a column entitled "As to My Candidacy." Here he posed a vital question, familiar to most Wobblies by this point: "Why doesn't the IWW grow?" From a high point of 55,000 members in 1905, the organization had declined to 6,000 by 1911. The IWW was languishing, and Foster thought he knew why. The dual union strategy had isolated the most conscious and militant workers, the critical "militant minority," from the workers' lives and had marginalized the revolutionary movement. Wherever syndicalists followed the dual union strategy, Foster argued, their movements had stagnated—not only in the United States but also in Germany and England. In France, Spain, and Italy, where the militants had followed a boring-from-within strategy, their movements were burgeoning, and workers were growing more revolutionary. Tom Mann's and Guy Bowman's efforts to import the strategy to England were bearing fruit in the form of the great labor unrest of 1910–11. While the IWW members were quarreling among themselves, French CGT militants "have made their labor movement the most feared one in the world" by "propagating their doctrines in the old unions and forcing them to become revolutionary."[50]

Most reactions to Foster's call for change ranged from constructive criticism to contempt. Some objected to the French analogy because most French workers were skilled, while in the United States the unskilled predominated. To enter the AFL, even if this were possible, would be, in effect, to abandon the mass of unskilled workers. Others described their expulsions from AFL unions for revolutionary activities. Those who tried to bore from within, they observed, would soon find themselves on the outside. Was it even possible, let alone advantageous, to follow Foster's scheme? J. S. Biscay, in one of the more thoughtful responses, argued that the problem with the IWW was not building from without but rather the virtual lack of any organizing in the workplace, where workers felt their deepest grievances and sought solutions. Most of the IWW's propaganda work was carried on in halls or on street corners. The AFL itself was growing by organizing on the job. "If the old line unions can get members on the job with an out-of-date plan of organization, we could do even better with modern industrial unionism," Biscay wrote. "What every worker wants is not theory or figures but demonstration." Disbanding the IWW without a firm base in the workplace, he contended, would retard the movement, not stimulate it.[51]

In response, Foster argued that radicals must fight for the best interests of the unions, "which are identical with those of the workers." He doubted that many Wobblies had actually been expelled from AFL unions, but even if they had been, this might be justified on the grounds of their hostility. "Workers are skeptical of the IWW," Foster concluded, because the organization was working to destroy their unions. Boring from within had never really been tried.[52]

Some members from the Pacific Northwest wrote in support of Foster's views. Jack Johnstone, who had met Foster in Spokane, had supported him at the convention, and had become a close collaborator from this point on, was convinced that "good results will be accomplished if the IWW follows Foster's plan." But most correspondents opposed the new strategy. To the *Industrial Worker*'s editor, the whole plan appeared futile. In December 1911, he closed the columns of his paper to the debate, effectively cutting Foster off from any potential base.[53]

Isolated from his natural constituency in the IWW but brimming with ideas and energy, Foster now struck out by himself. In a succession of organizations of his own design, he introduced American workers to the purest form of syndicalism the nation had seen.

3   The Militant Minority, 1912–16

FOSTER, deprived of his access to the IWW press, took to the road at the beginning of 1912 and for the next four years formed "syndicalist leagues." These leagues were never very large, but they were theoretically and organizationally significant because they combined Foster's syndicalist ideas and strategies with a practical approach to organizing. He put together a group of talented militants who built a base in several local labor movements. After working in the massive AFL organizing drives during World War I, they emerged in the early 1920s as the American Communist Party's most important group of industrial organizers. Through his writing and organizing in the prewar years, Foster provided links between the IWW's distinctively American anarcho-syndicalism and the roots of American communism in the World War I era.

Foster established a Syndicalist Militant Minority League at Chicago in January 1912 and set off at the end of the month to carry his boring-from-within message directly to the IWW membership. His speech before IWW Local 85 of Chicago shortly before departing suggests the message he took to the Wobbly rank and file throughout the West in the weeks to come: The spread of industrial unionism and the federation of existing unions within the AFL indicated a clear evolution of the mainstream labor movement. The main obstacle to the growth of a radical movement was dual unionism, which created "endless confusion in the ranks of militants," Foster declared. Militant minorities within the various AFL organizations would press for the abolition of contracts, closer affiliation between labor bodies, and lower initiation fees and would educate workers on the use of sabotage and the general strike. Such a strategy would end the radicals' long isolation. That few if any locals left the IWW must have discouraged Foster. But he made important contacts on the trip, and one by one individuals and small groups split off from the IWW to constitute independent syndicalist leagues.[1]

This long western trip reveals the depths of Foster's dedication to his new vision. He hoboed 6,000 miles across the country in the dead of winter to carry his message to small groups of radicals throughout the West. He was arrested by Mounties in the Canadian Rockies, ironically for being "one of those god-damned IWW's." Although he never mentioned it in any of his contemporary writing, he later recalled that this trip brought bitter deprivation and a close brush with death. Foster left Chicago without money, rode open freights in subzero temperatures, and averaged one meal a day. While he was crossing the plains of Nebraska and eastern Colorado, the temperature dropped to thirty degrees below zero. Riding in the midst of a blizzard in an open gondola loaded with bridge steel, he very nearly passed out and froze to death. Finally reaching a railroad junction, Foster ate, slept for eighteen hours, and then climbed back on an outbound freight to resume his speaking tour. That he regularly subjected himself to such extreme privation and danger in the interests of his organizing suggests not only dedication and toughness but also discipline and a methodical application of energy, all of which characterized his political life.[2]

With this organizing trip largely a failure, Foster paid his last dues to the IWW in February 1912. Relocated in Chicago, he took up railroading again that spring and joined the AFL's Brotherhood of Railway Carmen. Working long hours at his job as a car inspector, he also continued to write. With the IWW press closed to him, he began publishing in the *Agitator,* a Washington anarchist paper. Between April and July of 1912, he wrote a six-part series of articles entitled "Revolutionary Tactics." The IWW was failing, Foster argued, because it tried to mix two distinct functions in the same organization. It acted as a propaganda movement for industrial unionism, and in this regard—bolstered by the internal logic of industrialization itself—it had been extremely successful. Not only socialists and other radicals but also many rank-and-file unionists embraced the industrial union ideal. At the same time, however, the IWW tried to build an entirely new labor federation, which only divided, confused, and weakened the workers' movement. What was needed instead of a parallel movement, Foster argued, was a loose network of militants working within the various mainstream unions to transform them into revolutionary organizations. "There are to be found [in every union] a certain few individuals who exercise great influence over the thoughts and actions of the rest of the mass. They are natural leaders and maintain their leadership through superior energy, courage, intellect, oratorial [sic] power, organizational ability, etc.," Foster pointed out. These militant minorities would concentrate most of their efforts on strike organization and support and on educating the rank and file in the midst of such conflicts. Foster thought it important to have a national paper and some degree of coordination, but most of the important work would be carried on in a decentralized fashion by small groups of individuals in particular unions and localities. It was a model he held to over the next two decades.[3]

Foster spent that summer of 1912 with Earl C. Ford, an old friend from the Pacific Northwest, working as a canvasman setting up tents for a traveling theatrical show. The players staged melodramas and between acts filled in with song and dance numbers. Foster enjoyed the rural scenery of south central Illinois and Indiana and was fascinated by the isolated farmers' appreciation for the crude shows. This fascination for midwestern farm culture, a new world for someone reared in the urban slums, was not unlike the interest he had shown in various other regions of the country and in natural phenomena on his ocean-going adventures. With little formal education, Foster maintained a genuine intellectual curiosity about the diversity of human society and the physical world around him.[4]

In this rather unlikely setting, Foster produced the manifesto for his new syndicalist movement. Writing "during the long hot afternoons in the empty tent, on the shaking wagons pounding over rough country roads, or while loafing in the beautiful fields and woods," he hammered out a remarkable pamphlet called *Syndicalism,* probably the purest statement of syndicalist theory and strategy produced in the United States. He proceeded from what working-class intellectuals liked to call "the fundamentals." The gross inequalities and "monstrous poverty" that intelligent workers saw around them, Foster wrote, were products of the wage system, which he called "the most brazen and gigantic robbery ever perpetrated since the world began." "The thieves at present in control of the industries must be stripped of their booty," he wrote, "and society so organized that every individual shall have free access to the social means of production." This could be accomplished not by political organization, which he termed "worse than useless," but only by direct action, which he defined as "direct warfare—peaceful or violent, as the case may be—of the workers upon their employers, to the exclusion of all third parties."[5] To this point, there was really little in the pamphlet to distinguish Foster's perspective from that of the IWW.

The tract showed much stronger anarchist tendencies, however, than most IWW propaganda and was much more explicit in its blueprint for the new order that eschewed any notion of a central state authority. Workers would administer each industry through shop organizations, not unions, as both the IWW and the CGT envisioned. The functioning of such huge industrial units through autonomous shop organizations was foreshadowed, Foster argued, by the large industrial corporations that were already becoming almost "automatic in their operation." In the future, each monopolized industry would function autonomously, producing in accordance with demand, and its dealings with other industrial units would be limited to filling commodity orders. These shop organizations would administer not only industrial but also "social production," including medicine, education, criminal justice, and so on. For a fuller discussion of how the "social product" might be divided "from each according to his ability; to each according to his needs," Foster referred his readers to the Russian anarchist Peter Kropotkin.[6]

Clearly, Foster embraced his generation's affinity for technical knowledge and expertise. His language here and elsewhere is full of allusions to "scientific" reforms, "evolution" of industry and unions, and a reliance on technical skills. As Edward Johanningsmeier has noted, his vision of "automatic" production governed only by statistics and technical knowledge bore a resemblance not only to Daniel DeLeon's ideas but also to Kropotkin's and to those of the American utopian socialist Edward Bellamy. Foster was concerned with the "system" and how it operated, with objective facts, not sentiments. But the implications he drew from the "natural evolution" of industry in the direction of "automatic monopolies" were decidedly antidemocratic. It was technical expertise, he argued, that would allow the syndicalists to break out of the bourgeois system of political democracy: "In the Syndicalist society the ordinarily unscientific custom of majority rule will be just about eliminated. It will be superseded by the rule of facts and figures." These would be interpreted and executed not by rank-and-file workers but by technical experts in each industry. "Syndicalism and democracy based on suffrage do not mix," Foster concluded.[7]

How would workers achieve the transition to this new syndicalist society? The first step was simply organizing into trade unions, through which workers would carry on daily warfare against their employers by strikes and various in-plant strategies. For all its gigantic size and sophisticated technology, the "delicately adjusted" modern American industrial plant was, Foster shrewdly observed, remarkably susceptible to strikes and sabotage. Each large conflict was an educational experience that demonstrated the effectiveness of modern strike methods and the power of organized workers to control industry, "the greatest force in modern society." "But the vast mass of workers, because of their political, moral, religious, patriotic, craft and other illusions, have not learned this fact," Foster wrote. They would not come to the realization on their own. The militant minority must organize and coordinate these strikes and point out this critical lesson. Eventually, workers would realize their overwhelming power and expropriate all wealth through the ultimate working-class weapon—the general strike.[8]

Foster took pains to distance himself and the new organization from traditional American republicanism and from radical bourgeois ideology more generally. Indeed, he seemed to take great pleasure in flouting democratic values. The syndicalist recognized nothing that could be called "natural rights," he wrote. The freedoms individuals or groups enjoyed were not in any sense "natural"; "rights are only enjoyed by those capable of enforcing them."[9]

In a section entitled "Some Syndicalist Ethics," Foster observed that the syndicalist "has fathomed the current system of ethics and morals, and knows them to be just so many auxiliaries to the capitalist class. Consequently, he has cast them aside and placed his relations with the capitalists on a basis of naked power. . . . He knows he is engaged in a life and death struggle with an absolutely lawless and unscrupulous enemy, and considers his tactics only from the standpoint of their effectiveness. With him the end justifies the means." In answer to the predictable objection that the general strike was likely to result in bloodshed, Foster observed, "This is probably true. . . . But the prospect of bloodshed does not frighten the Syndicalist worker as it does the parlor Socialist. He is too much accustomed to risking himself in the murderous industries and on the hellish battlefields in the niggardly service of his masters, to set much value on his life. He will gladly risk it once, if necessary, in his own behalf. He has no sentimental regards for what may happen to his enemies during the general strike. He leaves them to worry over that detail."[10]

Two characteristics of *Syndicalism* are particularly striking. The first is the detail with which Foster tried to outline the syndicalist society and the revolutionary process from which it sprang. This represented a departure, if not in his thinking, then certainly in his writing, which up to this point had focused almost exclusively on practical issues of organization and tactics. Now he seemed to feel the desire to *see* the new syndicalist world and to show it to the militant minority: here, this is what we are fighting for. Foster's interest and faith in organization and technology, which appear so forcefully here and in much of his later writing, reflected a fairly common intellectual tendency of the time, but they undoubtedly also had a psychological dimension. From childhood, he had constantly faced a life of poverty, transiency, insecurity, and alienation. In visualizing the ideal society, he looked for system, order, precision.

Even more striking, however, was the extreme tone of much of the rhetoric in *Syndicalism* and in the theoretical formulations themselves. The insurrectionary Blanquist tradition, alive and well in the pre–World War I French syndicalist movement, was certainly a major influence.[11] This gave Foster a revolutionary lexicon, but his own experiences over the years may actually have been a more important factor. His language reflects a bitter, almost brutal worldview produced by years of hard work, frustrated plans, chronic insecurity and illness, and periodic brushes with death. He had long ago given up on the system and now was most interested in destroying it. Ironically, Foster had developed an extremely radical theoretical position and adopted ostentatiously violent rhetoric at precisely the moment when he and his colleagues were preparing to break out from the narrow dogmatism of the organized Left and immerse themselves—with some success—in the everyday world of the AFL. The contradiction between language and practice was one that returned to haunt Foster in later years.

Long after his return from Europe, Foster remained in contact with his French mentors. He wrote a regular column called "Lettre des Etats-Unis" for *La vie ouvrière* from early 1912 through the beginning of 1914, providing reports and analysis of the 1913 AFL convention, the sabotage debate and the expulsion of Big Bill Haywood from the Socialist Party, and a whole series of strikes in Michigan, West Virginia, Colorado, New Jersey, New York, and Chicago, which he described as part of a rebirth of the American labor movement. Foster's continued French connection made him an important interpreter of American labor activity for syndicalists abroad and reinforced the French influence in his own thinking as he went about building an American syndicalist movement.[12]

Foster issued a call for the new movement in the August 15, 1912, issue of the *Agitator,* specifically mentioning the CGT and Tom Mann's British group as models for what he hoped to achieve. *Syndicalism* became the program of the Syndicalist League of North America (SLNA), formally launched in Chicago the following month. At its height, the league maintained about a dozen branches with a total membership of perhaps 2,000, almost all concentrated in western and midwestern cities. The typical member was a skilled, native-born radical, recruited largely from two distinct groups—former Wobblies determined to work within the AFL unions, by far the largest of the two, and worker-anarchists.

The extremely decentralized structure of the organization, some of its strategies—including sabotage—and its blueprint for the new society all manifest a strong anarchist influence. In an article entitled "The Future Society," Foster outlined the league's vision for a postrevolutionary world. Like the Wobblies, he rejected any notion of state authority. For Foster, however, the key units were not the industrial unions but what he called the "producing organizations," preexisting formations in which workers produced all of society's commodities and services. With these organizations functioning effectively, the state simply had no role.[13] As in *Syndicalism,* Foster showed a fascination with the future and with technical detail.

In daily organizing work, however, most league members were happy to concentrate on the present. They focused on bread-and-butter issues and patiently worked to remake the unions into fighting organizations. League activists joined AFL local unions, helped organize the unorganized, and advocated higher wages, better conditions, and shorter working hours. For all of Foster's revolutionary hyperbole, it was an eclectic approach, a plan of action to which he himself adhered.[14]

League members shared with other syndicalists the idea of a natural evolution involving the amalgamation of individual unions and the federation of labor into ever greater and more powerful weapons in the class struggle. Foster constantly used the term *evolution* to describe this vital process and pointed to the building trades, metal working, the railroads, and the garment industry as obvious candidates for amalgamation. He was particularly impressed by the systems federations that railroad workers were developing, which coordinated the struggles of workers from the various shop and maintenance trades as well as the trainmen. These seemed to represent a natural step from craft organization and sectionalism toward industrial organization and one big union on the railroads. He also greatly admired England's so-called Triple Alliance of railroad, transport, and mine workers. Foster maintained contacts with syndicalists there and on the Continent. Tom Mann, the architect of the British movement toward industrial unions and that nation's foremost syndicalist, visited the United States for an extensive speaking tour in 1913. When his hostility to dual unionism and his advocacy of the boring-from-within strategy alienated Mann's IWW sponsors, Foster arranged his speaking engagements.[15]

The heart of the SLNA was certainly Chicago, where the league activists consciously thought of themselves as heirs to the tradition of the Haymarket martyrs—the working-class anarcho-syndicalists who had led the great eight-hour movement and general strike in the city in 1886. Eight leaders of this movement were imprisoned and four executed following a bombing and po-lice riot. They became powerful symbols of labor radicalism throughout the world. The league maintained contacts with several survivors of the events. Lucy Parsons, widow of Albert Parsons, one of the state's victims, provided Foster with a roof over his head and allowed the group to hold meetings and collect mail at her home at 1000 South Paulina on the city's old West Side. Lucy, who had been active in Chicago's radical labor circles since the 1870s, was at the center of its anarchist movement between the 1880s and World War I. She joined the SLNA in 1912 and eventually joined the Communist Party toward the end of her life in 1942.[16]

Jay Fox, another survivor of the Haymarket events, brought the organiza-tion not only many contacts and much experience in the anarchist labor movement but also a lively paper, the *Agitator*. Both the paper and its editor had colorful histories. Born just after his parents arrived from Ireland in 1870, Fox grew up in an immigrant neighborhood near Chicago's Union Stock Yards and had firm roots in the city's anarchist movement. In 1886, at the age of sixteen, he joined the Knights of Labor and was wounded during the events at Haymarket. He marched in the funeral cortege after the execution of the Haymarket martyrs and joined Eugene Debs's American Railway Union while working in the Illinois Central Railroad repair shops. Fox worked with the anarchist collective that published *Free Society* and was arrested in the wake of President William McKinley's assassination in the fall of 1901. He attended the IWW's founding convention in 1905, and in 1908 published the pam-phlet *Trade Unionism and Anarchism*, which clearly influenced Foster's own notions of the relationship between trade unionism and social transforma-tion. Fox had imbibed the "Chicago Idea," which mixed socialist, anarchist, and syndicalist ideas and strategies, from Albert Parsons and other working-class anarchists of the Haymarket era. The unions, they argued, could be fash-ioned as instruments for social revolution. Indeed, they represented the basic unit of organization for a new free society that would replace capitalism. It was this proletarian, union-focused anarchism that influenced Foster, who came to call his own syndicalist notions "anarchism made practical."[17]

Jay Fox remained active in Chicago's anarchist circles until leaving around 1908 for the Home Colony, an anarchist community of about 1,200 in Lake Bay, near Tacoma, Washington. During the early twentieth century, the Home group had been turning from the individualistic communism of the nineteenth century toward a labor-based anarcho-communism. As early as fall 1910 in the first issue of the *Agitator*, the group's bimonthly newspaper,

Fox called for an end to dual unionism and support for AFL unions that he felt were evolving in a revolutionary direction. But the colony itself remained a center for spiritualism, Hatha Yoga, nude bathing, and a bohemian lifestyle rather than for labor agitation. Fox printed the *Agitator* in his home on an ancient press inherited from the pioneer anarchist Ezra Heywood, who been jailed for his writings.[18]

Foster was a frequent visitor to the Home Colony during his years in the Pacific Northwest and in his later organizing travels. He stopped there several times in the course of 1912, and by the end of the year he had convinced Fox to move the *Agitator* to Chicago, the center for what he envisioned as a mass syndicalist movement, and to rename it the *Syndicalist.* In the course of the following year, Foster managed the paper along with Fox, but the *Syndicalist* ceased publication in September 1913.[19]

Given Fox's own remarkable trajectory and his devotion to libertarian ideals, Foster's influence on him is striking. After convincing him to switch from anarchism to syndicalism, Foster later won Fox over to a series of other syndicalist efforts and eventually to communism, a rather unlikely ideological home for a man who seemed to be an almost instinctive libertarian. Fox did eventually become disillusioned with the Party, but only after more than a decade. He and Foster remained lifelong friends.

Esther Abramowitz, Foster's future wife, was very much a part of this world. An immigrant garment worker from a Lithuanian Jewish family, she arrived in the United States in the early 1890s and came to the SLNA via anarchism. She had been married to a successful dentist, with whom she had two children, but she was divorced by the early 1900s. Her sister, Anna, married the West Coast anarchist labor radical Eric Morton and was apparently also active in the movement. Abramowitz probably became involved with Jay Fox around the turn of the century and lived with him at the Home Colony, where a third child was born, and in Chicago, where she worked with the IWW and an anarchist group. The writer Hutchins Hapgood described her in these years as a "beautiful jewess . . . melancholy and affectionate and gentle and sensual." He noted that she had had "an unhappy experience with men" and that she practiced free love, even during her ten-year relationship with Fox. At the Home Colony, Abramowitz worked with Fox and other anarchists on the *Agitator.* Here she met Foster, probably in 1909. Judging from the reminiscences of Lucy Robins Lang, who knew both of them, Foster and Abramowitz began an affair at some point during this period. Abramowitz, whom Lang recalled as "dark and voluptuous . . . a figure of Oriental romance," left Fox for Foster around the time she joined the SLNA in 1912, but the three remained friends. Foster eventually adopted her three children—Sylvia and

David, born about 1896 and 1898, from her first marriage, and Rebecca, still an infant, whom Fox had fathered. It appears that he had fairly close relationships with David and Sylvia, but Esther had no children with Foster, who had been influenced by the French syndicalist notion that children inhibited the actions of militants and furnished the capitalist with a "new supply of slaves."[20]

Given Esther's background as anarchist, free-love advocate, and syndicalist militant, her role in the couple's married life was quite remarkable. On the one hand, her relationship with Foster appears to have been very close and loving. He called her "an intelligent and devoted comrade . . . my constant companion and a tower of strength to me," and he dedicated many of his books and pamphlets to her. Friends recalled that they continued to talk politics and were interested in each other's opinions decades later. Yet Esther maintained a very low profile throughout their forty-nine years together, and friends recall that her political involvement was minimal during most of this time, perhaps partly because of her persistent health problems.[21]

The precise nature of the couple's early relationship is unclear. They were not officially married until 1918 and then perhaps only to secure Foster a draft deferment. From late 1911 through 1917 and possibly later, Foster rented a room in Lucy Parson's house, and it seems likely that Esther and her three children lived in their own place or perhaps with other members of Chicago's anarchist community. Foster went on at least two extended organizing tours, in 1912 and again in 1915, riding boxcars from Chicago to the West Coast and back, sleeping in flophouses or with friends. He spent the first several months of 1914 in the Pacific Northwest organizing the timberworkers and then represented them in Helena and Butte, Montana, that spring during a copper miners' strike. He never mentioned Esther in connection with any of these journeys. When Foster was in Chicago, he worked very long hours and often attended meetings in the evenings, so the couple probably spent minimal time together even when they were both in the city. His constant organizing and speaking tours and his frequent long trips to the Soviet Union monopolized much of their later married life as well. Foster was characteristically guarded in his remarks about Esther, as he was about all personal issues and relationships, which he appeared to view as tangential to the main theme of his life story. As a result, we know very little about this fascinating woman.

Like Esther, others in the Chicago group remained around Foster for many years to come. They included Joe Manley, a friend from Seattle and an ironworker who married Foster's adopted daughter. Sam T. Hammersmark was another veteran of the anarchist movement, which he joined as a teenager at the time of the Haymarket events. He had also been active in the IWW before joining the SLNA and helped Foster with his union organizing during World War I. For much of his life, Hammersmark ran the Radical Bookstore in Chicago. Both Manley and Hammersmark helped Foster develop extensive connections in Chicago's huge, heterogeneous labor movement, and both eventually joined him in the Communist Party, as did Jay Fox, Esther, and other SLNA activists.

If Chicago was the league's headquarters, however, some of its most successful organizing took place in Kansas City, St. Louis, and Nelson, British Columbia. The Kansas City group, probably the league's most effective, included Earl Browder, who went on to become the general secretary of the Communist Party and the architect of its Popular Front program. James Cannon, founder of American Trotskyism and an active Wobbly at the time, worked with Browder but was not a league adherent. Both men went on to play important roles in the radical labor movement of the following three decades. In Kansas City, the league helped launch the city trades council's "Labor Forward" movement, and in the process its activists led several important strikes and organized numerous AFL locals. The league's Kansas City paper, the *Toiler*, carried on syndicalist education by publishing editorials and articles by Foster and other league activists. The paper also translated and reprinted Emile Pouget's *Sabotage* and published Tom Mann's reports on British developments, his observations on the American movement, and his famous "Don't Shoot!" leaflet addressed to British soldiers. An auditing committee led by Earl Browder helped drive the Central Labor Council's head from office by uncovering irregularities in the council's finances. Foster might have been exaggerating the group's influence when he later recalled that it "virtually controlled the Central Labor Council," but there is no doubt that the league had sunk deep roots and earned a healthy respect among Kansas City's organized workers.[22]

St. Louis League members also published a weekly paper, the *Unionist*, and led a series of strikes among waiters, taxi drivers, and telephone operators. In Nelson, British Columbia, where Jack Johnstone had established one of the league's earliest branches from the remnants of an IWW local, activists "practically controlled the AF of L," according to Foster. Eventually, Browder, Johnstone, and other league militants from midwestern industrial centers joined Foster in Chicago.[23]

Foster himself spent the spring and summer of 1914 in the West. The International Union of Timberworkers had called a general strike in support of the eight-hour day for May 1, 1914. With Jay Fox serving as the union's vice president and other SLNA militants active, the league influence was strong in the timberworkers' union. For Foster, this organizing effort provided experience, but it also represented another instance of the ruinous effects of political strategies in industrial confrontations. In the midst of the organizing campaign and strike, the Washington State Socialist Party secured a referendum, which, if successful, would have mandated the eight-hour day. Naturally, the referendum strategy proved attractive to the tired strikers, who were facing heavy unemployment. Recognizing the plan's popularity, Foster advocated supporting both the referendum and the strike, but a special convention voted to end the strike and concentrate instead on securing passage of the referendum. In the end, both were defeated, and the union deteriorated in the wake of these failures, another victim, in Foster's eyes, of Socialist Party treachery.[24]

Dual unionism, the other great threat to labor militancy, surfaced that June in a revolt by Butte copper miners. Once again, Foster became involved. This was essentially a rank-and-file attack on an entrenched and corrupt bureaucracy, but in the midst of low wages, dismal health and safety conditions in the mines, and the rapid recomposition of Butte's population, the revolt took on an ethnic dimension and a desperate, violent quality that was not uncommon in the western miners' struggles.

Over the years, the conservative Irish American leadership of the Butte Miners' Union (BMU) of the Western Federation of Miners (WFM) had gradually developed a rather cozy relationship with the Irish American management of the Anaconda Corporation. The local union leaders were widely viewed as corrupt, but they maintained their grip on the organization so long as they could guarantee jobs to their settled community of miners. In the previous few years, however, the town's laboring population had been transformed by a massive influx of eastern Europeans, Finns, and Ethiopians as well as a new generation of young Irish immigrants. With unemployment rising, the newcomers were frozen out of the mines. These newer elements, together with an older radical group, constituted the base for an insurgent movement representing the vast majority of the town's miners. They declared war on the conservatives, and a violent struggle ensued. On Miners' Union Day, June 13, 1914, a large crowd attacked and destroyed the local's hall. The insurgents held a referendum in which over 95 percent of those voting disowned the policies of the BMU. In its wake, they formed the new Butte Mine Workers' Union. Although WFM president Charles Moyer and AFL president Samuel Gompers both blamed the IWW for the trouble, the new organization had no such affiliation, and Wobbly influence was minimal. It was with these fears in mind, however, that the AFL asked its constituent unions to send organizers to help Moyer reestablish some order in the town.[25] The International Union of Timberworkers sent Foster, who had worked briefly in the western mines.

There was little love lost between Foster and the local's leaders. He was aware that the militants "had exhausted every legitimate means to correct the abuses in the union" before the trouble broke out and had failed in all of their efforts. Noting the work that Wobblies and left-wing Socialists had done to build an opposition movement, he maintained that the revolt itself was largely spontaneous. Still, he believed that the dual union strategy would eventually destroy the miners' movement, as indeed it did. He succeeded in arranging a conference with the new rank-and-file leaders, urging them to remain within the WFM and take it over, but the insurgents dismissed him as Moyer's agent.

When Moyer tried to speak in Butte on June 23, a shoot-out developed between his gunmen and a large crowd of armed miners. Several in the crowd outside the union hall were shot, and at least two were killed. The miners riddled the hall with bullets, forcing Moyer and a small group of supporters to flee for their lives. Many years later, an old Wobbly described the scene that followed. As the miners exchanged fire with the gunmen in the union hall, "another gang had gone to a mine and got boxes of dynamite—boxes of it. And they were miners—they knew what to do." The skilled miners carefully planted twenty-six dynamite charges throughout the building "and just blew the thing to pieces—just dropped it." The new Butte Mine Workers' Union flourished briefly, but when another dynamite attack occurred at the end of August, the governor dispatched the state militia and placed the entire region under martial law. The troops and local authorities imprisoned the insurgent leaders and broke the new organization, and miners' unions virtually disappeared from Butte for the next several years.[26]

If the IWW had little to do with the Butte troubles, the Wobblies were certainly busy elsewhere, and for all of its feverish activity at the local level, the SLNA never had much of a chance in its competition with the older organization. While the SLNA's natural constituency lay within the IWW, the Wobblies' fortunes were rising, not falling, at the moment when Foster and his colleagues launched the league. After a notable success with the huge Lawrence, Massachusetts, textile strike in early 1912, IWW organizers fanned out into a number of industries in the East, South, and Midwest. During the next eighteen months, the Wobblies led dramatic strikes among black and white lumber workers in the Gulf Coast region of Louisiana and east Texas; silk workers in Paterson, New Jersey; rubber workers in Akron, Ohio; and at the Studebaker auto assembly plant in the open shop bastion of Detroit. Most of these strikes were lost, but they gave the organization a high profile and conveyed the notion that the Wobblies were on the move. Then, just as the IWW was reeling from its defeats in basic industry, organizers launched a successful drive among harvest hands and other itinerant agricultural workers, which carried over into the World War I era. The oft-asked question, "Why don't the IWW grow?" was far less relevant in the 1912–16 period than it had been in 1911, when Foster returned from Europe. His appeals for a new sort of labor movement fell on deaf ears; it was the SLNA that failed to grow. The organization simply faded out of existence in the course of 1914.[27]

No sooner had the SLNA disintegrated, however, than Foster organized another loose syndicalist group. On January 7, 1915, Foster gathered at a conference in St. Louis a dozen other SLNA militants from throughout the Midwest to establish the International Trade Union Educational League (ITUEL). The group designated him as its secretary, Chicago as its headquarters, and Max Dezettel of the Kansas City SLNA branch as editor of its new paper, *Labor News*. Though slightly more centralized than the SLNA, the new group clearly espoused many of the league's ideas and methods. There were still no dues, and local groups decided on their own structures, policies, and projects. The ITUEL even temporarily endorsed *Syndicalism* as a statement of its principles, though it soon became apparent that the new organization and its work represented an important ideological and tactical step for Foster and those around him.[28]

Foster outlined the new thinking in a remarkable pamphlet, *Trade Unionism: The Road to Freedom,* written in August 1915 and published at the beginning of the following year. Deeply influenced by the contemporary upsurge in the British and American labor movements, he took an even longer stride into the mainstream and went so far as to emphasize the spontaneously revolutionary character of trade union organization and experience. Although Foster later dismissed the pamphlet as a "sag into right opportunism," the work presented a fascinating vision of how workers could create through their own organizations a revolutionary movement capable of transforming society without the intervention of professional revolutionaries.[29]

Foster argued that whether animated by revolutionary ideas or not, the labor movement, with all its faults, was inherently radical. As unions grew larger and stronger, they also grew more aggressive and more expansive in their demands. Much of this initiative would be spontaneous and natural to unions' development. The union's "method is to take all it can," and the task of the militant minority in the unions was simply "to hasten their natural revolutionary development." Their most important activity would be to organize the great mass of unorganized workers into industrial unions.[30]

It was the unorganized, Foster argued, who "haven't the courage and ambition to fight their own battle," who "are the real enemy of Labor; the true obstacle to liberty." Even more than his earlier discussions of the militant minority, *Trade Unionism* seethed with a harsh revolutionary elitism. The unorganized masses were "sodden and inert," "stolid, stupid, spiritless," "human parasites." "The worst enemy of Labor is not the employer," Foster concluded, "but the unorganized workingmen."[31]

As he did in *Syndicalism,* Foster indulged his temptation to take "a glimpse into the future," where higher productivity and greater mechanization would bring shorter hours; distribution of necessities would be "from each according to his ability, to each according to his need"; and there would be little use for government. But there was nothing of the detail, the certainty, or the revolutionary hyperbole he had conveyed in *Syndicalism.* He admitted that all this was "little more than guesses."[32]

Foster closed his pamphlet with a ringing call to action that suggested both his gendered conception of labor militancy and his revolutionary elitism: "Brother Workingman:. . . . Become part of the American Federation of Labor! . . . In spite of its faults the Trade Union Movement is the greatest libertarian movement this planet has ever known. . . . Be a man! Join the Trade Union Movement and be a fighter in the glorious cause of liberty!"[33]

What is most striking in comparing this pamphlet with *Syndicalism* is not the ideas themselves. Although Foster later claimed that the pamphlet marked "radical changes" in the thinking of his syndicalist group, most of the basic ideas expressed in *Syndicalism* were still present—an emphasis on industrial organization rather than political organization and activism, the boring-from-within strategy, the libertarian approach to production and distribution, and a commitment to revolutionary change. Rather, the greatest difference was one of language and tone. *Trade Unionism* was simply far less shrill, far less extreme, and far more optimistic than *Syndicalism.* Foster was determined to get to the very core of the labor movement, even if it meant trimming his ideological and rhetorical sails.[34]

Here, even more than in his earlier formulations, Foster was driven by the events occurring around him. He later explained that his concept of the unions' natural revolutionary character was sparked by the evolution of the powerful Triple Alliance of miners, railwaymen, and transport workers in Britain and to a lesser extent by similar tendencies toward industrial alliances and amalgamations within the American labor movement. The federation movement among railroad workers of all descriptions, a more powerful role for local labor councils representing all the workers in a given locality, and the beginning of a wave of mass strikes by unskilled and semiskilled production workers all suggested to Foster the inherently radical quality of labor organization and encouraged him to sink his own roots deeper into the AFL. In turn, his ideas and the efforts that flowed from them helped reshape the labor movement in the World War I era.[35]

The ideas outlined in *Trade Unionism* explain a great deal about Foster's wartime behavior. Like many syndicalists, he sought above all to advance labor organization. Since radicalism would rise naturally from the movement itself, the important goal was to get workers organized, even if this meant considerable compromise with the conservative union leaders he had so long despised. Without organization, workers were worse than nothing; with it, they held the key to the future. And the key to organization was the militant minority.

To spread his ideas, Foster struck out once again for the open road in February 1915. Another 7,000-mile hobo trip through the plains states and the Far West left little permanent organization, however, and the only effective ITUEL group emerged in Chicago, where it was "pretty much . . . a local League."[36] This was Foster's last such trip. While he certainly remained mobile, he gave up the hobo's life and stuck close to Chicago for most of the next decade. Part of the reason for this change may have been personal. He was now almost middle-aged, with a wife and adopted children and both job and political connections in Chicago. Yet there is little reason to think that such personal considerations would have stopped Foster for long if he had felt that it was more politically productive to resume his transient life. The more important reasons for his rootedness in the coming years probably had to do with his evolving theories of revolutionary organization and with the characteristics of Chicago as a city.

From the time Foster had returned to the United States, his theory and his activism increasingly focused on the local. He had set out first to transform the entire IWW at the national level and then to change it from within through scattered locals. The SLNA consciously concentrated on particular locales. Each group had its own paper and activities, and the league's structure allowed for only a loose coordination between branches. In theory, the ITUEL was equally diffuse as a national organization; in fact, it amounted to a local group in Chicago. If the most important level of organization was local, if boring from within required time and contacts, then it made sense to sink roots in a particularly promising locale and concentrate one's work there.

Chicago, where Foster settled for the moment, seemed to hold out great potential for precisely such organizing. Situated on the Great Lakes in the middle of the nation, the city functioned as the center of the railroad industry and also supported a huge and diverse industrial economy. The size, strength, and progressive quality of its trade union movement was explained by a number of factors. It had a long and radical labor tradition that rendered the movement self-confident and relatively tolerant of new ideas. Throughout the early twentieth century, Chicago continued to be one of the most heavily organized cities in the country, and the top leaders of the powerful Chicago Federation of Labor (CFL) seemed supportive of new organizational initiatives.[37]

Even in Chicago, the ITUEL had less than a hundred people, but many of its militants soon occupied key positions as business agents and organizers for the painters, machinists, carpenters, tailors, retail clerks, garment workers, iron molders, and others. Some were elected as local union officials, and many held positions as delegates to the city's central labor body. Foster himself was hired in the Swift and Company car shops at the giant Union Stock Yards on the city's South Side. He was working there in August 1915 when he wrote *Trade Unionism*. Foreshadowing the next stage of his career, Foster noted that the "hopelessly and helplessly wretched, ignorant, starved-out and degenerate unorganized Stock Yards workers" he observed around him each day were the sort of people who badly needed organizing. He was elected as a business agent for the Railway Carmen in late 1915 and sat in the CFL as the union's delegate to that central body, quickly hatching a plan to affiliate all of the city's 125,000 railroad workers into one council similar to the building and other trades councils in the city.[38]

Even more loosely organized than the SLNA, the ITUEL never established a base outside of Chicago. By the spring of 1917 when the name was dropped, there was little left of the organization, though an important group of perhaps two dozen militants remained active in the city.

Both the SLNA and the ITUEL passed rather quickly from the historical record and left little trace of their work. Yet the organizations were vital to Foster's development, and each was historically significant as well. In terms of personal relationships, many in the group that coalesced around Foster in these syndicalist organizations remained with him throughout his active political life. They represented an ideological generation of sorts within the radical labor movement. Above all, they confronted the Left's disastrous policy of dual unionism and in the process brought a small but talented group of syndicalist militants into the mainstream. Long after the SLNA was gone, such people as Foster, Earl Browder, and Jack Johnstone played crucial roles in organizing basic industry in the United States and later in building the Communist Party. The group around Foster maintained personal contact and a degree of ideological cohesion throughout the World War I years and entered the Communist Party at a crucial point in its development, providing the Party with vital contacts in the factories, mines, and shops.

Foster and other syndicalists derived important lessons from their experiences during the war, which suggest the evolution of the American Left from the prewar syndicalist movement to the early Communist movement of the 1920s. Foster's failures and his successes in the great labor unrest that gripped the nation during and immediately after the war illuminate his adherence to communism better than an organizational history of the movement does.

4 The Chicago Stockyards, 1917–18

THE WAR YEARS offered Foster a splendid opportunity to test his boring-from-within strategy and to realize his goal of organizing the unskilled masses in American basic industry As defense plants geared up between 1915 and 1917, unemployment fell, prices rose, and workers through out the country grew restless With the U.S. entry into the war in April 1917, the federal government was forced to assume a more responsive attitude toward unions, if only to hold workers' loyalty to the war effort and avoid dam aging strikes in defense plants. Employers, faced with severe labor shortages but also the chance to make enormous profits, tended to be more pliant than would normally be the case. As Foster himself concluded, "The gods were indeed fighting on the side of labor."[1]

In this heady environment, workers took the offensive. The number of strikes soared between 1915 and 1916 as unemployment dropped. Trade union membership doubled between 1916 and 1920, peaking at over 5 million. Political radicalism grew along with the industrial unrest. The IWW, the Socialist Party, and local labor party movements all gained strength as the strike wave swept through one industry after another. General strikes broke out in several towns and cities, and industrial conflict remained high throughout the war years, peaking in 1919 with more than 4 million out on strike. In the course of the strike fever, Seattle, Washington, was shut down by a general strike and controlled briefly by a strike committee and the city's labor federation rather than by local government. Miners, the railroad brotherhoods, textile workers, machinists, and even Boston's police force were all out on strike. In the World War I period, the United States was very much a part of the worldwide labor insurgency.[2]

More important than the size of the movement, however, was its scope. A process of ethnic and racial integration began, as hundreds of thousands of workers never before touched by the labor movement were swept up in the organizing and strikes. Unskilled eastern and southeastern European immigrants flooded into the unions, where they mixed with old-line immigrants and the native-born. Progressive labor activists also tried to integrate another new element in the wage labor force: African American migrants from the Deep South who had journeyed to northern industrial cities and towns in search of steady work at high wages.

Foster's own position on the war suggests the continuing influence of syndicalism as well as, perhaps, a bit of opportunism. While most Socialists, Wobblies, and other labor radicals staunchly opposed U.S. involvement, often going to prison for their efforts, Foster was buying and promoting war bonds to support the enterprise. Why? Had he transformed himself from a revolutionary into a loyal trade unionist, a public image he sought to convey within the AFL? Whatever opportunism *was* involved, Foster's public declarations blended with his wartime politics. The apparent incongruity between his industrial militancy and his passive or even supportive attitude toward the war was not unusual among syndicalists. Like many of the French activists he admired, Foster saw the war as an opportunity to build and strengthen the labor movement. He argued, in retrospect, that he did oppose the war but also saw it as a real crisis for the system in which "capitalism was shooting itself to pieces," while labor was in a position to seize the initiative. Still holding firmly to his ITUEL notion that unions, not the Socialist Party, would bring revolution to the United States, he later wrote, "I logically arrived at the conclusion that the main revolutionary task in the war period was the building of trade unionism, the organization of the millions of unorganized," not creating an antiwar movement.[3]

Although Foster later dismissed his wartime position as "an opportunist compromise," it was consistent with his thinking since his break with the IWW. He still considered himself a revolutionary, but the place for a revolutionary was in the heart of the labor movement. If securing that place meant compromises with the labor bureaucracy and the government, Foster was prepared to make them in order to seize what he saw as an unparalleled opportunity for labor power.

While some of the positions Foster took during the war may have been opportunistic, it is difficult to fault his general argument about trade unions' radical potential. The rapid wartime organizing, the giant wartime strike wave, and radical activity in unions during the war all seemed to support Foster's view at the time—even if it was later disproved.

In Chicago, as elsewhere, Foster was at the center of things. For a while, he circulated on the margins of a fascinating Chicago Bohemian subculture revolving around Jack Jones. A former metal miner, hobo, and IWW activist loosely associated in local lore with both poetry and dynamite, Jones was the former husband of the Wobbly agitator Elizabeth Gurley Flynn. Foster knew him from the IWW and the Syndicalist League of North America, for whom Jones wrote a regular column, "Society Notes," instructing his readers on the finer techniques of sabotage. Jones had probably arrived in Chicago about the time Foster moved there, and he quickly became a local institution. Talking with him, the writer Sherwood Anderson once said, was "a little like being in the presence of Jesse James."[4]

Dressed in a green smoking jacket and flowing black tie, Jones presided over a motley group of artists and poets, union organizers and political radicals, thieves and prostitutes, politicians, lawyers, and newspaper reporters at his Dil Pickle Club. The repertoire included poetry readings, dancing, and the plays of Ibsen, Shaw, Strindberg, and Eugene O'Neill, but the place might have been best known for the bewildering range of ideas voiced over the years by all manner of thinkers. Just off Washington Square Park ("Bug House Square" to locals) on Chicago's Near North Side, the Dil Pickle and the park were both part of the city's rich heritage of free speech and radicalism.

Dil Pickle discourse was a jumble of Freud, Havelock Ellis, and Marx. Regulars heard not only from Ben Reitman, the "hobo doctor" and Emma Goldman's lover, and an assortment of Indian mystics and Bolshevik rationalists but also from University of Chicago scholars and other academics from around the country. At the Dil Pickle, Foster rubbed elbows with such writers as Theodore Dreiser and Carl Sandburg and the pioneers of American communism who also frequented the club. Foster's interest in the Dil Pickle probably had to do with politics more than with aesthetics. Yet the connection suggests that at least through the World War I era, he retained some affinity for the freewheeling lifestyle of his hobo years and his trips to the anarchist Home Colony.[5] Foster's visits to the Dil Pickle suggest a side of his personality that seems not to have survived his early years in the Communist Party. The club is never mentioned once in any of his autobiographical writings.

The focus of Foster's life remained where it had always been—on industrial organizing. In Chicago, he planted his deepest roots in a local labor movement. After a year as an elected business agent for the Chicago District Council of his own Brotherhood of Railway Carmen, he returned in late 1916 to his car inspector job on the Soo Line. Working seven twelve-hour days each week, he continued to serve as a delegate to the Chicago Federation of Labor (CFL).

Foster called the CFL "one of the bright spots" in an otherwise reactionary labor movement, and he reported it was "noted throughout the country for the cleanness of its leadership and the progressiveness of its policies." The key figure in Chicago's giant labor movement and in Foster's own situation over the next several years was the CFL's charismatic president, John Fitzpatrick, whom Foster called "one of the sturdy oaks of the labor movement." Fitzpatrick's story is that of the rise and decline of a class-conscious, progressive labor movement in Chicago. He was the spirit behind the movement and the personification of the city's militant labor traditions. A native of County Athlone, Ireland, Fitzpatrick had arrived on Chicago's South Side in 1871 at the age of eleven. A towering, husky man, a blacksmith by trade, an ardent Irish nationalist and anti-imperialist, Fitzpatrick was also a devout Catholic and a teetotaler. He refused to attend any union meeting held in a saloon, a common spot for such gatherings. He and a small group of reformers had battled an army of labor sluggers and grafters to wrest control of the CFL at the turn of the century from "Skinny" Madden and his gang amidst considerable violence. Since then, Fitzpatrick and his colleagues had built the movement's power and influence and had engaged in a spirited round of organizing and independent political work. The CFL progressives played a major role in the creation of both the International Ladies Garment Workers Union and the Amalgamated Clothing Workers of America. In a violent 1912 printers' strike, Fitzpatrick took the side of the rank and file against the international union. Particularly supportive of new initiatives among immigrant and women workers, Fitzpatrick was more an honest and dedicated trade unionist than a political radical. This is precisely what impressed Foster, for whom Fitzpatrick symbolized the sort of indigenous militancy that would transform the American labor movement.[6]

Chicago's long tradition of labor activism suggests that Foster exaggerated in contending that the ITUEL was "instrumental" in making the CFL "the most progressive labor council in the United States."[7] There is no doubt, however, that the city was the center for the radical labor movement in the

United States in the World War I era or that Foster had arrived at a propitious moment. Chicago became his element. He spoke to labor groups and at federation meetings. He became known and accepted as a radical labor activist willing to put his time and talents at the call of the local movement. When the city became the center for a national movement in defense of Tom Mooney, Foster joined the Irish revolutionary Jim Larkin and local activists in the campaign to free him. Mooney, who had organized on the West Coast for the SLNA, was arrested in 1916 and convicted on charges of bombing a San Francisco preparedness parade. At the end of 1916, Foster shared the speaker's stand at a Free Tom Mooney rally with Larkin, Bill Haywood, and the anarchist Alexander Berkman. The following March, Jack Johnstone, one of Foster's collaborators, organized a massive rally for Mooney under the auspices of the CFL, packing the Chicago Colosseum, which had a seating capacity of 12,000.[8]

In Chicago, then, Foster was part of an effervescent labor world. Between 1917 and 1919 federation activists led a campaign to free political prisoners, launched their own local labor party, played a key role in the creation of a national party and a labor news network, created the Chicago Railway Coun cil to link the efforts of disparate organizations in that industry, and coordinated the unionization of unskilled workers throughout the city's diversified and booming economy.

During the World War I era, CFL leaders became far more involved in electoral politics and far more international in perspective. John Fitzpatrick and those around him opposed U.S. entry into the war, supported the Irish struggle for independence, and warmly welcomed the Russian Revolution. They demanded recognition and trade for the new Soviet government and opposed American and Allied interference in Soviet affairs. As Foster himself began to move slowly toward greater interest in domestic labor politics and revolutionary movements abroad, he was surrounded by activists who shared this perspective. Above all, Fitzpatrick and the Chicago group remained militant trade unionists.[9]

Foster's relationship with Fitzpatrick was rather complex. In the war period and even after Foster was known as a Communist, Fitzpatrick seems to have had a deep, fatherly affection for the younger man. He supported Foster at numerous points when political expediency dictated separation. Foster's respect for Fitzpatrick shines through even his most intense criticism of Fitzpatrick in later years. Foster's main orientation to Fitzpatrick was characteristically political, but he may also have found him a suitable object for the respect he had never felt for his own father, for whom he had only pity. He placed Fitzpatrick at the very center of his rather ambitious plans for revamping the trade union movement. Successful union campaigns in such large industries as meat-packing and steel and progressive rank-and-file movements in existing unions, he reasoned correctly, would place Fitzpatrick in the limelight as the champion of militant trade unionism. This notoriety might then be used as a springboard into national labor politics, and Fitzpatrick might eventually succeed in dethroning the aging and conservative AFL president, Samuel Gompers.[10]

Foster eventually developed a rather patronizing attitude toward Fitzpatrick, referring to him in his autobiography as "slow-going Fitzpatrick" whom he was always "pushing forward." He could not "unfold all these plans and speculations," he claimed, because Fitzpatrick might get cold feet. Yet these observations came years after Foster's split with Fitzpatrick. In the war era, he appears to have had the highest regard for him and to have pinned his hopes for the labor movement on the old Irishman. Foster was shrewd enough to recognize the real article, an indigenous labor radical who had won the loyalty of thousands of workers.[11]

Foster's Chicago consisted of block after block of tenements and small wooden cottages, huge factories and construction sites, tangles of freight yards and car shops on the city's densely populated South Side and West Side. The key to wartime organizing in Chicago was the sprawling Union Stock Yards on the city's industrial South Side. The yards and adjacent packing and rendering plants were some of the largest industrial facilities in the world. Covering more than a square mile, the yards resembled a city unto itself, with its own police and fire departments, banks, hotel and restaurant facilities, and hundreds of miles of roadway, ramps, and railroad tracks.

Nowhere is this stark urban landscape described better than in Upton Sinclair's classic novel, *The Jungle:* "down a side street there were two rows of brick houses, and between them a vista: half a dozen chimneys, tall as the tallest of buildings, touching the very sky—and leaping from them half a dozen columns of smoke, thick, oily, and black as night. . . . There is more than a square mile in the yards, and more than half of it is occupied by cattle pens; north and south as far as the eye can see there stretches a sea of pens. And they were all filled—so many cattle no one had ever dreamed existed in the world."[12]

The upsurge of production to accommodate European and American war orders vastly increased the size of this operation. By the fall of 1917, hundreds of thousands of cattle entered the complex each week, and 45,000 workers toiled in the yards. Yet the entire complex remained virtually unorganized. The explanation lay in the power and psychology of the packers. Foster later told the story of a group of steamfitters with a particularly onerous grievance. They approached the company and were surprised to find themselves ushered into the office of an Armour vice president. The man simply ignored the group's pleas by discussing the weather. "So that's the answer of Armour and Company to its workers when they present a grievance," the group's leader asked, "you sneer at us by talking about the weather." "Yes, that's Armour's answer," the executive shot back. "Go back to your trade union friends and tell them Organized Labor will never get anything from this company that it hasn't the power to take." "I never forgot those cold, cynical words," Foster later recalled, "nor did I fail to draw the full class struggle logic from them."[13]

The campaign to organize the meat-packing industry unfolded in a rather dramatic setting. Tucked just "back of the yards" was one of Chicago's poorest working-class neighborhoods. Once populated largely by skilled German and Irish butchers, the "Back of the Yards" was now home to a bewildering ethnic mix of unskilled laborers, notably Poles, Lithuanians, Bohemians, and Slovaks. Smokestacks and the steeples of the community's various ethnic churches combined to create a memorable industrial skyline; saloons represented the community's largest single business interest. Infant mortality and contagious disease rates soared; wages remained very low. The fate of Chicago's packinghouse workers represented in many respects that of unskilled immigrant workers in industrial slums throughout the nation.[14] If the stockyards could be organized, perhaps the same might be done in Pittsburgh or Detroit, in one basic industry after another. Certainly this is what William Z. Foster had in mind.

The goal of organizing the stockyards had percolated in the city's trade union movement for more than a generation. The Knights of Labor and independent unions had led major organizing drives as early as the 1870s and 1880s. In 1894, during the great Pullman boycott, the packinghouse workers had joined the railroad workers and others in something approaching a general strike. Between 1900 and 1904, the AFL's Amalgamated Meat Cutters and Butcher Workmen had built a strong movement across all lines of race, nationality, gender, and skill to embrace virtually every worker in the yards. Yet the packers had destroyed each of these organizations, and the giant plants remained open shop on the eve of World War I. It would be remarkable, then, if many Chicago packinghouse workers and others were not thinking about a new drive as the United States entered the conflict in the spring of 1917. Sporadic strikes broke out among the restive immigrant workers. The summer of 1917 was an opportune time for a new assault on the yards.[15]

It was Foster who hatched the plan to realize this goal. By his account, the idea came to him one day, July 11, 1917 to be precise, as he walked to work. He presented the plan to his union that night and to the old Amalgamated's anemic cattle butchers' union two days later. On July 15, 1917, the Chicago Federation of Labor unanimously endorsed Foster's motion to organize the stockyards, cosponsored by Dennis Lane of the cattle butchers, and created the Stockyards Labor Council (SLC) a week later with Martin Murphy, a hog butcher, as president and Foster as secretary.[16]

Building such a movement in the American context would be no easy project. The ethnic and racial diversity of the labor force and the large proportion of unskilled workers in the stockyards, for example, presented Foster and his organizers with challenges that past movements had never overcome. This campaign represented the first large effort to organize unskilled workers in a major mass production industry. This could be achieved only through a new form of labor organization, a mass interracial movement organized along industrial rather than craft lines. The task in 1917 was to devise a strategy that would move toward such organization without violating the autonomy of the various craft unions represented in the yards.

Foster modeled the Stockyards Labor Council on the systems federation movement among the railroad workers. "We decided to move towards industrial unionism by setting up an industrial federation and by locking the various component craft unions so firmly together under one Council, one Executive Board, one set of Business Agents, etc. as to create a firm front in the whole industry."[17] Each of the thirteen craft unions with jurisdiction in the yards had a representative on the council, but the SLC staff did the actual organizing. Foster planned to draw as many workers into the drive as quickly as possible and later sort them out among the council's various constituent unions. Skilled auxiliary workers, such as the machinists and carpenters, joined locals of their craft unions, which were affiliated with the council, while workers in the various slaughtering and packing plants joined department units or mass, community-based laborers' locals of the Amalgamated Meat Cutters and Butcher Workmen. Cumbersome in structure, the Stockyards Labor Council nevertheless represented an important step toward industrial unionism, the ultimate goal of Foster and many other labor radicals.

For Foster, the plan was more than a matter of increasing the size of the labor movement and providing basic rights and decent conditions for the unskilled. He clearly saw it as an opportunity to transform the movement. "Such a great influx of members," he reasoned, "would, as I was quite consciously aware, change the character of the trade unions," and in this sense it was a part of a broader goal—"the revolutionization of the AF of L." This was perhaps a rather dubious proposition, but Foster assumed correctly that such a recomposition of the AFL's membership would have profound implications for the future of the labor federation. He hoped that the Stockyards Labor Council would provide a new model for organizing production workers in basic industries throughout the economy and that such sweeping organization would of itself create a new sort of labor movement. He still saw himself as a revolutionary, but the place for a revolutionary, he thought, was at the heart of the labor movement. Political parties could not accomplish a revolution; the unions would have to do it. "With such a conception," Foster later recalled, "I logically arrived at the conclusion that the main revolutionary task in the war period was the building of trade unionism, the organization of the millions of unorganized."[18]

The giant meat-packing companies had crushed earlier organizing efforts so effectively that the initial response was discouraging. The first public meeting attracted a throng of 10,000 packinghouse workers, but when Foster appealed to the audience to come forward and sign union cards, he observed "a dull silence for a moment—then many of those in attendance began to slip away."[19] Workers were intimidated by the packers' elaborate espionage network, which turned out to include two of Foster's own immigrant organizers.

As the workers did begin to pour into the unions in the fall of 1917, the response was particularly strong among immigrant laborers. Realizing that it was vital to win the immigrants' confidence, Foster established roots in the various ethnic communities, hiring foreign-language organizers and speaking before fraternal and other community groups. He found this mixture of volunteer and union-appointed organizers "the liveliest bunch he had ever come in contact with." The charismatic Polish orator John Kikulski seized the imaginations of the Slavic workers. Soon the campaign caught fire, particularly among the Poles, and swept through the densely populated immigrant neighborhoods surrounding the yards, "where the union became a household word." The council's largest local recruited 10,000 Polish and Lithuanian laborers within a month. Polish and Lithuanian women joined their own locals. By the end of World War I, more than 20,000 Slavic immigrants had joined the movement, and the white workers were largely organized.[20]

There was still "one big problem," as Foster put it when he spoke before the Chicago Federation of Labor on the progress of the campaign—"the organization of the colored men." With immigration falling by 80 percent between 1914 and 1918, thousands of African American migrants entered the industry. By 1917, nearly 12,000 black workers, about one-fourth of the industry's labor force, worked in the yards. As unionism grew apace among the immigrants, the growing number of African American workers in the yards represented a significant challenge, complicated by the poor state of race relations in the country at the time. Many national unions, particularly craft bodies, and more than one-third of the AFL affiliates in Chicago either drew the color line quite explicitly, their printed constitutions forbidding admission of African Americans, or segregated blacks into separate locals. The Amalgamated Meat Cutters and Butcher Workmen, the main organization for production workers in the industry, welcomed the newcomers, but even there integration was difficult. Major community institutions, welfare organizations, and religious and political leaders in the Black Belt opposed unionization, and many of the black workers themselves lacked any experience with the labor movement. In this context, the migrants came to distrust the unions, which many saw as a "white man's movement."[21]

Foster believed that these black workers would play a critical role in any coming conflict. Organizing blacks was "imperative . . . a place had to be made in the movement for every negro in the packing houses." "The first meeting we had we sat around a table and talked it over," he later recalled, "[and] we realized that to accomplish the organization of the colored worker was the real problem . . . we were determined to organize the colored worker if it was humanly possible to do so. . . . We found that we had tremendous opposition to encounter."[22]

The Stockyards Labor Council's first mass locals were interracial, but some black leaders complained that the minority would be submerged and their voices lost in such bodies. When Foster switched tactics and set up separate black locals, some attacked the Stockyards Labor Council as a Jim Crow movement. There were elements in the black community, Foster concluded, that would never welcome organized labor. "It seemed to make no difference what move we made, there was always an argument against it," he declared.[23]

Foster secured black male organizers from the AFL and the United Mine Workers of America and assigned Irene Goins of the Women's Trade Union League to recruit the industry's rapidly growing numbers of black women. SLC unions aggressively pursued African American workers' grievances, including those involving racial discrimination. Foster himself spoke before black community and civic groups. And he had some success. Perhaps four or five thousand African Americans joined the unions, and an active group of militants worked with Foster and the SLC, but the great mass of migrants held aloof. "Out in the stockyards we could not win their support," Foster testified before the Chicago Commission on Race Relations. "It could not be done. They were constitutionally opposed to unions, and all our forces could not break down that opposition." This failure would return to haunt Foster in the packinghouse workers' movement and elsewhere.[24]

Convinced that a showdown with the packers was inevitable, Foster argued that the unions should take the initiative while the labor market conditions still favored them. As the stockyards movement swelled through the late fall of 1917, the packers became more provocative. Superintendents victimized union members at several plants, and some workers called for a strike. Foster urged representatives from the various national unions to prepare for such a conflict, but the more conservative officials hesitated. Against this resistance, Foster secured votes demonstrating massive support for a strike, and workers poured into the unions in packing centers across the country, anticipating the fight. Fearing a disruptive walkout, federal officials were forced to mediate in late 1917. The government named federal judge Samuel Alschuler as arbitrator for the industry and set hearings for early 1918 to work out a compromise.[25]

The hearings marked the beginning of Foster's relationship with the brilliant Irish American trial lawyer Frank Walsh, who used the arbitration hearings to turn a spotlight on the misery back of the yards. Walsh, born in 1863 in St. Louis of Irish immigrant parents, had his own interesting career trajectory. He worked his way through high school as a messenger, factory hand, and railroad cashier and through law school as a stenographer, eventually creating a lucrative corporate practice in Kansas City. At the turn of the century, however, he dropped his corporate clients and increasingly devoted himself to a variety of reform movements, including woman's suffrage and civil rights. "Comfortable among Democrats and anarchists, among haughty AFL craft unionists and hardscrabble Wobblies, among Catholic prelates and Greenwich Village bohemians, Walsh was a unique figure," Joseph McCartin wrote. Appointed chair of the U.S. Commission on Industrial Relations, Walsh lined the committee and its staff with progressive reformers and academics and succeeded, McCartin concluded, "in using its investigations to raise a demand for the democratization of industrial life in the absence of a strong national political commitment to such an endeavor." During the war, Walsh turned his considerable talents to the cause of the packinghouse workers and others, and following the war, he involved himself in the labor party movement and the defense of a number of labor militants, including William Z. Foster. "For once," the *Chicago Herald* observed, "the humble day laborers who exist in the slums of Packingtown had counsel as adroit as that which their millionaire employers had been able to acquire."[26]

The attending publicity strengthened the workers' cause and forced the packers on the defensive. Polish laborers described industrial disease and accidents. Their wives, wrapped in shawls, spoke in broken English of dead babies and insufficient food. Foster rejoiced in the opportunity to expose the packers. "It was as if the characters in *The Jungle*, quickened to life, had come to tell their story from the witness chair," he declared. Comparing the laborers' average annual income of $800 with the United Charities estimate of $1,106.82 for a minimum budget for a family of five, the unions claimed that workers laboring long hours under dangerous conditions in a slaughterhouse earned well below the poverty level. Foster made the most of the scandal. "Has American industry ever shown a greater shame?" he wrote. "Workers paid less than paupers!"[27]

In March 1918, the packinghouse workers won a stunning victory in the government arbitrator's award, including a substantial wage increase, the eight-hour day, a ban on racial and gender wage discrimination, and a system for grievance arbitration. Wild celebrations erupted in the drab neighborhoods back of the yards, and John Fitzpatrick addressed a huge, racially mixed crowd in Davis Square, directly across from the packinghouses: "It's a new day, and out in God's sunshine you men and you women, Black and white, have not only an eight-hour day, but you are on an equality."[28]

Foster's boring-from-within strategy appeared to be paying off; the arbitration award brought another surge of membership. In July 1918, Foster wrote to Frank Walsh about the strength and stability of the new movement: "We are doing well in the Yards. The organizations maintain themselves very good. . . . I think the foundations of unionism have been laid in the packing industry for a long time to come."[29]

By this time, Foster had set his sights on an even more formidable target than the Chicago stockyards: the steel industry. His drive to unionize the "steel trust" between the summer of 1918 and the fall of the following year accomplished what the economist Philip Taft called "one of the greatest organizing feats in American labor history."[30] In the process, Foster built a national reputation, emerging as one of the most accomplished labor organizers in the United States.

5 The Great Steel Strike, 1918–19

DOMINATED BY UNITED STATES STEEL, one of the largest and most modern corporations in the world, the steel industry seemed impregnable. The power of the corporation extended beyond the plants' walls and into the mill towns, where it often controlled housing, local politicians and police, and even cultural and recreational facilities. Presiding over this "steel trust" was Judge Elbert Gary, an imposing figure, eloquent, dignified, and iron-willed. Philosophically, Gary was firmly wedded to the notion of the open shop, "which permits one to engage in any line of employment whether one does or does not belong to a labor union."[1] In practice, the corporation regularly fired activists and maintained elaborate blacklists to keep them out of its plants. "To trade union organizers," Foster wrote, "the steel industry had long symbolized the impossible."[2]

The workers appeared hopelessly divided and in disarray. Composed of literally dozens of nationality groups with vastly different backgrounds and experiences, the labor force was also segmented along skill lines, with native-born, British, and Irish craftworkers often despising the unskilled immigrant "Hunkies." How could such an organizing task possibly succeed? Encouraging Foster and other organizers was a sullen resentment of the steel trust that visitors sensed in the dingy mill towns. In many respects, the situation had seemed equally hopeless in meat-packing, where Foster and the Stockyards Labor Council had scored a brilliant success with a whirlwind organizing campaign aimed at the heart of the immigrant community.

Foster concluded that the only hope for the mammoth steel industry lay in an even more ambitious campaign. "The idea was to make a hurricane drive simultaneously in all the steel centers that would catch the workers' imagination and sweep them into the unions *en masse* despite all opposition, and thus to put Mr. Gary and his associates into such a predicament that they would have to grant the just demands of their men."[3]

That would be only the beginning. Several years later in an open letter to John Fitzpatrick, Foster described the master plan beyond the steel campaign.

> It was my aim to propose, if the steel strike had been a success, the formation of a great organization committee with branches in each of the big industries, to sweep the masses into the unions. We were in a position to insist that such a committee be formed. . . . With the prestige that had been gained through the unionizing of the steel industry and the general raising of the morale of the workers everywhere thereby this great organizing campaign must have been a tremendous success. It would have surely resulted in the organization of the broad masses of the working class.[4]

As ambitious as the steel organizing campaign appeared, it was but one part of an aggressive plan to realize Foster's vision of a militant new labor movement. Alliances with such indigenous progressives as Fitzpatrick provided a way to transform the movement from the inside out. Foster saw Fitzpatrick as Gompers's successor at the head of a giant new AFL. "The outcome of such a great campaign would have been to so enormously increase your prestige that you would have overshadowed Gompers," Foster later wrote, "and would have been in a position to deliver to him his long-needed *coup de grace,* which we would have known how to administer at the appropriate time."[5]

In the midst of the steel organizing campaign, however, any such grandiose plans were buried beneath Foster's methodical approach to the work at hand. The success of this mammoth undertaking depended on the cooperation of the AFL and all the international craft unions with jurisdictional rights in steel. The size and complexity of the campaign required large sums of money and coordination among unions in the various steel-producing regions.

Foster started once again where he was sure to get support, in Chicago.

On April 7, 1918, with the meat-packing campaign still in high gear, the Chicago Federation of Labor (CFL) unanimously passed Foster's resolution calling on the AFL to convene a national conference of unions concerned with the industry. Foster attended the AFL convention in June of that year as the CFL delegate and lobbied for such a conference to plan an organizing drive in steel, again securing unanimous support for the idea. He even persuaded AFL president Samuel Gompers to chair the conference. He then implored Fitzpatrick to take responsibility for the movement: "When that conference convenes, if the matter is left to me to put over I feel reasonably certain that the whole thing will fail, but if you will go to bat on it as you did in the stockyards project[,] then I am positive that it will succeed. . . . there absolutely must be someone at the head of it who will back up the organizing force to the limit in the drastic and unusual methods necessary. If it is some conservative or pussyfooter, then goodnight. It will be a noble cause ignobly lost."[6]

Fitzpatrick agreed to help, and the special conference finally convened in Chicago in early August and established the National Committee for Organizing Iron and Steel Workers. Precious time had been lost. Foster remained optimistic, but lukewarm support from the national unions threatened to destroy the plan. Each union pledged only $100, the total representing only a tiny fraction of the $250,000 he had expected. In addition, some unions contributed the services of organizers. Without sufficient resources to launch a simultaneous drive in each of the nation's steel centers but still determined to seize the initiative, Foster decided to target the most promising region, hoping to build on his success there.[7]

At the end of August 1918, Foster and his organizers swept into the steel towns along the south shore of Lake Michigan—South Chicago, Gary, Joliet, and Indiana Harbor. The results suggested what Foster's plan for a national campaign might have looked like with proper support. Large enthusiastic crowds filled the streets of the mill towns. Twelve hundred signed up in one day at Joliet, fifteen hundred at South Chicago. "You talk about spirit," read a dispatch from Gary, "why that is all these men out here are breathing. They have been hungering for the chance to get in."[8]

This Calumet region was not the biggest challenge facing Foster and his organizers, though. Off to a slow start and without enough money, the committee now moved into the solidly open shop heart of the industry, what Foster called "the den of the Steel Trust"—the Monongahela River Valley area around Pittsburgh. They did so under decidedly inauspicious circumstances. With winter fast approaching, a serious influenza epidemic broke out, ending all public meetings for several weeks. In November, the armistice was signed, government war orders were canceled, and layoffs started, extinguishing the favorable labor market conditions under which the original plan was conceived.

The mill towns themselves provided an ominous setting for the drama that was about to unfold. "For mile after mile the chimneys of the mills are like pipes of giant organs," the progressive novelist Mary Heaton Vorse wrote. "A pall of smoke forever hangs over these towns, and at night the darkness is perpetually shattered by the nightly hallelujah of the blast furnaces." It was this surrealistic glow emanating from dozens of blast furnaces up and down the Monongahela River that prompted the writer Lincoln Steffens to describe the area as "Hell with the lid off." "The district contains from seventy to eighty per cent of the country's steel industry," Foster wrote. "The whole territory is an amazing and bewildering network of gigantic steel mills, blast furnaces and fabricating shops."[9]

Foster ran the campaign to organize this giant industry from a small room in Pittsburgh that he shared with a stenographer; his daughter Sylvia Manley, who worked as his secretary; and Edwin Nedwick, his publicity director. His wife, Esther, was a frequent visitor. The place was often so crowded that impromptu conferences were held in the hallway near the doorways of surrounding brokers' offices. Later, the committee secured two additional adjacent rooms. Government propaganda and AFL recruiting posters and rally announcements covered the walls. One poster, headed "Americans All," showed various nationalities fighting together under the Stars and Stripes. A constant stream of visitors—steelworkers, organizers, women looking for missing husbands—flowed in and out, while Foster and his staff worked methodically. For all the activity, Mary Heaton Vorse found it to be "the quietest office I have ever been in. No one ever gets excited. Every one works ceaselessly and without flurry. All day long people came to see Foster. Foster talked with any one who wanted to talk with him. He was as accessible as the Post-Office Building opposite."[10]

Vorse left a memorable sketch of Foster at work in the midst of the campaign.

> He has a thin face, a kind mouth and eyes, and he can work from morning to night, interrupt his work to receive a hundred people, and never turn a hair. He is composed, confident, unemphatic and impeccably unruffled. Never for a moment does Foster hasten his tempo. . . . he seems completely without ego. . . . He lives completely outside the circle of self, absorbed ceaselessly in the ceaseless stream of detail which confronts him. . . . Once in a while he gets angry over the stupidity of man; then you see his quiet is the quiet of a high tension machine moving so swiftly it barely hums. He is swallowed up in the strike's immensity. What happens to Foster does not concern him. I do not

believe that he spends five minutes in the whole year thinking of Foster or Foster's affairs.[11]

This quiet intensity, selflessness, and the tendency to merge his own identity with that of his movement were qualities observed throughout Foster's career. It was partly his own quiet confidence that explains his enormous popularity among the steelworkers.

On the surface at least, Foster was not impressive. A reporter described him at age forty on the eve of the strike: "He is a slim man, about five feet nine inches tall, a typical Western railroader . . . he has worked hard in his life and must be under forty. He has a good head, small ears, keen, clear eyes, the jaw and chin of a leader of men, a small mouth with thin lips and the most leisurely way of doing things. His smile is quite engaging. . . . In the course of a day he gets away with a terrific amount of work."[12]

Much of this work involved the sort of detailed organizing on which Foster thrived. He scrutinized the smallest details of the campaign and clearly took pride in the efficient methods he devised to do the job. Characteristically, he emphasized the steel campaign's "logical and practical" qualities; he believed that he had developed an efficient *system*. Labor organizing, he said, was "a comparatively simple matter when it is properly handled." He described the campaign with the same technical and natural metaphors he had employed in much of his earlier writing. "It is largely a mechanical proposition. . . . The problem in any case is merely to develop the proper organizing crews and systems, and the freedom-hungry workers, skilled and unskilled, men and women, black and white, will react almost as naturally and inevitably as water runs down a hill."[13] Tellingly perhaps, Foster wrote little of the steelworkers themselves in his descriptions of the organizing. He seemed far more concerned with structure and strategy.

The success of the steel campaign depended almost entirely on the skills and abilities of Foster's organizers, a group of about 125 full-time organizers divided between experienced "stationary" or local secretaries and "floating organizers." The local secretaries were in full charge, controlling all funds, maintaining the local organizations, and reporting directly to the National Committee. Various unions contributed most of the floating organizers, who moved from place to place as the need arose. Composed largely of experienced unionists about Foster's age or perhaps even a bit older, this group included at least a few women, notably Fannie Sellins and Mother Jones, the eighty-year-old matriarch and nationally recognized symbol of the labor movement. While the organizers were a rather mixed lot, many were radicals Foster knew from his various political associations. His son-in-law Joseph

Manley and Sam Hammersmark had both been associated with the Syndicalist League of North America and later joined Foster in the Communist Party.
He knew J. G. Brown, his closest collaborator in directing the strike, from his
days as a timberworkers' organizer in the Pacific Northwest. The two crossed
paths again during the Labor Party agitation and the Trade Union Educational League organizing of the early 1920s. To maximize resources and guard
against any sign of malfeasance, Foster devised a unique accounting system
to keep track of membership income, disbursement of organizing expenses,
and other expenditures. He demanded that all organizers "adopt sound business principles of responsibility, standardization and general efficiency."
Whether out of pride in the movement's tight organization or as a defense
against any subsequent allegations of impropriety, Foster retained copies of
the National Committee's official audits, receipts, and elaborate financial records for decades.[14]

Among Foster's obstacles in the organizing was the structure of the committee itself, which demanded consultation with the various union execu-
tives for any major decision. "Everything, however small, except possibly de-
tailing organizers here and there, must be referred to that committee," Foster
explained to Senate investigators. "It is not bound together by any constitution or law or anything, except just common interest. The only way we can
maintain that committee together is to have a thorough understanding and
agreement among the organizations taking part in it, and in order to preserve
that agreement we find it necessary to continually refer back to these international heads."[15]

Anticipating claims that he was "using" the strike for his own ends, Foster
was scrupulous about such consultation, always sure that he had the support
of the AFL and the interested unions. He had to organize a huge, extremely
diverse, and far-flung labor force against overwhelming odds, using a jerry-
built structure with woefully insufficient resources, while always looking out
for the jealousies and suspicions of a dozen or more AFL craft unions. Bert
Cochran, a critic of Foster's later career, marveled at the coordination involved. "In the protracted, complicated negotiations required to maneuver a
dozen squabbling, narrow-minded and egocentric AF of L union heads into
cooperating in this major organization effort, and then to keep them from
undercutting each other during the bitterly fought strike, Foster displayed
tact and dexterity of a high order. In addition to being a capable strike organizer and tactician, he was a crafty politician; he had the streak of adapt-
ability in him." As the economist George Soule later noted, "It must have
been like driving a spirited twelve-horse team through No-Man's Land during an artillery barrage." "The disturbance throughout all the steel towns was

like a slow, heavy ground swell," Mary Heaton Vorse wrote. "There were very few organizers and a great number of steel workers. There was very little money for so great a campaign. And yet, steel was organized."[16]

Foster insisted that organizers concentrate not on the steelworkers' weaknesses but rather on improving "their own primitive organization methods." The workers wanted to get together and fight the companies, he said, and the success of the campaign depended on the organizers themselves, not outside forces. This argument "filled the organizers with unlimited confidence in their own power," Foster believed. "They felt that they were the decisive factor in the situation."[17]

Foster aimed first to establish basic civil liberties in the mill towns so that the organizing could proceed. "Western Pennsylvania is controlled body and soul by the Steel Trust," he wrote. "The whole district has the psychology of a company-owned town." Public speaking and large meetings were simply banned, and those who challenged the ban were quickly arrested. Foster and his staff launched a campaign similar to the IWW's free speech fights. In Monessen, Pennsylvania, they announced a public rally that was promptly banned by the burgess, who threatened to jail all those who attended. The local secretary, a miner, marched 10,000 miners in from the surrounding coalfields. Foster ensured a good turnout by securing several prominent speakers—Mother Jones; Phil Murray, the young president of District 5 of the United Mine Workers of America; James Maurer, president of the Pennsylvania Federation of Labor; and Foster himself. The burgess gave up. When merchants in Donora, Pennsylvania, demanded that the committee's local secretary leave town, workers organized a consumer boycott that forced the merchants to back down. A "flying squadron" of organizers circulated among the free speech fights waged in mill towns up and down the Monongahela Valley. Such flying squadrons were later employed when the Congress of Industrial Organizations (CIO) was organizing in the 1930s.[19]

By the spring of 1919, the National Committee had organized about 100,000 steelworkers. As the momentum grew, so did pressure for a strike. The National Committee adopted a series of twelve demands, including increased wages, the eight-hour day, a seniority system, one day off in seven, and the abolition of company unions, but the critical issue in the confrontation was union recognition and collective bargaining rights. As Gompers and the international presidents equivocated, Foster pressed for and secured a strike vote. The national ballot tabulated on August 20, 1919, indicated that 98 percent of those voting favored strike action if the companies refused to make concessions. Small stickers began to appear on buildings and lampposts throughout the steel towns: "Strike September 22."

Little more than a week after the ballot, Foster found himself in what must have seemed a rather incongruous situation, given his personal and political background. Summoned to the White House along with Gompers, Fitzpatrick, and others from the National Committee to discuss the impending crisis, he sat facing Woodrow Wilson, the president of the United States. Foster later recalled that the president tried to place the union men at ease by using what Foster called "roughneck talk." Wilson agreed to ask Judge Gary to meet with the union officials. Nearly two weeks passed, however, without a response; clearly, Gary had refused the president's request.[19]

The steel companies' attitude strengthened Foster's hand. It was vital to move quickly, he argued, or the national movement would disintegrate into local outbursts. In late August, Foster visited Gary's New York office along with Fitzpatrick and David J. Davis of the Amalgamated Association of Iron, Steel and Tin Workers, but Gary quickly rejected their proposal to schedule a conference to discuss the workers' demands. Meanwhile, organizers were attacked and jailed throughout the mill towns. On September 11, Gompers received a message from Wilson, asking him to postpone the strike until the President's Industrial Conference, due to convene on October 7. Inclined to honor the president's request, Gompers and numerous international union officials showered Foster's office with calls for a postponement.[20]

This put Foster and the steel organizers in a difficult position. To refuse the president's request would make them look unreasonable, yet Foster was convinced that any further delay would break the drive's momentum and squander a priceless opportunity: "if no action is taken now, our movement will rapidly go to pieces, through spasmodic strikes. To stop the movement now is out of the question." Desperate, he solicited testimony directly from organizers in mill towns throughout the country. A flood of telegrams confirmed Foster's impressions.[21] The National Committee finally issued 200,000 copies of its official strike call printed in seven languages. On September 22, 1919, 250,000 workers, about half of all American steelworkers, left their jobs, shutting down the industry in the country's first national steel strike and its largest industrial conflict to date.

Repression began immediately and was the worst in the Pittsburgh district. The companies built stockades, strung barbed wire around the mills, and placed machine guns at strategic points. To supplement the local police and deputies and the dreaded state constabulary, steel officials imported thousands of heavily armed "detectives" to intimidate the steelworkers. "Along the Monongahela River from Pittsburgh to Clairton, a distance of twenty-five miles," Foster claimed, "there were not less than 25,000 armed men in the service of the Steel Trust."[22]

The steelworkers desperately fought it out on the streets of the mill towns, where the strike was suppressed with considerable brutality from start to finish. Even before the conflict had begun, police systematically attacked open meetings. On Sunday, September 21, 1919, in Clairton, Pennsylvania, fifteen miles up the river from Pittsburgh, thousands of immigrant workers and their families gathered in an open field to hear plans for the strike set to begin the following morning. The crowd was listening to union leaders when half a dozen mounted state police charged into the audience at full gallop, cursing and flailing with their nightsticks at the screaming men, women, and children. Speakers who had discouraged the strikers from stoning the police were arrested, held without charge, and finally booked for disorderly conduct. "It was the beginning of the terror in the Pittsburgh district," the labor historian David Brody observed.[23]

The union's early civil liberties breakthroughs, Brody wrote, "were now ruthlessly swept away." Allegheny County authorities banned any public meeting of three or more in an outdoor public place. Even indoor meetings were permitted only in English and strictly at the discretion of local authorities, most of whom prohibited gatherings of any description. The county sheriff deputized some 5,000 vigilantes, who had been "selected, paid and armed by the steel companies." Most of them were businessmen and ex-soldiers.[24]

The results were predictable. On August 26 at Brackinridge, Pennsylvania, deputies led by a mine official charged a group of pickets in a mill yard, shooting as they came. When Joseph Strzelecki fell mortally wounded, the organizer Fannie Sellins came to his aid. Sellins, a forty-nine-year-old grandmother whose son had been killed in France during World War I, was clubbed, shot several times, and then clubbed again before she died. Despite many witnesses and discussion of the murderers' names in the press, the killers were not brought to trial until four years later and were then acquitted. Within ten days of the strike's beginning, fourteen people were dead, every one of them a striker or strike sympathizer.[25]

In addition to deputies and state police, strikers also contended with vigilantes. In those regions where the strike was solid, organizers could rely on protection. In Steubenville, Ohio, where Foster faced threats from the Chamber of Commerce and the American Legion, a large body of armed workers escorted him to the meeting hall and guarded the doors. He was not as lucky in Johnstown, Pennsylvania, where the strike was much weaker. A mob of about forty heavily armed men surrounded Foster as he walked from the train station to the union hall. According to the local organizer T. J. Conboy, the men included the general manager, several superintendents, and the assistant to the president of the Cambria Iron and Steel Company as well as members of the Chamber of Commerce and the Citizens Committee. With two detectives standing nearby, the group's leader stuck a gun in Foster's ribs and marched him back to the station, where he was placed on the train under armed guard. The same day, all other organizers were also physically driven from the town. Conboy returned to the town but had to be guarded day and night. He eventually suffered a nervous breakdown from the strain.[26]

Well-known in labor circles before the strike, Foster gained national prominence during this dramatic struggle in steel. Swimming against the conservative postwar currents in labor's mainstream, Foster was burdened by his syndicalist past. The steel companies, much of the local press, and even the *New York Times* portrayed the strike as the product of a Bolshevik conspiracy led by Foster. "For the first time in its history," the *Times* editorialized, "the American Federation of Labor turned over its vast power, its goodwill, its organization, to a wild revolutionary, an avowed advocate of violence and bloodshed." The *Wall Street Journal* held that Foster and the other leaders of the steel campaign were "apostles of violence with the destruction of law as a first principle." The steel companies discovered Foster's *Syndicalism* pamphlet with its class-war rhetoric and its plans for the destruction of the national government. They reprinted it and distributed thousands of copies throughout the steel regions in a clear attempt to embarrass the AFL and discredit the strike as a radical conspiracy.[27]

Subpoenaed in the fall of 1919 to appear before the U.S. Senate Committee on Education and Labor that was investigating the strike, Foster was grilled repeatedly regarding the pamphlet and his radical background, which quickly became the focal point for the investigation. Concerned that his radical past would damage the strike, Foster tried to defuse the senators' suspicions. *Syndicalism,* he said, "was written some eight or nine years ago . . . [when] I was a follower and an advocate of the Spanish, French, and Italian system of unionism, and since then I have become possibly a little less impatient, a little less extreme, possibly, in my views, considerably so, in fact; and today I will state that I am an advocate of the system of unionism as we find it in America and England." There was a limit to Foster's tolerance, however. Questioned about a passage in *Syndicalism* urging that scabs be "ruthlessly exterminated," he argued that he was advocating education, not execution, but admitted that "a workingman can do anything but scab . . . that is the lowest act of his life." When pressed, Foster repudiated the pamphlet and denied that he was any longer a syndicalist. His attitude during the war, he testified, was "that it must be won at all costs," and toward this end he had bought many Liberty Bonds and urged steel and packinghouse workers to do likewise. (In fact, Foster and other AFL organizers had used the Liberty Bonds to post bail for organizers, steelworkers, and even IWW members who had been arrested in the course of the strike.)[28]

Both Samuel Gompers and John Fitzpatrick, who were well aware of Foster's past, spoke up for him in their testimony before the Senate committee. "He is not preaching," Fitzpatrick testified, "and is absolutely confining himself to the activities and scope of the American Federation of Labor, and has done so for the years that I have known him . . . for probably six or seven years." When asked whether he had ever discussed *Syndicalism* with Foster, Fitzpatrick contended that Foster had "joked about the views he had in his younger days, . . . he had forgot all of those things that he learned when he was a boy, and is now doing a man's thinking in the situation." Asked about Foster's attitude toward the war, Fitzpatrick insisted that Foster was "absolutely loyal, and he did everything in his power to assist in every way. . . . I think that he rendered as great a service, not only to the United States Government, but to the Allies, as any man."[29]

Gompers described how surprised he was to learn that the delegate who had supported and flattered him at a meeting of the Chicago Federation of Labor was the same person who had denounced the AFL at the 1911 Budapest international trade union congress. "He was a man of ability, a man of good presence, gentle in expression, a commander of good English, and I encouraged him . . . I was willing to welcome an erring brother into the ranks of constructive labor."[30]

Both Gompers and Fitzpatrick had much at stake in the strike, and it was in their interests to defend its prime architect. Yet their contention that Foster was now a loyal AFL trade unionist was consistent with his scrupulously responsible behavior during the strike and the revised version of syndicalist ideology he had developed in *Trade Unionism; The Road to Freedom*. Four years before the strike and perhaps even earlier, Foster had concluded that the greatest chance for change lay within the movement and that the single most important activity in which a radical might engage was simply to organize unions.

Despite this strong testimony from such labor statesmen as Gompers and Fitzpatrick and Foster's own statements about his ideas, the committee reported that as "a man of excellent education, a thinker, and prolific writer," he was all the more dangerous. "If labor is to retain the confidence of that large segment of our population which affiliates neither with labor organizations nor capital," the committee concluded, "it must keep men who entertain and formulate un-American doctrines out of its ranks and join with employers of labor in eliminating this element from the industrial life of our nation."[31]

Mass circulation magazines also probed what was behind "The Red Radical of Great Steel Strike." *Current Opinion* found Foster "as mild-mannered a man as ever plotted to scuttle an industry," while the *New York Evening World* argued that his influence was second only to President Gompers himself in the AFL, where "he has popped up with the effect of a submarine popping up in the middle of a convoy in mid-Atlantic during the war."[32]

Ironically, while government investigators, the steel corporations, and the press tarred Foster with his radical past, revolutionaries denounced him for his class collaboration. Testifying before the same Senate subcommittee, Jacob Margolis, a Pittsburgh Wobbly, claimed that boring from within robbed a radical like Foster of his potential. "Instead of becoming a leader in the movement," Margolis argued, "he becomes a follower . . . he must lose his identity, and . . . that is exactly what happened with Mr. Foster; he lost his identity." To the new Communist movement, "he was little short of a renegade and a traitor," Theodore Draper wrote. The Party attacked Foster "ferociously," according to Earl Browder, ridiculing him as "E. Z. Foster" and denouncing his decision to sell Liberty Bonds during World War I as the crassest kind of opportunism.[33]

Within the immigrant communities, however, Foster was a celebrity. Here the strike effort was solidly supported, and, in spite of all the intimidation, workers poured into the unions. John Fitzpatrick estimated that at their greatest strength in the weeks immediately following the strike call, the unions had enrolled about 350,000 steelworkers, most of whom were immigrant laborers. The National Committee's red, white, and blue initiation receipts were big favorites in the ethnic communities, and immigrant workers displayed them proudly. Foster found that the spirit of the Slavic laborers "compared favorably with that shown in any organized effort put forth by working men on this continent. Beyond question, they displayed trade union qualities of the very highest type."[34]

Foster and his organizers employed patriotic symbols and language, stressed the democratic quality of the movement, and wherever possible tied their efforts to American war aims. In turn, the union movement introduced many immigrants to democratic values and practices: the importance of working with others in mass democratic organizations and the significance of free speech, public assembly, voting, and majority rule. For these workers, the experience represented a kind of "Americanization from the bottom up," a process of socialization and acculturation in which they came to terms with and began to understand the society in which they found themselves. Under the headline, "Why Are Strikers Called 'Foreigners'?" the National Committee's *Strike Bulletin* addressed the issue in four languages:

Everyone in America is either foreign born or a descendant of foreign born. . . . The papers say you foreign workers ought to be "Americanized." What does that mean? It means—at least it ought to mean—to make Americans of you, to teach you American ideals and to teach you respect for American institutions. . . . the right of workmen in America to belong to labor unions and to bargain with their employers through union representatives of their own choosing . . . is an *AMERICAN* right and the strike is an *AMERICAN* method, recognized constitutional and legal. . . . If you believe in *FREEDOM*, you have *AMERICANISM* in your heart, wherever you were born and whatever language you speak. You will make a good American if you are willing to *FIGHT* for freedom by *PEACEABLE, LEGAL* methods.

When the immigrant steelworkers had organized and beaten the steel trust, the bulletin concluded, then *"YOU WILL HAVE TAKEN A BIG STEP IN YOUR OWN AMERICANIZATION."*[35] "The democratic theme made unionism comprehensible," according to David Brody. In addition to the material advantages that unionism seemed to offer, this ideological dimension created a strong bond between immigrant workers and the nascent labor movement in steel. "The steel workers' meetings," Foster said, "were schools in practical Americanization."[36]

But the unions were less successful with other elements of the labor force. Many of the native-born or old immigrant skilled workers, with long memories of earlier defeats and contemptuous of the "Hunky strike," remained at work. Their loyalty to the steel firms crippled the unions' efforts. As in meatpacking, African American workers occupied a critical position in the balance of power. Again Foster reached out to the black community. In Pittsburgh, he spoke in African American churches, worked with the Urban League, and debated anti-union community leaders in public gatherings. Here, however, the campaign failed even more miserably than it had in packing.[37] In a few places, such as Cleveland, black workers responded well, "but in most places and exactly where their support was needed the worst," Foster wrote, "they made a wretched showing. . . . The indifference verging on hostility with which Negroes generally regard Organized Labor's activities manifested itself strongly in the steel campaign. Those employed in the industry were extremely resistant to the trade-union program; those on the outside allowed themselves to be used freely as strikebreakers." At Homestead, where they represented an estimated 12 to 14 percent of the labor force, only eight of the 1,737 African American workers joined the union, and only one struck. Both Duquesne and Braddock had several hundred black workers, but there were no black strikers in either town. Foster insisted that the numbers were similar in Chicago, Buffalo, Youngstown, and elsewhere. The companies imported thousands of Mexican immigrants and southern black migrants, who, as in the Chicago stockyards, appeared "almost immune to the union appeal."[38]

Foster placed the onus for this failure on anti-union, middle-class elements and on community institutions that relied on the steel companies for their livelihood. In the case of one African American church where he was allowed to speak, the minister explained afterward that the congregation had paid dearly for his lecture. The Carnegie Corporation canceled its $2,500 annual contribution. "As soon as the colored man becomes a factor in industry," Foster concluded, "he is going to be organized, providing he does not become a victim to the line of tactics that are laid out by the employer. In the steel strike he lined up with the bosses."[39]

In some respects, Foster's failure to mobilize African American workers was not surprising. The committee's strike call came in the wake of dozens of race riots in industrial towns and cities throughout the country. Black workers were mobbed on their way to work, "deadlined" out of white working-class neighborhoods, and lynched. A great deal of water had gone under the bridge by the time Foster and his organizers appealed to black workers in September 1919 to join with their white "brothers" in this strike.[40]

The unions themselves were also to blame. For years AFL unions had excluded or segregated black workers. "The great number of Negroes who flowed into Chicago and Pittsburgh plants were conscious of strikebreaking," the Interchurch Commission reported. "For this attitude, the steel strikers blamed American organized labor. . . . Through many an experience Negroes came to believe that the only way they could break into a unionized industry was through strikebreaking." "Race prejudice has everything to do with it," Foster told the Chicago Commission on Race Relations, and as a result, "they don't feel confidence in the trade unions."[41] These and other early experiences convinced Foster that racial segregation was one of the most serious obstacles to working-class solidarity.

To maintain morale in the face of these problems, Foster spent a good deal of his time on three key elements of strike organization: fund-raising, material support for the strikers and their families (both of which were crucial in a long strike of poorly paid unskilled immigrants), and dissemination of reliable information. He successfully appealed to the International Fur Workers Union, the Amalgamated Clothing Workers of America, and other unions, particularly those in the needle trades, and spoke before a throng of labor activists in Madison Square Garden in New York. In all, Foster and his staff generated $418,000—only a small fraction from the AFL unions actually involved in the dispute. With this, they established a commissariat. "Imaginatively conceived, efficiently administered, and adequately financed, the

Commissariat served its purpose," David Brody concluded, "no one starved during the steel strike."[42]

To counteract the sweeping bias of the local press and to bolster workers' support, Foster hired a public relations expert, printed a regular strike bulletin, and held mass meetings continually. In one regard, the union may actually have had an edge. The National Committee produced much of its propaganda in a wide array of immigrant languages and provided translators at meetings, while much of the mainstream press and the pronouncements of corporate leaders remained opaque to the foreign-speaking workers. Many of the immigrants' own foreign-language newspapers appear to have been more sympathetic to the strike than their English-language counterparts were.[43] In the long run, however, the employers held the advantage. In many minds, the ethnic quality of the strike reinforced a xenophobia and growing fear of radicalism that characterized the postwar "Red Scare." Union offices and private homes were raided in an attempt to uncover "Red" influence, and immigrant strikers were commonly assumed to be "Bolsheviks."

Throughout the industry, workers were intimidated into returning to the mills. After a minor skirmish between strikers and strikebreakers, the state mobilized the militia at Indiana Harbor, and at Gary 1,500 regular federal troops with fixed bayonets entered the fray under the command of General Leonard Wood. Wood arrested leaders and activists and paraded his troops through the streets. He used troops to break up meetings, harass pickets, and coerce the immigrants back to work. Judging Gary "a hotbed of anarchy," Wood brought machine guns and field artillery into the city and kept the troops in place until, as Raymond Mohl put it, "The military restrictions simply destroyed the strike." By November 1919, the movement was collapsing throughout the Midwest.[44]

In the Pittsburgh area, strikers were evicted from company housing, and their mortgages were foreclosed. Here and elsewhere, company officials formed "back to work" committees to recruit strikebreakers, whom police and soldiers escorted into the plants. By the middle of December, the strike was disintegrating in most of the steel centers, though support remained solid in isolated spots. In early January, Foster and the other members of the National Committee met in Pittsburgh and voted to abandon the strike.

In the meantime, many of the same forces that had hobbled the steel strike—economic depression, nativism, racism, police repression, and the conservative political atmosphere of the Red Scare—had also led to the destruction of the labor movement in the meat-packing industry. Although organizers were busy in packing centers around the country, Chicago was the key. In the spring and summer of 1919, the Stockyards Labor Council had launched a giant "100 percent union" campaign to sweep the last recalcitrant elements into the union, and for a brief moment it seemed that even the color line had finally been breached. The Slavic immigrant community "Back of the Yards" blazed with activity, and by July about 95 per cent of white workers had joined the union. Although many blacks, particularly recent migrants from the Deep South, were continuing to hold back, the council was beginning to build a core of activists in "Black Belt" neighborhoods.

On July 6, in a conscious effort to break the color line once and for all, the council staged a giant interracial march, beginning in the immigrant community Back of the Yards and climaxing with a rally in the heart of Chicago's Black Belt. Jack Johnstone, Foster's longtime friend and ally from IWW and Syndicalist League days, had assumed leadership of the Stockyards Labor Council. He addressed the crowd. "It does me good to see such a checkerboard crowd," Johnstone hollered. "You are all standing shoulder to shoulder as men, regardless of whether your face is white or black."[45]

Three weeks later, however, Chicago's South Side exploded in a bloody race riot, resulting in millions of dollars worth of damage and the loss of thirty-eight lives, twenty-three African Americans and fifteen whites. Rampaging white street gangs assaulted blacks at random, while black mobs attacked whites who ventured into the Black Belt. The conflict had its roots in racially contested neighborhoods more than in the workplace, but it had a devastating effect on the labor movement. In its wake, black membership plummeted as the meat-packing corporations solidified their hold on African American community groups and replaced white union activists with nonunion blacks. It became virtually impossible to sustain interracial labor organization.[46]

At the same time, factionalism emerged in the Chicago Federation of Labor, and right-wing elements used nativism and patriotic appeals to assail the federation's progressive leadership and Foster's left-wing group. Conservative dual unions were established in the stockyards and elsewhere. While the Left retained control of the labor federation, the stockyards workers themselves divided along skill, nationality, and racial lines. Aggravating these tensions, unemployment set in during 1920, as thousands of returning veterans, immigrant unionists, and black migrants competed for fewer and fewer jobs.[47]

At this opportune moment, the packers took the offensive. They declared a substantial wage cut, forcing the union into a disastrous strike at the end of 1921, and recruited thousands of black strikebreakers, seriously aggravating the tense racial situation on the South Side. When strikers tried to stop the scabs, thousands of mounted police moved in to suppress virtually all picketing. At least one striker was killed, and hundreds of people were injured. By the time the strike was abandoned in February 1922, the Stockyards Labor Council, Foster's model for organizing basic industry, lay in ruins.[48]

In the immediate aftermath of the steel strike, Foster resigned his position as secretary of the battered National Committee and returned to Chicago, turning over the reins to Jay Brown, with whom he had worked most closely during the strike. Foster urged the National Committee to continue its work by publishing a regular organizing bulletin in several languages, leaving its organizers in the field, educating workers, and preparing the way for the next confrontation in steel. Instead, most unions soon withdrew support, and the National Committee faded away.[49]

The strike's defeat had personal implications for Foster. When he sought work on the railroads, he found himself blacklisted. He worked briefly for the *New Majority,* the Chicago Federation of Labor newspaper, but remained unemployed for many months. During the summer of 1920, he traveled through the Dakotas, Montana, Utah, and Washington, speaking on behalf of the nascent Farmer-Labor Party movement.[50]

Foster used his time off to evaluate the steel strike and produced his first major book, *The Great Steel Strike and Its Lessons.* That he analyzed this experience in the form of a book is revealing. Foster was a genuine labor intellectual, someone who studied his experiences, considered their broader implications, and tried to place them in a context that would mean the most to other activists.[51]

Foster took pains to detail the repression in the mill towns, but he placed the greatest blame for the strike's defeat on the labor movement itself. One obvious problem was the lack of resources, not only money but also organizers. Bitter about the lost opportunity, Foster often referred to "sabotage" by labor conservatives who refused to provide vital support. Another obstacle was the movement's decentralized structure; most unions retained authority over their own organizers and demanded constant consultation with the leadership of the committee. Only a much more centralized organizational structure and more authority for a national committee would allow the sort of coordination necessary to defeat the steel trust. But Foster projected an even broader basis of institutional cooperation. An alliance between the steelworkers, miners, and railroad workers would ensure victory in the event of a future strike because sympathetic action by these groups would stop the movement of both raw materials and the finished product, strangling the industry even if corporate managers did manage to recruit strikebreakers.

In his conclusion, Foster was remarkably sanguine. The strike, he argued, marked an important evolutionary stage in the development of American trade unionism, and the unprecedented cooperation among so many unions should encourage progressive unionists to pursue similar campaigns in the near future. He ended the book with an appeal to American radicals to get back into the labor movement and to help transform it with a vision of a powerful industrial union movement in steel and elsewhere. Foster's optimism must have sounded strange amidst the staggering defeats of the postwar years, but the birth of the CIO in the late thirties suggests that it was not misplaced. By the World War II era, strong industrial unions, populated by African American and second-generation white ethnic workers, appeared in the Chicago Stock Yards, the steel mill towns, and other industrial communities throughout the United States.

In the light of the resounding defeats in meat-packing and steel, what had Foster and his colleagues accomplished? Over a period of less than three years, they had organized well over half a million workers against the opposition of two of the most impressive concentrations of corporate wealth and power in the United States, the United States Steel Corporation and the Big Five packers. Even more impressive was the character of the labor forces involved, for the unionization of the steel and packinghouse workers represented several key breakthroughs in labor organizing. These were the first national efforts to unionize unskilled laborers in basic industry, a project the AFL had studiously avoided up to this point and the IWW was never capable of achieving. In the process of creating structures equal to the task, Foster and his colleagues also took a giant step beyond craft unionism and toward industrial organization. Finally, perhaps most important in the context of a multiracial and multiethnic society, the steel and packinghouse organizers faced the issues of racial and ethnic divisions squarely, trying—though failing—to fashion movements to bridge these enduring barriers.[52]

His wartime organizing experiences had two important effects on Foster. First, in spite of his problems in working with the national AFL, the explosive response of workers in both steel and packing strengthened his resolve to pursue his bore-from-within strategy. "A mere handful of syndicalists," he later wrote, "had been instrumental in launching and leading movements that had organized over half a million workers—native and foreign born, Negroes and whites, skilled and unskilled, women and youth—in two of the most highly trustified industries in the United States. . . . and the whole job was done in the face of the crassest incompetency, indifference and downright sabotage of the AF of L leadership." "Even though the movement was not successful, it was a triumph of organization," George Soule wrote. "And this is what Foster took particular pride in."[53]

Second, the defeat of the steel strike and the ultimate destruction of the unions in meat-packing convinced Foster that "the lack of a strong left wing had been a disastrous handicap to us," because it left the important machinery of the labor movement in the hands of conservatives who seized every opportunity to discredit Foster and the radical activists around him. "The loss of the steel strike killed the plan to revolutionize the AFL through the medium of a great organizing campaign," he later wrote. "It was necessary to take a new tack to arrive at the goal of the reorganization and modernization of the trade union movement." What was needed, Foster reasoned, was a more effectively organized "militant minority" that could win control of the unions and lead the sort of organizing drives that the new situation in American industry required. In late 1920, Foster set out, as a syndicalist, to build such an organization. When he returned to the task the following fall after visiting Russia, he did so as a Communist.[54]

6   *From Syndicalism to*
     Communism, 1920–22

HIS EXPERIENCES IN World War I and the revolutionary era following it brought William Z. Foster to American communism. The Russian Revolution held a great attraction for him, as it did for most labor radicals, but his own trade union experiences also helped place Foster in a political trajectory that led gradually away from a strictly industrial orientation and toward a greater concern with state power and politics. This shift away from an exclusive concentration on direct action and toward a practice that embraced both industrial and political organization was one that Foster shared with a generation of syndicalists and working-class anarchists. In the years following World War I, the Communist movement seemed to represent the most promising path to a revolutionary labor movement.

Foster's experiences during the war and the steel strike sent him back to his original project of creating a national organization of militants grouped around a coherent program and set of strategies but working within the mainstream unions to seize control of them and transform them into more effective fighting machines. The new organization that Foster modeled on his wartime experiences was far more durable and influential than any of his earlier creations. The Trade Union Educational League (TUEL), formed in Chicago in November 1920 by Foster and perhaps twenty associates, emerged as the main opposition to the AFL leadership, keeping the cause of labor radicalism alive throughout the conservative twenties and at the same time providing the new American Communist movement with its first opportunity to exert some influence within the labor movement.

Though Foster launched the league at the end of 1920, it made little headway at first. Early in 1921, he identified a thousand "live wires"—radicals in various unions around the country—and sent them circulars outlining his plans for the TUEL. They would be joining not a dual union but a network of militants aiming to "infuse the mass with revolutionary understanding and spirit."[1]

At about the same time that Foster was beginning to organize the TUEL, his old Syndicalist League associate Earl Browder was on a search for labor radicals. Browder had joined the Workers Party, the American constituent of the new Communist International, and was charged with recruiting a North American delegation for the first congress of the Red International of Labor Unions (RILU), the Comintern's industrial arm. Solomon Lozovsky, the RILU's general secretary, expected a delegation of genuine labor activists. Given the American Party's isolation from the union movement in these years, Lozovsky's command was easier said than done. Charles Ruthenberg recalled that at the time it would have been difficult to gather a handful of Communists "who knew anything about the trade union movement."[2]

Browder, one of the few Party members with valuable labor contacts, succeeded admirably. The American delegation to the first RILU congress in the summer of 1921 included a diverse group of genuine trade union radicals: Pascal Cosgrove of the Shoe Workers' Union in Haverhill, Massachusetts; Joseph Knight of the Canadian "One Big Union" movement; Hulet Wells of the Seattle Central Labor Council; Dennis Batt of the Detroit Central Labor Council; Ella Reeve Bloor of the Minneapolis Trades and Labor Council; and George Williams of the IWW. Browder, listed as a representative of the Kansas miners, served as the delegation's secretary. He had known Foster from the ITUEL and invited him to join the group. All of the delegates had left-wing backgrounds, and all had long been associated with unions, but Bloor and Browder were the only Party members. Collectively, they represented the prospect of linking the nascent American Communist organizations with the labor movement. But, as Theodore Draper observed, Foster, with his extensive contacts, experience, and talents, "was a far more important catch than any of the delegates or indeed than all of them combined."[3]

Foster's perspective on the eve of this Russian trip is perhaps best conveyed in *The Railroader's Next Step—Amalgamation,* one of the TUEL's first pamphlets published in March 1921, shortly before he left the country.[4] What is particularly striking about this pamphlet is the continuity with his arguments in *Trade Unionism: The Road to Freedom* and his own brand of syndicalism. On the eve of his conversion to communism, Foster still did not reflect much on the importance of political organization, and he clearly did not embrace the Leninist concept of a vanguard party. For Foster, the revolutionary potential of workers emerged spontaneously from their experiences at work and in unions; his attention remained focused on practical questions of organization and strategy facing the militant minority. The continuity between *The Railroader's Next Step* and his earlier writing and its contrast with much of Foster's later work suggest the impact that the Russian trip had on his outlook.

Browder's invitation could not have reached Foster at a better moment. At the age of thirty-nine, he had reached a turning point in his life. "He was through with the Socialist Party, through with the IWW, through with the AF of L," Theodore Draper wrote. "Isolated except for a small band of devoted followers, yet still full of tireless ambition," he was a dedicated militant looking for a way to vitalize the TUEL and to implement the lessons from his wartime experiences.[5]

Up to this point, there had been little reason for him to look to the Communists for any help in this project. He still had reservations about Soviet Russia and deep suspicions regarding the new American Party, largely because of the Communists' adherence to dual unionism. In late 1920, Ralph Chaplin, the Wobbly writer and newspaper editor, had accompanied James Cannon, a recent convert to communism, to Foster's apartment on Chicago's South Side. Cannon felt that the Party was badly weakened and its perspective skewed by its lack of industrial contacts. He hoped that he might interest Foster in directing these kinds of initiatives and thereby balance the Party leadership with the inclusion of a genuine labor militant. Foster, however, expressed contempt for the Party leadership and displayed no interest whatsoever in joining the movement. "Once a Wobbly, always a Wobbly," Cannon said in disappointment as he and Chaplin waited for their streetcar.[6]

For their part, Party leaders had ridiculed Foster's accomplishments in packing and steel, denounced his support for the war, and dismissed him as a reformer or, worse, a typical labor bureaucrat. Divided into feuding parties, in early 1921 the Communists remained underground, emulating the intrigue of the early Bolsheviks and trying to avoid government agents. One of the few issues on which the dueling parties agreed was the need for separate revolutionary unions to fight the AFL, which the Communist Party of America called "reactionary . . . a bulwark of capitalism." "Trade unionism is the arch enemy of the militant proletariat," the *Communist* declared. "This is one of the tasks of the Communist Party—the destruction of the existing trades union organizations."[7] From Foster's perspective, the Communists had failed miserably in the only test that meant much to him—the postwar labor struggles that represented the revolutionary potential of the great mass of workers.

By the spring of 1921, however, this situation was changing quickly. The Comintern demanded that the American Communists emerge from the underground, fuse the squabbling parties, and enter the labor movement. Lenin had admonished Communists worldwide to work in the mainstream unions. He already knew about Foster and his reputation. The American Communist writer John Reed had sent Lenin a copy of *The Great Steel Strike* in late 1920, enclosing a brief description of Foster's work and Reed's opinion that Foster was the best informed of American working-class leaders. Sometime early in 1921, Foster read Lenin's *Left-Wing Communism: An Infantile Disorder* with great enthusiasm, recognizing in it a vindication of his own arguments against dual unionism and a blueprint for the radicalization of the labor movement. In establishing the RILU, the Comintern seemed to be taking concrete action to realize this goal. "It appeared that our ten-year fight for work within the conservative unions was at last going to be successful," Foster later recalled.[8]

Still suspicious or simply worried that too close an identification with the Party might jeopardize his contacts, Foster agreed to go to Moscow as an observer rather than as a delegate. He served also as a correspondent for the left-wing Federated Press. On his way to Moscow in April 1921, Foster stopped in England, where a general strike loomed. The Miners Federation of Great Britain, faced with an attack by the mine owners, struck on April 1, 1921, and called on its partners in the Triple Alliance, the National Union of Railway men and the National Federation of Transport Workers, for support. After failing to negotiate a compromise and under considerable pressure from their rank and file, the leaders of the alliance set a strike date of April 15. The resulting conflict would have closed down the United Kingdom's ports and railroads as well as its coal mines, virtually strangling the nation's economy. Foster was particularly interested in the alliance. Its origins lay in a 1910 decision by Tom Mann and other British syndicalists to work within the existing unions. First, between 1910 and 1913, they pushed the individual craft organizations toward amalgamation within their respective industries. Then they built the Triple Alliance "brick by brick" over the following two years. The process was precisely the sort Foster had envisioned for the United States, and he saw the alliance as "the great movement long looked forward to by the syndicalists." The alliance had already backed employers down with a strike threat on "Red Friday" in 1919. Now, however, the leadership clearly feared the prospects of such a giant conflict. They first postponed and then called off the strike at the last possible moment on "Black Friday," August 15, 1921. The result was widespread demoralization, further attacks by the employers, and the collapse of the Triple Alliance. By the end of the year, British union membership had declined by more than 20 percent, and strike activity fell off drastically.[9]

The Triple Alliance had occupied a vital place in Foster's wartime theory that increasing concentrations of union power would eventually destroy capitalism without resort to parties. His explanation of this "great betrayal" suggests his evolving view of strategy as he visited Moscow that spring and summer. He had at first been attracted to the British movement by its "modern methods" and the deliberate building process that had resulted in an impressive level of coordination. In the end, however, Foster saw the failure as one of leadership. "The unfortunate consequence of right-wing officials at the head of a left-wing movement, of reformists trying to direct a revolutionary upheaval, had resulted in the usual, nay inevitable, tragedy." The future, Foster concluded, in the United Kingdom and elsewhere, lay with the militant minority now grouped around the Red International of Labor Unions, which would remove the conservative officials and install the new revolutionaries.[10]

Once among these revolutionaries in Moscow, Foster kept a low profile. Alfred Rosmer, a French delegate and a former syndicalist who knew him from his days in France, recalled that Foster's visit was "notable for its discretion." Foster reported on economic conditions, the reorganization of Russian society, and the functioning of the Russian trade unions for Chicago's *Voice of Labor* and other labor papers. His observations eventually appeared in *The Russian Revolution,* which he described as "a brief workers' history of the revolution," published by the Trade Union Educational League in late 1921.[11]

By his own account, Foster's three and a half months in Russia represented a transition in his thinking. "It was soon as plain as a pike-staff to me that in Soviet Russia there had occurred a truly socialist revolution," he later wrote, "just what I had been fighting for all my adult life." "Once in a while," he wrote back to the States, "one has an experience that can never be forgotten so long as life lasts . . . it seemed as though I saw the soul of the revolution."[12]

It was the power and discipline of the Soviet Communist Party that most impressed Foster, appealing to the revolutionary elitism he had nurtured since his IWW days. The Russian labor movement was comparable to the American, Foster argued, but the Russian radicals possessed "infinitely better understanding, determination, discipline, and power." He concluded at this point that "a strong state, sternly enforcing the will of the revolutionary proletariat was indispensable to the transition from capitalism to socialism and from socialism to Communism." "The Russian Communist Party is the most marvelous organization that has been constructed by beings," Foster told a Detroit crowd soon after his return to the United States in late 1921. "It is on a new principle of organization. It is not a mass organization. It is an organization of militants alone." A small group of Party members controlled a factory of 900 "just as completely as though the 900 were members. In this fact is the great strength of the Communist Party. They do the thinking for the Russian working class. . . . Ten good men acting together, absolutely relying on one another, are as good as 10,000 unorganized."[13] Each of these conclusions was a vital step in his evolution beyond syndicalism and toward an industrially oriented communism.

Yet if his Russian experiences moved Foster, his transformation into a Communist did not occur overnight. His later claim that "my whole experience of many years in the revolutionary movement had prepared me to readily become a Communist" oversimplifies the process.[14] Looking for the roots of Foster's Communist politics in his earliest ideas and tactics can distort his political and intellectual evolution, which were shaped by a wide range of contexts and experiences. But later factional claims that Foster remained a syndicalist who simply used the Communist Party as a focal point for his industrial organizing also miss an ideological evolution that began long before Foster's Russian trip and continued long after he joined the Party. It is certainly possible to identify early influences that led him eventually to embrace this outlook. His experiences in the meat-packing and steel campaigns had convinced him of the importance of state power and disciplined, centralized organization, while his work with the Chicago Federation of Labor brought him into the movement for an independent party based on the unions, a labor party. Seeing the collapse of the Triple Alliance, long a model for Foster and other syndicalists, shook his faith that unionization on its own would lead inevitably to the collapse of capitalism. Foster concluded that even very large federated trade union blocks were not sufficient; political organization was essential.[15]

Finally, the spectacle of the Russian Communists creating the first socialist society in history appealed to Foster's long-held fascination with labor organization and strategy as well as the value he placed on "systematic" approaches to the solution of social problems. His Russian visit undoubtedly represented the catalyst for Foster's conversion, but his new adherence to communism in the fall of 1921 was not a leap in the dark.

Nor did Foster's turn to communism entail a total rejection of his earlier syndicalist views. In the fall of 1921, as he first digested what he had seen in Russia, Foster explained the spectacle in trade union terms: "To me the Russian Revolution did not seem difficult to understand. It is only our own labor movement carried to its logical conclusion . . . the Russian Revolution is only a strike raised to the nth degree."[16]

During his early years in the Party, he continued to focus his energies on industrial and trade union work, which he still saw as the key to revolutionary change. Certainly Foster's factional opponents in the Party viewed him as tainted with syndicalist tendencies long after he joined, and they employed their greater theoretical sophistication to combat what they saw as vulgar influences. For his part, the "workerism" and distrust of intellectuals he had first exhibited during his years in the Wage Workers Party and the IWW, values that were characteristic of syndicalists throughout the world, shaped his attitudes toward political conflicts within the Communist Party. Through much of his first decade as a Communist, he surrounded himself with old friends and comrades, people he had learned to trust during a lifetime of trade union work. He carried his syndicalist past with him into the new movement, even as he became a disciplined Communist, an American counterpart to the Russian Bolshevik.

Foster's experience at the First Congress of the RILU in July 1921 encouraged him to see the Communist movement as the only logical context for his industrial work, a conclusion he shared with many other syndicalists worldwide. Syndicalist organizations, including the IWW, were invited to the congress, though their delegates split on a variety of issues, particularly dual unionism. Some syndicalists dropped out when the congress voted overwhelmingly for the strategy of boring from within against strenuous protests from the IWW, but most supported the policy. This latter group included such prominent leaders as Pierre Monatte and Tom Mann, who had exercised a decisive influence on Foster's own political evolution. Mann's experience may have been the closest to Foster's. Mann argued for a great deal of continuity between his Industrial Syndicalist League and the British Communist Party's Minority Movement, a group similar to Foster's TUEL in structure, membership, and goals. Foster's adherence to communism must therefore be seen in the broader context of a generation of syndicalist activists who entered the new movement in this era.[17]

There was no mistaking the implications of the new line for Foster's plans to transform the American labor movement. The TUEL became the American section of the RILU, "the logical, ready-made instrument for Communist activity in the American trade union movement," and Foster, as logical director of the Workers Party's trade union activities, became "a Communist figure of top rank."[18] The arrangement invested the TUEL with the prestige and support of a large international and revolutionary labor movement, while it provided the Party with its first genuine link to the working class and Foster with a vehicle for his plans to revitalize the labor movement.

Earl Browder later recalled that the arrangement to make the TUEL the RILU's American constituent and, in effect, the industrial arm of the Workers Party was cast at the RILU congress without consulting the leadership of the Party in the United States. Ruthenberg and other Party leaders were thus faced with a fait accompli regarding Foster's status as director of trade union work. The circumstances of Foster's sudden rise to influence in the Party, with his own base of support in the TUEL and with his own mentor in the person of the RILU leader Solomon Lozovsky, undoubtedly complicated his relationship with the official Workers Party leadership. But these factors also afforded him some autonomy, and Lozovsky's support in particular sustained Foster through the factional conflicts of the following decade.[19]

Foster stayed on in Moscow after the RILU congress to observe the Communist International's Third Congress. The city had been devastated by World War I, the revolution, and the civil war. Successive drafts had depleted the city of much of its male work force, and Foster found "the whole population, except the children, . . . living on the edge of starvation." As disease spread, medicine became scarce. Streets, homes, and shops remained dark, and many industrial plants were idle for want of fuel. Since so many of the city's buildings had deteriorated or had been plundered for firewood, housing was scarce, despite the decline in population. Local transportation had been disrupted and crippled.[20]

Foster and other foreign guests of the Soviet government lived on the "diplomatic ration," which was luxurious by the standards of common Muscovites—one pound of bread per day and occasionally a bit of meat. Foster claimed to have lived for several days on apple parings and black bread. As a result of such a diet, he lost twenty-five pounds in the course of his three-and-a-half-month stay in the city. Visiting the apartment of the anarchists Emma Goldman and Alexander Berkman with Earl Browder, Foster was scandalized to find a sumptuous meal on the table—meat, fish, butter, and white bread. Goldman explained that the precious food had been passed on to them by friends abroad, but for Foster the spread reinforced his impression of Goldman as "an inveterate self-advertiser and publicity hound . . . a petty bourgeois political adventuress."[21]

For all the suffering in the city, Moscow was also alive with the "spirit of the revolution," or so it seemed to Foster. His interpreter recalled his asking questions incessantly as he went about the city. He was deeply impressed with Lenin—the more so since he was then immersed in Lenin's writings for the first time. Seeing him at the Comintern Congress "was one of the most inspiring moments of my life," Foster recalled. "I regarded him so intently as he went about the Congress that his whole makeup and characteristics literally burned themselves into my memory. . . . After more than twenty years of intellectual groping about," Foster later wrote, "I was at last, thanks to Lenin, getting my feet on firm revolutionary ground."[22]

Foster joined the Communist movement soon after returning to Chicago in the late summer of 1921, though he kept his membership secret until the spring of 1923. This organization to which Foster devoted the remainder of his life was a highly structured, hierarchical party based on the Soviet model. In spring 1921, two distinct Communist groups had merged at the insistence of the Comintern to form the underground Communist Party of America. Then in December 1921, a new legal organization emerged. Originally called the Workers Party of America, the new party was renamed the Workers (Communist) Party in August 1925. It did not become the Communist Party, USA, until 1929. In its early years, much of the Party's membership was concentrated in its foreign-language federations. The organizational autonomy of these units, reinforced by their distinctive cultural lives, separated immigrant activists from one another and from the small group of native-born radicals and considerably complicated Foster's union projects. He complained often and loudly about the failure of immigrant members to support the Party's industrial programs or even to join unions. In 1925, as part of the Comintern's plan to "Bolshevize" its constituent parties, the Workers Party was ordered to centralize and reorganize on the basis of "street nuclei" and "shop nuclei" attached to particular neighborhoods and factories. These small local units were grouped into sections and sections into districts, which usually included a large urban concentration but also embraced a number of states. (The exception was the New York metropolitan area, which was organized into two separate districts.) District executive committees oversaw activities at the local level. Each layer of organization had its own meetings and leadership and reported to the next higher body. Large districts had elaborate committee structures with numerous paid functionaries. A head organizer assumed ultimate responsibility for all work at the district level.

The Central Executive Committee (or Central Committee from 1929 on), was usually elected in the districts and represented the Party's top leadership at the national level. A smaller political committee, or "Polcom," met regularly and determined policy between Central Committee meetings, while a secretariat of three or four people ran the Party on a day-to-day basis. Charles

Ruthenberg, an old Ohio Socialist, served as executive secretary (later general secretary) of the Party until his death in 1927, but until the mid-1930s, power on the Central Committee derived not from the authority of one individual but from a series of shifting alliances—a situation ripe for factional conflict. The precision and effectiveness of this elaborate hierarchical structure can easily be exaggerated, but the structure is important to understanding Foster's experience. During his first decade in the Party, he was one of a very few top leaders who shuttled between Party headquarters and the nation's various industrial battlefields.[23]

The Party's new turn to industrial organizing created a suitable place for Foster at the top of this hierarchy. He was immediately elected to the Political Committee, and for more than a year he directed the Party's trade union work from the TUEL's Chicago headquarters, while Party secretary Ruthenberg directed its political activities from the national headquarters in New York City. Two distinct factions developed around these men. When Foster won a majority on the Party's executive committee in 1923, he succeeded in moving the Party headquarters to Chicago. Ruthenberg's New York group, including Jay Lovestone, Benjamin Gitlow, and Max Bedacht, came out of the Socialist Party's 1919 split over the Soviet Revolution. They had their roots in Europe and were well grounded in Marxist theory.

Most of those close to Foster were western or midwestern, native-born trade unionists who had been strongly influenced by anarcho-syndicalism or the revolutionary industrial unionism of the IWW. The division was not strictly along ethnic lines, however. Foster developed strong support among Finnish miners and other workers in the upper Midwest and among Yiddish-speaking garment workers in New York and elsewhere. The Jewish and Finnish-language federations were among the largest in the Party.

Both Browder and Cannon came from Kansas families. Browder was born in 1891, the son of a populist preacher steeped in the sort of agrarian socialism made famous by the Girard, Kansas, *Appeal to Reason.* Four of the seven children in the family eventually joined the Communist movement. Browder joined the Socialist Party at Wichita in 1907 and first came into contact with Foster through the Syndicalist League of North America in Kansas City, although he claimed never to have been a member of the organization. In Kansas City, he developed very solid contacts in the local labor movement and gained valuable organizational experience through the "Labor Forward" movement, which organized from ten to fifteen thousand workers in the city's basic industries during 1916. He broke with Foster over the war. Browder actively opposed the conflict as an imperialist venture and went to prison for his views, while Foster took the syndicalist position of focusing all efforts on industrial organization, using the war as an opportunity to strengthen the labor movement. Browder rejoined the Socialist Party in 1918 and worked with James P. Cannon and a group of left-wing Socialists on the *Workers' World* newspaper. Imprisoned for draft resistance in June 1919, he joined the Communist movement soon after emerging from prison at the end of 1920.[24]

James P. Cannon's background was similar in some respects to Browder's and Foster's, though he was a very different sort of person. He had grown up in a radical midwestern environment. His parents were English-born Irish nationalists who had met and married in the United States and settled in Rosedale, an industrial suburb of Kansas City. Like Browder, Cannon grew up reading the *Appeal to Reason* and *Wilshire's Magazine.* His father passed through the Knights of Labor and the Populist Party and wound up with the Socialists. His mother was a devout Catholic. Cannon attended parochial school and shared her faith until her death when he was fourteen, at which point he began reading more about science and socialism. Like Foster, he lost his faith more through the confrontation with science than through politics. The boy worked sixty hours a week in a Kansas City meat-packing plant from the age of twelve and spent much of his leisure time shooting pool with his mates. Unlike Foster, he later returned to finish high school, which he marked as the turning point in his life, and briefly attended evening law school classes. He joined the Socialist Party at the age of eighteen in 1908 and the IWW three years later. Cannon traveled throughout the Midwest as an IWW organizer from 1912 to 1914 and was jailed briefly during a strike in Peoria, Illinois. For the next five years, he was active in the IWW's Kansas City local before rejoining the Socialist Party in 1919 and the Communist Labor Party (CLP) later that year. Although Cannon was not part of the Chicago group, he supported Foster's emphasis on the Party's industrial work, and he lined up with Foster in the factionalism of the mid-1920s. As a native-born worker with considerable labor experience, Cannon was a rare resource in the early Party and rose quickly in the national leadership, joining the Central Executive Committee in 1920 and the Political Committee as chair in 1922.[25]

Several other western labor activists who had gravitated to Chicago joined Cannon, Browder, and Foster in the Party. Jack Johnstone, another veteran Wobbly, had organized for the IWW in British Columbia before joining Foster's Syndicalist League and the packinghouse workers' movement. In 1920, he helped Foster establish the TUEL. Johnstone joined the Communist movement in 1920 against Foster's advice and worked as his right arm in the TUEL throughout the twenties. Earl Browder claimed that much of Foster's early success in Chicago was due to Johnstone, who was held in high regard by the CFL leadership.[26]

Sam Hammersmark was born in Norway shortly before his parents immigrated to the United States, and he grew up in Michigan and Chicago. Like Johnstone and Foster, he also spent time in the Pacific Northwest. Active in working-class anarchist circles there and in Chicago, he later organized for the retail clerks and in Foster's steel campaign. After several years in the labor party movement, the CFL, and the Labor Defense Council, he joined the city's Communist movement in 1923 and ran a radical bookstore for many years.[27]

Arne Swabeck, a Danish immigrant and another Socialist Party and IWW veteran, edited a Scandinavian Socialist newspaper before the war and became a leader in the 1919 Seattle general strike. Elected as a delegate to the CFL from the painters' union, he served in the early twenties as the Workers Party Chicago district organizer. Charles Krumbein, like Swabeck a founding member of the CLP and a CFL delegate, was a steamfitter and served as the Chicago Party's industrial organizer. Joseph Manley, an Irish-born structural ironworker with roots in the anarchist movement, the IWW, the SLNA, and the ITUEL, probably met Foster at the Home Colony. He also worked as an organizer in the steel campaign. In the early twenties, he headed the Trade Union National Committee for Russian Famine Relief, married Foster's daughter Sylvia, and became the TUEL's most important organizer until he was killed on the job.[28]

Perhaps the most colorful figure around Foster was William F. Dunne, who was born in 1897 at Little Falls, Minnesota. The son of an unskilled Irish railroad worker and a French-Canadian mother, he was the oldest of seven children. Dunne worked his way through the University of Minnesota, studying engineering, playing football, and boxing, but he dropped out shortly before graduation and worked for several years on the West Coast as an organizer for the International Brotherhood of Electrical Workers. He married and settled in Vancouver, where he worked as a skilled electrician and joined the Socialist Party in 1910. He first heard of the Russian Revolution from a group of Russian soldiers in a German prisoner of war camp. After his release from the camp, Dunne moved to Montana, where he witnessed the June 1917 mine explosion near Helena in which 160 miners were burned alive. The accident galvanized a bitter strike. As it spread, Dunne assumed leadership of a joint strike committee and editorship of the Montana State Federation of Labor's popular newspaper. With the strike's defeat, he was elected a state legislator on the Democratic ticket, secretary of the electricians' union, and vice president of the Montana Federation of Labor. In 1919, he became a charter member of the new Communist Labor Party.[29]

The writer Joseph Freeman remembered Dunne as having a body "like a retired prize-fighter's . . . short and stocky, with a tremendous barrel-chest, solid as a rock" and "a dark, heavy Irish face." He mixed an interest in writing with a reputation for drinking, profanity, and womanizing. In 1924, he became editor of the new *Daily Worker.* He supported Foster's industrial policies on the Party's Central Executive Committee in the early twenties, though he opposed Foster in later factional conflicts.[30]

Alexander Bittelman was the odd man out when he joined Foster's group in 1923. Born in 1890 in Odessa, Bittelman attended a heder and later a government school, joining the Jewish socialist Bund while still a teenager. By the time he immigrated to the United States in 1912, he had already spent two years in Siberian exile. After studying engineering at the Cooper Union, he devoted himself full-time to revolutionary politics, first as a member of the Jewish Socialist Federation's Harlem branch and then, after the creation of the Communist movement, as secretary of the Workers Party Jewish Federation. Studious and formal in style, steeped in Marxism-Leninism, given to long theoretical discourses, Bittelman was sometimes called "the pope." He offered Foster's group fluent Russian and a keen eye for political shifts in the international movement.[31]

In the early twenties, the Communist delegates were both a sizable and an important influence in the Chicago Federation of Labor, representing perhaps 20 percent of the body's delegates. More active than most other delegates, they were integral rather than marginal elements and were involved in a number of organizing efforts, particularly the resistance of the city's building trades unions to a massive open shop drive in the spring of 1922.[32]

These and other Communist trade union organizers around the country occupy an important place in Foster's own story and in the Communist Party's. Their recruitment marked a turning point, indicating, as Draper concluded,

> that the Communists had scored some success in linking up with an older, more indigenous radical tradition. These men had gone from one radical movement to another; if they ended up as Communists, it signified that communism succeeded with them in taking over the radical tradition. They were not bookish, ideologically punctilious types. They adopted communism emotionally long before they mastered it intellectually. They were less interested in the party's abstract principles than its day-by-day practice. The change in line enabled them to make the transition from old-time radicalism to newfangled communism with a minimum of shift in practical activity.[33]

Draper may have underestimated some of these labor radicals. Many were worker intellectuals, not only gifted in their line of political involvement and union work but also intellectually engaged and already familiar with Marxist theory. This was increasingly true of people like Foster, Cannon, and Browder by 1921. The intellectual sophistication of this group of workers who had so little formal education is impressive. As early as 1916, the labor economist W. F. Hoxie invited Foster to lecture to his class at the University of Chicago and urged him to bring the iron worker Joe Manley along to provide a discussion of Schopenhauer and Hegel. The eminent economist John R. Commons was extremely impressed with Foster's intellectual capacities when he spoke before two thousand students and faculty at the University of Wisconsin. Commons thought Foster gave his labor economics class "the most scholarly account I have heard of the evolution of Communist doctrine from Marx to DeLeon and Lenin."[34]

The TUEL's *Labor Herald* reflected this sophistication. It was a highly polished journal aimed at a literate and politically sophisticated working-class audience—Foster's militant minority, not the typical immigrant industrial worker.

But Draper is undoubtedly correct not only about the group's training its political focus on the day-to-day world of trade union struggles but also about the fundamental difference between such radicals and the more cerebral immigrant group that emerged from the left wing of the Socialist Party. Nor is there any doubt that many Communists saw Foster and the group around him as extremely valuable links to the real world of the American worker. James P. Cannon called these trade unionists "nuggets of gold." "This was in my eyes and in the eyes of most of us, a tremendous acquisition for American communism," the Party veteran Alexander Bittelman later recalled. "For here were revolutionary socialists with great experience in organizing and leading significant working class struggles . . . with much prestige in the unions, and with broad mass contacts." Bittelman, a Party intellectual, was impressed by this group of Communist trade unionists "because they were building an American movement out of American traditions."[35]

For all the promise these activists brought to the Party, their arrival also introduced an element of tension. Foster's faction used its proletarian background as leverage in the emerging Party conflicts. Vera Weisbord, then a new member in the Party's Harlem branch, had trouble following the issues in the debate, as did many rank-and-file members, but she noticed that "the Foster faction prided itself on being proletarian, and on having a monopoly on this distinction, for they were always denouncing the others as petit-bourgeois and intellectual (a term uttered with scathing contempt)." More commonly, the "Fosterites" referred to Jay Lovestone, Bertram D. Wolfe, and the other young intellectuals around Ruthenberg as "the City College boys," because several of them had graduated from the College of the City of New York.[36]

Foster's apparent anti-intellectualism might have been more complex than it appeared. Much of his early life and his later commitment to research and writing suggest that he had a strong intellectual curiosity and great respect for learning. His animosity toward "the City College boys" might have derived partly from the frustration he felt at not having a better education himself and from a certain insecurity when it came to theory and ideology. He craved but seldom received recognition as an original thinker. This would account for the otherwise improbable alliance between Foster and Alexander Bittelman, the Foster group's "theory man." Foster maintained great respect for Bittelman, his friend Sam Darcy noted, partly because of his own feelings of intellectual inadequacy. "He was not sure of himself as a political leader," Benjamin Gitlow recalled, adding that "his inferiority complex in this respect was so apparent that we of the opposition took full advantage of it, making his life on the Central Executive just as miserable as we could. We were the bright boys who knew how to sling the Communist lingo; he was the shamefaced dullard."[37] Yet Foster was also genuinely impatient with the abstract quality of much of the endless discussion of theory, a characteristic of Party life that frustrated many other working-class Communists involved in mass organizing.

For its part, the Ruthenberg faction dismissed Foster and his colleagues as "half-educated workers" and "syndicalists," politically inarticulate and rather vulgar people. Vera Weisbord recalled that "Ruthenberg made a much better impression than Foster," whom she found "overwrought, easily provoked, and contentious." Weisbord was onto something. Few of the people around Foster worried much about decorum. Normally very controlled in his behavior, Foster himself had a bad temper. He could be impatient and rude even toward friends and allies and savage in his attacks on factional opponents. Bittelman noted that "most of the Cannon-Foster circle were a rather rough-and-ready group. . . . few niceties in mutual relations. . . . they would use what they chose to call 'trade union language' . . . four letter exclamations were a dime a dozen." There were also frequent parties with "food and drink and song." Foster, a vegetarian who neither smoked nor drank much (apparently for health reasons), never took part in these festivities. This is rather revealing of his personality. Most Communist cadres were serious about their politics but none more so than Foster. Older and more reserved than most of his supporters, he may also have viewed such gatherings as informal meetings of a Cannon grouping within his faction. For whatever reason, he chose to steer clear of the parties. The more intellectual, New York–based leadership continued to resent not only the policies of Foster supporters but also their lifestyle and mannerisms. Apart from important political differences, then, the struggle represented a clash of subcultures within the Party.[38]

To call the "Fosterites" syndicalists, as their opposition often did, is perhaps an oversimplification, but their union experiences weighed heavily on their political orientation, and they clearly valued industrial initiatives over electoral politics. Many of Foster's supporters were longtime colleagues from Syndicalist League days. Jack Johnstone, Sam Hammersmark, Joe Manley, Earl Browder, and James Cannon all had trade union roots and backgrounds in syndicalism or anarcho-syndicalism. They were joined by Jack Carney, editor of *Voice of Labor,* originally an independent labor paper and later a Party-oriented weekly, and Tom O'Flaherty, another radical journalist and organizer. These two Irish immigrants, both present at the creation of American communism, maintained connections with Chicago's large Irish American community and provided the Communists with some entree to the world of radical Irish nationalism.

For Foster, Dunne, and the others around what Communist contemporaries referred to as "the Chicago trade union group," radical politics was rooted not in texts but in the factories and coal mines and in the streets of working-class communities throughout the country. They saw themselves, as Browder wrote, as "the real Bolshevik bunch in America."[39] If the contention between Party factions had worked itself out independently of international influence and had been determined by an approach that was effective in the industrial and political environment of the United States, the history of American labor radicalism might have been very different. But resolution of the "American Question" was shaped and reshaped by the politics of the international Communist movement as well as the Party in the United States. The division of labor between Ruthenberg's group of political Communists in New York and Foster's trade union Communists in Chicago made sense. For the time being, Comintern authority rested with the former group, while the Party's prospects for a mass following clearly depended on the latter. But the theoretical and more explicitly political perspective of the New York leadership clashed with the practical and industrial inclinations of the Chicago trade unionists around Foster. The widely divergent backgrounds, experiences, and interests of the two distinct groups accentuated the Party's inherent tensions between immediate domestic issues and the theory and politics of the international movement, laying the foundations for a decade of bitter factional conflict.

7 *Boring from Within, 1922–25*

"NOT OFTEN DOES ONE find an organization so completely dominated by the philosophy and personality of one man," Earl Beckner wrote of the Trade Union Educational League (TUEL). "William Z. Foster has been the moving spirit of the League from the very beginning; without him it would probably have gained very little influence."[1] Beckner was undoubtedly right that Foster's personality dominated the TUEL, but the organization and its fortunes were shaped by a number of influences, and the interplay between these explains the character of Communist industrial policy in the 1920s.

Foster's own interests and his genius lay in the practical trade union world—organizing and strike strategy, labor union politics, and an instinctual understanding of workers from widely divergent social backgrounds. He understood that the potential for labor radicalism lay in the real grievances of workers, particularly in such troubled industries as garment manufacturing, textiles, and coal mining and in the conflicts between these rank-and-file workers and their leaders. Foster's TUEL gained a following by concentrating on concrete concerns and providing leadership and a program for indigenous militants.

Historians have tended to analyze the TUEL's work primarily from an organizational perspective, as the reflection of the Communist Party's industrial policy, its successes and failures.[2] Clearly, Party policies and politics *did* shape the league's history, sometimes with disastrous effects, but this perspective neglects the broader context for the TUEL's activity and the significance of workers' own efforts to gain control over their unions and to resist the erosion of labor organization and standards. As the union movement declined throughout the 1920s, thousands of workers supported the TUEL's activities at one point or another as a means of reversing this collapse.

The ideas guiding TUEL policy and practice grew naturally out of Foster's experiences and were the logical extension of his earlier thinking—develop rank-and-file opposition groups in the conservative unions; organize the unorganized; fight strikes over key industrial issues; and develop new strike strategies. Such initiatives were not the *creation* of the Communist Party but products of Foster's own development based on experience, lessons learned in almost two decades of labor radicalism. As a result, they produced struggles over the most fundamental questions facing the labor movement in the twenties: What was the purpose of the unions? What should their policies be? Was it possible to work out compromises with employers? Should the labor movement steer clear of politics or develop its own independent political voice? No one had to impose these questions on workers; they emerged from the dismal situation facing unions in the decade following World War I. There was a potential for labor radicalism in the midst of the "normalcy" of the 1920s.

But how would the Communists exploit this potential? Here a different impulse was at work: the central planning and direction that was characteristic of the Leninist vanguard party. Throughout the early twenties, Foster maintained a considerable degree of autonomy in his trade union work, and he left his mark on the Party by concentrating much of its attention and energy in the industrial sphere. In turn, his TUEL provided the Communists with their first genuine base in the labor movement.[3] But increasingly, the TUEL's position and policies had to be squared not only with orders from the Party's Central Committee but also with the Comintern's international line, for these two were clearly linked. Although the Comintern might speak of its policies as the application of scientific socialism, the policies were the products of decidedly unscientific influences: the collective wisdom of Soviet and other experienced revolutionaries; their own sometimes faulty perceptions of international, particularly American, political and economic conditions; and the power struggles within the American Party and the Comintern itself. As a central figure in the Party leadership, Foster became increasingly em-

broiled in these conflicts, and TUEL policy was shaped as much by Comintern and Party factional conflicts—the class struggle in theory—as by real
conflicts in the workshops and in the streets.

Communist Party policies and factionalism undermined the TUEL's potential and eventually cut Foster and his followers off from their natural constituency in the unions. Foster found his strenuous efforts to build the league
stymied by not only conservative labor leaders but also his opponents within
the Party. Life as a Communist leader drew him into another world, where
decisions and planning relied as much on Party politics in New York and
Moscow as they did on conditions and events in Detroit and Chicago or in
the coalfields of Pennsylvania and West Virginia. Pursuing the strategies he
thought most effective in such places depended on maintaining his leadership in the Party, and holding onto leadership brought him into intense factional conflicts and led him to positions that gradually isolated him from the
mainstream labor movement he had long seen as the proper context for all of
his activities. Foster's behavior in the 1920s was thus shaped by a tension between his own distinctive brand of Communist activism—heavily influenced
by his earlier industrial experiences and contacts—and the exigencies of political life in a highly centralized international Marxist-Leninist movement.

Finally, the mainstream union leadership, generally conservative and on
the defensive throughout the twenties, had a major impact on Communist
fortunes in the labor movement. In particular situations and at particular
moments, TUEL activists might make alliances with local, district, or even
national leaders; more often, particularly from the mid-1920s on, they were
under attack. Foster described the American labor leadership to his Soviet
mentor Solomon Lozovsky as "the most reactionary trade union bureaucracy
on the face of the globe."[4] Quite apart from any ideological aversion union
leaders might have felt for the TUEL, its activists threatened them in an era
when they felt particularly vulnerable, pressed on one side by aggressive employers and on the other by disgruntled rank-and-file members. Such leaders
had formidable weapons at their disposal in the civil wars that erupted in
unions between left and right. They could and frequently did expel individual radicals and even entire locals. Where unions could enforce a union shop
or where leaders were willing to collaborate with management, expulsion
from the union could mean blacklisting from the industry.

Such repression within the unions reflected and to some degree was a
response to the conservative political atmosphere in the country at large during the 1920s. Part of the TUEL's problem, of course, was that Foster and his
comrades made their arguments amidst prosperity and stability. Particularly
for those skilled workers who retained union affiliations through the twen-

ties, it was not difficult to believe that the system was working. For workers who *did* embrace the TUEL's more radical perspective, often in troubled industries where wages and standards were falling, there was the threat of pervasive political repression. Foster's task of radicalizing the labor movement was vastly complicated because he was organizing the TUEL in the midst of the Red Scare. Particular policy decisions undoubtedly weakened the Party position within the labor movement, but, as in subsequent periods of crisis and decline, the Party did not simply crumble from within; it was relentlessly attacked by conservative union leaders, employers, and the state.

The TUEL's fortunes are best understood, then, by the interaction among these factors: the practical problems facing workers in various industries and employers' efforts to rationalize work and undermine labor organization; the vagaries of Communist strategy and factional politics; the responses of trade union officials to the challenge TUEL activists represented in several important organizations; and the repressive political atmosphere of the time. During the twenties, Foster emerged as the central figure in the Party's industrial work, if not in the Party generally, but the policy he mapped out was a product of not simply "orders from Moscow" but all these influences. The force of each emerges from an analysis of the TUEL's roots and its situation in particular industries.

As always, Foster concerned himself with avoiding any appearance of dual unionism. He objected to Soviet requests that he build a mass membership. "On pain of being driven out of the movement we must . . . make the membership proposition as diffused as possible," he argued. "This is a major point that should always be borne in mind. . . . To disregard it will be to wreck our movement." The TUEL therefore had neither dues nor membership. Foster raised money through collections at public meetings; the sale of league literature and subscriptions to the *Labor Herald*, the TUEL's rather impressive journal; and more or less regular Soviet subsidies. Writing in the Chicago Federation of Labor's *New Majority* at the end of 1921, Foster envisioned the organization eventually constituting "from 500 to 1,000 groups of trade union radicals and progressives in the many localities to put spirit and fire into the labor movement." The TUEL, Foster declared, "has nothing in common with dual unionism," which had "greatly injured the labor movement."[5]

Instead, TUEL militants remained in their own unions to win them over to a radical program. As the organization evolved, the key units were local industrial committees made up of activists in the same trade and affiliated with one of the TUEL's fourteen national industrial groups, each with its own secretary. To coordinate activities on a regional basis, four district committees serving Canada and the eastern, central, and western states each sponsored periodic conferences to develop regional programs and strategy. A Mexican committee also eventually emerged. A yearly national conference elected a committee that met regularly and ran the national organization on a daily basis, and from 1922 on, the TUEL was affiliated with the Red International of Labor Unions (RILU) at the international level. As national secretary of the TUEL, Foster oversaw the whole operation.

The TUEL structure was actually less elaborate than this suggests. The league was strongest in Chicago, where its first public meeting at the end of February 1922 drew an audience of perhaps 400. This number probably better suggests the broader sympathy for the local movement, however, than actual membership. Like Foster's earlier efforts, the league was loosely organized and relied for its day-to-day needs on a fairly small core of militants, perhaps twenty to twenty-five, all in Chicago. But the organization grew quickly in the course of 1922. That summer Foster reported local organizations in forty-five to fifty cities. Nationally, the *Labor Herald* had about 4,000 subscribers, but the group was selling 10,000 to 15,000 issues in about 115 cities by the summer of 1922, and the league had about 500 hard-core activists at the movement's height in late 1923 or early 1924, according to Earl Browder. By the mid-twenties, Foster could call on thousands of local activists, but his Chicago group still represented the key element.[6]

Foster's labor radicalism still revolved around the *militant minority* and *boring from within,* both concepts heavily influenced by French and British syndicalist models. His notion of a militant minority represented a major ideological link between his earlier syndicalism and the revolutionary elitism of his 1920s Leninism. In reports to Moscow, he maintained that most American workers, when left to their own devices, were "tame and stupid . . . so ignorant as to be almost unbelievable." The key to energizing the labor movement, making it "an instrument of working class emancipation," lay in organizing "the thinking and acting part of the working class, the very soul of labor." "Revolutions are not brought about by the sort of far-sighted revolutionaries you have in mind," he told the radical economist Scott Nearing, "but by stupid masses who are goaded to desperate revolt by the pressure of social conditions, and who are led by straight-thinking revolutionaries who are able to direct the storm intelligently against capitalism." The purpose of the TUEL was to provide a channel through which these militants could "bore from within"—coordinate their activities, educate the rank and file, and transform the unions. In these and other respects, the league represented a logical culmination of Foster's theory and practice, what some Party critics called "Fosterism," long after his adherence to communism.[7]

The league's program, hammered out in a series of Foster's articles and pamphlets, looked quite radical: class struggle unionism rather than class collaboration; development of industrial unionism through amalgamation of existing unions; organization of the unorganized; opposition to dual unionism; the shop delegate system of local union organization; an independent labor party; affiliation with the Red International of Labor Unions; abolition of capitalism and the establishment of a workers' republic; and support for the Russian Revolution and recognition of Soviet Russia. In daily work, however, TUEL activists emphasized practical issues and often developed reputations as honest, progressive trade unionists.[8]

Foster served as TUEL national secretary throughout its existence and wrote extensively for the *Labor Herald* in the league's early years. Foster and Earl Browder built the magazine on reports from worker correspondents in various industries, editorials, and analysis of labor politics by the two of them and other league leaders. It was a sophisticated publication in many respects, featuring graphics by the celebrated cartoonist Fred Ellis and other radical artists, a regular international column, and occasional articles by British and European labor radicals.

From the founding of the Party in 1919 through 1921, the Communists had little support in the unions. Their few contacts were largely through small independent left-wing unions in New York City. When Foster became a Communist, he brought with him the TUEL, its program, contacts, and some of those activists who had not yet joined the Party. From late 1921 through late 1923, the TUEL made significant headway through painstaking efforts to build opposition movements within the various unions. By the mid-1920s, however, the organization was faltering because of factional conflict within the Party and attacks from conservative trade union leaders. During the late 1920s, the Party gradually settled into a dual union strategy dictated not only by the official Comintern line but also by the conservative opposition the TUEL faced in the unions.

In the early twenties, the TUEL's greatest successes were based on two central demands: the amalgamation of existing unions and a labor party based on the unions. The labor party movement emerged from union organizations throughout the United States—in New York City and Seattle; the industrial towns of Pennsylvania, Ohio, and Connecticut; and Chicago, the heart of the movement, where a national conference in November 1919 established the National Labor Party, later renamed the Farmer-Labor Party. The new party declared that "throughout the world, workers have reached the determination to . . . take control of their own lives and their govern-

ment." Parley P. Christensen, the party's 1920 presidential candidate, garnered over 290,000 votes, running on a platform calling for nationalization
of banks, natural resources, public utilities, and basic industry.[9]

Although Foster was originally skeptical of the labor party venture on
syndicalist grounds, his "old syndicalist anti-politics," as he put it, "had
started to collapse" by 1920 as a result of wartime organizing experiences. He
was gradually won over to the idea and became active locally in Illinois by
mid-1920, long before visiting Russia. The change of heart may have been
rooted in his experiences in the great steel strike, where he saw the practical
implications of corporate control of local government in the form of devastating legal and physical assaults on strikers and labor organizations. He was
also impressed with what appeared to be considerable trade union support
for the movement. Yet Foster still placed far more emphasis on industrial
organizing than on political activity, and it seems that he rationalized the
labor party effort as a natural outcome of industrial conflict.[10]

In early 1922, at the invitation of the railroad brotherhoods, a large number of union, farm, socialist, and Farmer-Labor Party delegates met in Chicago to constitute the Conference for Progressive Political Action (CPPA).
With a program all of these groups might support, the movement now promised to take the form of a mass party with the broadest possible base.

International Communist strategy also had been evolving toward coalition politics since Lenin's declaration of the "United Front" at the Comintern's Third Congress in the summer of 1921. As the revolutionary tide
receded during the next year, the United Front proved increasingly attractive,
particularly to such activists as Foster, who prized their contacts with the
broader working-class movement.[11]

In November 1922, the Workers Party formally supported John Fitzpatrick, president of the Chicago Federation of Labor (CFL), and his Illinois-
based Farmer-Labor Party. The new party came into the CPPA's Second
National Convention the following month demanding the immediate formation of a national labor party and was quickly alienated from the mainstream CPPA leadership. First, despite strenuous objections from the CFL and
the Farmer-Labor Party, the CPPA's more moderate elements refused to seat
Foster and Ruthenberg as Workers Party delegates. Then the CPPA dropped
the demand for nationalization of the railroads and refused to commit itself
to the formation of a national labor party. At this point, the CFL and Farmer-
Labor Party delegates withdrew and laid plans for their own national convention at Chicago in July 1923. It was Fitzpatrick who proposed the united
front, in effect, by inviting the Workers Party to the convention. "Quite a
victory," Foster reported to a Soviet colleague.[12]

Still, Fitzpatrick was wary. As Theodore Draper observed, "The Chicago trade unions had taken the lead in creating the Farmer-Labor movement and only those Communists familiar to them were welcomed in their political movement." Fitzpatrick saw the Chicago group of "trade union Communists" first and foremost as militant trade unionists. He knew Jack Johnstone, Foster, and several others in the group around them rather well, and he approached the Workers Party through them. A classic united front emerged. A committee composed of Fitzpatrick; Jay G. Brown, an old friend of Foster from the Pacific Northwest and the steel strike; and Edward Nockels, the CFL's secretary, conferred regularly with a committee of Communist unionists designated by the Workers Party leadership: Arne Swabeck, the Party's district organizer and a CFL delegate from the painters' union; Charles Krumbein, the steamfitters' delegate; and Earl Browder, editor of the TUEL's *Labor Herald* and a member of the Party's Chicago district executive committee. Swabeck later recalled that Fitzpatrick bluntly warned the Communists at the first meeting about any effort on their part to control the new party: "Let's get this straight—we are willing to go along, but we think you communists should occupy the back seat." The remark underscored the complexity of the united front in practice. The Communists prided themselves on the vanguard character of their own party, but to form alliances that brought them into the mainstream movement, they had to acknowledge the natural leadership of such progressives as Fitzpatrick. The Communist unionists went along with what Swabeck called "a left wing minority" position within the movement. By spring 1923, however, the Workers Party was at the center of the labor party movement.[13]

To demonstrate support for the labor party idea, Foster hit on what he termed "the greatest referendum vote in the history of the American labor movement." The TUEL mailed ballots directly to 35,000 union locals, asking them to endorse the move, and 7,000 did so. The labor party idea was brought before thousands of industrial workers, the AFL leadership was pressed to face the issue, and the TUEL received credit for its efforts to build the movement.[14]

If the labor party campaign helped to put the TUEL on the map, the league's plan for transforming the labor movement ultimately depended on its success in the unions. Here league activists struck a responsive chord with their motto of "amalgamation or annihilation." The amalgamation campaign provided the TUEL with prospects for a broad-based movement. Aside from the obvious strategic advantages to organizing, bargaining, and, if necessary, striking together, separate crafts in the same industry stood to gain in financial and other practical ways from coordinating their activities through amalgamation. Eventually, amalgamation would lead to the reconstruction of unions along industrial rather than craft lines, a goal that increasingly made sense to workers. This growing enthusiasm was reflected in the league's early successes.

Foster started the amalgamation campaign on friendly turf—the Chicago Federation of Labor—in March 1922. Delegates warmly embraced his argument that "amalgamation is not enough. . . . Labor must go further and prepare its ranks for a revolt against capitalism." His motion put the CFL on record in support of amalgamation and called on the AFL to convene a national conference on the issue. Fitzpatrick and other progressives spoke in support of the motion and defended Foster against red-baiting by conservative delegates. The amalgamation resolution, cosponsored by Foster's protege Jack Johnstone, passed by a vote of 114 to 37.[15]

In May, Samuel Gompers attended a special conference on amalgamation sponsored by the CFL. He denounced the campaign and claimed that Foster wanted to become "the Lenine [*sic*] of America." Once again Fitzpatrick defended Foster, who lectured Gompers and the others for half an hour on the virtues of industrial unionism and invited Emmet Flood, an AFL organizer, to debate the amalgamation issue. Gompers offered himself instead, and "amid a storm of cheers and angry shouts," Foster accepted. Foster published an open letter following up on Gompers's challenge, but Gompers ignored him. In retaliation for the CFL's role in the amalgamation movement, the AFL executive committee threatened to cut off its subsidy of half of the Chicago central body's expenses. The Chicago movement's progressive stance was beginning to cost something. Still, the amalgamation movement rolled on. In the eighteen months following the March 1922 CFL meeting, TUEL activists succeeded in getting their model resolution adopted by sixteen international unions, seventeen state federations, scores of city labor councils, and thousands of local unions—organizations representing perhaps half of organized labor in the United States. Foster wrote to Lozovsky that "on the basis of this issue alone, the communists have sprung into great prominence in the trade union movement."[16]

The amalgamation and labor party campaigns provided the TUEL with contacts and visibility, but Foster's plans depended largely on the ability of indigenous militants to radicalize each union from the inside. The TUEL built its strongest and most durable movement in the needle trades—the International Ladies Garment Workers Union (ILGWU) and the Amalgamated Clothing Workers of America (ACWA), as well as the capmakers' union, the fur workers' union, and other smaller unions. Throughout the clothing industry, workers' activism had deep roots in radical immigrant culture, particularly in such Yiddish-speaking enclaves as the Lower East Side of New

York and Chicago's West Side ghetto and in the wretched wages and working conditions the garment workers confronted. The unions themselves were the creations of worker radicals, and the Socialist Party and other radical groups maintained followings in them throughout the early twentieth century. In the wake of World War I and the Russian Revolution, small left-wing groups formed in several unions in opposition to the more conservative Socialist leadership, eventually providing the nucleus for Communist trade union activity.

In the ILGWU, for example, the left wing's roots went back to 1917, when radicals in Waist and Dress Makers' Local 25 organized a current events committee and agitated against the union's leadership. The committee soon disintegrated, but loosely knit opposition groups remained in a number of locals, merging in the fall of 1919 into a shop delegate movement modeled on the Shop Stewards' and Workers' Committee Movement among British metal workers. They aimed to shift organization and authority from the bureaucratic leadership of the union to the rank-and-file members in the shops. The movement spread throughout the ILGWU, attracting not only Communists but also radical socialists, syndicalists, anarchists, and others who saw it as a way to build a militant and more democratic union. In early 1922, as the TUEL reached into the industry, the shop delegate activists provided a base for the league, and extremely popular rank-and-file leaders, such as Charles Zimmerman and Rose Wortis, carried its message. The birth in April 1922 of *Freiheit,* a new Yiddish-language daily close to the Party, provided radicals in the needle trades with a valuable weapon in their conflicts with the union's right wing. Through the TUEL's and later the Party's needle trades committees, Foster worked in close cooperation with these rank-and-file radicals and encouraged them to base their own campaign on grievances regarding industrial conditions and on popular demands for greater democracy and rank-and-file control in the union. As long as the league stuck to these issues, it continued to build a strong following. In its early years, the TUEL attracted the support of non-Communist radicals, and, by 1924, the left wing controlled several locals as well as the union's joint boards in Philadelphia and Chicago. Comparable movements developed in other sections of the industry, particularly among fur workers, where the Communist Ben Gold emerged as a heroic figure and the left wing won control of the national union in 1925 after a long and bitter struggle.[17]

In the men's clothing industry, Party influence actually *inhibited* a rank-and-file revolt. Foster and other Workers Party leaders were sympathetic to Sidney Hillman's administration in the ACWA. Hillman had supported the great steel strike, underwritten Foster's 1920 national speaking tour, and even offered to hire him as an organizer when he was blacklisted in the wake of the strike. Earl Browder recalled that the ACWA contributed $1,000 to the TUEL in 1922. Hillman tended to line up with the left wing in its disputes with the old-line Socialists in the Jewish community and helped finance the *Freiheit*. The strongest bond between Hillman and the Communists was undoubtedly the ACWA's consistent and substantial support for Soviet Russia. The union contributed large sums for famine relief and even launched a cooperative clothing manufacturing venture with the Soviet government. Although there were rank-and-file grievances against Hillman, who often cooperated with employers on productivity schemes, Foster and other Party leaders counseled league militants against any open break with the ACWA leadership and disciplined those who were disinclined to accept such advice. "In some instances," the national committee of the TUEL's needle trades section reported, "such as the support of the Hillman machine in the Amalgamated, the National Committee differed seriously with the policy of the CEC [Central Executive Committee], objecting to the many compromises made with the Hillman administration. In all cases, however, the policy laid down by the CEC was loyally carried out by the National Needle Trades Committee." The alliance with Hillman came apart in the course of 1924, first because of his collaboration with employers in the wake of a successful 1924 strike and later because of his support for Robert M. La Follette in the 1924 elections. Relations deteriorated in the mid-twenties, but the TUEL was never able to generate the sort of strong opposition it built in the ILGWU.[18]

As in the needle trades, the coal industry was under severe pressure to cut costs in the twenties, and as in the ILGWU, the United Mine Workers of America (UMWA) radicals built their own organization on a deeply rooted indigenous rebellion. In the coal mines, trade unionism had a compelling, almost desperate quality about it that invested the UMWA factional conflicts with an endurance and intensity seldom matched in other organizations. "Their bulwark—almost their church—was the union," David Montgomery wrote of the miners. "No other AFL union of the 1910s evoked such loyalty from members, such fervent responses to strike calls from miners who were not members, such rank-and-file fury at leaders' misdeeds, such factionalism, or such a blend of locally directed struggle with the conviction that outside the international union there was no salvation as did the UMWA." It was on such long-established traditions of rank-and-file insurgency that TUEL activists built their own movement, the miners' leader John Brophy explained.[19]

At stake was the organization itself. In 1920, more than half of America's 785,000 miners were in the UMWA; in the following decade, as large parts of the industry went into decline, employer attacks and factional conflicts decimated the organization. John L. Lewis, the union's autocratic president, had successfully resisted a wage cut in the course of a 1919 strike, but only at the cost of a weak agreement and continuing rank-and-file opposition. Radicals in Illinois, Pennsylvania, and elsewhere demanded more organizing, greater internal democracy, and a tougher stance against the employers.[20]

Lewis's typical response to such opposition was expulsion. In Illinois District 12, a radical stronghold, he revoked the charters of twenty-four local unions for an unauthorized 1919 strike that he blamed on Socialist Labor Party agitators. When British Columbia miners voted overwhelmingly to join the radical "One Big Union" movement the same year, Lewis simply expelled their leaders and reorganized the union's entire western Canadian district. Lewis's most celebrated victim was Alexander Howat, president of the UMWA's Kansas District 14, who was imprisoned for refusing to cooperate with the Kansas Court of Industrial Relations, a system of compulsory arbitration. When miners throughout the state walked out in support of Howat, Lewis demanded an end to the strike. When Howat refused to cooperate, Lewis removed him and all other district officials and ordered the miners back to work. By the end of 1921, he had revoked eighty-three local union charters and had expelled 2,500 Kansas miners. Far from ending the rebellion, however, Lewis's action stimulated greater rank-and-file opposition, which now focused on the struggle to reinstate Howat and to drive Lewis from the leadership. It also brought Howat much closer to the TUEL and the Workers Party.[21]

Foster and the TUEL built the Progressive International Committee of the UMWA from these and other disparate opposition elements at a Pittsburgh conference in February 1923. They focused their attention on western Pennsylvania District 5, where Foster addressed local unions throughout the region. The Communists also received strong support in Nova Scotia, where the district leadership, expelled by Lewis, was under TUEL control. What the league contributed to this rank-and-file rebellion was organization and a program. By the time the UMWA assembled for its 1924 convention, the most tumultuous in the union's history, the league had managed to project a clear set of demands around which the opposition might rally: direct election of organizers, committees, and officers; simultaneous expiration of all coal contracts; reinstatement of the Nova Scotian leadership and Howat; nationalization of the mines; a six-hour day and five-day week; and Foster's pet project of an alliance between miners and railroad workers. Although each of these resolutions was defeated, the left wing garnered significant support. Their Communist presidential candidate in the union's December 1924 elections secured almost one-third of the votes, despite apparent ballot irregularities.[22]

On the railroads, where Foster maintained numerous contacts, TUEL activists played important roles during the long 1922 shop crafts strike, which involved more than 256,000 machinists and maintenance workers. The strike's failure, which Foster considered "the greatest single defeat ever suffered by the workers in this country," was clearly related to the segmented character of craft unionism in the industry. The railroad brotherhoods generally failed to support the machinists; their members ran trains while the machinists walked picket lines. The strike thus provided dramatic justification of the league's demand for the amalgamation of the sixteen railroad unions. Its defeat fueled opposition movements in both the machinists' union and the railroad brotherhoods. At the end of 1922, the TUEL sponsored an extremely successful national amalgamation conference, which drew 400 machinists and railroad workers to Chicago to lay out a plan for linking the unions.[23]

In the International Association of Machinists, which had seen its membership drop from 273,000 in 1921 to 97,300 in 1923, the TUEL supported William Knudsen, who endorsed the league's entire program, including the formation of a workers' republic, and won 30 per cent of the vote in his 1922 run against incumbent president William H. Johnston. As on the railroads, amalgamation was a vital issue among machinists even before the TUEL launched a campaign around this demand. The league also organized groups and contested elections in the carpenters' and other building trades' unions, particularly in Chicago, where they benefited from a bitter fight against the open shop; in New York City, where Morris Rosen, the TUEL building trades' national secretary, organized the Progressive Carpenters' Committee; and in Detroit, where Bud Reynolds, an open Party member, was elected district president of the carpenters' union and vice president of the city labor federation. In addition to the groups in the building trades and in the railroad, mining, and metal-working industries, league organizer Joe Manley established industrial sections in the printing, boot and shoe, food processing and service, and textile industries by the end of November 1922.[24]

These successes were built on Foster's years of practical experience in creating alliances with the large number of non-Communist labor progressives. Long after James P. Cannon became a foe, he recalled Foster's accomplishment. "Foster's work and achievements in the early days of the TUEL under the Communist Party, were no less remarkable than his stockyard and steel campaigns. His rapid-fire organization of a network of effective left-progressive groups in a dozen or more different unions demonstrated most convincingly that his previous successes in the AFL were no flukes," Cannon wrote. "It proved, for a second time, under different auspices, that given the forces and the machinery to work with, Foster was a trade union organizer without a peer." Foster counseled league activists to attach themselves to broad reform movements and establish reputations for hard work on concrete issues. He was impatient with Communists who thought they would win the masses with "talk" and urged them to do less of that and more "day-by-day detail work." "Let the militants offer a practical program," he counseled in the spring of 1922, "participate in labor's everyday struggles with concrete demands, let them learn how to handle the masses and . . . [their] task will be accomplished soon." As Draper concluded, "His approach was matter-of-fact, down-to-earth, straightforward."[25]

By the middle of 1923, the TUEL had sunk deep roots in the labor movement and was active throughout the country by following this formula. Yet at the end of 1924, Foster himself acknowledged that the TUEL's pace had slackened and that its effectiveness had been reduced. The league's early successes suggest that Communist efforts to build progressive blocs in the unions and exercise some influence over them were not preordained to fail. What explains the league's decline in spite of its auspicious beginnings in the early twenties? Part of the explanation involves repression—by the government, employers, and especially trade union officials. Raids, arrests, court cases, firings, blacklisting, and mass expulsions of activists and whole local unions made it increasingly difficult for the league to operate. The success of these attacks, however, was related to the Communist industrial policy and the position of Foster and his group of "industrial Communists" in the Party. Some Party initiatives helped isolate league activists and facilitate attacks by conservative union officials. These policies most often had their origins in official Comintern politics and in the U.S. Party's factional conflicts, which often reflected those of the international movement.

Foster's own prospects for transforming the labor movement and those of the Workers Party for building a mass following were circumscribed by the political atmosphere of the 1920s. The decade opened in January 1920 with the infamous Palmer raids in which an estimated 10,000 people, including most of the leaders of the young Communist movement, were arrested. Hundreds of foreign-born radicals were deported, while simultaneous raids shut down political organizations and publications throughout the country. The TUEL was under attack from the moment it became active. Government documents from early 1922 indicate that Foster and his colleagues were under surveillance by Justice Department agents working with business groups to identify and blacklist railroad militants. In August 1922, the state's attorney's agents raided the TUEL's Chicago headquarters, wrecking the place in the process and carting away documents, manuscripts, and subscription lists. Police also raided the group's first national conference a few weeks later and arrested some of the delegates.

Justice Department agents, often working with local authorities, followed Foster all over the country. In August 1922, he was kidnapped by Colorado state rangers while on a speaking tour in connection with the railroad shop crafts strike. Seized at his hotel room and jailed briefly as "one of the most dangerous men in the country today," he was handed over to Wyoming authorities and dumped on the open range near the Nebraska state line. If he should ever return, the Cheyenne sheriff warned Foster, he would go home "in a box."[26]

Within a few days of the Colorado kidnapping, Michigan state police raided a secret Communist Party convention in the forest near Bridgman, Michigan, arresting fifteen Party leaders and again seizing a large quantity of documents. Ironically, the most important discussion at the convention involved liquidation of the secret, underground Party and the formation of a program that would help the Communists establish links with the labor movement. At the precise moment that Communist leaders concluded it was essential to work openly, they were arrested. Foster, of course, was a crucial part of this new strategy. He addressed the group in rather dramatic surroundings—out in the forest, illuminated by torches and lanterns. Long after Benjamin Gitlow had become an anti-Communist and a government informer, he remembered that Foster "had made a tremendous impression," arguing that the " 'fate of the Communist Party depends on the control of the masses, through capture of the trade unions, without which revolution is impossible.' " Foster eluded arrest by leaving immediately after lecturing the group on union tactics, but he was picked up in Chicago shortly afterward. At first, he was held under suspicion of being involved in an Indiana train wreck. These charges were eventually dropped, but he and ten other Communist leaders were charged with criminal syndicalism under an extremely broad state conspiracy law. If convicted, Foster faced a five- to ten-year prison sentence, a $45,000 fine, or both.[27]

For all of the disruption that these legal problems caused, Foster received impressive support from progressive, non-Communist labor activists, who tended to view such attacks as part of a general offensive against the labor movement. Following his arrest for criminal syndicalism, the Chicago Federation of Labor and major central bodies defended Foster and other Communist trade unionists. Until Foster's arrest, the *New Majority* noted, the Palmer raids had "seemed something remote," but the raids on the TUEL and the

Michigan convention were a "direct attack upon the labor movement as a whole, particularly upon the progressive trade union movement." The CFL passed a ringing denunciation of the arrests and an endorsement of those unionists involved. Federation activists organized protests and collected money for a defense fund. CFL leaders were instrumental in setting up a defense committee for Foster, the first of the defendants to face trial. Out of this effort, local labor defense councils emerged in cities around the country, the basis for the International Labor Defense, which later provided legal assistance for labor radicals throughout the twenties and thirties. The Workers Party was heavily involved in organizing the councils, but the groups also included prominent liberals and labor progressives, and their propaganda emphasized the indicted Communists' "genuine trade union backgrounds." Fitzpatrick arranged for Frank Walsh to serve as Foster's defense counsel, and he attended the trial himself on a regular basis. The Michigan Federation of Labor supported legislation to repeal the law under which Foster had been indicted, viewing it as an infringement of the constitutional right to free speech and a threat to the labor movement. The Socialist leader Eugene Debs served on the original Labor Defense Council's national executive committee and wrote warmly in Foster's support. Through the defense work, Foster joined the American Civil Liberties Union and served briefly on its national committee. Even as he was on trial for his radical politics, then, Foster maintained broad contacts with a variety of organizations across the country.[28]

Foster stood trial in Michigan on the criminal syndicalism charge during the spring of 1923. The government's decision to proceed with his trial first was probably a tactical error because its case against him was the weakest. It may be that the federal government, working with the Michigan authorities, concurred with the *New York Herald's* assessment that he was the "ablest and most vicious Red" and that he posed the greatest threat because of his poten tial as a labor leader. The defense maintained throughout the trial that Foster had never joined the Party and had attended the convention as an observer rather than as a delegate. Although he was secretly a Party member, the prosecution never succeeded in proving this. In his testimony, Foster estimated that perhaps only 10 per cent of the TUEL's membership consisted of Com munists but when asked about his relationship with the Party admitted that he "fully sympathized with its aims." The jury—nine farmers, a nonunion railroad worker, a grocery store clerk, and the wife of a factory superintendent—finally deadlocked over the question of whether the Communists actually advocated the violent overthrow of the capitalist system and the government or simply predicted it. Minerva Olson, the superintendent's wife, argued that Foster was being prosecuted "because of his union activities rather than through fear of his Red agitation." The Communists celebrated Foster's acquittal as a great victory.[29]

In April 1923, soon after his acquittal, Foster announced his membership in the Workers Party. The original division of authority between Foster's direction of trade union affairs and Ruthenberg's control of the political apparatus in the Party allowed Foster considerable autonomy during his first two years in the Party. The Central Executive Committee assumed much greater influence over trade union policy after 1924, often with negative results, but throughout the early twenties policy and strategy derived from Foster and the TUEL activists around him, a group well connected with militants in and outside the Party in industries around the country. These Chicago-based "trade union Communists," with their exclusive emphasis on industrial work, were quite distinct from the more theoretically grounded group at the Workers Party headquarters in New York. Although Foster occupied a position on the Party's Political Committee almost from the moment he became a member, he prized his connections in the mainstream labor movement, tended to be preoccupied with union rather than Party politics, and preferred to deal with the New York group through intermediaries, notably Earl Browder, during these years.[30]

While the TUEL was increasingly successful and growing, its relationship with the Party remained tenuous. "We have succeeded in building a trade-union machine for the party," Earl Browder explained to a 1922 gathering, "but we have not been able to build a trade-union machinery OF the party. We have created a movement for you which is in your hands and which is completely dominated and controlled by you, but 90% of the movement is outside of the party and not more than 5% of the effective manpower of the party has been put into that movement. . . . if you do not establish an actual functioning connection between the Workers Party and the Trade Union Educational League, the latter will be out of your control. . . . once it begins to gather momentum, if you are not right down in the ground . . . in every local group, it will escape your control. . . ." This was precisely the problem some Party leaders had feared in the wake of Foster's admission.[31]

The fact that Foster was quite autonomous in his trade union work in the early twenties and that the TUEL developed in the context of indigenous rank-and-file movements does not mean that it operated without Party direction. Party influence became increasingly intrusive over the course of the decade. Throughout the mid-twenties, Foster chaired both the Party's Trade Union Committee and the TUEL's national committee meetings, which meant that there was not only a close but also a personal relationship be-

tween the two organizations in the persons of Foster and his closest colleagues. The Trade Union Committee minutes demonstrate Foster's domination of the industrial work—drafting position papers, sponsoring resolutions,
and debating policies, as well as working out in the field, raising funds, speaking before strikers, and consulting with TUEL leaders on organizing and
strike strategy.[32] Since Foster also sat on the Political Committee, which directed the Party's own affairs, he had to deal regularly with the professional
revolutionaries in the Party's Union Square headquarters.

On the Trade Union Committee, Foster concerned himself with the most
minute and practical details of work in the various industries and regions,
taking great interest in precisely how issues were raised with the rank and file
and how alliances could be established with non-Communist progressives.
He could often be seen in the balcony at union conventions, signaling left-
wing delegates on critical votes. On the Political Committee, he often criticized Party activists for ineptitude or lethargy. At times, Foster clearly felt
that politics were getting in the way of effective industrial work.[33]

Foster could not have remained aloof from the Party's factional politics
even if he had wanted to—and at times it seemed that he did. His industrial
work was increasingly shaped by Party policy, which was a product not of
science but of politics—within the Party in the United States and ultimately
in Moscow. To draw distinct lines in a narrative of the Party's factional conflict would be misleading. Foster was usually under siege from one or another
factional opponent throughout the twenties. Still, it is possible to identify
three related periods of conflict, each of which found Foster in the center of
the fray, constrained in his industrial work.

As late as the spring of 1923, Foster's perspective, strongly supported by
the Party chair James P. Cannon, held sway on most labor-related matters.
Jay Lovestone complained that the Central Executive Committee was dominated by the group around Foster and Cannon, who placed "too strong an
emphasis on the party being in the good graces of certain progressive labor
leaders—particularly Fitzpatrick and Nockels of the Chicago Federation of
Labor." The Party's industrial policy was set by the TUEL, "Foster's League,"
rather than vice versa. There was also some tension over Foster's tendency to
emphasize local industrial issues to the exclusion of broader ideological concerns. When RILU chief Lozovsky complained about the lack of international
news and analysis in the *Labor Herald,* Foster insisted that "we must deal with
living problems in this country." The Comintern's preposterous 1923 estimate of 2 million TUEL members and Lozovsky's demands for more coverage
of international Communist activities suggested to Foster that the Soviets
were too optimistic about American prospects.[34] As a result of Foster's influ-

ence, the Party treaded warily in the trade union world—until the summer of 1923.

Foster's first involvement with factional conflict grew out of a conflict over the Communist position on the Farmer-Labor Party. This experience at once cut him off from many of his most valued labor connections, drew him deeply into the factional life of the Party, and opened the TUEL to the charge that it really was a foreign body directed by the Party rather than a genuine rank-and-file union movement.

Still more oriented toward industrial organization than electoral politics, Foster nevertheless viewed the Farmer-Labor Party as an important opportunity to link the Communists with a genuine mass movement. Until the summer of 1923, the prospects for this seemed bright. During the following year, however, two factors combined to destroy this opportunity and to isolate Foster and the Communists from their labor support. First, the AFL leadership launched a systematic effort to separate the Communists from Fitzpatrick and other progressives. At the same time, the Workers Party's own internal conflicts and those of the Comintern facilitated this strategy and prevented Communist activists from salvaging the alliances they had painstakingly built in the postwar era.

Throughout the spring of 1923, Gompers placed increasing pressure on Fitzpatrick and other labor progressives. In April, he cut the AFL's monthly subsidy to the CFL and threatened to reorganize the federation unless it severed its ties with the Workers Party. He also threatened to revoke the Seattle Central Labor Council's (CLC) charter unless it toed the AFL line. Specifically, the AFL's executive committee objected to the Seattle body's position on organizing women workers, its involvement with the Washington Farmer-Labor Party, and its demands for recognition of Soviet Russia. More generally, the AFL claimed that the CLC was directing "the Seattle labor movement to conform to the policies and principles enunciated by Soviet Russia."[35] The two major city federations that the Workers Party had earmarked as centers for their organizing were now under attack.

At this critical juncture, Fitzpatrick began to waver. Foster, with whom he had a close and supportive relationship, was now out in the open as a Communist, and, in the Red Scare atmosphere of the time, this undoubtedly complicated matters for Fitzpatrick and other non-Communist progressives. The union support upon which Fitzpatrick had always predicated his labor party project appeared to be evaporating as more union activists were attracted to Robert M. La Follette's independent presidential campaign. Fitzpatrick approached the Communists and asked that the Farmer-Labor Party's projected July convention be postponed until he could shore up union support. Significantly, Fitzpatrick did not seek an end to his collaboration with the Communists but pursued an ongoing propaganda campaign in lieu of the immediate formation of a party.[36]

The Chicago Communists proceeded with caution, realizing that labor support for the project was at stake. Foster himself and most Party activists around him were far more interested in the movement's potential for mobilizing progressive unionists than they were in farmers' involvement. They feared a loss of their valuable contacts with progressives in Chicago and elsewhere. Cannon, Browder, and others in Chicago warned that with the refusal of the Socialist Party to take part and the danger that unions were bending to Gompers's pressure, there was a real danger that the convention would lack a mass base, that it would alienate progressive allies, and that the Workers Party would become isolated. The Party's New York leadership chose to force the issue.[37]

Foster's main antagonist was John Pepper, a Hungarian Comintern representative who had enjoyed a meteoric rise in influence during his one year in the country. Cannon later remembered Pepper as a "phony, but by far the most brilliant phony I ever knew." He had "a rich European political experience, plus a European culture—which distinguished him among the American shoemakers," but he had little if any understanding of the American political situation or labor movement. Pepper and the majority on the Central Executive Committee demanded that Communist unionists identify more closely with the Party and distinguish themselves from labor reformists. If Fitzpatrick would not act immediately, then Foster and his colleagues must abandon the CFL group and go it alone. Foster argued that the Party should follow such a course only if the Communists themselves could generate enough labor support without Fitzpatrick. Even Ruthenberg opposed the break, but a majority supported Pepper, who appeared to have the Comintern's blessings.[38]

Once the decision was made, Foster supported it, but he feared that it would cost dearly in organizational terms and that he would be made to look a fool or traitor in the eyes of old and trusted labor friends like Fitzpatrick and others around Chicago. Fitzpatrick, perhaps believing that he could muster a majority at the convention, refused to even meet with Workers Party representatives.[39]

When the moment of the Farmer-Labor Party convention arrived on July 3, 1923, Foster at first believed he had been mistaken. The convention represented a humiliating defeat for John Fitzpatrick and, on the surface at least, a victory for the Communists. At the end of 1922, Fitzpatrick had bolted the CPPA convention when the body refused to establish a national labor party immediately. Now he fought the majority of Farmer-Labor Party delegates from the opposite side of precisely the same issue. Foster confronted Fitzpatrick with the contradiction before the assembled delegates. Robert M. Buck, editor of the CFL's *New Majority,* who had played an instrumental role in Foster's defense following the Bridgman arrest, was in a minority of three on the convention's organizing committee. He opposed the majority position at length, but he was voted down. The Communists, well organized and well represented through an array of radical labor, fraternal, and farm groups, exerted disproportional influence over non-Party delegates through group captains and runners carrying information and instructions from one group to another, an accomplishment Foster described privately as "an inspiration to our movement." They easily defeated Fitzpatrick on the floor of the convention, and he walked out in abject defeat, losing even some of his old supporters. In the new Federated Farmer-Labor Party (FF-LP) that emerged from the convention, Communists controlled most of the key positions. They converted the old Workers Party Chicago newspaper, the *Voice of Labor,* into the *Farmer-Labor Voice,* which became the new party's mouthpiece.[40]

Publicly, Foster was optimistic, and he hailed the Communist success at the convention as a "landmark in the history of the working class . . . striking proof of the vital fact that American workers will follow revolutionary leaders, even as their forebears did in 1886, once these leaders participate in the mass organizations and supply them with practical proposals." For a while at least, Foster told Cannon, he "got carried away myself and was convinced against my will and better judgement."[41]

But he and others with experience in the labor movement soon understood that this was a hollow victory. As Jay G. Brown, secretary of Fitzpatrick's national Farmer-Labor Party, noted, "It is one thing to capture a gathering in the Ashland Auditorium in Chicago and quite another to capture the imagination of the rank and file of the workers."[42] Although organizations allegedly representing 600,000 members had voted to form the FF-LP, the number of members actually voting to affiliate with the new party was only 155,000, and most of these were from organizations close to the Workers Party. As Foster himself later concluded, the FF-LP "amounted to a united front with ourselves."[43]

Fitzpatrick, humiliated and feeling betrayed, complained that the Communists' behavior was "on the level of a man being invited to your house as a guest and then once in the house seizing you by the throat and kicking you out of the door."[44] In turn, the Party attacked Fitzpatrick, appearing to confirm Gompers's warning that the Communists were devious disrupters who would turn on him when the opportunity arose. Fitzpatrick distanced himself from not only the Federated Farmer-Labor Party but also most other progressive causes and threw his enormous prestige behind conservative labor politics.[45] In Chicago at least, the Communists' strategy had done more to kill progressive labor politics than to promote it.

Writing to Lozovsky in early September, Foster feared the split would drive progressives like Fitzpatrick "right square into the arms" of the AFL leadership. "We will surely find ourselves isolated and discredited even in the eyes of our own friendly unions." The AFL leadership took the split with Fitzpatrick as the signal for an attack on the TUEL on several fronts. The September 1923 Illinois Federation of Labor convention demonstrated how far the breach between the Communists and the labor progressives had already widened. It is difficult to judge the merit of Foster's contention that the convention was packed by the conservatives, but certainly they had planned for the confrontation. The CFL distributed an announcement, what Foster called "a dagger in the back," disassociating itself from the TUEL. Labor leaders, hardened by what they saw as Foster's betrayal of the venerable Fitzpatrick, were ready for battle. The convention, Foster wrote, "was one of the bitterest clashes that has yet taken place between revolutionaries and reactionaries." There was no doubt who came out on top in the confrontation.[46]

"I'm a sailor," Victor Olander, the federation's conservative secretary, announced, "and to me 'boring from within' has a very significant meaning. It means scuttling the ship."[47] Olander went on for more than an hour excoriating Foster. The convention chair, John Walker, an old socialist miners' leader who had always strongly supported the labor party movement, denied Foster the right to respond to the charges leveled against him. Foster's two amalgamation resolutions—one calling on the federation to sponsor a conference to begin the process at the state level and the other asking it to recommend the plan to the AFL's national convention, both of which the CFL had overwhelmingly supported before the split—were denounced as "TUEL propaganda" and soundly defeated. Resolutions that the federation had routinely passed a year or two earlier, such as the one supporting Soviet Russia, were resoundingly defeated.[48] The channels through which Foster had always operated were now closing.

Fitzpatrick and most other Chicago delegates now supported the positions of the conservative leadership. Fitzpatrick even opposed the CFL's own resolution calling upon the AFL to support an independent labor party. The Illinois Federation of Labor had a reputation for facing questions squarely, Foster observed, and it should not be distracted by red-baiting. "Let us not duck the issues," he argued. "Let us say whether we are for a labor party or against it." To the argument that the resolution was a Workers Party ploy,

Foster responded, "We must consider this resolution on its own merits where the devil himself wrote it. . . . Our leaders are abandoning these big issues and leaving it to the radicals to fight them through. . . . The American workers at this time are practically a political zero." He put his case forcefully, and numerous miners and machinists as well as the delegates from the Chicago high school teachers' union supported him. In the end, however, the labor party resolution was killed 456 to 65, which was a clear reversal of the federation's earlier position on the issue.[49]

The other shoe dropped at the AFL's national convention in Portland, Oregon, the following month. "The left-center split on July 3rd," Foster later wrote, "was one of the basic reasons why the Gompers bureaucrats could ride roughshod over the left wing at the AFL convention a few months later." The point of departure was AFL president William Green's motion to unseat Foster's close associate William F. Dunne, a duly elected delegate from Butte, Montana, strictly on the grounds of his political affiliation (i.e., his membership in the Workers Party). The TUEL was expecting this attack. After two hours of attacks on the Party and Foster himself, Dunne provided a spirited defense that the TUEL later published as a popular pamphlet. When the question was called, William Hutcheson, president of the carpenters' union and a frequent TUEL target, insisted that every delegate rise to be counted in a roll call. The tactic resulted in what David Montgomery termed "a lynch-mob atmosphere" and a vote of 27,837 to 108 against Dunne. Samuel Gompers noted that it was only the second time in the organization's history that a delegate had been expelled, but he failed to note that it was the first time someone had been excluded solely on the basis of his or her politics. The convention overwhelmingly rejected all progressive resolutions, including those supporting recognition of Soviet Russia, industrial unionism, and independent labor politics. In addition, the AFL leadership demanded that the Seattle, Minneapolis, Detroit, Cleveland, and other city central bodies cleanse themselves of Communist influence or face revocation of their charters. Foster carried the fight back to Chicago. But where the Communists had once been at the very heart of a powerful progressive movement, they were now clearly on the margins, discredited and distrusted. "Lines were now so bitterly drawn," the historian Eugene Staley concluded, "that there was virtually no middle ground; progressive trade unionists found themselves forced to choose between going to the extreme left with Foster and the Communists or back to the right with Gompers and the American Federation of Labor."[50]

"Our Party is in the most dangerous position it has occupied since it was an open organization," Earl Browder wrote to the Workers Party Central Executive Committee in the fall of 1923. The labor party fiasco "was merely the culmination of a well thought policy which has been leading us directly for isolation for the past eight months. The fundamental fault in our leadership has been the practical abandonment of the strategy of the United Front."[51]

For Foster, all of this meant that the TUEL's campaign had reached a new phase and that it would now be necessary to confront the conservative union leadership directly. "To break the reactionary resistance of the bureaucracy and to release the revolutionary forces of the rank and file," Foster wrote in the fall of 1924, "is the latest task of the TUEL."[52]

As the TUEL stepped up its attack on union leaders, league activists were expelled from unions throughout the country, cutting the movement off from the rank and file. The repression did not always work. In the ensuing struggle in the ILGWU, for example, the Socialist leadership sent Vice President Mayer Perlstein to clean out the Reds in Chicago, where the league had an especially strong presence. But when Perlstein expelled many of the area's most prominent needle trades activists, a giant protest movement emerged. It was at this protest meeting of 2,000 garment workers in August 1923 that Foster was nearly assassinated. When he rose on stage at the Ashland Auditorium to address the throng, shots rang out from the back of the hall and a near-stampede occurred. Foster was unharmed, but the episode underscored not only his notoriety but also his vulnerability. The ILGWU national leadership tried to proscribe Workers Party and TUEL membership and then launched an all-out attack on the union's left wing in New York City, expelling individual activists, unseating delegates at the union's 1924 convention, and dissolving and reorganizing whole locals to reassert control.[53]

League militants also came under attack in the ACWA, where the TUEL had enjoyed an effective alliance with Sidney Hillman. After its disagreement with him over the La Follette campaign, the Party gradually took the lid off, and league militants quickly turned on Hillman. They set up a Joint Action Committee similar to the one in the ILGWU but were never able to generate the support the Left found in the women's garment industry. The TUEL and the Party had considerable support from Lithuanians and Italians, but ethnic divisions within the union tended to cut both of these constituencies off from the union's mass Jewish membership. In turn, Hillman attacked the Left. He declared the Joint Action Committee a dual union and suspended the leaders of left-wing locals. One of the earliest casualties was Benjamin Gitlow, already a rising star in the Party.[54]

By the end of 1924, conservatives in one union after another turned on the TUEL opposition with increasing fury. In the UMWA, the attack started with Lewis's decree that all Communists should be expelled from the union. In the carpenters' and machinists' unions, where the league had a smaller presence, trials and expulsions followed in 1924 and 1925. Gradually, the movement was driven out of the trade unions and underground. Writing in 1926 of the attacks on the left wing throughout the labor movement, the labor scholar David Saposs concluded, "We are today witnessing a desperate struggle for control and domination where the usual rules of the game are discussed and war measures are invoked."[55]

These defeats represented more than a rout of Foster and the TUEL. They also had profound implications for a key element in Foster's theory—the notion that the labor movement could be transformed and harnessed to the class struggle through a process of boring from within the unions. The TUEL's decline undercut Foster's arguments against those in the Party who were pushing for independent Communist unions. Not only did the mainstream unions prove resistant to the boring, but the Left found itself doing its boring from without. In nearly every trade union throughout the country, Foster later concluded, the attacks had virtually left the TUEL "an underground organization."[56]

Foster analyzed the growing intensity of right-wing attacks on the labor Left as part of the general crisis of the labor movement in the mid-twenties. By 1924, Foster argued, the conservative labor leadership and even many progressives were on the defensive. A new open shop campaign threatened to annihilate them, and they saw various labor-management cooperation schemes as a way out. To save their organizations, they were often willing to collaborate with employers, even if this meant sacrificing the interests of their own membership. The league and the left wing in the various unions threatened this strategy by urging workers to replace their conservative leaders and to confront their employers over any deterioration of wages or conditions.[57] The "civil wars" occurring in various unions throughout this era represented the confrontation between two fundamentally different models of unionism. The ferocity of these wars derived from the fact that each side was fighting for survival.

The decline of the labor party movement paralleled the attacks in the unions. At the beginning of 1924, Foster had accepted the break with Fitzpatrick as final and publicly repudiated him, publishing an open letter in the TUEL's *Labor Herald.* He claimed that the split was "altogether due to your weakness and complete lack of real leadership," and he accused Fitzpatrick of red-baiting and "treason to the labor party movement." Foster now saw Fitzpatrick's determination to preserve his connection to the labor mainstream as a "localist weakness." "You will not break completely with the official family and become an outcast, a disrespectable in the movement." This, Foster wrote in a revealing passage, was "the fate which every real progressive leader must undergo at our present stage of development." Fitzpatrick, he claimed, had not only abandoned all his progressive ideas but also yielded control of the Chicago Federation of Labor to the conservatives. "I have watched with interest and grief the rapid swing of the Chicago Federation of Labor to the right. . . . The fact is," Foster concluded, "you have gone back to Gompers politically and dragged the Chicago Federation of Labor with you."[58] The tone of the letter denoted more than sectarianism, though that is certainly present; it underscored the genuine crisis that the split with Fitzpatrick represented for Foster. Quite apart from whatever personal feelings he had for Fitzpatrick, the situation had confronted him for the first time with a conflict between Party discipline and personal judgment.

Even after the disastrous rift with Fitzpatrick, events in Minnesota offered one last chance to salvage some connection with progressive labor and to broaden the base of the FF-LP. The Minnesota Farmer-Labor Party, headed by the Minneapolis labor editor William Mahoney, had already displaced the Democrats and recently elected both the state's senators and two of its congressional representatives. Here the regional Farmer-Labor Party with strong roots in the unions and the Farmers' Non-Partisan League was willing to work with the FF-LP to create a truly national Farmer-Labor Party, with progressive Wisconsin Senator Robert M. La Follette as its standard-bearer. A national convention was set for June. Foster regarded La Follette and other middle-class reformers with considerable antipathy, but the strategy had the potential of bringing the Communists back into a broad coalition with some labor support, a prospect he welcomed. Once again, however, Comintern politics intervened.[59]

In the spring of 1924, with the Farmer-Labor Party convention fast approaching, Foster and Pepper journeyed to Moscow, along with Mosaige Olgin, editor of the left-wing Yiddish paper *Freiheit*. Ostensibly observers at the plenum of the Comintern's Executive Committee, in fact, they were looking once again for a resolution of their own conflicts. To varying degrees, both Foster and Pepper supported some form of third-party initiative. But once in Moscow, they found that, with Lenin's death, the emerging power struggle between Stalin and Trotsky had produced an abrupt shift in the Comintern line away from the United Front concept. Both men tried to use the Comintern conflicts to enhance their own positions in the U.S. Party. On the surface, Pepper seemed to have the edge.

In the name of his majority on the Workers Party Central Executive Committee and at the last Workers Party convention, Foster asked the Comintern for two measures: a sanction for the emerging third-party strategy and the removal of Pepper, who, he claimed, was "gambling with the life and health of the Party" in "a reckless struggle for power." "It is an impossible situation," Foster argued in his letter to Gregory Zinoviev, who chaired the Comintern's Executive Committee. "If allowed to continue it will surely wreck our promising party." The Comintern leadership recalled Pepper, but on the labor party issue it decided to compromise with Trotsky, who denounced any cooperation with La Follette. It declined to support the new labor party strategy unless La Follette would be willing to endorse the Communist program—clearly a dead end.[60]

Foster accepted the inevitable break with La Follette and even proposed a separate Workers Party slate, an idea the Comintern endorsed in the event that La Follette rejected the Communist demand for his support of its program. Why did Foster give in so readily to the effective termination of a third-party strategy, having invested so much time and effort in it over several years? One possible explanation is opportunism. It is difficult to avoid the suspicion that Foster saw his own interests within the Party best served by this turn of events. Rather than fight the emerging line, probably a lost cause in any case, he accepted it in return for Pepper's removal, which left Foster in a stronger position on the Party's Central Executive Committee. Yet his decision was not inconsistent with his earlier thinking regarding a labor party. He had always envisioned this as a "class party" based largely on the unions, but the July debacle in Chicago had effectively ended that possibility. The Minnesota movement relied heavily on farmers, and La Follette's emerging campaign would undoubtedly include numerous petty-bourgeois reformers and a very moderate reform program, elements for which Foster had a profound distaste. If it were not possible to have a "real" labor party at this time, perhaps it was better for the Communists to run their own slate.[61]

La Follette made things easier for the Communists by denouncing them and refusing to associate himself with the Minnesota group, which he viewed as contaminated by its association with the Workers Party. At the Farmer-Labor Party convention in June, Foster spoke of the new party as a genuine united front: "for a Farmer-Labor party to be serious, it cannot be Communist. . . . We don't expect a Communist program, a Communist organization, or Communist candidates."[62] In fact, between them, La Follette and the Comintern had ended any chance for the Minnesota-based group to form a viable party. In the wake of La Follette's denunciation and the Comintern's decision, the Minnesota movement disintegrated as some of its constituents remained with the independent Farmer-Labor Party and others flocked to La Follette. The Workers Party quickly nominated a slate reflecting its factional divisions—Foster for president and Benjamin Gitlow for vice president—and liquidated the FF-LP. Like Fitzpatrick before him, Mahoney felt betrayed and thereafter opposed the Communists, seriously hindering their efforts to work in the Minnesota movement during the 1930s and 1940s.[63]

Following this newest split, Foster now attacked not only La Follette and Mahoney's Minnesota group but also Eugene V. Debs, the great symbol of American socialism, whose reluctant support for La Follette Foster termed "capitulation to this petty-bourgeois reformer." Debs responded, "You may be right in your criticism of my position and I may be wrong. . . . Having no Vatican in Moscow to guide me I must follow the light I have."[64] Foster was unrepentant. "We make no apology for accepting the guidance of the Third International," he replied. "On the contrary, we glory in it. Our party is proud to be a section of the revolutionary world organization, the Communist International." "Debs has long been a militant figure in the labor movement," Foster wrote, "but his militancy rested principally upon sentimentalism." It was this that kept Debs in the Socialist Party when he should have gone with the Communists and this that led him to support La Follette. Foster wrote him off, as he had Fitzpatrick: "Debs has finally wound up by losing completely the leadership of the left wing. He has destroyed his usefulness to the revolutionary workers."[65]

Predictably, the new turn was disastrous for Foster and the Workers Party in terms of not only the election results but also the isolation that resulted. Foster polled 33,316 votes, while La Follette, who finished third, polled just under 5 million.[66] Notwithstanding La Follette's loss, his movement turned out to be extremely broad-based, including the bulk of organized labor, and Foster later conceded that the decision to oppose La Follette had been a serious error. By supporting the coalition, even from the outside, the Communists "could not only have carried on effective work among the masses in motion, but could also have avoided much of the Party's relative isolation."[67]

At the end of 1926, the left wing labor journalist J. B. S. Hardman took stock of Foster, the TUEL, and the Party in assessing the damage inflicted by sectarianism: "The TUEL is not a party unit. . . . The league was to be a clearing house for *all* progressives in the movement. . . . Foster himself permitted the Communists . . . to make him responsible for the very things he has steadfastly opposed. . . . The immense value of his reputation and the access his former achievements and name gave him . . . was largely blotted out by party tutorship over an effort that should have been kept off party tracks."[68]

It is difficult to exaggerate the significance of this failure for the Party's development or for Foster's own. It lies in the short-term destruction and isolation it produced and in what it represented in terms of the relationship between the Party's mass work and its internal politics. As Paul Buhle argued, "By the early 1920's ordinary Communists had learned to put ideological questions aside in trade-union matters. They could, with favorable conditions and leadership, mobilize significant numbers behind their positions." A broad left movement based on the unions, as the labor party movement was, offered the best chance for translating this local influence, considerable in Chicago and a few other places, into leadership at a national level. Foster was crucial in this effort because of his judgment and instincts as well as his extensive contacts and solid reputation, which rested on more than a decade of union activism. Until the fall of 1923, the labor party movement and the TUEL's own involvement in rank-and-file insurgencies seemed to offer the Communists a real home in the labor movement and an opportunity to build a radical base. The strategy dictated by the Party and ultimately followed by Foster destroyed their credibility and cut them off from their most valued allies. In a period of less than two years, the Communists had managed to isolate themselves from key labor progressives in two important militant centers and open themselves to massive attacks from conservative union leaders. As Buhle concluded, "American Communism had bungled its first attempt at sustained influence."[69]

Foster himself analyzed the breach with the progressives in terms of the strength and aggressiveness of the employers' offensive against the unions. By the end of 1924, Foster argued, employers had opened a broad attack against all labor organizations and had begun to erect alternative structures in the form of welfare systems and employee representation plans. They left a small opening for "responsible" labor elements who would be willing to collaborate with them through productivity deals and labor-management cooperation plans. On the defensive and striving to save their own positions, many labor leaders were prepared to take the deal, Foster argued, even if it meant sacrificing the interests of their members. This crisis heated up the conflict between the mainstream—even many of the progressive labor leaders—and the left wing, represented by the TUEL, which was determined to resist such practices.

The collision between Foster's long-term goal of building a radical labor movement and the dictates of the Party presented him with a dilemma. In his first two years or more in the Party, he operated with a rare autonomy. "Foster's original design," thought James Cannon, who knew him well, "had been to play the part of the outstanding mass leader, . . . operating with a wide area of independence and getting the full support of the party on his terms." He was reluctant at first to become involved in factional politics, partly because he lacked the intellectual confidence of the key figures in the New York leadership.[70]

But Foster eventually concluded that a more central leadership role was essential. Party factionalism had created the break with Fitzpatrick in the first place, but a factional fight represented his only chance of winning support for a realistic industrial policy, which he saw as the key to a revolutionary movement. Cannon recalled, "Foster saw that when the showdown came . . . if he really wanted to control the trade union work and keep it within the bounds of realism, he would have to have a big hand in the control of the party itself. . . . to shift the main axis of his activity from the TUEL work to the party . . . that's what it came to in a very short time."[71] This showdown came in 1924.

Foster brought considerable prestige to the task. Long after joining the Party, his proletarian credentials and his long experience as an organizer and strike leader suggested to some Party and even some Comintern leaders the potential for a mass base in the unions. This provided Foster with a certain cachet in his conflicts with the more intellectually sophisticated Party leaders based in New York.

8   *Factionalism, 1925–29*

THE DEBATE OVER labor party policy not only isolated the Communists but also accentuated the factionalism that had characterized the Party from its birth and drew Foster into the heart of the conflict. While he had confronted Fitzpatrick in public, he had attacked his factional opponents for causing the debacle. Whatever hopes Foster had held for the FF-LP vanished in the months following the convention as he saw his political space in the labor movement close and his work with the TUEL washed away in a flood of expulsions. Pepper, far from recognizing the extent of the damage he had caused, had projected a bright future for the FF-LP, and Party secretary Charles Ruthenberg had supported him. Pepper had written a series of articles in 1923 making great claims for the FF-LP as a "revolutionary party," the beginning of a "Third American Revolution" represented by the emerging La Follette movement. Such hyperbole suggested the Party leadership's rather tenuous grasp of American political realities.[1]

Convinced that a continuation of Pepper's reign would kill the prospects for any sort of mass movement, Foster and his group of union-minded Communists had determined to fight. Foster, lacking the experience and confidence for a sustained factional struggle, had turned to James Cannon, the Party's chairman who had generally supported Foster on the Central Executive Committee (CEC). In November 1923, the two had produced a remarkably clear and detailed postmortem, assessing the damage caused by the split and laying responsibility for the disaster at the door of Ruthenberg's majority. "These comrades see more revolutionary potential and more Workers Party strength than exists," Foster and Cannon had argued. Their dogmatic position had destroyed much of the Party's influence. It was essential now to rebuild united front alliances with progressive elements, especially those in the labor movement, wherever possible. Cannon had carefully constructed a coalition representing diverse Party elements. By December 1923, a majority of the CEC had supported the Foster-Cannon position on the FF-LP. The new faction had succeeded in moving Party headquarters to Chicago, the heart of the Party's mass work, and had won control of the CEC and the Political Committee at the Workers Party's third convention in early 1924.[2] But Foster's temporary ascendance hardly ended the warfare. Factional conflicts raged throughout the late twenties, as Ruthenberg and later his protege Jay Lovestone struggled with Foster for power.

The fate of the labor party movement remained a major source of contention between the two factions. Foster and his followers thought the movement was a dead issue in the wake of the disastrous 1924 strategy, while Ruthenberg's group sought to sustain it. "Our minority would have peace only on terms of unconditional surrender," Browder wrote to Solomon Lozovsky, the RILU chief, in November 1924. "We told them to go to hell. We are going to have a Bolshevik party, not a goddamned job trust or priesthood." Immobilized by these deep divisions, the American Party once again turned to the Comintern, which set up an American commission to break the cycle of factionalism in the American Party.[3] Its report reversed the Comintern's previous instructions, steering the Americans back in the direction of a farmer-labor party effort, a repudiation of Foster's position. The report was inconclusive, however, on the vital question of control in the American Party. Though it appeared to give Ruthenberg the edge, Foster maintained his leverage through support from Lozovsky, who made sure that the commission endorsed the TUEL.[4]

On the eve of the Workers Party August 1925 convention, the factions remained as far apart as ever, and the Comintern intervened once again, appointing the Parity Commission to settle questions of policy, representation, and, ultimately, Party control. The old Bolshevik Sergei Gusev served as impartial chair, and the rest of the commission consisted of representatives from each of the factions in equal number. On the convention floor, Foster emerged with a clear majority of 40 delegates to Lovestone's 21 and prepared to consolidate his hold on the Party by removing Ruthenberg from the Secretariat and Lovestone from the Central Executive Committee. In addition, he aimed for complete control of the *Daily Worker*. The convention was in an uproar, with fistfights breaking out in the aisles, but Foster had the votes. On the eighth evening of the convention, however, Gusev dropped a bombshell, obliterating Foster's plans by simply reading a telegram from Moscow. The cable accused Foster's group of "ultra factional methods," declared that "the Ruthenberg Group is more loyal to [the] decisions of the Communist International," and demanded an arbitrary 40 percent representation on the Central Executive Committee for Ruthenberg's faction and continuing shared control of the *Daily Worker*. "Those who refuse to submit," the cable concluded, "will be expelled."[5] In a moment, the Comintern had stripped the American Party of its own control and subverted the will of the convention majority.

Foster exploded, refusing even to serve on the Central Executive Committee under these conditions. Cannon was more careful, recognizing Foster's outburst for what it was—a revolt against Comintern orders. Cannon upped the ante by insisting on a fifty-fifty split, and a majority of Foster's caucus voted with him. Faced once again with isolation from the Comintern and his closest comrades, Foster yielded publicly to Party discipline. "We are Communists," he wrote in the *Daily Worker* a few days later, "and realize that when the Communist International speaks it is our duty to obey." But at the same time, he complained bitterly to Lozovsky, "We cannot understand what it is all about. . . . The minority has been given the party and we have been widely discredited. . . . They are out to crush us completely. Our effectiveness has practically been destroyed for the time being."[6]

Foster considered appealing the decision directly to the Comintern leadership when the Parity Commission handed over control of the Party's main committees to Ruthenberg's faction. Gusev now publicly attacked Foster in the name of the Comintern. This left Foster nowhere to go, and he capitulated: "like soldiers we must obey the CI. I am for the Comintern from start to finish . . . and if the Comintern finds itself criss-cross with my opinions, there is only one thing to do and that is change my opinions to fit the policy of the Comintern."[7] Ruthenberg assumed the chairmanship from Foster, Party headquarters eventually moved back to Union Square in New York, and the following two years saw what Browder termed a "war of extermination in the districts," as functionaries and organizers were reshuffled to reflect the control of the newly manufactured majority.[8] The lesson was not lost on Foster:

Party control ultimately depended more on Comintern support than on a majority of the membership.

While he was losing control of the Party, Foster also faced a serious threat to his leadership in trade union work. As the TUEL declined and became more isolated during 1924 and 1925 because of AFL attacks, it became increasingly identified with the Party. To some degree, this was a natural process. By the end of 1924, most of those still associated with the league were in or very close to the Party, and the TUEL journal had been consolidated with the Party's as *Workers Monthly*. But Foster's factional opponents now sought to dismantle the league entirely and absorb it into the Workers Party. Quite apart from the threat this posed to Foster's status, the change also meant abandoning the notion of boring from within. Without the TUEL structure, the Party would assume direct control of trade union work in its own name. In Foster's view, this would completely undermine its already weak position in the labor movement and cut any remaining ties with non-Communist progressives.[9] Foster's fate once again lay in Soviet hands. He traveled to Moscow in late 1925, and in the meantime the Workers Party Central Executive Committee, under Ruthenberg's control, assumed direction of the Party's trade union program.

The initial results confirmed Foster's fears. Communist organizers in a 1925 anthracite coal strike spent much of their time in local jails, and the strike disintegrated. In the various needle trades unions, where prospects for left-wing control were quite good up to 1926, Communist influence declined precipitously. In the fur workers' union, Party conniving undermined a small but unusually effective group of left-wing activists. When the fur union's convention opened, Ruthenberg sent "secret" instructions to left-wing delegates in a Western Union telegram, describing how they could seize control. The telegram quickly fell into the hands of the union's leaders, who used it to discredit the radicals. The Party's activists in the fur industry recovered from this blunder to lead the union through a string of successes, including a resounding victory in an industrywide strike in 1926, but their achievements were exceptional.

The one bright spot surfaced in the textile industry, where a strike broke out under Communist leadership at Passaic, New Jersey, in January 1926, while Foster was in Moscow appealing his case. Even here, however, Communist influence dissipated in the course of a year or so. Originating in a walkout over wage cuts, the Passaic strike was eventually well organized and received considerable publicity. A United Front committee, with strong Party ties, coordinated picketing and welfare work and held the strikers together for almost a year. In the end, a combination of factors undermined the Party's control of the strike. Foster's objections to dual unionism, the employers' refusal to deal with the Communist organizers, and Comintern intervention all led the Party to relinquish leadership to the AFL's United Textile Workers Union, which eventually arranged a weak settlement. But Passaic was the first mass strike waged under the Communist banner, and it undoubtedly strengthened Foster's factional foes. Its leader, Albert Weisbord, a bright young Harvard Law School student who gave up his career to work in the mills and organize, was a rising star in Ruthenberg's camp.[10]

In Moscow, the Comintern refused Foster's request to restore his control over the Party, but it did endorse the TUEL as a separate body to facilitate united front efforts in the unions. Its resolution called for the TUEL to become a "broad oppositional bloc in the American labor movement" that would embrace non-Party elements and use "slogans of the broadest program." The American Party leadership agreed that "substance and mass strength shall be given preference over ideological clarity." By the summer of 1926, Foster had regained control of union work through the Comintern's restoration of his group's majority on the Party's Trade Union Committee, but this did not bring an end to factionalism that continued to hobble work in the unions.[11]

In the ILGWU, where the TUEL had built a strong following, the league maintained majority support and established the Joint Action Committee (JAC), based, in effect, on a parallel union leadership. In the many shops where it had strength, the committee collected dues, negotiated with employers, called strikes, and continued to attack the leadership. The JAC had the potential to become a dual union, but Foster fought this tendency among embittered left-wing activists. The committee's strength was emphatically demonstrated by the 40,000 cloakmakers and dressmakers who filled Yankee Stadium to protest the union leaders' attacks on the left wing. By the end of 1925, the left wing had won control of the joint boards in New York and Chicago and enjoyed strong support in several other garment centers.[12]

In New York, the new left-wing leaders were inclined to accept a government-sponsored reorganization scheme as a basis for reopening negotiations. But both rank-and-file cloakmakers and a large section of the employers opposed this plan—the cloakmakers because the scheme threatened longer hours, lower standards, and layoffs, the employers because they held even these lower standards to be too expensive.

A strike began on July 1, 1926. As national secretary of the TUEL and chairman of the Party's Trade Union Committee, Foster involved himself throughout the strike, with Lovestone sniping constantly. The left wing's policies in the union were discussed extensively at the meetings of the Political Committee as well as the Trade Union Committee and the TUEL's National Committee.

Serious industrial issues produced the strike, but the growing factional conflict between Foster and Lovestone clearly shaped its conduct. The dispute dragged on, emptying the union's treasury, until September, when the chance came for a compromise settlement with one section of the employers. But neither Foster's faction nor Lovestone's wished to weaken its position by supporting the compromise, and both pressed the ILGWU's left wing to reject it. Hundreds of workers and the union's entire New York leadership were arrested for violating injunctions.

The conflict finally ended in November with a weak contract, discrediting the leftist leadership. In the wake of this defeat, the union's right-wing General Executive Board assumed direct control of the New York Joint Board and revoked the charters of several left-wing locals amidst more expulsions. John Fitzpatrick cooperated with the ILGWU leadership to achieve a similar effect in Chicago. Communist workers in the needle trades remained an organized force within the union and a base of Foster's support within the Communist Party for a generation to come, but the ILGWU itself was greatly weakened, and the Left lost much of its influence in the needle trades.[13]

In coal mining, as in the garment industry, league activists tried to insulate themselves and their supporters by emphasizing issues of broad concern and by creating alliances between the TUEL and other opposition elements. To achieve this end, Foster himself raised the "Save the Union" slogan in late 1925 and spent five months on the road in early 1926, helping to organize a movement that took this slogan as its name. In contrast to the increasingly radical international line, the "Save the Union" movement based its appeal on an effort to salvage labor organization in the industry by breaking John L. Lewis's control and reversing his policies. "The situation is desperate in the UMWA," the rank-and-file radical Powers Hapgood wrote his parents. "It is gradually bleeding to death." Foster grew impatient with the abstract and hyperbolic revolutionary language of the official RILU formulations in the midst of this crisis. "There are plenty of obstacles to organizing work in America without introducing the worst of all," he wrote to Lozovsky, "namely, the bogey of Communism." "We say that the trade unions are in danger of being wiped out and we propose to mobilize the organized workers for their defense. . . . The RILU resolution and your article ignore the whole matter." While the Communists worked closely with indigenous rank-and-file movements in the industry, Foster and the group around him took the initiative in establishing the "Save the Union" movement and planning its strategy. Foster described three phases of the movement's work. First, activists tried to pressure Lewis into organizing nonunion mines in West Virginia, Kentucky, and other parts of the South. This effort failed. Next, in 1926, the Communists worked closely with Hapgood to rally the various UMWA dissidents behind the candidacy of John Brophy, a Pennsylvania progressive. Foster persuaded Brophy to support a labor party, nationalization of the mines, and other league positions in exchange for Communist help. Hapgood drew closer to the Party over the next two years. Brophy clearly mistrusted the Communists, but he had considerable respect for Foster and worked closely with him in his campaign. Brophy took more than a third of the votes, amidst more claims of massive vote fraud.[14]

When the union finally collapsed in the spring of 1927 in a long strike concentrated in the soft coal regions of Pennsylvania and Ohio, the "Save the Union" movement made strike-support work the focus of its final phase. The miners put up a desperate struggle to save their union in these regions; every effort on Lewis's part to compromise seemed to strengthen his rank-and-file opposition. Foster discussed the strike's importance in terms of preserving the UMWA, but he also recognized its value for Party recruitment and building a base in the coalfields. He toured the fields for months, directing league activists and speaking to groups of miners. He put Alfred Wagenknecht, who had long directed league work on the railroads, in charge of a system of commissaries modeled on those Foster had created during the 1919 steel strike. With their support for the conflict, the Communists built a solid reputation among the miners and established branches throughout the region. But the strike was defeated with considerable violence after more than a year. By March 1928, Foster reported, many of the organizers were in jail, including both John Brophy, the leading progressive, and Pat Toohey, the key Communist organizer. Five miners were dead, unemployment was widespread, and the movement was broke. Lewis took the opportunity to attack the Communists and their progressive allies. Once again, thousands of miners were expelled and dozens of charters revoked. Many of the remaining progressives broke with the Communists, and the "Save the Union" movement was crushed.[15]

As these attacks spread in the labor movement, factionalism resurfaced in the Party. When Charles Ruthenberg died suddenly in March 1927, his last words were said to be, "Tell the comrades to close the ranks and build the party." Instead, Communist leaders turned on one another with renewed vigor. Foster's opposition claimed his "Save the Union" approach constituted a "Native Dictatorship" that disregarded the international line. Comintern politics once again shaped the conflict, resulting in the expulsion of several

Foster allies. Stalin had been orchestrating a campaign against Trotsky for several years, and American Communists tailored their own positions in relation to this emerging conflict. As early as September 1925, Foster warned the radical writer V. F. Calverton, "One can easily break his political neck on the Trotzky [*sic*] issue." Some of Foster's closest associates showed sympathies for Trotsky's position, and the new turn of events placed Foster himself in an awkward situation. "Why, in spite of repeated warnings," Stalin later demanded, did Foster "not repudiate them at the time? Because he behaved first and foremost as a factionalist." When Stalin finally demanded the expulsion of Trotsky at the Sixth Comintern Congress in the summer of 1928, James P. Cannon sided with the opposition and returned home to establish the American Trotskyist movement. Foster himself brought charges against his former factional partner. Cannon, who had designed and built the Party's International Labor Defense and maintained extensive union contacts, took perhaps only a hundred other activists with him when he was expelled in October of 1928, but this number included such key intellectuals as Max Schachtman and such union activists as Arne Swabeck, Martin Abern, Bill Dunne's brothers, Vincent, Grant, and Miles, and others in Chicago and Minneapolis who had worked with Foster. Aside from the disruption this caused in the Party's work, it certainly weakened Foster's standing in the midst of a major confrontation with Jay Lovestone.[16]

With Ruthenberg's death, Jay Lovestone assumed control of the majority faction. His ascent introduced the most bitter stage of the factional conflict. In many respects, Lovestone embodied the cerebral, urbane wing of the Party that held Foster in such low regard. The feeling was mutual. Foster called Lovestone a "petty-bourgeois intellectual" and "professional factionalist and intriguer." In fact, Lovestone *was* the consummate factionalist, always fighting ruthlessly for control. He was not above rifling an opponent's mail for incriminating evidence of political improprieties, and he closely watched Comintern politics to maximize his leverage in the American conflict.[17]

Lovestone is most commonly associated with the concept of American exceptionalism, the notion that the character of class relations was unique and the prospects for revolution dimmer in the United States because of the stability of its capitalist system. He certainly elevated this concept to a higher theoretical level and began to develop policy accordingly, but comparable ideas had been around for years and continued to be a major influence on the Party's program long after Lovestone's demise. The Comintern line was always based on the notion of *general* characteristics of capitalism and the class struggle worldwide, but the actual experiences of American Communists always seemed to lead them back to the unique characteristics of their own society. Foster himself had bordered on a belief in American exceptionalism in discussing the weakness and conservative nature of the American labor movement. Much of Earl Browder's thinking during the Popular Front era to follow was shaped by the assumption that Party policy must be based on the unique political and cultural character of the United States. The same dynamic conflict between the international line and domestic characteristics reemerged in later efforts to democratize the Party.[18]

Lovestone's emphasis on American conditions helped turn the Party in a new direction. Under the rubric of a Comintern decree to "Bolshevize," he engineered a complete reorganization, which took the emphasis away from the Party's foreign-language federations and ethnic cultures and placed it on shop and neighborhood branches. In the short run, the move cost the Party support among immigrant radicals, for whom the cultural dimension of communism was vital, but, in effect, Bolshevization was also Americanization. It focused greater attention on American political and cultural traditions and brought activists from various ethnic backgrounds into contact with one another and with native-born workers. It represented an opportunity to overcome the ethnically segmented character of the Party and to create a truly national organization based on American realities. In the 1928 national elections, for example, the Communists reached into many areas of the South for the first time. Traveling 18,000 miles and visiting forty states between September 9 and November 7, Foster spoke to campaign rallies in Louisville, Birmingham, Atlanta, New Orleans, Norfolk, and Richmond, and in some cases, he was the first Communist speaker to have addressed a public gathering. In analyzing the experience, Foster emphasized the potential for recruiting black workers and the importance of developing a coherent southern program based on the peculiar character of class conflict in the region. To be sure, the reception was not always enthusiastic. He was arrested in Wilmington, Delaware, and charged with using an inflammatory slogan on his campaign poster: "Abolish Lynching!" But as in other respects, the Party was making a halting effort to reach out to mainstream America.[19]

What was different about Lovestone's American exceptionalism of the late twenties was its timing and significance in relation to Comintern politics. Having attacked Trotsky from the right and having successfully pressed for his expulsion, Stalin now turned 180 degrees to the left to attack his remaining opponents for "right opportunism." The new Comintern line that emerged at the Sixth World Congress in the summer of 1928 in the course of this conflict posited the "Third Period" of capitalist crisis and revolutionary ferment. In these new conditions, it was essential for constituent parties to take a position of "class against class"—uncompromising independent Communist leadership of unions and other mass organizations and forthright attacks on not only capitalists but also "social fascists"—Social Democrats and other reformists. For both theoretical and internal political reasons, Lovestone had aligned himself with Nicolai Bukharin, who emerged as the leading target in Stalin's new campaign. Usually very sensitive to the nuances of Comintern politics, Lovestone had made a disastrous choice.[20]

As late as the Workers Party's sixth convention in early March 1929, Lovestone seemed to be in control. With the support of more than 90 percent of the delegates, he fended off a Comintern effort to install Foster as general secretary and resisted the Comintern representatives' demands for a thorough Party reorganization. In the wake of the convention, however, the Soviets insisted that leaders from both factions report to Moscow. In April 1929, Foster left for Moscow to plead his case, while an official delegation of ten represented Lovestone and the CEC majority.

Foster complained about the nonproletarian character of Lovestone's CEC and about racism on the part of Party organizers in the South. He was interrupted constantly by heckling from the other faction. Lovestone embarrassed Foster by reading aloud from a personal letter in which Foster claimed victory in advance on the strength of a personal interview with Stalin himself. Gitlow also read into the commission's official record the stories of Foster's sale of war bonds and professions of patriotism in his 1919 testimony before the U.S. Senate. Speakers shouted directly at one another, often profanely, ignoring the chair. Tom Myerscough, a miner who had come up through the TUEL, called Foster "yellow." Foster jumped to his feet, shouting, "You're a god damn liar and you know it!" Lozovsky patiently lectured each side on proletarian civility but with little effect. Foster and Gitlow continued the personal attacks in their closing speeches.[21]

In Foster's long speech before the commission, he used the fear of a "Right Danger" to castigate Lovestone, but he also developed three other specific lines of argument that would characterize his attacks on "Browderism" twenty years later. First, in emphasizing the dynamic quality of the bourgeoisie and the decrepit quality of the working class, Lovestone borrowed heavily from bourgeois theorists, Foster argued, notably Thorstein Veblen and the modern industrial engineers of the "new capitalism." Lovestone thus showed himself susceptible to the illusion of a progressive capitalism, while he ignored the growing working-class radicalism exemplified in the textile and mining strikes. Second, Lovestone and his followers ignored the danger of "white chauvinism" by glossing over cases of racial discrimination by southern organizers and by failing to pursue the official Comintern line of national self-determination. Finally, Foster returned to an old theme, the importance of maintaining a proletarian membership. Lovestone's approach had accentuated the Right Danger, Foster argued, by diluting the Party with skilled workers and petite bourgeoisie instead of concentrating on the recruitment of industrial workers. "The CI must take a firm hold of the American party," Foster argued.[22] Sensing that his political future was once again in question, Foster closed with a ringing declaration of loyalty to the Communist International: "I came to the CI and I stayed with the CI and I shall be with the CI when many of those comrades who had had the guts to stand up and criticize me will be on the other side of the barricades."[23]

The significance of the American factionalism in the broader context of Comintern politics is suggested by the fact that Stalin himself and seven other prominent Russian leaders served on the American commission. Indeed, Stalin's first appearance as an international leader came in his confrontations with Bukharin over the nature of American capitalism. The Americans' problems furnished the context for a major turn in the history of world communism. As the Bukharin biographer Stephen Cohen has argued, the years 1928 to 1929 "were a turning point in the conduct of Soviet leadership politics. They marked the transition from predominantly overt intra-party politics of the twenties . . . to the covert politics of the thirties and after." The "American Question" thus occupied a peculiarly important moment in the "Stalinization" of the Soviet Party and the Comintern. The American commission's report criticized both factions but came down particularly hard on Lovestone and his followers, effectively stripping them of their control. Once labeled "right opportunists," they were expelled by the American Party in June 1929. Lovestone set up a small opposition party, which developed some following among radicals in the clothing and auto industries, but the group had little long-term influence and disbanded in 1941. Ever taken with international intrigue, he ended his days as a staunch anti-Communist AFL operative, with close ties to the Central Intelligence Agency.[24]

Ironically, Lovestone's defeat did not signal Foster's rise to power. In the same period that they were destroying Lovestone, Stalin and his supporters confronted Foster with the most serious crisis yet in his ongoing struggle to build a radical labor movement on the shifting sands of Comintern policy. The same ultrarevolutionary line of "class against class" that eventually cost Lovestone his control also required all parties to establish independent revolutionary unions. The new policy represented an impulse Foster had been fighting throughout his political life. His aversion to dual unionism rose directly from his considerable labor experience and was deeply embedded in his approach to politics. Yet adherence to the principle of dual unionism emerged as a critical ideological test of one's "Stalinism." Foster resisted the new line tooth and nail, even though his mentor Lozovsky had designed it. In doing so, Foster risked his position in the Party. "The American unions are reactionary and difficult to work in," he wrote to Lozovsky at the end of 1927. "But we cannot surrender them to the employers. We must fight for them . . . a general dual union policy would be wrong for the United States."[25] Having supported Foster's boring-from-within strategy for years, Lozovsky now accused the American Party of making opposition to dual unionism a "fetish." Foster was enmeshed in a bitter mining strike when Lozovsky unveiled the new line at the RILU's Fourth Congress in early 1928. Foster's closest associates carried the fight against the new line to the congress floor but eventually abandoned the fight.[26]

Foster himself opposed the policy throughout the spring and summer of 1928, going so far as to support his bitter rivals in the Lovestone faction against his own supporters who had come to embrace the necessity for the new unions. In the process, he faced one of his most bitter experiences. Lozovsky now repudiated Foster, who found himself totally isolated. He lost control of his own faction, which regrouped around Alexander Bittelman. Even Jack Johnstone—Foster's closest ally since the Syndicalist League days and his staunchest supporter in emphasizing the Party's industrial work—became convinced that the TUEL was damaged beyond repair and that it was time for new unions. Foster undoubtedly saw this as a gross betrayal; still he held out. He had always acknowledged the possibility of new unions in industries where there was no organization at all. In response to attacks on the TUEL (and, presumably, in deference to the new line), he went a step further in the spring of 1928. Writing the Party's trade union resolution for the Central Executive Committee plenum in May, he acknowledged that separate unions might be justified in textiles, where there was little organization, and perhaps in mining, where mass expulsions provided a natural base and no possibility of continuing to work in the UMWA. But he still saw such a new miners' union as the exception, a regrettable situation dictated by Lewis's extreme repression and not the model for a new industrial policy. (In fact, Foster contacted activists in both the UMWA and IWW about establishing a new miners' union before the Comintern's declaration of the new line.) Otherwise, he concluded, radicals belonged in the AFL. As late as July, he attacked many of Lozovsky's criticisms of the TUEL as "manifestly incorrect." "Our basic trade-union policy remains the same," Foster argued. "It was right in the past and it is right now."[27]

In the midst of this conflict, Foster ran for president, touring the country during the summer and fall. Under enormous pressure to change his line, he caved in toward the end of 1928. In the *Communist* the following month, he observed the AFL's general decline and concluded that building new revolutionary unions was the Party's "main task." This was not good enough. Max Bedacht, editor of the *Communist,* inserted an editorial comment attacking Foster: "This 'theory' of comrade Foster's is a very dangerous one. . . . [It] *is in reality an opportunist conception, a Right deviation from the correct line of the Communist International.*" Bedacht's language was particularly damning in the light of Stalin's campaign against Bukharin's "Right deviation." The attacks continued in the columns of the *Daily Worker,* and at the end of February Foster finally conceded, "We are now entering upon a prolonged period of dual unionism." By the summer, he saw the main danger coming from "rightists" who sought to shift the emphasis back to work in the reformist unions. In his assessment of the Party's ten years of trade union work, Foster included a long list of TUEL errors, most of them related to the "basic error" of "trade union legalism."[28]

Foster's behavior regarding the question of dual unionism is crucial for two reasons. To some degree, the new unions represented the Communists' response to a real dilemma facing them in their industrial work. Vast areas of industry remained virtually unorganized, and the AFL showed little inclination to undertake the task. In auto manufacturing, steel, food processing, and other mass production industries, there would be little competition with mainstream unions simply because so little organization of any kind existed. Many Communists argued, rightly as it turned out, that the AFL would never organize these industries and that new industrial unions had to be established to do the job. Eventually, in the late 1930s and World War II era, the CIO filled this role, with the support of the Communists.

In some industries where union organization did exist, mass expulsions, the unseating of Communist convention delegates, and other attacks by conservative union leaders had deprived the Party of its contacts and made it virtually impossible for radical activists to function. Such conditions had also produced a membership for separate organizations in coal mining and the needle trades, for example, by placing thousands of solid unionists outside the ranks of the mainstream unions. In this sense, the weakness and conservative character of the labor movement in the late twenties is as important as the new Comintern line to understanding the history of the Trade Union Unity League, which replaced the TUEL in 1929 as the Party's industrial arm.[29]

On a personal level, however, Foster's capitulation to dual unionism represented the final stage in his shift away from a sort of syndicalist communism, what some in the Party called "Fosterism," toward a more orthodox

Stalinist position. It suggests the struggle that raged inside him when Party policy seemed to contradict his own experience and to threaten the industrial work that he had always taken as the focal point for his radicalism. Foster's spirited resistance to the new line threatened his prospects for leadership at the very moment of Lovestone's demise and actually raised the danger of Foster's expulsion. For years afterward, his resistance to the new line and his reputation for bitter factional conflict tarnished his image among some Comintern leaders. His ultimate reversal on the issue, conditioned as it was by the AFL's unrelenting attacks on the TUEL, was a clear indication that he now saw little choice but to subordinate his own instincts to the collective will of the Party. Powers Hapgood, who had consistently supported Foster's trade union work and provided a vital link between the Party and progressives in the UMWA, once challenged Foster on this about-face: "you denounced dual unionism and I agreed with you one hundred per cent. I still feel the same way. Now I am told that you and the Communist party have come out for dual unionism, and frankly, Bill, I just don't understand it." Clearly, he touched a sensitive spot. Foster looked away and responded quietly, "Powers, the Communist party decided that policy. As a good Communist, I just have to go along." Within a year, Foster was denouncing Hapgood and his old friend Alex Howat, both dedicated militants, as "fascist tools."[30]

In later years, Foster maintained that "a constructive process was quietly in operation" beneath the maelstrom of factional conflict in the twenties. The ideological level of the Party was raised "through the tireless instruction of the Comintern." Bolshevization and "ideological unification" purged "harmful, non-Communist elements from the ranks." The expulsions of Cannon and Lovestone, Foster declared, "broke down the factional walls practically overnight. Like magic, almost, the factional fight disappeared and the Party started rapidly along the path to unity."[31]

To some degree, Foster was right. The Party had been purged of its factional problems, but only at the cost of most of its membership and virtually all of its influence in the labor movement. In the coming crucial decade, the decline of open debate within the Party worked to Foster's detriment. The fights also engendered great bitterness among comrades who might otherwise have put their efforts into more constructive pursuits. One activist recalled, "Our factional loyalties turned all Party meetings into screaming conniving sessions that often ended in fist fights." Drawing on numerous interviews with veterans of these factional battles, Paul Buhle described their effects on the people and the Party:

Whatever headway they could make by leading strikes of workers in "sick" industries like textiles and coal, Communists lost through the sickness of their own internal party life. It is difficult now, for the ordinary participants in those melees, to understand what the argument was all about. They recall finding themselves lined up on one side or the other . . . glad to see the trouble end through Russian-commanded bureaucratic fiat. . . . [They] made their own low profile adaptations to the stubborn phantasmagorias of the Party leadership on the one side and the stubborn realities of American working-class life on the other.

Each shift in power brought a reorganization in the Party, reassignment of functionaries, and disruption of work in the districts. Many of those not expelled simply dropped out in disgust. By the end of 1929 there were only 7,000 Communists left, and they had succeeded in separating themselves from the great mass of American workers.[32]

The factional conflict and Lovestone's downfall did not bring Foster control of the Party. Instead, the Comintern put a secretariat of four, including Foster, in charge. On the eve of the greatest crisis ever to face world capitalism, the Communist Party had once again shrunk to a small revolutionary sect, and Foster was still out of power.

In this process, Foster had undergone an "ideological purification" of his own. Over the next three decades, he continued to oppose some Party policies with which he disagreed, but always as the loyal opposition. His only chance to continue his work lay in the Party, and so he conformed. Yet the discipline he displayed was more than opportunism. He had embraced the Bolshevik model of organization; once the Party made a policy decision, he held to it. Indeed, it was perhaps always the Party's discipline and organizational effectiveness that he had most admired. By 1929, a rigid adherence to the Party line emerged as Foster's most striking political characteristic.

William Z. Foster, one of the "militant minority," probably in early 1912. (Courtesy of Russian Center for the Preservation and Study of Documents of Recent History, Moscow [RTsKhIDNI])

Esther Abramowitz with her children, Sylvia and David, at Home Colony, Washington, around 1912. (Courtesy of Joseph Manley Kolko, Just Black and White, Inc., Portland, Maine)

Foster with other leaders of the great steel strike at a free speech demonstration in Monnessen, Pennsylvania, April 1, 1919. *From left:* William Feeney, organizer for the UMWA; William Z. Foster; Mary "Mother" Jones; James Maurer, president of the Pennsylvania Federation of Labor; unidentified flag bearer; Phil Murray, vice president of the United Mine Workers of America; J. M. Patterson, vice president of the Brotherhood of Railway Carmen. (Courtesy of RTsKhIDNI)

Mounted Pennsylvania state constables attack steel strikers on the streets of a mill town, 1919. (Courtesy of RTsKhIDNI)

Farmer-Labor Party Convention, Chicago, July 3, 1923. *Insert:* John Fitzpatrick, president of the Chicago Federation of Labor. (*Labor Herald,* 1923)

Executive Bureau of the Red International of Labor Unions (Profintern), Moscow, 1924. *From left:* C. E. Johnson (USA), Josef Hais (Czechoslovakia), A. Kalnin (USSR), Tom Mann (UK), A. S. Lozovsky (USSR), W. Z. Foster (USA), Andres Nin (Spain), A. Herclet (France). Absent: M. Hammer (Germany) and C. Carametto (Italy). (*Workers Monthly,* 1924)

William Z. Foster working at the American Commission of the Communist International, Moscow, 1925. (Courtesy of Library of Congress)

Esther and Bill Foster in the Soviet Union in 1926. (Courtesy of RTsKhIDNI)

Opposite page: Foster with National Textile Workers Union delegates and organizers, Charlotte, N.C., 1929. (*Seated, from the right:* Rebecca Grecht, Foster, and Bill Dunne. Other individuals are not identifiable.) (Courtesy of RTsKhIDNI)

Foster on the campaign trail for the presidency, New York City, 1928. (Courtesy of RTsKhIDNI)

Foster speaking at a huge outdoor rally at Union Square, New York City, on International Unemployment Day, March 6, 1930. (Courtesy of RTsKhIDNI)

Robert Minor (*far left*) and William Z. Foster being led away in handcuffs in New York City, March 6, 1930. (Courtesy of RTsKhIDNI)

Hugo Gellert's illustration of Foster and James W. Ford, his running mate in the 1932 presidential election, from *New Masses*, July 1932.

Foster with William Weinstone at the Barvicha Sanitarium, USSR, June 1933. (Courtesy of RTsKhIDNI)

Earl Browder (*behind the drummer*) proclaiming the Popular Front's motto, "Communism is Twentieth Century Americanism," at a July 4, 1937, celebration in Chicago. (Courtesy of Syracuse University Library)

Candid photo of Foster, Detroit, 1940. (Courtesy of RTsKhIDNI)

Foster with his his great-grandson Joey and his daughter Sylvia Manley Kolko, Crompond, New York, in the early 1950s. (Courtesy of Sophia Smith Collection, Smith College)

William Z. Foster shortly before his death in Moscow in 1961. (Courtesy of RTsKhIDNI)

9   *Class against Class,*
1929–35

BY EARLY 1930, the Communist International's Third Period forecast for world capitalism's demise appeared to be unfolding on schedule. The American stock market had collapsed the previous fall, the banking system was following in its wake, and by January more than 4 million Americans were out of work. In the next three years, the economy largely disintegrated, eventually idling 15 million, one of out of every three workers, and dragging millions of American families into poverty. Children starved, public health plummeted, the suicide rate climbed. Huge encampments of the homeless sprang up around cities and industrial towns throughout the country. Long soup lines formed, and crowds of desperate people congregated in parks and on street corners. Millions of men, women, and children, displaced farm families and city folk, rode the rails and tramped the highways and fields in search of work. The depression's most striking quality in its early stages, however, was not the physical deprivation but peoples' inability to comprehend or find a way out of the catastrophe that gripped them. The collapse produced an atmosphere, the writer Edmund Wilson observed, in which "people were crying out for leadership, for almost anyone to organize them."[1]

In this context of mass unemployment, deprivation, and mounting so-cial unrest, the Third Period line did not always sound so far-fetched. "As the depression burst across the world," Irving Howe and Lewis Coser wrote, "it seemed for a time to the Communist followers in Europe and America that the ultra-leftism of the Comintern had been justified, for they assumed that the severity of the crisis would automatically lead to revolutionary concious-ness among the masses."[2] To many in and outside the Party, this seemed to be precisely what was happening.

With capitalism facing its greatest crisis and the Communists their great-est opportunity, William Z. Foster confronted his own crisis in the thirties. Poised on the verge of assuming Party leadership in a moment of great social upheaval, Foster once again felt power slip from his grasp. With Earl Brow-der's rise to leadership and the advent of the Popular Front by the mid-thirties, Foster became increasingly marginalized. He continued to enjoy great prestige among the Party's proletarian elements, and he represented the only significant opposition to Browder's regime throughout the depres-sion and war years. But his efforts and ideas had little influence until the end of the war, when Soviet intervention and domestic politics combined once again to reshape the American Party, providing Foster with an opportunity to regain the initiative with his more orthodox brand of Marxism-Leninism.

The Communists' earliest successes came in organizing the mounting legions of unemployed. At the beginning of 1930, Foster traveled to Moscow for a meeting of the Communist International, which focused on, among other problems, the rising tide of unemployment in the advanced capitalist countries. He returned carrying the Comintern call for mass demonstrations throughout the world on International Unemployment Day, March 6, 1930, but he denied AFL vice president Mathew Woll's claim that he had also brought $1.25 million back from Russia "to fan the fires of class hatred and to destroy all civilized governments of the earth." With or without Moscow gold, small groups of Communists clashed with police in several cities during January and February as Foster planned for the big demonstration. On March 6, millions of unemployed workers marched in Paris, London, Berlin, and other cities to demand bread or jobs.[3]

In New York City, where between fifty and a hundred thousand protesters waited in Union Square across from Communist Party headquarters for per-mission to march, the mood was tense. Foster led a committee in negotia-tions with Police Commissioner Grover Whalen, who offered his car to trans-port the committee to city hall but refused the Party's request for a parade permit. Foster mounted the speakers' stand. Al Richmond, a young Commu-nist, later recalled the scene: "Foster stood on the central platform, tall and erect, his figure etched against the sun." The city authorities, he said, had handed over the streets to "every monarchist and militarist exploiter of Europe and America" but had denied them to the unemployed workers of New York. "Will you take that for an answer?" Foster asked. The crowd roared, "No!" "Then I advise you to fall in line and proceed," Foster shouted, pointing in the direction of city hall. Thousands poured out into Broadway, singing the "Internationale" and starting what the *New York Times* called the city's "worst street riot in generations." One thousand policemen immediately waded into the crowd, flailing away with blackjacks and night sticks with what the *New Republic* called "indecent savagery." The crowd pelted them with bricks. "What followed," Richmond recalled, "is a hazy jumble in my mind . . . the roar of motorcycles, the whine of sirens . . . shouts and screams, and the thud of police clubs against human bodies . . . mounted cops swinging away with their clubs as trained horses maneuvered through the crowd." Armored motorcycles, tear gas, and machine guns appeared, and firemen doused the crowd. The square was filled with screams. Demonstrators and bystanders, some of them drenched in blood, ran in all directions. By the time the bloody fighting had subsided, four policemen and more than a hundred civilians were injured. Amidst the melee, Foster and his committee made their way to city hall, where they were promptly arrested and charged with serious felonies—incitement to riot, assault in the second degree, and conspiracy.[4]

Earl Browder later termed the March 6 demonstration one of "the first big steps" in the Communist Party's resurgence during the thirties. For all of its violence, or perhaps partly because of it, the event attracted public attention to the plight of the unemployed. "Overnight, by the initiative of the Communists," Browder recalled, "the nation became conscious of the problem of mass unemployment." It also provided an effective launching pad for the Party's unemployed campaign, a major focus of its organizing in the coming years. Foster, with his dramatic appeal to the crowd and his arrest, once again emerged as the Party's premier mass leader.[5]

As soon as Foster and his comrades were released on bail, they were arrested once again on new charges, and this time Foster was held without bail on the strength of his 1909 Spokane conviction. When he was finally released, he quickly confronted New York City's Mayor Jimmy Walker at a public hearing and presented him with the list of demands adopted at the March 6 demonstration. Foster employed his most aggressive language with the slick Walker, the sort of politician for whom Foster had the utmost contempt. "You cannot cure unemployment except by the overthrow of capitalism and the establishment of a Soviet government in the United States," he declared, adding that "only by violence finally can a revolution be accomplished." He denounced the Socialist leader Norman Thomas for a "gratuitous slander against the Soviet Union" because Thomas had suggested that the Russians also had problems with unemployment, and he closed with salutes to the Communist Party, the Comintern, and the "revolutionary struggles of the workers of the world." Later at his trial, Foster predicted that the growing army of unemployed "are not going to starve upon the streets. They are going to fight." "The problem of unemployment, in the final analysis," Foster argued, "can only be solved . . . by the abolition of the capitalist system and the establishment of a workers' and farmers' government. . . . [and] the Communist Party and the Trade Union Unity League organize the unemployed, not only for the purpose of these immediate demands, but for this ultimate revolutionary goal."[6]

The court reduced the charges with the American Civil Liberties Union's intervention, eventually sentencing Foster, Israel Amter, and Robert Minor to six months, and two young unemployed seamen, Liston and Phil Raymond, to one month and ten months, respectively. Foster entered prison in late April and emerged on October 31. Nearly fifty years old at the time of his sentencing, Foster spent his months in the infamous city jails on Riker's, Hart's, and Welfare islands. For Foster, the prison islands, Potters' Field, the workhouses, the orphanages, and the insane asylums that lined the East River just off Manhattan represented a metaphor of capitalism—"a long panorama of human sickness, defeat, misery, hopelessness and death." Though Foster showed genuine sympathy for his fellow prisoners, he saw most of them as tragic figures, like Skittereen's denizens—beyond hope, "drug wrecks," "sexual degenerates," and others "swept into the vortex of crime through a slum environment," their lives destroyed by capitalism. Confined to cells four by six-and-a-half feet in size, Welfare Island's sixteen hundred inmates suffered stifling heat in the summer and damp cold in the winter. On the other islands, overcrowded dormitory conditions facilitated the spread of disease and led to numerous fights. Foster also witnessed at least one race riot during his imprisonment. With no plumbing, unsanitary eating facilities, spoiled food, inadequate medical care, and brutal discipline, the prisons took their toll in contagious disease and death.[7]

Although he never drew the connection himself, Foster's six-month term under such conditions undoubtedly weakened him. Amidst all the descriptions of the place and its inhabitants, Foster includes very little of his own experience or the personal problems he faced, as if he expected no better. Like the rest of his autobiographical writing, his prison memoirs are impersonal, detached. He and the other Communists labored regularly out in the sun on the prison farm, subject to the same unhealthy food and physical conditions as the other prisoners. Foster and his comrades seemingly got along well with other inmates, who either respected them or feared the large, militant forces they seemed to have at their command.[8]

The psychological effects of the confinement are more difficult to gauge, but the bitter edge and grim determination that had always permeated Foster's personality probably were accentuated by prison. He was particularly frustrated with his isolation from the growing conflicts over wage cuts and unemployment. Nominated for governor of New York while still in jail, Foster helped Amter draft an unemployment bill, and he and Amter carried on a running critique of Party policy from their jail cells. They complained of Browder's pulling key activists out of union and other mass work. Writing with a pencil on the floor of his cell, Foster produced a whole string of articles for the Party press and was angered to find that they were "allowed to lie around." Browder would not respond to his letters.[9] When Foster emerged from prison toward the end of 1930 still on parole, he embarked on an extended speaking tour of the West and the Pacific Coast, speaking in more than a score of cities to help establish unemployed councils and promote the Party's drive for federal unemployment insurance.[10]

To organize the unemployed, the Party created a loose national movement, the Unemployed Councils of the USA, while Foster was still in prison in the summer of 1930. Nominally under the auspices of the Trade Union Unity League (TUUL), the movement's strength was based on hundreds of neighborhood councils in cities and towns throughout the country. Local organizers represented the heart of the movement, marching on relief agencies, moving evicted families back into their homes, and confronting landlords, local officials, and the police. Lines of hungry workers converged on state capitals, and in December of 1931 and once again a year later, the Party led large hunger marches on Washington, D.C., to lobby for national unemployment insurance. The Communists' unemployed councils were not the only unemployed organizations during the early years of the depression, but they were the most effective, leading hundreds of demonstrations and marches, fighting evictions, and counseling welfare recipients. In the mid-thirties, with the advent of New Deal programs, Communist organizers worked increasingly with other radicals and in 1936 cooperated in the foundation of the Workers' Alliance, which functioned as an advocate for the unemployed and as a union for workers involved in Roosevelt's massive New Deal public works projects.[11]

While Foster's heart still lay with industrial organizing, he contributed to the unemployed movement by speaking at rallies and demonstrations and by planning at the national level. He was particularly proud of the organization achieved in the first of the national marches, which he later termed, with typical modesty, "the best organized march in the history of the American proletariat up to that time." The different roles Foster and Browder played in the march suggest their roles in the Party at this time. On December 6, 1932, Foster addressed the National Hunger March delegates in Washington and was part of a delegation turned away the following day at both the White House and the Capitol while trying to deliver a petition for the Party's workers' unemployed insurance bill. On December 7, the assembled delegates elected him and three other prominent Communists to establish a new center for organizing the unemployed independent of the TUUL, but Foster's main function seemed to be touring the country to boost the unemployment insurance bill. Browder was also in Washington during this march, but he never appeared publicly, seeking instead to negotiate indirectly with federal officials to reduce the prospect for bloodshed.[12]

Two years after his arrest, on the evening of March 6, 1932, Foster was in Detroit speaking to the city's Unemployed Council, which was mobilizing for a march on Henry Ford's giant River Rouge plant the following morning. With the auto industry operating at 20 percent capacity, Detroit had become a major center for the Party's unemployed organizing. By the time of Foster's visit, the Detroit Party had a membership of about five hundred in thirty-five to forty shop and street nuclei and had organized at least fifteen unemployed councils. In his speech, Foster emphasized the symbolic importance of confronting Ford, but he also warned against provocations to violence. The next day he went on to a meeting in Milwaukee, where news reached him that Ford guards and city police had opened fire on the marchers, killing four and wounding dozens. A crowd estimated to be between 20,000 and 40,000 attended the funeral, where the four bodies lay beneath a red banner bearing the likeness of Lenin and the words "Ford Gave Bullets for Bread." The press carried stories insinuating that Foster's speech had been responsible for the bloodshed, and the court issued a warrant for his arrest under the old charge of criminal syndicalism. He returned to New York expecting to be indicted, but the Ford authorities apparently wished to let the matter die. Instead, Foster was simply restricted to New York City under the revised terms of his parole.[13]

Although nominally related to the TUUL, the unemployed organizing stood increasingly on its own from early 1932. Foster was chronically frustrated by this division between the Party's union and unemployed work and urged local TUUL groups to cooperate directly with the unemployed councils. His effort to coordinate industrial and unemployed organizing was one source of his increasing conflicts with Browder, who feared that Foster was trying to incorporate the unemployed councils into the TUUL so that he could direct them. Although Foster was frequently called on as a speaker, a group of younger activists directed most of the actual organizing.[14]

In contrast, Foster's involvement in the Party's trade union work during the early thirties was far more extensive and direct. Having at first strongly opposed the concept of dual unions, he remained at the center of the Party's industrial work once the TUUL was established. The 690 delegates to the league's founding convention in Cleveland in late summer 1929 suggest the character of the activists involved. Almost half came from the first three industrial unions—the National Miners Union, the National Textile Workers Union, and the Needle Trades Workers Industrial Union. About 10 percent were women and another 10 percent black. The activists were young, averaging about thirty-two years of age. The league eventually chartered additional revolutionary unions in steel, metal working, and other industries and among maritime and automobile workers. Its national industrial leagues, which Foster saw as "industrial unions in embryo," were loose groupings of local unions, shop committees, and individual activists working in coordination with the TUUL. Such leagues functioned in the food industry and among several other groups. A national committee of fifty-three elected at the league's yearly convention made policy, while a national executive board of ten, composed of Foster's closest associates, met monthly to oversee the day-to-day work. The TUUL's program reflected its roots in the new "class against class" line: opposition to labor-management cooperation; militant strikes; organization of the unorganized; full equality for blacks; the seven-hour day and five-day week; defense of the Soviet Union; social insurance; world trade union unity; organization of youth and women; and defeat of the misleaders of labor.[15]

In practice, the new organization's prospects were severely limited by a lack of local membership, organization, funds, and the sort of creative networking with non-Communist progressives that had made the TUEL successful in its early years. By its very nature, the TUUL's membership, most often garnered and lost in the midst of bitter strikes, fluctuated enormously over the organization's life. Not unlike the Wobblies, league organizers tended to sweep into areas and lead spectacular strikes against the odds, but they seldom managed to build lasting unions. In 1931, the TUUL briefly enrolled at least 25,000 miners in Pennsylvania and Ohio and thousands of textile workers during strikes in New England. Thus, Foster's 1932 estimate of 40,000 TUUL members might have been accurate, depending on the month in which the count was taken. Yet much of the textile and coal membership was wiped out within a year as a result of lost strikes. Membership in the Needle Trades Workers Industrial Union was somewhat more stable, probably around 10,000 in the early thirties, perhaps as high as 30,000 in early 1934. Several thousand Communist unionists worked in textiles, steel, metal working, and maritime, and smaller groups operated in the printing, meat-packing, auto, and boot and shoe industries. The league was also geographically concentrated. Foster's estimate of 45,000 TUUL members in the New York district at the end of 1933 seems reasonable, given the strike activity at the time and the large groups in the city's needle trades, hotel, food, and maritime industries. But New York was certainly the exception. Even at its high point in the 1933–34 strike wave, the TUUL was probably never larger than 100,000. Certainly the Party's April 1934 estimate of 125,000 was inflated.[16]

Yet the TUUL had a lasting significance. It supported organizing among the unemployed and led a series of important strikes in the textile, coal, and steel industries and among migrant farm and food-processing workers on the West Coast and sharecroppers in the Deep South. Like the IWW before it, the TUUL reached out to many groups largely untouched by union organization up to that time. By the summer of 1931, local league activists were producing more than a score of shop papers, with a circulation of about 30,000. Young Communist activists acquired experience and contacts that proved vital to building new industrial unions during the late thirties and World War II. In steel, meat-packing, electrical manufacturing, the maritime trades, and elsewhere, Communist militants did much of the earliest organizing under the auspices of the TUUL, and after its dissolution, they entered the mainstream movement as organizers, local officers, and national leaders in some of the new industrial unions of the late thirties.[17]

It is also vital to put the TUUL's failures into the broader context of labor organizing in the early 1930s. Facing massive unemployment that created a seemingly endless supply of strikebreakers and often brutal opposition from employers and a hostile government, any labor organizer had a daunting task. Communist unionists also had to contend with widespread fear and hostility toward their movement, even among workers, and the vagaries of changing Party and Comintern policies. Their strikes failed less because they politicized them than because they were often waged by the poorest and least organized workers against overwhelming odds and amidst remarkable levels of repression and violence. As Howe and Coser noted in their highly critical history, "TUUL leaders and members often displayed a heroism and self-sacrifice which no amount of political disagreement should deter anyone from admiring; they were repeatedly beaten by police, company agents, and vigilantes; they worked as volunteers or at subsistence wages; several of them were killed during strikes and demonstrations. But not all their passion and selflessness could prevent the increasing isolation of the Communists in the trade-union field."[18]

The Labor Research Association counted twenty-three workers killed in TUUL conflicts—eight in strikes and fifteen in unemployed demonstrations—between September 1929 and March 1933.[19] Most of these organizing efforts failed, but they placed TUUL activists in a strategic position on the eve of the successful industrial union movement of the late 1930s and World War II years.

As in the twenties, the Communists found their best prospects for union organizing in textiles and coal, both declining industries, where they led important strikes in the early depression years. By the end of 1930, more than half of the New England textile workers were completely unemployed, and many others were on short-time. The annual tonnage of bituminous coal had fallen from 535 million in 1929 to 310 million in 1932, the lowest level in more than thirty years. Neither the National Textile Workers Union nor the National Miners Union competed directly with its AFL counterpart. Both organized in areas where there was no organization of any kind or where the mainstream organizations were disintegrating. The history of Communist unions in these industries demonstrates two major obstacles they faced in these years—severe employer and state repression and the liabilities of the dual union strategy itself. It would be misleading to attribute their failures to one factor or the other, since the two were clearly linked. Isolated, the revolutionary unions were even weaker and more vulnerable than AFL organizations, while they projected more militant programs and demands and usually faced more violence.[20]

The National Textile Workers Union (NTWU), founded in September 1928 in the wake of an unsuccessful strike at New Bedford, Massachusetts, was the earliest of the independent Communist unions, established while the TUEL was still in existence and Foster was still fighting the dual union line. In April 1929, the new Communist union launched its first major strike in what seemed rather unlikely surroundings, but the timing was propitious. By the late 1920s, the heart of the textile industry had shifted from the birthplace of the industrial revolution in New England's mill villages to the textile company towns in the Piedmont region of Tennessee, Virginia, and the Carolinas. Faced with severe competition in a tight market, southern textile employers cut costs by continually intensifying the speed and productivity of their workers while maintaining or even cutting wages. Textile workers called it "the stretch-out" and launched a series of desperate fights against it in 1929.

"They are looking for a Moses to take them out of the wilderness," the

NTWU's Fred Beal, a veteran of the union's New England strikes, wrote to Albert Weisbord in February 1929. "With three of us working down here we would have a strike on by next summer." Instead, the outbreak came only a few weeks later. "This strike will be the spark that will set the whole South ablaze," Beal wrote on the eve of the conflict. "It will put us on the map." A general strike throughout the South is certainly what Foster had in mind, and events quickly moved in that direction. Spontaneous strikes swept through the Piedmont, closing plants across Tennessee and the Carolinas. In Tennessee, the AFL's United Textile Workers moved in to direct the action. In Gastonia, North Carolina, where Beal had organized a local, the superintendent closed the mill, and five companies of National Guard troops moved in. Weisbord urged a separate organization for the small number of black workers in the area, but the Communist organizers insisted on integrated locals. Foster and other Communists openly advocated complete racial equality in public speeches throughout the strike. As an interracial Communist union advocating equality for blacks, the NTWU struck fear in the hearts of Gastonia's city leaders. Above a cartoon of the American flag with a snake coiled beneath it, the headline of the *Gastonia Daily Gazette* screamed, "Communism in the South. Kill it!"[21]

The conflict spread, in spite of intimidation and hundreds of arrests. Strikes were settled in other towns, but Gastonia area employers resisted any settlement with the Communists. The conflict dragged on through the summer and early fall amidst considerable violence. Evicted from company housing, the strikers huddled in a tent camp organized by the Party's Workers' International Relief. When police and company guards invaded this refuge, an armed conflict erupted. The town's police chief was killed in the conflict, and Beal and the rest of the strike leadership were jailed on murder charges. The NTWU's Ella May Wiggin was killed when vigilantes fired into a truck full of unarmed strikers. "Altogether," Foster recalled, "it was a situation of fierce class struggle." After touring the area, speaking to strikers, and helping organize the relief effort, Foster was convinced that the only way to salvage the strike was to expand it. He urged the Party to extend the conflict into a general textile strike throughout the South, and in October he organized a regional conference in Charlotte toward this end. But the Gastonia strike remained isolated and was largely crushed by the end of the summer.[22]

The NTWU also led strikes in the declining New England textile industry. In early 1931, Edith Berkman, a twenty-six-year-old, Polish-born knitter, gradually built up small union groups in several of the largest mills in Lawrence, Massachusetts, an old textile town with a history of labor radicalism stretching back to the heyday of the IWW. At the end of February, when the

NTWU led a strike of 10,000 workers over a speedup, the entire strike committee was arrested, and the upsurge was crushed. Short of organizers and eager to spread the movement, the TUUL sent its best cadre on to other New England towns. By October 1931, when a new strike broke out in Lawrence, the NTWU found itself in competition with two other organizations, the AFL's United Textile Workers and a new group formed by the pacifist radical A. J. Muste. The TUUL refused to have anything to do with these reformists, and the divided effort resulted in multiple strike meetings, competing picket lines, and a disastrous defeat. By the end of the year, two of the NTWU's key organizers had been deported, and Berkman was in prison. Other organizers struggled to hold the movement together, but the NTWU had only 2,000 members by the beginning of 1932.[23]

The Communists waged by far their largest and most important strikes in the coalfields of western Pennsylvania, eastern Ohio, West Virginia, and Kentucky. The Communist union also built locals in central Illinois, long a hotbed of anti-Lewis sentiment. In some of these areas, the National Miners Union (NMU) developed a genuine mass following, and Foster took an active role in directing and maintaining these strikes. Where it was possible to do so, the NMU attached itself to an indigenous revolt against wage cuts, Lewis's autocratic policies, and the decline of the UMWA. Between 1919 and 1930, the proportion of bituminous coal mined under union-wage contracts had fallen from 70 percent to 20 percent, and even many loyal UMWA members believed that Lewis's policies were killing the union. Between 1928 and 1931, the NMU built locals in the fields around Pittsburgh and in a few other areas. A strike against wage cuts at one Pittsburgh area mine in late May 1931 spread quickly throughout the region. Foster estimated that the NMU had drawn more than 40,000 out by July, including a large number of African American miners. Writing from the coalfields in the midst of this revolt, he called the strike "by far the greatest mass struggle conducted by revolutionary unionists in this country . . . a brilliant exposition . . . of the growing radicalization of the workers," and he argued that its rapid spread "fully supports the program of building the new unions." He complained that Party nuclei became "more or less paralyzed at the outset of the strike and have played little or no leading role." Foster encouraged organizers to spread the strike by establishing broad united front committees that would include UMWA members. He insisted that the strike could be won and criticized the Party for providing too few organizers and too little relief.[24]

Foster directed the 1931 coal strike from start to finish, frequently working eighteen-hour days and spending a total of five months in the region. As in the southern textile conflicts, his main goal was to broaden the strike. "Foster, expecting something big to happen, thought he was right to call the strike," Party veteran Myra Page recalled. Facing sweeping injunctions, the union organized hunger marches and aggressive picketing, which elicited considerable violence. In early August, the *New Republic* reported three miners killed, fifty-five hospitalized, and thousands gassed or wounded. In mid-July, the NMU called a conference, which by Foster's count drew 685 delegates from 270 mines in eight states, a testament to rank-and-file opposition within the UMWA and, Foster believed, the potential for Communist unionism. The strike was already beginning to crumble by this point, however, under the weight of injunctions, violence, and extreme deprivation for the miners and their families. In the Pittsburgh area, Pennsylvania's second largest operator signed a sweetheart contract with the UMWA, which had actively opposed the struggle. A state study indicated that nearly all of the strikers and unemployed were in deep debt. Food was scarce even among those who continued to work, while "a typical meal for the children and families without work was bread and coffee." The Party leadership counseled a strategic retreat, but Foster resisted, as did many miners. When Arthur Ewert, the German Comintern representative, tried to coax the strikers back to work, the organizer Harry Haywood recalled, "Some organizers looked at him as though he were a scab. . . . Even Foster seemed unfamiliar with the idea of a voluntary retreat. . . . If we are facing defeat, we should go down fighting." Foster and the NMU leaders persisted until the strike was on the verge of collapse. On August 18, 1931, the general strike committee advised the miners to return to work, if possible, on the best terms available.[25]

Ironically, the 1931 coal strike paved the way for the UMWA's recovery. Some companies signed contracts with Lewis, "risking the chicken pox from UMW," as Irving Bernstein wrote, "to avoid the smallpox from NMU." When UMWA organizers returned in the spring of 1933 to those fields where the strike ended without any contract, they found the miners ready to move.[26]

The strike also affected Foster's relationship with Browder in his role of newly emerging Party leader, bringing the first major confrontation between the two and laying the foundations for ongoing conflict. "The strike was a dreadful mistake," Myra Page recalled. "The issue divided the Party." Foster complained that the strike was lost because headquarters failed to provide an adequate number of organizers; Browder insisted that Foster was neglecting his Party work in pursuit of a lost cause, a charge he repeated a few months later before the Anglo-American Secretariat of the Comintern. In assessing the strike's many faults, Browder detected "a slowness and hesitation in bringing the Party forward." A close friend recalled that Foster was "hurt bitterly" by Browder's criticisms. When William Weinstone returned from an extended assignment in Moscow halfway through 1931, he found "an extreme, sharp situation" between the two men.[27]

Finally, this 1931 defeat seemed to end whatever enthusiasm Foster had generated for the dual union strategy during the first two years of the depression. Remaining in the coalfields for months at a time, rising at 5 A.M. to speak and organize, he was physically and emotionally drained by the end of the strike. The conflict resulted in 25,000 new members (most of them short-term) for the NMU and 1,000 for the Party, but Foster himself later admitted that its defeat dealt the NMU "a deadly blow" and that he himself was "almost finished."[28]

Fresh from this defeat, Foster turned immediately to organizing the December 1931 National Hunger March. He saw off the New York delegation of 10,000 on December 2 and then addressed the national delegates in Washington four days later.[29]

A new mine strike broke out at the beginning of 1932 in Harlan County, Kentucky, where the miners' plight was even more desperate than in the Ohio and Pennsylvania fields. In the spring of 1931, the UMWA had abandoned a long, violent fight against a 10 percent wage cut at the Black Mountain Coal Company, leaving bad feelings among many of the miners, who believed they had been sold out. The UMWA failed to provide relief or legal aid and to defend miners blacklisted in the wake of the strike. Local authorities charged indigenous activists with being Communists even before NMU organizers entered the fields that summer. It would be difficult to imagine a less promising organizing situation.

The NMU leadership tried to discourage a badly timed strike while it organized relief and legal aid, but the district NMU convention, faced with a spontaneous movement against wage cuts, voted overwhelmingly to strike all southeastern Kentucky and Tennessee mines on January 1, 1932. With inadequate planning and resources, the miners waged the fight in the face of daunting violence. The authorities quickly raided the NMU headquarters and arrested its organizers. Mine owners blacklisted the union's members and escorted strikebreakers in under guard. As he had in the Pennsylvania strike, Foster turned to Theodore Dreiser to generate publicity and relief through the National Committee for the Defense of Political Prisoners, which established the "Dreiser Committee," including Malcolm Cowley, Edmund Wilson, and other famous writers, to investigate conditions in Harlan County. A church group led by Reinhold Neibuhr and a Senate subcommittee followed. Focusing nationwide attention on the strike, the strategy boosted NMU fortunes briefly, and the miners received considerably more support from the International Labor Defense and the Workers' International Relief than they had from the UMWA. Local vigilantes, however, turned back relief columns staffed by students and other sympathizers, assaulted reporters and others, and drove one of Dreiser's writers delegations out of town. Race as well as class hatred animated the violence directed at the Communist union. Facing what the Communists called the "Negro Question" squarely, the NMU insisted on interracial solidarity and the integration of all meetings and soup lines, a policy the owners used to divide white miners from the NMU. Armed vigilantes spread throughout the region, killing several miners and a young Communist organizer, Harry Simms. Foster urged a crowd of 10,000 at the young man's funeral in the Bronx Coliseum to "make the capitalist class pay dearly for the murder of Simms," declaring that "it will not be long before they will face workers' courts in America." But with its membership blacklisted in the midst of heavy unemployment, the NMU was frozen out of the mines, and the strike collapsed by the spring of 1932. Foster's involvement in the mining strikes and other organizing probably weakened his standing in the Party. When he appeared with Browder again before the Comintern in 1932, Browder criticized Foster for his distance from the daily leadership, which was clearly the result of his greater involvement in the Party's mass work. Browder also noted that the Kentucky strike brought what he characterized as "serious political differences" between him and other members of the leadership, notably Foster and William Weinstone.[30]

The NMU had to compete with not only the UMWA but also several other organizations in the anthracite region, West Virginia, and Illinois. Federal authorities deported the union's president, Frank Borich, in October 1933. Internal problems also plagued the NMU. A field organizer, writing in late fall 1932, complained of "top heaviness"; an average of 500 members in Pennsylvania, Ohio, and West Virginia supported eighteen full-time organizers. While Foster emphasized the importance of "partial demands" and working in united front arrangements with other unionists, in practice the NMU approach was often long on revolutionary rhetoric but short on the concrete analysis of industrial issues. Finally in December 1933, long before the declaration of the Popular Front and the shift back to boring from within, a Party conference on mining decided to scrap the NMU and go back to work wherever possible in the UMWA.[31]

In the midst of organizing the revolutionary unions, Foster never abandoned the idea of working within the AFL, and the defeats in mining and elsewhere seemed to push him further back in this direction, though he continued to support the dual union line publicly. He criticized Communist activists for failing to emphasize "daily problems and demands," instead falling back on "general slogans and simple agitation." Because of extremely high unemployment and wage cuts even among the most skilled workers, he argued in the spring of 1932 that the "situation in the reformist trade unions now presents an exceptionally favorable opportunity for revolutionary work" and that every one of the revolutionary unions should have a committee devoted to working within the old unions.[32]

One result of the Party's revolutionary line in this union activity and its unemployed work was to strengthen conservative arguments for a special congressional committee to investigate and root out Communist subversion. The new committee, established on the day of Foster's March 6, 1930, arrest, eventually became the House Committee on Un-American Activities (HUAC) and provided the government with a powerful weapon against domestic radicalism, particularly the Communist Party. The committee's sixteen-volume report on its 1930 hearings included some rather strange theories about the origins of American radicalism and finished by recommending that alien Communists be deported and the Party outlawed. One expert witness, the right-wing extremist and anti-Semite Father Charles Coughlin, testified that he could trace the American Communist Party all the way back to 1776 and the Order of the Illuminati and that the international labor movement was led by Henry Ford. Another professional Red-hunter estimated the Communist Party's strength at "slightly over two million."[33]

In December 1930, Foster, fresh from prison, was subpoenaed to appear before this new committee, where he read a powerful prepared statement. If the committee really wished to understand the growth of communism, Foster argued, it should look into "the miserable situation under which the masses live and from which only communism shows the way out." The Party's aim was to organize and lead the masses of workers in their struggles against such conditions and to transform the American system into the Soviet model. "The only possible guard for the future security of the working class," he concluded, "is the dictatorship of the proletariat and the establishment of a Soviet Government." In answer to the predictable questions, Foster declared the Communists supported complete racial equality, including interracial marriage, and international proletarian solidarity against nationalism. At times, he appeared to be intentionally provocative. In answer to a question about Communists' loyalty to the United States, he replied, "The workers of this country and every country have only one flag and that is the red flag . . . the flag of the proletarian revolution."[34]

All of this impressed the writer Edmund Wilson, who witnessed Foster's confrontation with Hamilton Fish, the committee's conservative Republican chairman. Wilson found Foster "an incongruous figure in the marble chamber of the Capitol. . . . his peculiar kind of eloquence is a new one to congressional committee rooms." At first Foster appeared nervous, seemingly out of his element. "Yet never once," Wilson wrote, "in the course of the three hours' grilling does his courage or his presence of mind fail him . . . and as soon as he meets the question, he is the dominating figure in the room." He never flinched from the Party's ultrarevolutionary line, and the congressional committee room rang with the rhetoric of class war. Wilson noted that "an element appears in his language which is quite alien to anything which has hitherto been characteristic of even the militant American workman . . . it is the idiom of Russian communism."[35]

During the Comintern's Third Period (1928–35), Party ranks were saturated with such class-against-class rhetoric, a language in which Foster excelled. Long after the Party had made the turn toward the more moderate and flexible Popular Front form of organization and strategy, he still used the rhetoric of class warfare. Why did Foster embrace this language and view so readily and stick to it so persistently? Certainly part of the explanation lies in his own disposition and experiences. From his young adulthood on, class conflict was not simply an element of theory but the central experience in Foster's life from which he developed his ideas. His strength was not in the area of theory but in the realm of organizational and strike strategy. His role in the Party's policy discussions continued to be as a voice for militant industrial organization and struggle. In this sense, his syndicalist background continued to influence his language and orientation to politics; his confrontational style remained as well. Earl Browder complained that Foster, even in his fifties during the 1930s, worried far less about confrontations with the police than other Communist leaders did. He seldom advocated violence, but he seemed to accept its prospect as a matter of course. For all the changes he had lived through in the transformation of revolutionary syndicalism into communism, there is a striking resonance between the class warfare rhetoric of his Syndicalist League days and the Third Period years. He took so well to such language because it reflected his own personal experiences and his natural orientation to politics.

But if the impetus for the new line originated in the Soviet Union and Foster's own hyperbolic rhetoric tended to inflate the revolutionary prospects, the language sounded less peculiar than it might have in the turbulent and often violent political climate of the early thirties. If Foster accepted some degree of violence as given, he certainly saw enough of it about him. In its unemployed and union organizing, the Party faced something like "class war."

No document exemplifies the Party's sectarianism and its radical hyperbole better than Foster's own *Toward Soviet America,* published in the spring of 1932 by a commercial firm. He described the book as "a plain statement of

Communist policy," and in it he outlined the apparent collapse of the economy, which he thought portended capitalism's ultimate demise. "Capitalism is doomed," he wrote, and its decline would lead "irresistibly towards the proletarian revolution."[36]

Foster saved most of his fire for reformers. "The policy of Social Democracy," he wrote, "is basically that of Fascism." The Communists would wage "a ruthless fight against the Social Fascist leaders, especially those of the 'left.' . . . They must be politically obliterated," he declared. Under the pressure of the severe depression, workers and other elements would turn their backs on these parasites. "The Negro masses," he wrote, "will make the very best fighters for the revolution," but farmers, businesspeople, and "even the intellectuals are being compelled to think." The key to organizing the masses was to lead them in their everyday economic struggles and make "every shop a fortress for communism."[37]

For worried conservatives who were apt to take his blueprint seriously, Foster added the specter of a growing Communist movement. Membership stood at 15,000 in the Party and 5,000 in the Young Communist League, but Foster suggested the Communists' influence was much broader, and he was probably right. They published twenty-nine papers and journals with a circulation of over 300,000. He claimed 40,000 members for the TUUL and listed the major strikes led by the Communists. Their influence was growing quickly, Foster argued, and soon it would be time to settle accounts. "The working class cannot come into power," Foster concluded, "without a civil war."[38]

There are two striking characteristics of this book. The first is Foster's highly detailed, almost surreal prognostication of what "The United Soviet States of America" would look like. In this highly centralized state, ruled by a presidium and council of commissars and linked to other soviet governments through a world soviet union, special courts would try counterrevolutionaries, who would be dealt with by Red Guards. The new state would abolish not only all other political parties but also the Masons, the American Legion, the Rotary Club, and, of course, the YMCA. The state would end all forms of social inequality (something absent, presumably, in the USSR) and abolish all restrictions on interracial marriage. The government would control the media, yet culture would flower. The new organization of society would encourage human biological evolution. The TUUL would become the nucleus of labor organization (something AFL leaders has suspected all along). As if to reassure his bewildered reader, Foster noted in an aside, "Such a program is not a matter of mere speculation. This is the line that developed in the Soviet Union and it is the one that will develop here."[39]

As strange as Foster's forecast might sound, it was in character. He had always shown a keen interest in questions of organization and production, and these passages resemble his sketch of the syndicalist society in his little red book, *Syndicalism*. His early pamphlets and columns on the Russian Revolution also tended to be consumed by detailed descriptions of economic, political, and legal organization.[40] It was as if he needed to visualize this new society in all of its workings to legitimate his ideological path. But the difference between his communist and his earlier syndicalist model for the new society was crucial. The state now had a central role in its creation and operation, which suggests the ideological distance Foster had traveled since his syndicalist days.

The nature of the state and society Foster envisioned was never really in doubt, for the other striking feature of *Toward Soviet America* is the persistent, overwhelming presence of the Soviet Union. Foster held up Stalin's regime as a model for the chaotic world in every aspect of life, not simply a blueprint but a touchstone for all analysis. The five-year plans had brought great prosperity to Soviet workers, Foster argued, while Stalin's cultural programs produced greater education and literacy. The dictatorship of the proletariat brought a "whole series of restrictions of liberty in the case of the oppressors, exploiters and capitalists," but it meant, as Lenin had said, an "immense expansion of democracy—for the first time becoming democracy for the poor." Foster denounced stories of widespread violence and repression as "gross fabrications" and defended the GPU, Stalin's secret police, as guardians of the state. Stalin's purges of his opponents, left and right, Foster saw as testaments to the democratic character of the Soviet system.[41]

As early as the mid-thirties, with the advent of the Popular Front, the Party disavowed such class-war rhetoric and emphasized the constructive role the Party had to play in cooperating with other progressive groups. At the time of its publication, however, *Toward Soviet America* was an accurate reflection of the Communist line. Foster was clearly in step. Earl Browder called the book an "extended statement of the Communist Party platform in the coming National Election struggle."[42]

Foster's arrest, his congressional testimony, and the roles he played in the National Hunger March and the coal strikes meant that he remained the Party's most visible public figure and its most popular leader among the rank and file. As America's most familiar Communist, he emerged as the Party's natural standard-bearer in the 1932 election. In May, Foster's parole board agreed to let him travel, and the Party nominated him once again for the presidency at a wild convention in Chicago's Coliseum, where delegates carried him around on their shoulders amidst a sea of red banners. Foster hit the campaign trail the following month. He was certainly not on his way to the White House, but this time the prospects seemed brighter. In the context of the depression, his candidacy generated far more interest than in previous elections; more people seemed willing to hear what he had to say.[43]

In an unprecedented move, the Communists slated James Ford, a black postal worker, as Foster's running mate. A migrant to Chicago from Alabama, a trade unionist, and a trusted Party activist, Ford was meant to symbolize the black proletariat to whom the Communists hoped to make a special appeal. Although the Party had recruited blacks almost from its inception, the commitment was much stronger during the depression years. Between 1928 and the early 1930s, the Communists developed a new policy based on Stalin's theories concerning the Soviet national minorities. It called for the self-determination of blacks as a distinct national minority in the United States and the eventual establishment of a separate black nation in the Deep South. It is questionable whether the new theory itself won many recruits, but it did suggest the Party's commitment to facing the distinctive problems of African Americans, as did the Party's efforts to cleanse its own ranks of "white chauvinism." Far more important to recruitment were the efforts at organizing the unemployed in urban black ghettos and sharecroppers in the Deep South and the defense of the "Scottsboro Boys," nine young black men put on trial in 1931 for allegedly raping two young white women. In these situations, the Party offered black workers a rare opportunity to get organized and fight back. It was its practical program, then, more than its ideology that drew most of them.[44]

In the short run, Ford's candidacy and the Party's more general appeal to black workers had an effect. Between 1929 and the spring of 1935, the Party's African American membership rose from approximately 150 to more than 2,200, and black representation in its leadership increased significantly. The Party actually recruited much larger numbers, but the turnover in black membership was quite high. In the long run, the Communists generated mass bases in only a few black communities, notably Harlem and Chicago's South Side.[45]

At the other end of the social structure, the Party began to attract more intellectuals and professionals, and Foster's 1932 campaign became a focal point for this work. His own attitude toward intellectuals was deeply ambivalent. He read and did research constantly. Part of what attracted him to Marxism were the ideas themselves, yet he was profoundly suspicious of intellectuals as a social group. At about the same time that the Party was beginning a serious effort to recruit them, Foster had shown contempt for such people, arguing that only "a small percent of these intellectuals, especially those with a proletarian background, will become genuinely revolutionary and real Communists." The rest he considered natural recruits for fascism or, about the same thing, social fascism.[46]

Now, however, Foster made a bid for the support of intellectuals, with some success. His list of supporters read like a Who's Who of the nation's most prominent writers, including Edmund Wilson, Theodore Dreiser, Langston Hughes, Sherwood Anderson, and John Dos Passos. These and dozens of others joined the League of Professional Writers for Foster and Ford, and some worked actively for the ticket. Dreiser, who had admired Foster's organizing skills during the steel strike and had worked closely with him in Harlan County, regarded Foster as the great symbol of the American working class and referred to his "Christ-like devotion" to the nation's poor. A few of these writers, including Dreiser and Hughes, supported the Party over a fairly long period. Most, however, found its intellectual atmosphere stifling and departed, some to become staunch anti-Communists (confirming in Foster's mind, no doubt, intellectuals' unreliability in any revolutionary movement). In the course of the election, though, they lent Foster's campaign credibility and notoriety.[47]

During the campaign, Foster followed a grueling itinerary, traveling more than 20,000 miles from coast to coast and speaking to almost 200,000 people between early June and early September, 1932. Organizing most of his speeches around the Party's demand for unemployment insurance, he turned out large crowds not only in Detroit, Buffalo, Cleveland, and other large cities but also in Great Falls and Butte, Montana, and respectable audiences even in small mining and industrial towns along the way. He attacked both Herbert Hoover, the Republican incumbent, and Franklin D. Roosevelt, the liberal Democratic challenger, but in Third Period style, he seemed to train more fire on Roosevelt.[48]

As always, Foster had his problems with the law. When he arrived at Ziegler, Illinois, in the midst of a violent wildcat strike, armed deputies forcibly turned him away. In Lawrence, Massachusetts, police arrested him for obstructing a highway and disturbing the peace. In Los Angeles, he became the focal point in a major free speech conflict. Foster had intended to lead a demonstration to protest the police shooting of an unemployed worker, but authorities refused to grant the Communist candidate a permit, and police announced in advance that he would be arrested if he attempted to hold the meeting without it. The American Civil Liberties Union argued that the city's position was unconstitutional and petitioned for an injunction to avoid a police attack. Judge Gates joined the ACLU in its skepticism, if only briefly. How could it be determined, he asked city attorneys, that Foster would behave illegally before the meeting had ever taken place? The chief prosecutor reassured him, however, focusing on the threat posed by the Communist Party's program and indeed its very existence, and the injunction was denied. Hundreds of supporters assembled in front of the Open Forum Hall chanting "We Want Foster!" Denied a permit and a hall, Foster simply held the rally outside in a working-class neighborhood, under the watchful eye of the Los Angeles Red Squad.[49]

The *Daily Worker* described the scene as an "armed camp" with at least a hundred mounted policemen and an even larger crowd of armed American Legionnaires and vigilantes. Undeterred, Foster mounted a car to address the crowd, but the moment he said, "We protest the suppression of free speech in Los Angeles," police rushed in from all sides. Launching tear-gas bombs and clubbing members of the audience, they dragged Foster off to jail. The Party's mayoral candidate climbed a lamppost to continue the speech, but ten policemen quickly pulled him to the pavement. Foster received rough treatment. Police charged him—once again with criminal syndicalism—threw him into a cell, and displayed him before an American Legion group and other professional patriots before finally dropping the charges and releasing him at 3 A.M.[50]

Foster started the campaign exhausted and showing signs of heart trouble. He complained often about poor organization and a schedule that was overloaded with events and subject to constant change. Aside from the obvious practical problems, campaign manager Clarence Hathaway's bungling offended the candidate's sense of efficiency. At times, Foster had no idea where he was headed next; at others, he literally arrived on the wrong date. "It is impossible for a speaker to know what in hell he is doing," he complained, "if dates are changed without notifying him."[51]

The highlight of the campaign was to be a huge rally on September 12 on Chicago's South Side, one of the Party's few strongholds. A crowd of 12,000 gathered for the event, but the candidate never arrived. A physician who had examined Foster on August 28 when he complained of chest pains found him completely exhausted and under extreme stress: "A careful survey of Mr. Foster's activities for the past year indicates a total disregard for his health and reserve." The pains became more severe and spread through Foster's entire left side, but he pressed on. On September 8, while speaking at a campaign rally in Moline, Illinois, Foster collapsed. He insisted on going on to Chicago but collapsed again, and his personal physician ordered him to bed. "Even such activities as dictation and the reception of visitors," Dr. Solon Bernstein wrote to Earl Browder, "are fraught with danger." Two months later, the Foster-Ford ticket received a little over 100,000 votes, while the hated Socialists took nearly 900,000. The defeat once again measured the limits of the Communists' appeal, even in the midst of a severe economic and social crisis.[52]

One dimension of Foster's personal crisis was purely physical. Arteriosclerosis had closed one of the branches of the artery supplying blood to the heart, producing a severe heart attack. "In addition thereto," a court-appointed physician later explained, "he apparently suffered a spasm or temporary closure of one of the arteries supplying blood to the left side of his brain with resulting symptoms and physical signs on the right side of his body from head to foot." Aside from the heart attack, then, Foster had also suffered a fairly serious stroke. Later diagnoses noted related symptoms—hypertension, high blood pressure, an enlarged heart. Now over fifty, with a lifetime of hard work and physical deprivation, Foster had been operating at breakneck speed for almost two decades. He had spent months at a time out in the coalfields, organizing strike activity and welfare work, speaking before large groups of strikers and unemployed. His prison experiences, followed quickly by the whirlwind election campaign, the arrests, and a beating, had undoubtedly drained him. As Foster later recalled, "The pitcher had gone once too often to the well."[53]

Beyond his coronary and neurological crisis, Foster's illness involved emotional and psychological problems. Some of his symptoms suggest nerve damage, probably related to the stroke or oxygen deprivation at the time of the coronary attack. He was also deeply frustrated and disappointed with Browder's newfound power and popularity. All of this contributed to a severe psychological and emotional crisis. A close associate described Foster's collapse as a "nervous breakdown," and Foster himself called it "a smash-up: angina pectoris, followed by a complete nervous collapse."[54]

The illness took him out of action entirely for almost three years. He spent five months in bed and most of the next two years resting under a doctor's care. Even after long bed rest, he remained plagued by anxiety attacks and a whole host of physical and psychological problems. "What ails me now," he wrote William Weinstone in June 1933, "is the tail end of a bad nerve shattering—and believe me it was real hell. The heart symptoms have quite disappeared. What I need now is quiet, rest, and general health building." He was in such poor shape, he explained, "that Party questions of all kinds have been kept away from me. For 7 months I did not even read the *D[aily] W[orker]*. I have not been in the Party or the TUUL since last August. But I am firmly convinced that in a few months more I'll be as good as new, with some reservations, as I am now really making progress toward recovery."[55]

Foster was wrong. In the summer of 1933, he traveled to the USSR, accompanied by his daughter Sylvia Manley Kolko, who had to be with him at all times. His recovery was excruciatingly slow and incomplete, a particularly frustrating and discouraging experience for someone with Foster's drive and rather impatient disposition. Eventually, Esther Foster joined him, but she was also ill, partly because of the strain of his sickness. By the fall, Foster was in despair. In October, while recuperating in the Black Sea resort town of Sochi, he wrote an unusually revealing letter, asking his old friend and mentor Lozovsky for help. "One of my basic troubles," Foster wrote, "apart from nights without sleep and nervous attacks, is involuntary inactivity. . . . I was very active, and now I am almost completely isolated. . . . I cannot talk to people, especially about politics. I have no self-confidence to speak more than two minutes."[56]

The recovery would have been difficult for anyone, but Foster's self-image as a vigorous, selfless revolutionary made the emotional and psychological dimension of the illness more complicated. What he described to a friend as the "killing boredom" of the recovery was "real hell." Yet when he tried any sort of activities for more than two minutes, all of his symptoms returned, so that he was constantly in fear of exerting himself at all. "I don't know how to spend my days," he wrote to Lozovsky.

> The result of this endless isolation and frustration is that I am constantly agitated and nervous. . . . This agitation is deepening because of the struggles in the States, while I can do nothing to help. . . . What should I do now? . . . I feel that I cannot go on this way. . . . Lying here, I'm of no value to the movement, and the isolation is eating me up. In the past, my strength had no limits. I could and for many years did work sixteen hour days without a rest, even on Sunday, not to mention a vacation. But now even unimportant things get me down. . . . Inactivity is just overwhelming me.[57]

Foster's anxiety attacks, inability to concentrate, persistent irritability, and feelings of helplessness and despair all suggest clinical depression.

Still weak and depressed, Foster returned to the United States by sea in January 1934, but a long period of recovery lay ahead. He admitted later that "my nerves were badly shattered" as late as the summer of 1934. Foster's physician insisted that he stay out of New York and out of politics. Sam Darcy, who was close to Foster before, during, and after the illness, described his symptoms when he arrived on the West Coast in early 1934 to recuperate: "He was in shocking physical condition. His head shook constantly, his hands trembled, and he walked with great difficulty."[58]

Foster remained on the West Coast for several months. In the spring of 1934, the Party assigned a secretary to him so that he might work for short periods, but he wrote to Browder that "after two days work—one hour each day—I simply had to give it up." He tried to follow the San Francisco, Minneapolis, and other big strikes that spring, but he found it difficult to concentrate on the issues, let alone take any part. "I am just like one in chains," he wrote Browder. "I am desperately restless." In the midst of the San Francisco strike, he wrote, "It grieves me beyond expression not to be able to sit in and help work the thing out. I tried to for a bit, . . . but the results on me were so bad we agreed I had better stay out. . . . I have given up all writing now. . . . If I did any writing in the USSR it was because I was so terribly tense . . . so horribly cut off and isolated that I had to do something or bust."[59]

It "just about breaks my heart," he wrote, "to be laid up in the midst of this developing struggle." Foster was clearly in bad shape, but Browder seemingly never responded to his many letters. By summer, Foster was still quite isolated and seldom read even the *Daily Worker.* In June, perhaps to raise his spirits or to remove him entirely from the scene of the West Coast labor conflict, Esther took him back to the place they had first met, the Home Colony near Tacoma, where they stayed with their old friend Jay Fox. "Am slowly picking up," he wrote, "but very slowly. I must have almost killed myself."[60] Very gradually, Foster regained some of his mobility, though he never fully recovered from the illness.

Foster tried to keep in contact with the movement in the mid-thirties through dictated statements, but for three years he was unable to make even a short speech. Very gradually, he regained some of his strength, but for the entire period between late 1932 and 1937, he later told a doctor, he was "practically helpless."[61]

The crisis involved more than Foster's health. Politically, his prison sentence and subsequent illness came at the worst possible moment. Earl Browder, Foster's lieutenant from the early TUEL days, rose quickly in the Party during the early thirties. His only serious rival for Party leadership, Foster was removed from contention at precisely the moment Browder made his move.

Browder's break with Foster over the question of dual unionism in 1928 had left some bitterness between the two, but Browder remained abroad, first as a Comintern representative in Asia and then for consultation in the Soviet Union, for most of the period from 1926 to early 1929. When he finally returned to the United States, there was no reason to suspect that he would be favored over Foster, who was still viewed as the major figure in the Party. The first leadership arrangement following Lovestone's demise in 1929 did not even include Browder. Apparently in an effort to undercut the factionalism, the Comintern named a temporary four-person secretariat consisting of Foster, Max Bedacht, William Weinstone, and Robert Minor.

Browder, a small-town midwesterner and bookkeeper by trade, looked the part. Until his meteoric rise, he had assumed a decidedly minor role in the movement and was best known as Foster's subordinate and aid. Perhaps because he had been out of the country during the late twenties, he seemed an unlikely choice, on the surface at least, as leader of the revolutionary movement in the United States.

Yet the fact that Browder had missed the worst of the factional fighting that tarnished Foster's reputation was an advantage. For years afterward, Comintern officials continued to record in Foster's official personnel file his sharp resistance to Lozovsky's dual union line and his vigorous factional conflicts with Lovestone in the late twenties. In 1932, Browder contributed a long memo dealing with the Party's leadership problems, including Foster's various weaknesses. Comintern leaders clearly held all of this against Foster in the early thirties, when they made their decisions about the American Communist Party's new leadership. J. Peters, an American Comintern representative, wrote a confidential January 1931 Comintern report regarding Foster's suitability as Party leader. It was largely negative:

> Foster has never had a definite worldview. He's a poor Marxist. . . . If you analyze his activity, you might conclude that he is still more a syndicalist than a Communist. . . . Foster is able to work extremely hard and he might prove very useful, but someone must direct him in the areas of theory and organization. He is a good speaker and pamphlet writer. Thanks to his unsteadiness and confused views, he could hardly become Party leader. As a comrade he is good, simple, modest. It is rumored that he has a weakness for women.

Whether the Soviets accepted Peters's assessment, Stalin's own 1929 claim that Foster's "factional blindness blunts his party feeling and solidarity and makes . . . [his] methods unscrupulous" would have been enough to diminish his prospects for top leadership.[62]

Perhaps realizing that his stock was low in Moscow, Foster actually proposed Browder for the Secretariat, which Browder joined in the summer of 1930 when Bedacht and Minor were dropped. At this point, Foster may still have thought of himself as the prime mover and Browder as his spokesperson, what Sam Darcy called "Foster's creature." But if Foster did hope to control Browder, events confounded him. Foster was named national chairman sometime in 1930, but he remained in prison, while Weinstone, the other Secretariat member, spent thirteen months during 1930 and 1931 in the Soviet Union on extended assignment. Their absences and the openings in the bureaucracy occasioned by the departure of Lovestone's adherents gave Browder and his organizational secretary, Jack Stachel, an opportunity to reshuffle the

Party cadres. Foster missed the crucial July 1930 convention, where Browder laid out his plans to reshape the Party and began his rise to ultimate power. By the time Foster emerged from prison in October, momentum was shifting toward Browder. Foster's work on the unemployed movement, the coal strikes, and the 1932 presidential campaign occupied him for most of the next two years. Weinstone engaged Browder in a nasty, unsuccessful power struggle throughout 1932. Late in the year, the Comintern dissolved the old Secretariat, named Weinstone its American representative, and proposed to build the Party around Browder and Foster. But the Soviets' optimism for Foster's quick recovery proved unfounded. His prolonged illness put him out of commission until at least 1935, while Browder consolidated his control. As Harvey Klehr concluded, "Foster's illness paved the way for Browder's emergence as undisputed party leader." At the 1934 convention, Browder was acknowledged as the Party's main spokesman and was formally named general secretary, an administrative position that carried enormous power and prestige.[63]

The choice of anyone but himself might have been difficult for Foster to accept, but Browder's rise to power must have been especially galling. The relationship between the two men throughout the twenties had been one of respected leader and devoted follower. While Browder resisted this characterization in his memoirs, contemporaries clearly saw him as Foster's protege. James P. Cannon knew both men well. "The original relationship between Foster and Browder, and the proper one, considering the personal qualities of each, had been the relation between executive and first assistant," Cannon recalled. "The appointment of Browder to the first position in the party, with Foster subordinated to the role of honorary public figure without authority, really rubbed Foster's nose in the dirt. It was not pleasant to see how he accepted the gross humiliation and pretended to submit to it."[64]

While the personal tension between these two men shows an important side of Foster's personality, there is a danger in analyzing Communist Popular Front politics in terms of personality conflicts among Party leaders. Though Foster's conflict with Browder remained a factor in Party politics, the Party's history in the thirties and the forties is best understood in terms of broad changes in its social base, the historical context within which it operated—the depression, the New Deal, and the conflict with fascism—and, as always, the changing politics of the international Communist movement. Foster's marginalization for more than a decade between the early thirties and the end of World War II paralleled a transformation in the Communist Party's membership, policies, and strategy. As the new Popular Front Party emerged, Browder took the field, and Foster was relegated to the sidelines.

10 On the Margins of the Popular Front, 1935–45

BY THE TIME William Z. Foster returned to Party work in 1935, the organization itself was in the midst of a dramatic transformation. The impetus derived not only from Moscow but also from a crucial conjuncture in the histories of the Communist Party, the American labor movement, and electoral politics in the United States. The biggest single factor in the Party's ideological transformation and the catalyst for many other changes was the rise of fascism and the Comintern's response to this threat in the form of the Popular Front. Several constituent parties, including the Communist Party, USA (CPUSA), had been moving toward a more flexible policy for some time, one that would allow them to work with other political groups in industrial and unemployed organizing and in antifascist work. But the Comintern's new Popular Front line was not formally implemented until its Seventh World Congress in the summer of 1935.

From the perspective of the Communist Party's history, the Popular Front represented a crucial departure. It freed Communists throughout the world to merge with diverse elements in a "broad left." But the Popular Front was, as Michael Denning has argued, neither the Communist Party nor its alliance with sympathetic liberals. Rather, it was a genuine social democratic mass movement, "a central instance of radical insurgency in modern U.S. history." Its base was not the Party but the labor movement, particularly the emerging industrial union movement of the late 1930s.[1] Yet as in other moments in the CPUSA's history, it is vital to consider the international context for this movement, as well as the rapidly changing domestic situation between the mid-thirties and the end of World War II.

Foster's personal and political situation help explain his marginal status during this "heyday of American communism." While Foster never openly opposed the Popular Front line, he seemed uncomfortable with it from the beginning. He was strong enough to attend the Seventh World Congress as a member of its ruling presidium, but his illness still severely limited his activities. It was Browder who made the American delegation's major address and Browder who emerged as the Party's standard-bearer in the 1936 election. Even if there had been an inclination to choose Foster (and there is no evidence of this), he was not in any condition to carry on such work.[2] He was too weak to deliver his own speech that emphasized the radicalization of American workers and the dangers of war and fascism, including "fascist elements" within Roosevelt's New Deal government. "In the United States now there is a race between the fascists and the Communist Party, for the leadership of the politically rapidly wakening toiling masses," he wrote, "[and] the fascists are at present far ahead in this race." Foster also emphasized the need to field an independent farmer-labor party slate in the 1936 elections. In tone and substance, Foster's speech reflected the Party's Third Period conception of the New Deal.[3]

The focal point for the congress was Georgi Dimitrov's dramatic declaration of the new Popular Front line, which stood in striking contrast to Foster's more confrontational tone. Dimitrov and other Comintern leaders emphasized cooperation with all progressive elements in the struggle against fascism and called specifically for support of FDR in the coming presidential elections. While both Browder and Foster were shaken by the dramatic implications of Dimitrov's speech and declined to respond immediately, Browder recovered more quickly. In his speech, delivered later in the proceedings, he embraced the new line, despite some misgivings.[4]

The Popular Front strategy's most important contribution may have been simply to unleash Party activists to follow strategies and tactics that developed rather naturally from the situations in which they found themselves and to base the Party's policies to a greater extent on the domestic situation in the United States. As Mark Naison noted, "If changes in Comintern policy and party rhetoric helped create such a world view, the energies it unleashed far transcended their [Comintern] control."[5] The new line ushered in a renaissance of American radicalism, with the Communist Party at its center.

It is not difficult to recognize the opportunity presented by the Popular Front. As Irving Howe and Lewis Coser noted, "It was the first approach the CP [Communist Party] had found that enabled it to gain a measure of acceptance, respectability, and power within ordinary American life."[6] But if the Popular Front brought Communists into the mainstream, it also changed the Party, bringing in new blood in the form of young cadres recruited from the unions and other mass organizations within which the Party now worked. As Paolo Spriano has described for the European parties, "It was the Popular Front experience, the persistent search for unity at both rank-and-file and leadership levels, the education of cadres and masses in the practice of 'doing politics' in the thick of events . . . of dealing with the great issues of national life, that finally created mass Communist Parties." As a result of this new approach, the Party's face was transformed. Veterans who had built and remained with the movement through all the factional struggles and twists and turns of the twenties were now joined by a new generation of Communists drawn from Popular Front mass movements, shaped by their experiences in these movements—unemployed and industrial union insurgencies, student and peace organizing, struggles against fascism during the Spanish Civil War and World War II. As an organization, the Party might have been no more and perhaps even less democratic than it had been, but these younger activists experienced democratic politics and worked with individuals and groups from a broad political spectrum in organizations in which they were often important leaders.[7]

If Foster's own inclinations and temperament seemed ideally suited to Third Period language and strategy, Browder's seemed natural in the Popular Front atmosphere. He enjoyed the Party's growing acceptance and prestige in the broader society and the status and power that such success brought him in the American Party and to some degree in the international movement. By the late thirties, Comintern general secretary Dimitrov was calling Browder "the foremost Marxist in the English-speaking world." "After years in the shadows," Mark Naison noted, "Browder discovered long-suppressed ambitions to become a public figure." An opportunist, Browder experimented in the interests of gaining greater acceptance, and this quest for acceptance propelled him toward social democratic formulations. He was constantly reacting to the changing political situation in the United States during depression and war. By comparison, Foster never seemed entirely comfortable with the more expansive applications of the Popular Front line. His own thinking remained what the political scientist Joseph Starobin, himself a former Communist, described as "an amalgam of his trade union origins and his 'fundamentalist' understanding of Marxism." As the veteran Party activist Gil Green later recalled, "Foster had his eyes set in one direction, how to organize the working class into industrial unions." Here he had great insight, but he "often had a much narrower approach in the political arena."[8]

During Foster's gradual recovery in the mid-thirties, the Party's industrial work with which he had been so closely identified was transformed. The TUUL was gone by the end of 1934, its activists dispersed to various AFL unions, and a new union movement was beginning to emerge. When Foster did return, he was unable to engage in such organizing and instead spent a good deal of his time writing.

In the course of organizing radical unions and waging the violent strikes of the early thirties, Foster had remained convinced of the importance of working in the AFL. As long as the Party placed most of its scant resources in the new unions, his pleas to continue boring from within the AFL had little effect. The death of both the NTWU and the NMU by late 1933, however, brought a general decline of TUUL activity. The strike wave beginning late that year and extending through 1934 took the Communists and virtually everyone else by surprise and provided openings for radicals to work with other activists on a local level. As late as June 1934, Jack Stachel, a Browder loyalist who took over the TUUL helm at the time of Foster's collapse, assured league activists that the Party was not liquidating the TUUL. Late in 1934, the Party did finally disband the last of the revolutionary unions, but even before the league was liquidated, hundreds of its militants had entered the AFL— before the declaration of the Popular Front. They merged with the nascent industrial union movement that culminated in the formation of the Committee for Industrial Organization within the AFL in fall 1935. This new committee agitated for industrial organization and strategies and for a giant drive to organize the open-shop basic industries. The Congress of Industrial Organizations (CIO) was launched in the fall of the following year when AFL leaders suspended those unions adhering to the committee's program. In the following decade, this new federation revitalized the American labor movement, embracing millions of black, immigrant, and women workers in the nation's large-scale mass production industries and in the process introducing new strategies and organizational forms. Communist activists were at the very heart of this historic movement from its beginning.[9]

Just as the new industrial union movement appeared, badly in need of experienced organizers willing to undertake the momentous and often dangerous task of organizing basic industry, the Communist Party was emerging from the restraints of the Third Period. The new line freed thousands of Communist activists to reenter the mainstream labor movement. Under the auspices of the Popular Front, Communist unionists, sometimes whole locals of the old TUUL organizations, entered the AFL and joined with other militants to create the new CIO. Communists surfaced as rank-and-file and even national leaders in the new labor federation, and for the first time since its inception, the Party achieved a major influence in the American labor movement. Foster clearly saw all of this as a vindication of his perennial position on working within the mainstream unions, though he never said as much publicly.[10]

The declaration of the Popular Front also coincided with the leftward drift of the New Deal Democratic Party and the emergence of a new coalition that included organized labor, small farmers, and a variety of ethnic groups. As Maurice Isserman concluded, the new line allowed Communists to "continue to think of themselves as revolutionaries even as they immersed themselves in reform-oriented day-to-day politics."[11]

As the Party moved closer to Roosevelt, Foster grew more uncomfortable. In assessing the significance of the Popular Front for the Party in 1937, Foster contrasted the spectacular growth of the French and Spanish parties with the stagnancy of the CPUSA and emphasized the importance of systematic recruitment and training. Working in front organizations, Foster insisted, was not enough: "The party must find the ways and means to stand out clearly . . . as the real leader of the masses in the daily fight as well as in general theory." The Party's main weakness, he observed, "consists of making too little criticism of progressively-led movements . . . inadequate criticism of Roosevelt and Lewis, and . . . a failure to put forward our own program." The Party had a "liquidatory tendency" "to lose its identity in the general work."[12]

Foster also worried about the implications of the Party's expanding social base. If the trend went too far, the Party's proletarian character might be overwhelmed by a flood of middle-class recruits. "Their entry," Foster wrote, "present[s] to the Party many problems and tasks . . . [These] boil down to the issue of how to make use of the . . . [professionals] to further our central objective of broadening and strengthening the proletarian base."[13]

Yet in organizational terms, the Communist Party thrived under Browder. As a result of its work in progressive coalitions, the Party achieved unprecedented support and influence by the eve of World War II. At the time of the Seventh Congress and the declaration of the Popular Front in 1935, Party membership stood at about 30,000; by the summer of 1939, it had reached a high point of 80,000 to 100,000, including the Young Communist League.

The proliferation of Popular Front organizations and high turnover in membership mean that American communism influenced many more than this number suggests.[14]

Browder did not allow much room for Foster or anyone else to raise questions in the midst of all this apparent success. Ironically, as the Popular Front emerged during the mid-thirties, with its greater tactical and ideological flexibility and its democratic rhetoric and symbolism, internal debate in the Communist Party declined, at least at the national level, an effect of Stalinization that helped Browder consolidate his position. Gone was the bitter factionalism of the twenties, but with it, it seemed, went any discussion of alternative views. As Howe and Coser concluded, "A pall of unanimity fell upon the party."[15] A cult of personality very much in keeping with the Stalin years grew up around Browder. "As the party's membership and influence expanded," Isserman wrote, Browder's "self-regard grew proportionally." The general secretary's position achieved much greater status and garnered more organizational power than it had ever enjoyed in the past. Foster undoubtedly lost in the course of these innovations. Wherever possible, Browder curtailed Foster's direct involvement in decision making, reducing his chairmanship to what Alexander Bittelman called "a kind of glorified dog house."[16]

Although Edward Johanningsmeier argued that Foster faced the events of the mid-thirties with a "dogged and tenacious optimism," it seems instead that he emerged only very gradually from the profound physical and emotional crisis he suffered for several years following his 1932 breakdown. Throughout the late thirties and the war years, Foster remained weak and was rather easily exhausted. He experienced shortness of breath after the briefest walks. Unable to speak publicly for more than a few minutes, he also had trouble sitting through long meetings. "I am getting along pretty good ordinarily," he wrote his friend Sam Darcy in late 1937 or early 1938, "but don't stand up under the least pressure." It often became necessary for him to recline on a couch installed in the meeting room for this purpose and participate in discussions while lying flat on his back. While Foster still displayed the grim determination that had driven him throughout his life, he simply lacked the stamina and perhaps also the confidence to assume an influential position. Foster admitted to a group of Party leaders in 1939 that "as soon as there is any excitement coming along I am practically out of the running. . . . the only way I can work is when things are perfectly quiet and [I] can work by myself, writing, etc."[17]

To cope with the physical crisis, Foster summoned up remarkable, perhaps obsessive self-discipline. He established a new work regime, which he maintained for most of the rest of his life. He rose early in the morning—by

5:30 or 6 o'clock—usually skipped breakfast, read the morning papers, and began to write. He set himself a quota of one thousand words per day, which normally absorbed several hours, and then had lunch around 11 o'clock. In the early afternoon, a driver usually delivered him to Party headquarters, where he submitted his *Daily Worker* or *Communist* articles and discussed them and future assignments with editors and other comrades. Foster also often conferred with Browder, though they were certainly not on cordial terms. If there was a meeting of the Party's Central Committee or National Board, Foster attended in the afternoon and then headed home, usually by 3 o'clock. Normally, the Party's meeting schedule accommodated Foster's medical condition: no late night or excessively long meetings. Except for going to an occasional Yankee game or a cowboy movie, Foster stayed at home. Unless he was obligated to speak at a public gathering, Foster spent most of his evenings reading, usually history, biography, or popular science, and listening to classical or folk music in his flat near Yankee Stadium in the South Bronx. The cramped, poorly furnished, three-room apartment on the fifth floor of an old building was overflowing with books and often in disrepair, but it was a quiet place to work, and Foster did most of his writing there by hand, usually with a pencil on a yellow legal pad.[18]

Beyond the obvious physical toll that the heart attack and stroke had taken, his crisis also had had a profound psychological effect that shaped Foster's perspective and behavior long after the collapse. Like many stroke victims who had enjoyed great physical strength before their illnesses, Foster now lost confidence in his abilities. He was often nervous, a condition that stood in stark contrast to the coolness he had so often displayed in long and difficult organizing situations before the mid-thirties. Gil Green, who served with him on the Party's National Board from the late thirties through the World War II years, remembered that long after his recovery, Foster required assistance crossing the street and was visibly frightened by the heavy traffic around the Party's Union Square headquarters. When he spoke publicly, he always asked that a small glass of gin, indistinguishable from water, be on the speaker's rostrum, apparently to steady his nerves. Oddly, Foster never seemed to take a drink but clearly derived some sense of security just from having the glass there. Some of these peculiarities diminished over time, but observers agree that he never recovered the stamina and critical edge he had exhibited before his illness. Foster himself later estimated that he never regained more than half of his original physical capacity, although he eventually "learned to live with himself." The transformation made a deep impression on Green and presumably others. A man who had long been acknowledged as the premier symbol of the Party's more aggressive masculine image, someone who had exuded great drive, determination, and confidence, was now diminished not only physically but emotionally. The stroke haunted Foster for the next two decades, and he carefully measured his every effort so he would not have another collapse. A *Saturday Evening Post* reporter visiting Communist Party headquarters in the summer of 1938 characterized Foster as "respected, but somewhat worn."[19]

Too weak now for his usual traveling and organizing, Foster had resumed his writing on a regular basis upon his return from the Soviet Union in the fall of 1935. To some degree, this was a natural development. Gerhardt Eisler, the Communist International's representative to the CPUSA, encouraged Foster along this course. Foster could now indulge his early attraction for study and reflection. Yet his shift from organizer, director of the Party's industrial work, and possibly the Party's leading public figure to radical writer was also part of the process of marginalization. Browder supporters in the Party headquarters cautioned Foster against taking too active a role, lest he suffer a relapse. Certainly Browder was happier relegating Foster to this new role than he would have been sharing power with him.[20]

Foster first produced two major articles, one on the dangers of fascism in the United States and the other an extended critique of syndicalism. Both pieces were orthodox in tone. In the first, Foster complained that most workers and even some Communists tended to see fascism as quite distinct from the more general assault of big capital on labor. In fact, he argued, the fascist tendencies exhibited by such groups as the Ku Klux Klan and the American Liberty League and even some AFL leaders were products of the current evolution of American capitalism. One should not expect the same characteristics as those exhibited in Italy and Germany. Foster located a native American variant of fascism, which wrapped itself in patriotic rhetoric about democracy while attacking democratic movements and institutions. He saw the New Deal itself as part of the state's general turn to the right. Fascist tendencies were dialectically related to the growing working-class revolt evidenced by the great strike wave of 1933–34, continuing unrest among the unemployed, and the growth of the Communist Party. As big business and its political representatives, including Roosevelt and the New Deal, tried to stem this tide of revolt, the dangers of a fascist reaction increased. Foster accepted the Comintern's new Popular Front policy as the proper response to this threat, but he still thought in terms of a new farmer-labor party, not a coalition with the New Deal Democrats.[21]

Such ideas did not contradict the Party's official position in the early years of the New Deal, but they suggest another breach between Foster and Browder. Once the Party assumed a more conciliatory attitude toward Roosevelt and his policies from early 1936 on, Foster was much less comfortable with the arrangement than Browder was.

In the article on syndicalism, Foster traced its historical development, delineating the objective and subjective factors accounting for its strength in the United States and analyzing its significance for the American revolutionary movement. Syndicalism, or more properly anarcho-syndicalism, he defined rather simply as "that tendency in the labor movement to confine the revolutionary class struggle to the economic field, to practically ignore the state, and to reduce the whole fight of the working class to simply a question of trade union action. . . . In short, syndicalism is pure and simple trade unionism, using militant tactics and dressed up in revolutionary phraseology."[22] Foster shared the ideological journey from syndicalism to communism with a whole generation of labor radicals, men and women who made the ideological leap in the faith that the Communist Party represented a more suitable vehicle for achieving a working-class revolution. Yet Foster's critique of syndicalism was strikingly simplistic. He was in a unique position to analyze the movement's strong attraction for some of the most sophisticated radicals of the early twentieth century. More important perhaps, with his intimate knowledge of the movement throughout the world, he might have provided a very useful discussion of the creative strategies and forms of organization that syndicalists developed in the face of increasingly integrated and bureaucratic capitalist structures and sophisticated systems of mass production. Foster had a better feel for this movement and a greater understanding of it than perhaps anyone else in the United States. But rather than subject the movement to a rigorous analysis and probe the obvious connections between it and early communism, Foster devoted the article to arguing the weaknesses of syndicalism compared with communism. For Foster, syndicalism was now simply a primitive form of labor radicalism, exposed in all of its weakness by the triumph of the Russian Revolution and Lenin's theoretical genius.

There is no reason to doubt that this was Foster's true perspective. Yet the syndicalism article, in its logic, language, and style, confirms the trajectory of Foster's thinking away from the creativeness of the World War I and TUEL era and toward an increasingly mechanistic and formulaic version of Marxism-Leninism. It was as if, detached from direct contact with the movements and conflicts that had sustained him over the past thirty years, he settled for orthodoxy. This tendency, somewhat muted at the height of the Popular Front and the struggle against fascism in the late thirties and World War II years, burst forth in full force in the political repression of the postwar era. The theoretical rigidity that helps explain the eventual decline of communism as a political force was already characteristic of Foster's thinking by the mid-thirties, if not earlier.

This rigidity facilitated Earl Browder's success in relegating Foster to an inferior position during the thirties. "I reduced handling Foster to a system," Browder later claimed. "I let him put forward his opposition on every issue in the top committees and used the opportunity to argue it out before rather than after the fight."[23] That Foster felt himself "a mass leader against cockroaches and New York intellectuals" undoubtedly embittered him. Yet he had little choice but to conform; Browder held all the cards during the Popular Front era. In the vital reaches of the Comintern, Foster's optimism about the prospects for cooperation not only between the Soviet Union and the United States but also between contending classes within the capitalist societies was consistent with the official Soviet line throughout the war years. Bound by the discipline he had come to embrace, Foster did what the Party asked of him and waited for a chance to challenge Browder. He may not have been "a thoroughly shorn lion," as one study suggested, but Browder and the Popular Front had undoubtedly diminished his roar.[24]

Still Foster commanded considerable support among Communist trade union activists. In this milieu, the key question for the Communists was what role they would play in the emerging industrial union movement. The answer was far from clear in the mid-thirties. First, there were fears of conflict within the labor movement. While industrial union advocates aimed to organize millions of workers virtually ignored by the AFL, their establishment of a separate new movement brought with it all the dangers inherent in dual unionism, a strategy Foster still resisted. Then there was the matter of the Party's own labor militants who had worked to build the now dismantled TUUL. What role, if any, would these valuable cadres play in a new movement?

In early 1936, before the new federation was launched, John L. Lewis and other top CIO leaders met with Earl Browder, Clarence Hathaway, and the auto activist Wyndham Mortimer to be sure they had the Communist Party's support. Browder eagerly promised whatever support the Party could give the movement, and the Communists eventually provided the CIO with important organizing and leadership support. But there is no doubt that the Party hesitated in publicly supporting the break with the AFL.[25]

The prospect of yet another split in the labor movement particularly bothered Foster. The Party's policy in the mid-thirties, Foster later wrote, was very similar to the one he had set out for himself a generation earlier—to revolutionize the AFL by "systematic work within its ranks."[26] In early 1936, Foster attacked the AFL leadership and sided with the CIO's demand for industrial organization, but he was clearly uncomfortable with the idea of the split when it came later that year. In mid-1937, he warned the Party's Central Committee that Lewis might one day turn on them, as he had on the TUEL in the 1920s. The Transport Workers Union, the National Maritime Union, and other organizations led or influenced by the Party gradually joined the new federation in the course of 1937. As late as August 1938, however, Foster was still hoping for a reunited labor movement (an aim he pushed once again during the war). As Bert Cochran noted, the Party's early wariness was not surprising, given the fluidity of the situation until the fall of 1936, when the AFL suspended those unions constituting the Committee for Industrial Organization. Certainly Foster's misgivings were predictable. He and other Communist Party leaders worried about finding themselves isolated once again from the mainstream labor movement if the CIO's gamble did not work out.[27]

The top CIO leadership included numerous longtime foes, ranging from John L. Lewis of the UMWA, who led the new federation, to David Dubinsky and Sidney Hillman of the ILGWU and the Amalgamated Clothing Workers, with whom the Communists had tangled during the battles in the garment industry. There were also numerous practical problems with making the switch. Having just dismantled the TUUL, many Communist labor activists were enmeshed in major AFL organizing drives, sometimes now as local leaders. Jack Stachel, the Party's organizational secretary, reported at its ninth convention that the number of Communists in the AFL had grown from 2,000 to 15,000 between 1934 and the summer of 1936, including delegates to every state AFL convention and 20 delegates to the AFL's national convention.[28]

But in assembling the new movement, the CIO leaders badly needed the experience and dedication of Communist militants. The CIO's reliance on the Party and those close to it offered the Communists a priceless opportunity. Lee Pressman, the CIO's general council, became Lewis's main contact with the Communist Party. John Brophy, Lewis's longtime enemy in the UMW and a former Communist ally, became the CIO's vice president, and he hired Len DeCaux as director of publicity. DeCaux, a British immigrant and former Wobbly, had helped edit the radical *Illinois Miner* during the twenties and knew Brophy from the progressive opposition to Lewis's regime. By the mid-thirties, DeCaux was very close to, if not a member of, the Communist Party. At ground level, Communist activists filled organizer positions in a number of industries.[29]

The steel industry provides an example of the Party's importance in the CIO drive and of Foster's continuing influence on Communist organizers. As early as 1934, TUUL activists had gained some influence by working in the company unions that flooded steel and other industries in the wake of Section 7A of the National Industrial Recovery Act, which asserted workers' right to organize. Through its fraternal group, the International Workers' Order, and other organizations, the Communists also had contacts with the various ethnic communities of the steel towns and sometimes with the black community. Once the CIO had established the Steelworkers Organizing Committee (SWOC), John L. Lewis, Foster's old enemy in the coal struggles of the twenties and early thirties, turned to the Party as a source for dedicated and experienced organizers. Brophy, who had collaborated with the Communists in Foster's "Save the Union" movement, acted as intermediary, probably because he was familiar with some of the Communists. He met with Browder, who pledged the Party's full support, and Communist Party and Young Communist League staffs were incorporated into the organizing drive in steel areas. For his part, Brophy promised that there would be no discrimination against the Communists. Foster himself estimated that at least 60 of SWOC's 200 full-time staff organizers were Party members. One source indicated that 31 or 32 of the 33 SWOC organizers in the Chicago area were Party members. In addition to these official organizers, the Party contributed its own resources and the time and energy of volunteer organizers and rank-and-file Communist steelworkers.[30]

Far less mobile and energetic from the mid-thirties on because of illness, Foster continued to play a role in these efforts to build a new, more progressive labor movement, and younger activists respected him for his experience and accomplishments. Dorothy Healey, a young labor organizer at the time, later recalled, "Although Browder supervised the behind-the-doors contacts with top CIO leaders, most of us in the unions assumed that the Party's chairman, William Z. Foster, was an equal spokesman when it came to trade union affairs." It was Foster's experience and reputation that earned and held this respect. "I remember a collection of his pamphlets that was very influential among us called *Organizing the Mass Production Industries,* published in 1936. . . . In our eyes he remained the authoritative public spokesman on issues confronting the labor movement. It is an oversimplification to assume that just because Browder was general secretary and he said or did something, that's what filtered down to us in the rank and file as the last word on Party policy," Healey observed.[31]

Several organizers mentioned Foster's series of pamphlets on industrial organization, particularly in the steel industry, in interviews and memoirs. His *Organizing Methods in the Steel Industry* (1935) became what the labor historian Lizabeth Cohen called a "blueprint for CIO policy," not only in steel but among organizers in many other industries as well. In it, Foster advocated special strategies for organizing black workers, women, and youth and was also sensitive to the newer trends in popular culture, particularly emphasizing the importance of the radio in steel mill towns and other industrial communities where corporations exercised tight control of life in the community as well as in the plant. The radio, Foster explained, "takes the union message directly into the workers' homes."[32]

Organizers recall meeting with Foster, who discussed strategy and suggested valuable contacts in steel and coal towns and among packinghouse workers in Chicago. The very success of the CIO organizing in contrast to the massive defeats of the era following World War I suggests that conditions had changed significantly in such places and elsewhere. But some of Foster's early contacts were still there, and some of the ideas and strategies that he advocated on the basis of considerable experience were still quite relevant. Herb March, a Party activist and perhaps the leading figure in the CIO's Packinghouse Workers Organizing Committee, remembers that Foster stressed an escalation of very specific, practical demands as a way of drawing workers into the CIO campaign in the Chicago stockyards. Foster recalled an old Russian formulation of the strategy: "First you fight for hot water for tea, then you fight for tea for the hot water, and then you fight for sugar for the tea."[33]

Because the labor movement remained the Party's main source for recruitment and mass organization, Foster's prestige among key industrial activists was significant. With the new industrial unions assuming ever greater importance in the American labor movement and with Communists assuming ever greater influence in the industrial union movement in the late thirties and forties, first as field organizers and rank-and-file activists and later as union officers and representatives, Foster's standing with this wing of the Party provided some degree of authority. At the least, it probably inhibited Browder from moving too aggressively against Foster when he did voice opposition to Browder's line. Any move against Foster had to be weighed in terms of his enormous popularity with the Party's rank and file.

If Earl Browder held the reins of power firmly, controlling the Party bureaucracy throughout the late thirties and World War II years, Foster remained the CPUSA's most potent symbol of its proletarian roots and constituency. "Had CPUSA members selected their general secretary democratically," Browder's biographer concluded, "they certainly would have chosen Foster."[34]

To some extent, Foster's transition, from the mid-thirties on, from active labor organizer and major Party spokesman to writer and symbol was natural, given his illness. Through his own life and experiences, he linked the Communist Party to older American radical traditions and to the working class. More than any other individual leader, he represented the Party's potential to become a mass revolutionary working-class party, and so he continued to be honored.

Whatever his symbolic importance, Foster could do only so much in his weakened physical condition. In this situation, he began to "reinvent" himself. Always somewhat insecure about his own intellectual abilities but deeply committed to learning, Foster indulged his interest in writing and research as never before. In the next few years, he produced at least twenty pamphlets, including the series on industrial organizing, which to some degree stood in for the actual organizing and speaking now well beyond Foster's physical abilities. The pamphlets allowed Foster to feel he was contributing to the political work he most prized.

In the late thirties, Foster turned to a far more ambitious writing project—his own life story. Autobiography, as Phillipe LeJeune wrote, "is necessarily in its deepest sense a special kind of fiction, itself and its truth as much created as discovered realities"; that is, we can tell a great deal about people from their biographies, but less from the details than from the way in which they choose to describe their lives.[35] In Foster's autobiographies, we find little definition of himself as an individual and little description of his relationships with those around him.

In 1937, Foster published *From Bryan to Stalin,* which he accurately described as not so much an autobiography as "a contribution to the history of left wing trade unionism in the United States during the past forty years" and an "outline of the development of the Communist Party."[36] Two years later, he produced *Pages from a Worker's Life,* a series of fascinating, often humorous, and occasionally touching sketches drawn from his experiences at work and on the road. Both books, rather well reviewed in the mainstream press, served important functions for the Party.

Organizational in form and tone, *From Bryan to Stalin* stood in for an official Party history until Foster himself produced one in 1952.[37] Reflecting Foster's explicit goals in writing it, as well as whatever problems he had in understanding his own life story, *From Bryan to Stalin* is peculiarly impersonal. Foster enters the story only through his organizational efforts and has no independent role. Even then, the real genius he displayed in some of these efforts is subordinated to the narrative of movement development, with all roads leading toward communism. As Elizabeth Gurley Flynn noted in a review, "*From Bryan to Stalin* . . . was a veritable guide book to the American labor movement of the past half century." If you wanted to know about the "actual experiences of Bill Foster," however, they had to be "glimpsed between the lines."[38]

Pages from a Worker's Life offered a far more personal perspective, full of anecdotes, but Foster seemed to value these for what they showed about what he called "the forces that led me to arrive at my present opinions." Again Foster's experiences are portrayed as those of a more or less typical worker. Because of this objective and the organization of the book in the form of brief episodes, it is difficult to chart any pattern of personal development, a problem that held little interest for Foster.[39]

Neither book is introspective in the least, suggesting why Foster seemed to suffer so much when he was isolated from the movement in the mid-thirties. His personality was fused with the Party's own. As Flynn wrote, "There is no ego here; no cultivated 'complex'; no soul-searching 'to find himself'; no personal glory, amorous conquests nor 'success' recipes." "This is the key to Foster," Flynn argued, "He lives and moves and has his being as a worker; conscious of his class and its struggles, its needs and what its final aims must be. He has no personal life nor ambition outside of theirs." The writer Joseph Freeman made a similar observation about Foster around the same time. He seemed to have no personality independent of the movement, Freeman said: "Anything he said about himself was an illustration of a parenthetical general law of revolutionary strategy or a trade union principle. . . . personal characteristics emerged by accident. . . . the problem of personal conduct . . . did not seem to interest him. He was ascetic by a standard which determined all his actions. The class struggle was the most important thing in the world. For that struggle he wanted to keep physically, mentally, and morally fit." Freeman also noted that Foster's illness tended to accentuate this asceticism, "obliged him to be especially careful."[40]

To the extent that *Pages from a Worker's Life* can be taken in some sense as a reflection of Foster's life, what is perhaps most remarkable about its episodes is the almost total absence of women. The most striking case is Esther Abramowitz Foster, the remarkable woman he had met thirty years earlier and with whom he lived until his death in 1961. A strikingly beautiful woman, Esther was a free-love advocate and anarchist militant in her early years, the mother of three children, and apparently a fascinating person. Foster dedicated *From Bryan to Stalin* to her, "An intelligent and devoted comrade, . . . my constant companion and a tower of strength to me in all my activities for these many years," but he mentions her only once in the 345-page book, and this acknowledgement comes in a brief paragraph concerning her role in the Syndicalist League of North America. Esther was not mentioned at all in *Pages from a Worker's Life*. FBI reports suggest that she was a semi-invalid by at least the early 1940s as a result of severe arthritis, that she appeared nervous, and that she seldom if ever left home.[41] Esther's low public profile can thus be explained partly by her health. Her absence from the pages of Foster's memoirs is more puzzling. Some acquaintances might describe their relationship as warm and loving, but she was invisible here and in the rest of Foster's voluminous writing.

Foster's silence about Esther and heterosexual relationships more generally is explained at least partly by the homosocial worlds he inhabited for much of his life. Virtually all of his early work environments, typical of a generation of unskilled western migratory workers, were exclusively male, often rather dangerous settings—isolated lumber and mining camps and sawmills, deep-water sailing ships, and railroad freight yards and boxcars. His life as a hobo between jobs and on organizing trips was an experience calculated to accentuate both the male bonding and the violence and alienation of an unskilled worker's life. His few references to personal friends and companions from these early years and beyond are virtually all to men.

Likewise, although he certainly encountered and even worked with women, Foster's political spaces resonated with an ostentatiously proletarian and "muscular" form of trade union politics. This was as true of his TUEL circle and his "Chicago" Party faction in the 1920s as it had been of his earlier political engagements with the Seattle Socialist Party, the Wage Workers Party, the IWW, and his own succession of syndicalist groups. By the standards of Foster's lifetime, the Party integrated women rather well into its leadership, including the Central Committee, but few served in the top leadership during his first decade in the Party and none at all between 1923 and 1927. The proportion of women on the Central Committee rose throughout the 1930s, reaching a high point of one-fourth in 1940, but Foster had been incapacitated for several years before turning to his autobiographies in the mid-1930s. Foster maintained a very warm friendship with Elizabeth Gurley Flynn, another "old Wobbly," and Harvey Klehr asserted that Rebecca Grecht, a district and union organizer in the 1920s, was Foster's "girlfriend" during these years. Still, Foster's worlds of work and politics were largely male worlds, not simply in the sense that they were inhabited almost exclusively by men but also in the sense that they projected a masculinist language that valued industrial work and strikes over all other forms of political action.[42]

Foster's changing role reflected new political realities in the Party. He emerged as the central figure in a small left opposition within the Party leadership to Browder's increasingly expansive rendering of Popular Front theory and practice. Several times over the next decade, he challenged Browder on key policy issues. Indeed, he represented Browder's only true opposition, carrying on what Browder characterized as "constant guerrilla warfare" against his policies. Whatever fault one might find with Foster's role in the late thirties and forties, he was fairly consistent in his politics.[43]

One of the earliest of these confrontations came when Foster and Browder were summoned to Moscow to discuss the Communists' 1936 election strategy. This time, it was Foster who urged direct support for Roosevelt, while Browder advocated a Communist ticket, concentrating most of the Party's criticism on Alf Landon, Roosevelt's Republican opponent. The idea was to strengthen Roosevelt without risking too close an identification of his policies with the Communist Party. After considerable discussion, Comintern leaders left the details to be worked out by the American Party, but they clearly sided in principle with Browder, whom the Party chose as its candidate. In a pattern he continued to follow in the coming decade, Foster publicly supported the decision, functioning as chair of Browder's campaign.[44]

Throughout the late thirties, Foster returned to Moscow to criticize Browder for what he viewed as an uncritical attitude toward FDR and for "tailing" rather than leading the progressive forces in the political mainstream. Foster tended to stress the American workers' revolutionary potential and the strategy of developing a farmer-labor party that could provide the Communists with a genuine Popular Front grouping, in which they might exercise considerably more influence than they could over the Democratic Party.

With the return of depression conditions in late 1937, Foster pressed his case for a more independent and militant Party position. At the end of the year, on his way to Moscow, Foster attacked Browder's line before the annual Congress of the French Communist Party. He contrasted the American Party's uncritical attitude toward the New Deal with the French Party's decision to enter the Popular Front government on its own terms.[45]

He sounded this theme in a long speech before the Comintern in April 1937 and returned to it during a major confrontation with Browder at the beginning of 1938. In this case, Foster received considerable support from the Soviet economist Eugene Varga. Browder vigorously defended his policies, noting that Foster's disagreements with the Politburo had "increased in number and intensity" over the previous nine months. He publicly accused Foster of "wavering" on the international line, a serious charge that Foster recalled bitterly more than a year later. Claiming that the Moscow confrontations with his old mentor represented the "most painful experience of his life," Browder asserted that he was now "learning from even greater teachers, from the greatest teacher of all, Comrade Stalin." The dispute divided the Comintern's executive, which took a week to issue its report. Although the Comintern chastised both men, cautioning them against identifying too closely with the New Deal, it clearly sided with Browder. The Comintern decision noted certain "sectarian remnants" in Foster's formulations, an ominous allusion to his factional struggles with Lovestone a decade earlier, and concluded that the "Right Danger" lay in the threat of isolation due to such

remnants. Bolstered by this victory, Browder dubbed his own expansive reading of the international line and the Party's close identification with the
New Deal, the "Democratic Front." In the months to follow, he packed Madison Square Garden and Carnegie Hall with enthusiastic audiences and became the only American Communist leader to appear on the cover of *Time*
magazine.[46]

Browder and Foster traveled to Moscow again in February 1939 as the
Spanish Republic appeared to be collapsing. Browder had had his own problems in Spain. A year earlier, on a poorly timed trip while returning from
Moscow, he had visited exhausted Lincoln Brigade volunteers on the Spanish
front. The usually glib Browder drew thunderous boos and hooting with ill-
considered remarks about poor morale. In early 1939, on his last Russian trip
before the outbreak of World War II, Foster pointed out the failure of Browder's original policy of supporting nonintervention in the Spanish conflict
and argued that this and other recent setbacks justified a change in leadership. But again, as in every other confrontation between the two, the Comintern leadership supported Browder. Some were clearly losing patience with
Foster. Dimitrov, architect of the Popular Front and a man with enormous
prestige in the international movement, urged that Foster simply be removed
from all major offices.[47]

Browder later argued that a pattern developed in these Moscow trips.
About once a year, the two journeyed there for consultation, often in the
company of other Party leaders, and stayed for six weeks to three months.
Foster appeared as what Browder called "a complaining witness," formally
presenting objections to Browder's policies and leadership and appealing to
the Comintern leadership to correct these. Often Foster received some support, particularly from leaders of other constituent parties, whom Browder
characterized as "more orthodox than the pope." But the Russians tended
to support Browder, who prized the long discussions and consultations as
a means of thinking through and hammering out American Party policy.
"With what soon became monotonous regularity," Browder later recalled,
"Foster took his complaints to the Comintern, and was overruled." Even Foster's role as "permanent opposition" was useful, Browder recalled, "since he
provided a convenient anvil upon which to hammer out the plow." His biographer James Ryan suggests that Browder so enjoyed his pummeling of Foster
that he declined Dimitrov's offer to find a Comintern position for Foster overseas, passing up an opportunity to displace his only serious opposition.[48]

These Russian trips had the effect of vindicating Browder's leadership in
the eyes of the international movement, and they probably damaged Foster's
standing at home. Since other American leaders were usually present during
the discussions and the formulation of policy and since, as Harvey Klehr

concluded, "[Foster's] frequent appeals to the Comintern got him nothing but criticism," they further tarnished his image among the Party leadership. He may still have been respected for his long years of service to the labor movement and the Party, but Browder always seemed to be judged right and Foster always wrong.[49]

Foster, having committed himself to Party discipline so often in the face of severe misgivings about such policies as dual unionism and the break with Fitzpatrick and having embraced Third Period sectarianism and class-war rhetoric, now found it difficult to take the logic of the Popular Front as far as Browder did. Whatever personal animosity he harbored toward Browder, he also seemed genuinely concerned about too close a cooperation with bourgeois parties and such conservative labor leaders as John L. Lewis, whom he had been battling for two decades. Gil Green remembered that when Lewis approached the Party with a plea for organizers in steel, Foster was wary, noting, "You can't trust that son-of-a-bitch." Browder favored collaboration with Lewis on practical grounds and in the spirit of the Popular Front.[50]

Browder later claimed that Foster was a sheer opportunist, devoid of any particular ideological inclination. Certainly Foster was opportunistic, as was Browder, but Foster stood to gain little in opposing Browder at this juncture, since the odds were so against him. Moreover, his opposition, right or wrong, was quite consistent and usually left wing in nature. He thought Communist writers were too easy on Roosevelt and Lewis. In 1937, he sided with William Weinstone's efforts to support rank-and file opposition and wildcat strikes in the United Automobile Workers Union but once again lost the argument. Above all, Foster feared that if the Communists failed to establish their own distinctive perspective within the mass movements of the Popular Front, they might be submerged in a morass of bourgeois reformism and lose their revolutionary identity. Theirs was "not only a party of progressive immediate demands," he insisted, "but also the Party of proletarian revolution."[51]

Foster represented a coherent orthodox left-wing opposition within the Party. Although Browder effectively marginalized this critique throughout the late thirties and the war years, its potential was enormous if the political context itself shifted back to greater ideological and class confrontation in the wake of the war.

Some historians have argued that the Popular Front was strictly a tactical proposition and represented no fundamental change in the essence of the American Communist Party, which remained essentially an instrument of Soviet policy.[52] Foster, however, saw the Popular Front as a major departure that might permanently transform the very nature of the Party. The subsequent history of the organization suggests he was right.

The experience with the so-called influentials in the trade union movement represents an example of what worried Foster. These were Communists who maintained a discreet distance from the Party and whose membership remained a personal matter so long as they functioned as leaders in major unions. The liquidation of Party fractions and shop papers in the CIO and elsewhere in 1938; the rise of many of these "influentials" to leadership positions in international unions and the CIO itself; and their political alliances with non-Party elements all accentuated the distance between these members and the Party. Historians concerned to show continuing Communist intrigue in the labor movement have noted secret meetings with and directives from top Party leadership, but often these meetings took place precisely because influentials were resisting Party policies. When pressed, some followed the line, often with disastrous consequences; others continued to drag their feet or even to ignore the directives; and still others left the Party entirely and in some cases turned against it. "During the crucial organizational periods, in the turmoil of directing strikes and fighting other factions for control," Harvey Levenstein wrote, "the directives of the party leadership were often simply ignored . . . so swept up did party members become in union affairs that it was difficult for them to perform any party functions at all."53

The heavy turnover in Party membership, particularly during the Popular Front years, was partly because of friction between on the one hand, broad, mass work, with its diverse political alliances, practical issues, and flexible methods, and on the other, efforts to maintain the Party as a centralized, disciplined, Marxist-Leninist vanguard. The Party clearly aimed to put its mark on its Popular Front organizations and the reform movements it sought to lead, but there was always the danger that the opposite would occur: that Communist activists, particularly those who were new to the Party, would come to see their trade union, or antifascist, or electoral work as their prime focus and the Party, with its notorious reputation and revolutionary trappings, as an impediment to success in these crucial efforts. There was some danger that such activists would become, in a word, "reformist" and either leave the Party—as so many did—or remain to transform it into a much more moderate organization, as some tried to do in the mid-fifties. While Browder hitched his wagon to the Popular Front star, Foster spoke rather consistently for those who feared this reformist threat.

Even during the Popular Front of the late thirties and the war years, Foster occasionally advanced this view, though it was muted by the fascist threat, which provided the rationale for the new policy; by the Party's success in membership and influence; and by the international line, which favored Browder's perspective and policies. But if and when the Party turned back

toward a more revolutionary line and orthodox methods, it would be difficult for even some of the most trusted cadres to return to Foster's perspective.
In the crisis following World War II, it turned out that Foster's fears were
justified in the sense that the Popular Front had indeed transformed the Party
and much of its membership.

Many of Foster's conflicts with Browder came in private or in Moscow,
beyond the eyes of the rank and file. Even other American leaders, while they
were undoubtedly aware of the friction, may not have understood the depths
of Foster's hostility. The storm broke closer to the surface at a closed March
1939 Political Committee meeting, for which we have an unusual verbatim
transcript. Browder noted Foster's "very strong disagreement" with some aspects of the Party's work and suggested that "more or less the same problems"
had surfaced several times in the past. Confident of his own control, Browder
was flushing Foster out into the open to crush his opposition. Foster took the
bait, complaining bitterly that "the Party was [not] making the best use of my
services." In a very revealing statement of his grievances, he spoke of the
frustration he had been feeling since his illness, which kept him from the
work he most valued.

> . . . I am by no means working at one hundred per cent . . . ever since I had
> anything to do with the labor movement and the revolutionary movement, I
> always had a natural inclination towards mass organizational work . . . practi-
> cal organizational work. And while I was laid up sick, it was the real grief to me
> that here during the years when the Party had only a limited opportunity to
> carry on active mass work, . . . I was able to function, but as soon as the situa-
> tion broke in such a manner that the masses got into action, where I always
> figured I could function the best, here I had to be laid upon my back, unable to
> do anything, and I will assure you that was a pretty bitter thought for me. . . . I
> slowly began to limp back into the work and naturally my inclination turned
> right towards practical steps of mass organizational work . . . where my most
> fundamental experience is, the thing that I turn to most naturally as a worker
> in the movement. . . . I haven't sat so easy. . . . I made pretty sharp complaints.

But since that time, Foster complained, "practically every proposal of any
importance that I made . . . was voted down." On a recent trip to the Soviet
Union, Browder had accused him of "wavering from the main line of the
Party" and had suggested that he had little to offer as Party chair in terms of
"practical work." In the context of the Comintern, these were very serious
criticisms. Browder opposed his every initiative, and the reason, Foster believed, was Browder's personal animosity toward him.[54]

Other speakers denied that Foster had been ignored, but he was able to cite numerous instances when he had vocally opposed Browder's position and failed to get a hearing. During the Spanish Civil War, he had urged the Party to push for American intervention on the side of the Republic, but Browder had held firmly to the concept of nonintervention. Foster also unsuccessfully opposed Browder's concept of a "Sit-down Strike of Capital," an analysis that he felt lent uncritical support to Roosevelt's administration. He had protested Browder's ouster of Sam Darcy, perhaps the only other vocal Browder opponent, from the National Committee, but the leadership once again ignored him and backed Browder.

Frustrated by his health problems, Foster yearned for greater responsibility but seemed to be hemmed in at every turn. His tone seemed sad, almost pathetic. He sensed that the movement he had helped create was leaving him behind. "I am something of a veteran in the Comintern. . . . I think that EB [Earl Browder] has got to take the padlock from my hands," Foster pleaded. But there was still a note of bitter resentment: "I don't think he has to watch me at all, no more than he was watched after he made serious mistakes in the Comintern."[55]

In response, Browder was fairly quiet. Knowing that he retained the committee's support, he had forced Foster to bring their continuing conflicts before the collective leadership, which now proceeded to thrash him. One after another the committee members supported Browder. Roy Hudson, who directed the Party's union work, told Foster he had "the closest thing to a persecution complex of anybody I ever saw." Robert Minor suggested that Foster's illness had affected his mental faculties. Eugene Dennis accused Foster, not Browder, of injecting personal feelings into Party affairs. He insisted that all of the disagreements Foster had described were essentially political and that they must be straightened out by the Political Committee. Except for rather vague promises to better "integrate" Foster and take advantage of his vast experience, no action was taken on his complaints.[56]

By the end of the meeting, Foster's lack of confidence resurfaced, and he retreated, criticizing himself: "I want to say that I recognize one hundred percent that EB is the leader of this Party. He is the outstanding leader, the number one leader. It is our task to build his prestige among the masses and in every way to strengthen his hands. . . . As far as me being a leader of the Party, I have no such ambitions. . . . I think my outstanding weakness is a lack of theoretical growth. . . . I have been a practical worker and I have neglected to pay enough attention to this. . . . I don't know as I am the easiest guy to work around." He concluded, "I don't think I am in any shape to do any considerable executive work."[57]

Foster obviously had genuine political reservations about the direction

Browder was taking the Party, which were duly registered by the Comintern leadership, but he also resented Browder's leadership on a more personal level. Such confrontations must have been not only frustrating but also deeply humiliating. For nearly a decade, Browder had been thought of as Foster's "clerk," his "man Friday," or, at best, his protege. Now Foster was the subordinate in a political world very different from the one that had shaped his ideas and values. As the political scientist and former Communist Joseph Starobin wrote, "Foster had been outdistanced by his junior, and felt this lapse in status keenly."[58]

In August 1939, foreign policy issues provided the source for yet another confrontation between Browder and Foster when the Soviet Union signed a nonaggression treaty with Nazi Germany. The following month, shortly after the Nazis invaded Poland from the west, the Soviets invaded from the east, occupying the Baltic nations and part of Poland. When Great Britain and France finally abandoned their strategy of appeasement and confronted Hitler by declaring war in September 1939, the Soviets held firm to their treaty with the Nazis and denounced the war as imperialist.

The Hitler-Stalin Pact staggered the Party, creating severe disaffection in several of its constituencies, particularly among intellectuals. Jewish members were greeted on the streets of New York's garment district with cries of "Heil Hitler!" By 1940, the position had produced anti-Communist sanctions and agitation in the mass organizations that represented the lifeblood of the Popular Front. Unions and other voluntary organizations passed "Communazi" resolutions, outlawing membership in either group; mobs attacked Communists on the street; some CIO organizations purged Party members from their staffs; HUAC launched another series of investigations into subversive activities. Although the Hitler-Stalin Pact seems not to have contributed much to anticommunism among rank-and-file workers, it helped provide the basis for CIO factional conflicts that eventually undermined the Party's position in the labor movement.[59]

Neither Foster nor Browder opposed the Hitler-Stalin Pact, but the new line, with its more militant rhetoric and a quasi-syndicalist emphasis on broadening economic struggles into political ones, brought Foster back into his element and made him a more formidable opponent. He and Browder clashed immediately over the issue of American neutrality. Browder briefly tried to walk a fine line between the old antifascist policy and the new one of opposition to the war, while Foster, who may actually have anticipated the pact, vigorously condemned the "imperialist war" and called for strict neutrality. At a September 14, 1939, Political Committee meeting, Foster and Alexander Bittelman, now on firmer ideological ground because of the Soviet position, argued that the Party should resume the offensive, formally changing its goal from "peace" to "socialism." Bittelman eventually withdrew his motion, but the Party's October 1939 manifesto on the war crisis suggests that Foster's and Bittelman's arguments had some effect. Sharp clashes continued at Political Committee meetings during the fall of 1939, though none of this was apparent to the membership.[60]

The ambiguity of Foster's new situation was underscored at a celebration of his sixtieth birthday, which drew 18,000 Party members and other admirers to Madison Square Garden on St. Patrick's Day, March 17, 1941. Foster's symbolic importance and genuine popularity were apparent. The evening included testimonials from labor organizers as well as such prominent radical intellectuals as the writers Richard Wright and Theodore Dreiser, who called Foster a saint—"my first and only contact with one." From a stage covered with flowers and gifts, the black baritone Paul Robeson sang the Bill of Rights, Russian and German folk songs, and "The Purest Kind of Guy" from Marc Blitzstein's labor operetta *No for an Answer.* Browder spoke at length about Foster's reputation, and a left-wing theater group performed *One of Us,* an original play based on Foster's contributions to the labor movement. But the evening also served to launch a new "Free Earl Browder" campaign. Convicted of a passport violation, Browder was about to enter prison, and Foster was forced to share the spotlight with him.[61]

When Browder entered federal prison in Atlanta for a year in March 1941 to serve his sentence for passport violations, it was not Foster but Robert Minor, a far less distinguished but more loyal Party functionary, who assumed leadership. Foster recommended Gil Green for the temporary position, but Green thought he lacked the experience to take over, while Foster himself would not accept the job for health reasons. Foster's influence, however, increased during 1940 and 1941, first with the new, more aggressive line occasioned by the Hitler-Stalin Pact and then with Browder's imprisonment. A confidential 1941 Comintern memo, in observing that Foster had been "very reliable and loyal to the CI [Communist International]," noted that he had been "first to take new position on international situation [the war]." The Party vigorously attacked Roosevelt, and Foster pronounced Browder's collaboration with New Deal forces a failure.[62]

In his *Daily Worker* columns and a series of pamphlets, Foster condemned any American effort to support the Allies. "The war between the Allies and Germany," he wrote, "is a struggle between rival imperialist powers for the mastery of the world; hence the workers have no interest in supporting either side in the contest. . . . There is no reason to suppose that the Allies in victory would be more just or democratic than Germany would." The Popular Front's antifascist and peace campaigns had been important. "Now, however, with the beginning of war between the Allies and Germany, the former distinction between the 'democracies' and the fascist countries has lost its significance." The cure for war, Foster concluded, was socialism.[63]

The new line facilitated a renewed militancy among Party activists in the CIO and what Maurice Isserman called "an ideological mood resembling syndicalism." Concentrating on economic issues and building strikes around such issues would help draw workers into the peace movement, Foster argued at the end of 1940: "economic questions relating to the living standards of the people . . . are the main starting point in the struggle for peace." The Communists backed a large strike wave in defense plants during the first half of the following year, including disputes at Vultee Aircraft and North American Aviation in California, as well as new organizing drives at Ford and elsewhere.[64]

These industrial conflicts represented familiar terrain for Foster, who also led the Party's campaign against war preparations. No one embraced the critique of "imperialist war" more firmly. "The fight to keep America out of the war is of historic importance," Foster wrote in June 1940. He called the interventionist lobby, which included many liberals and labor activists, "warmongers." A year later, he was still publicly equating the British and American governments with Hitler's.[65]

With Hitler's invasion of the Soviet Union on June 22, 1941, however, Foster and the Communist Party found a new appreciation for American "warmongers." Speaking at the Chicago Stadium in August 1941, Foster noted that "one step after another, they [the American people had] endorsed lifting the arms embargo, the Lend-Lease bill, conscription, use of navy patrols, the transfer of service planes and ships to Great Britain, and many other increasingly vigorous measures." He and the Party now supported all of this and much more—indeed, any action that might speed the destruction of the Nazi war machine. One Comintern memo actually criticized the American Party for making too abrupt a turn and failing to allow time to educate Americans on the new line on the war. Another singled out Foster for his pro-Soviet hyperbole and his failure to explain adequately Soviet war aims in terms of workers' own interests.[66]

The invasion had dramatically transformed the Party's attitude toward the war and, in the short run, muted the conflict between Foster and Browder. It led to an alliance between the Soviet Union and the western democracies in what the Comintern now termed a "just war of defense." The new alliance permitted, to use Perry Anderson's phrase, "a unique fusion of international and national causes on the left." "Hitler's attack upon the Soviet

Union changes the character of the world war," Foster observed, speaking before an emergency meeting of the Party's National Committee a few days after the German invasion, "and thereby makes necessary changes in our Party's attitude toward that war. Previously the war had been a struggle between the rival imperialist power groupings. . . . We correctly did not take sides. . . . But now, with Hitler's war against the Soviet Union, the whole situation is basically altered."[67]

After Browder's release from prison in 1942, both he and Foster spent the rest of the year explaining the nature of the war to the Party membership and pressing for a second front to defend the Soviet Union and defeat the Nazis. Because of his reputation, Foster was particularly important to the Party's industrial policy during the war, which emphasized industrial peace, labor-management cooperation, and high productivity. The center piece of this policy was the no-strike pledge. In his 1949 Smith Act deposition, Foster proudly recalled that the Party had "enforced this pledge perhaps more rigidly and more firmly than any organization in the United States." He wrote a long series of *Daily Worker* columns entitled "The Unions and the War." For more than a year, his question-and-answer column responded to members' concerns about war policy. Always in Browder's shadow in the Party hierarchy, Foster remained an important symbol of the Communist contribution to the war effort, especially among Party labor activists. In the midst of the 1943 UMWA strike, he addressed a Pittsburgh meeting of 150 Party labor militants, apparently as part of a speaking tour aimed at defusing the strike. Labeling Lewis a "man who wants fascism in this country," Foster denounced the strike and appealed for a new Party membership drive to counter Lewis's sinister influence. Foster relished the opportunity to indulge his old hatred of Lewis, whom he accused of anti-Semitism, red-baiting, and racism as well as sabotage of the war effort.[68]

As the war progressed, Browder's increasingly expansive interpretation of the Democratic Front tested Foster's loyalty. As early as 1942, Browder was probing beyond the official line. His formulations represented a remarkable departure in American Communist thinking. But his efforts to forge a new conception of Communist politics on the basis of the wartime experience also led to the final conflict between the two major figures in the Party's history, to Browder's political demise, and to Foster's final, untimely ascendance.

The earliest indications of Browder's optimistic vision for the postwar order came in *Victory and After,* published shortly after his release from the Atlanta penitentiary in May 1942. As Maurice Isserman observed, the pamphlet was "a frank justification of the case for class collaboration during the war—and, as the title suggested, in the postwar era as well." This was a notion that was bound to draw Foster's fire eventually. Browder further developed his analysis and projected his postwar vision at the beginning of 1944 in the most important work of his career, *Teheran and America*.[69]

In part, Browder's new thinking was the product of world events and the domestic political situation. In November 1943, Stalin, Churchill, and Roosevelt met at Teheran to reaffirm their wartime alliance but also to project a postwar reconstruction based on cooperation and mutual respect. Browder saw the agreement as a dramatic turning point in the history of both international politics and domestic class relations—in fact, "the greatest, most important turning point in history." "Capitalism and Socialism," he concluded, "have begun to find the way to peaceful coexistence and collaboration in the same world." To help ensure a peaceful international and domestic social order, Browder argued, Communists "must help to remove from the American ruling class the fear of a socialist revolution in the post-war period." The Communist Party was publicly abandoning the goal of socialism for the foreseeable future. For good measure, he said he would shake hands with the (long dead) millionaire banker J. P. Morgan if that would advance the cause of Soviet-American cooperation. It soon became clear that Browder's small gesture regarding the handshake had real symbolic significance for Foster, who retained his deep hatred of the system Morgan represented.[70]

Browder's ideas also derived from the Party's own transformation in the course of its Popular Front odyssey and from Browder's driving ambition and his deep desire for acceptance, which, as Johanningsmeier observed, "melded with the needs and desires of a whole generation of Communists who had come into the Party during its 'heyday' " and "were dissatisfied with the old, conspiratorial sectarian style of Communist politics, and yearned for a measure of acceptance and legitimacy." "Teheran," as Isserman noted, "finally gave Browder the confidence he needed to take that dramatic historical leap which, he hoped, would bring him and the party all the way to the public acceptance and influence he wanted so badly."[71]

Browder spoke emphatically about the prospects for long-term cooperation not only between the Soviet Union and the United States but also between the Communist Party and the big capitalists. The American political scientist Barrington Moore observed at the time, "In this fashion the party has recently completed a full circle in its official ideology, swinging from open advocacy of violent revolution in the United States to strong support for the capitalist system."[72]

Although Foster heralded the Soviet victory over the Nazis on the eastern front as "one of the greatest (if it is not the greatest) military achievements in all the annals of war," his evolving vision of the postwar prospects stood in stark contrast to Browder's. As early as March 1941, he saw the war unleashing a postwar revolutionary cataclysm. At about the same time Browder was outlining his vision of peaceful coexistence in December 1943, Foster described a resurgent right-wing Republicanism in Congress, new attacks on the labor movement, and the reversal of New Deal legislation—political expressions of a "rampant American imperialism" that would confront Soviet power "and sow seeds for World War III." In early 1944, evidence for Foster's formulation was just below the surface of wartime solidarity: a spirited, conservative Republican opposition to Roosevelt's policies in the 1944 election, antilabor legislation in Congress, factionalism in the labor movement over the no-strike pledge and other issues, and a reassertion of management prerogatives on the shop floor and in the society at large. In the face of this onslaught, Foster's postwar projections included a much more militant program than Browder's: merger of the AFL and CIO, renewed industrial organizing, greater political mobilization, expansion of social welfare programs and public works, and the nationalization of the banks and basic industry.[73]

However abrupt and even naive Browder's shift appears in retrospect, in 1943–44 he was in closer step with both contemporary international and domestic events as well as with current thinking in the Soviet Union than was Foster. As Geoff Eley noted, "Most of the European CP's experienced a dramatic surge of creativity. . . . The exceptional circumstances of war and the conditions of an effective antifascist resistance loosened the tightly drawn bonds of Moscow-oriented conformity long enough for certain independent departures to occur." In May 1943, when the Communist International dissolved itself in the interests of solidifying the Grand Alliance, American writers and politicians called on the CPUSA to follow suit in the interests of domestic wartime solidarity. The Party systematically shifted members from shop branches to larger, more public neighborhood branches, and in October 1943 Young Communist League delegates voted to disband their organization entirely. The Allies' firm statement of continued cooperation at Teheran, the prospects for a second front in the West, and the Soviet defeat of the German offensive in the East all encouraged optimistic views of the prospects for peace and postwar progress. Browder's ideas were endorsed by Dimitrov, the Italian and French Party leaders Palmiro Togliatti and Andre Marty, and, by implication at least, Stalin himself. Browder took such acquiescence as a sign that the American Party was "standing on its own feet for the first time."[74]

As a next logical next step, Browder proposed at an enlarged January 7, 1944, meeting of the Party's National Committee to dissolve the Communist Party. He would replace it with the Communist Political Association (CPA), which would simply work in coalition with other organizations. The association aimed "to secure to its membership adequate information, education and organized participation in the political life of our country in cooperation with other Americans for the advancement and protection of the interests of the nation and its people." As Barrington Moore observed at the time, Browder was transforming the Party from a revolutionary organization into a "pressure group." A Communist presence—in the unions, labor parties, and other mass organizations—was vital to the war effort, Browder reasoned, but a Communist party might inhibit the national unity essential to the postwar domestic and international peace. Isserman noted that Browder's sweeping proposal "repudiated much of the party's traditional outlook without solving any of the problems the Communists had long faced," notably their perennial isolation from the political mainstream. Remarkably, there was no opposition whatever to this stunning change of course, possibly because of the public character of the meeting to which Browder had invited more than a hundred guests. Open opposition in this setting would have caused considerable embarrassment and would, in fact, have represented a breach of Party discipline.[75]

This was too much for Foster. Clearly troubled for some time over the direction of Browder's thinking, he was galvanized by the sweeping implications of the Teheran speech and the prospect of the Party's dissolution. At a closed National Committee meeting prior to the January 7 public event, he alone voted against Browder's proposal. He had also been prepared to speak against Browder at the public meeting but was dissuaded from doing so by other members of the Political Committee, who feared the effects of such an open confrontation. They promised a full discussion of the issue, and Foster relented. In the meantime, just days after he had presented Browder's only opposition, Foster was delegated to introduce and explain the new line on a national radio hook-up. Sam Darcy, who was perhaps closest to him at this time, suggested the sort of pressure Foster was under. He wavered repeatedly about whether to confront Browder. "He complained that I was pressing him too hard; that he couldn't sleep even with pills; that he was afraid of another breakdown," Darcy recalled.[76]

While Browder had emerged from prison full of even more confidence in himself than he had when he entered, Foster was still showing signs of insecurity. But by the third week in January, when it became clear that there would be no critical discussion of the proposals unless he spoke up, Foster launched his attack. He addressed a seventeen-page letter to each member of the Party's National Committee, locating seven "serious errors of an important nature" and emphasizing the decisive theoretical and political turn represented by Browder's thinking.[77]

Most of Browder's errors derived not from particular aspects of his analysis, Foster argued, but from its very basis—the projection of a postwar economic boom that would provide the material foundation for maintaining the alliance that the capitalist powers and the Soviet Union had forged in the heat of battle. On the contrary, Foster maintained, the end of hostilities would bring depression, domestic political reaction, imperialist expansion, and the threat of war between the United States and the Soviet Union, problems that were "insoluble under capitalism." Likewise, Browder's whole notion of the Democratic Front was flawed. The layer of "intelligent capitalists" representing some of the largest corporations in the country, who Browder thought would continue to support the New Deal and the Grand Alliance, would instead attack the coalition of workers, farmers, and small businesspeople who had achieved the New Deal reforms and were winning the war. Recognition of this harsh reality had profound policy implications, Foster argued. The Party would need to abandon, not extend, the no-strike pledge and be prepared to fight in the immediate postwar period. While he agreed that victory, not socialism, was the immediate issue, he urged more discussion of socialism as an ultimate goal. Finally, in a bid to expand support for his critique, he called for a full discussion before the Party membership. "I for one am convinced," he concluded, "that if we give this attention to Comrade Browder's report, adopted by the National Committee, we will find it necessary to alter [it] in the general sense of the several points raised in this letter." Foster had focused primarily on what he saw as Browder's revisionist analysis of the postwar order, but the Party's dissolution undoubtedly had great symbolic importance for him, accentuating his aversion to Browder's abrupt decision.[78]

In an effort to save the Party from what he saw as a disastrous course, Foster now climbed out on a limb. Gambling that others on the National Board would support his position or at least the notion of a full discussion among Party members, he confronted Browder directly by circulating the letter to the members of the Political Committee. Foster's action showed great political courage; he had reason to feel insecure. A discussion of the letter at an enlarged Political Committee meeting on February 8, 1944, demonstrated the depth and breadth of Browder's support and the weakness of Foster's. Browder allowed Foster to summarize the letter, after which Foster was assailed unmercifully from all sides. Morris Childs, the Illinois Party chairman, called the letter "an insult to the Party membership." Gil Green called Foster's performance "tragic" because it indicated the effects of his isolation from the Party's mass work. There could be no compromise on the differences between Browder and Foster, Green said, leaving no uncertainty about where he stood.[79]

Except for Sam Darcy, Philadelphia's inveterate left-wing organizer and an old friend, Foster stood alone. One after another, each member of the National Committee rose to Browder's defense. Isolated and under blistering attack, Foster at first refused to retreat. He emphasized what he saw as Browder's basic error—the notion that "decisive sections of finance capital . . . are now, particularly since Teheran, playing a progressive role and can be, must be, therefore, included in the national unity that is supporting Teheran." This showed excessive optimism, Foster said, which would have tragic consequences.[80]

Eugene Dennis, a key member of the Party's National Board, called Foster's position "confused, nondialectical, and anti-Marxist." "Comrade Foster has become, consciously or unconsciously the victim of a factional approach," Dennis declared. "Comrade Foster has no faith in, and no confidence in, Comrade Browder or in the National Committee. . . . Comrade Foster has raised on a number of occasions . . . doubts about the leadership of our Party and particularly Comrade Browder. . . . Comrade Foster does not accept nor understand that Comrade Browder is the foremost, the outstanding leader of our Party. . . . And there is also the danger that Comrade Foster . . . may destroy his own prestige and usefulness in and to the Party."[81]

In his own response, Browder alternated between sneering condescension and direct threats. Foster was "tragically confused; I think he has lost his way. The world has become too complex for him," Browder declared. Then, lest there be any ambiguity in the thrust of Dennis's remarks, Browder let Foster know what was at stake: "Anyone who goes out to combat before our Party the line that we have presented in our National Committee is taking the line of struggle against our movement; he is standing in front of an army moving into battle." Widening the debate to include the Party rank and file, Browder suggested, would be viewed as a move toward factional struggle, a grounds for expulsion. Any leak of information concerning Foster's opposition, he warned, would greatly weaken the Party. In the subsequent vote, every member present rejected Foster's critique except Foster himself and Darcy.[82]

Browder's concern that the disagreement might leak out was well founded. While the Communist leadership discussed Foster's arguments, FBI agents sat next door to Party headquarters, patiently taping the meeting with a sophisticated listening device. They leaked news of the Browder-Foster confrontation to the *New York World Telegram,* which printed a version of the story a month after the National Board meeting. Foster still placed the Party's image above principle; he immediately issued a statement denying any opposition to Browder's line.[83]

The leak and Browder's threats probably discouraged Foster from any public opposition, but Soviet intervention was also a factor in the dispute. At Foster's behest, Browder conveyed the text of the letter, a shorter appeal drafted by Foster, and the minutes of the two crucial meetings to Moscow. That the Comintern no longer existed, at least not on paper, did nothing to dissuade Foster from his appeal. He summarized his letter, objecting to a continuation of the no-strike pledge and Browder's "serious underestimation of the danger of American imperialism." In reply, Dimitrov asked Browder whether he was "not going too far . . . to the point of denying the theory and practice of class struggle . . . ?" He asked Browder "to reconsider all this," but in the end the Soviets continued to back Browder.[84]

As Harvey Klehr and his collaborators noted, "Had Foster seen Dimitrov's cable, he would never have agreed to stifle his objections." Instead of showing Foster the cable, however, Browder sent Gil Green to Foster's Bronx apartment with the message that Dimitrov simply had advised Foster to withdraw his objections. In a word, Browder lied.[85]

Foster's choices were now clear. He could pursue his struggle on a factional basis, risking expulsion and a split in the Party, or he could concede in the name of discipline. Since the leadership overwhelmingly opposed him and the international line supported Browder, this was really no choice at all for Foster. He confined his opposition to the National Board. His letter attacking Browder's line was suppressed for the next seventeen months.[86]

Sam Darcy's fate suggests not only Browder's strength but also Browder's determination to humiliate Foster. Later that spring, Darcy, one of the few people in the Party who might be characterized as a close personal friend of Foster, was accused of factional activity. When a special commission convened to hear his case, Browder appointed Foster to chair it. Darcy later claimed that Foster tearfully urged him to capitulate and asked forgiveness for what he was being forced to do. The Party expelled Darcy, a talented and experienced organizer who had devoted all of his adult life to the cause. Because of the rank and file's continuing loyalty to Foster, it would have been difficult for Browder to have moved directly against him in this fashion, but Darcy's trial sent Foster a clear message. Browder had forced him to oversee his closest ally's political destruction. As Joseph Starobin notes, "Although Browder attempted in both 1944 and 1945 to place the issue on the level of strategy and theory, his contempt for Foster was obvious."[87]

Browder's bold stance had personal as well as broader political implications for Foster. The Party's demise and the rise of the new Communist Political Association stripped Foster of his role as Party chair; he was simply one of fourteen *vice presidents* in the new organization. His articles in *Political Affairs* and columns in the *Daily Worker* appeared far less regularly. At the beginning of 1945, Foster submitted a lengthy article for publication in the Party's theoretical journal. In it, he tried to reconcile his own position with Browder's Teheran analysis, making important concessions in the process. He still believed, however, that the fate of domestic peace lay in "the relations between workers and employers." This was Foster's effort to make his peace without utterly abandoning his own perspective. Browder scribbled critical comments throughout the manuscript, which the journal then rejected. From early 1944 through the spring of 1945, Foster was effectively silenced.[88]

Throughout most of 1944, the international and domestic situation favored Browder's vision of the postwar order. Teheran was followed in early 1944 by the Yalta Conference, where Roosevelt, Churchill, and Stalin laid firm foundations for a continuation of the wartime alliance.

But just at the moment when Browder seemed invincible, international affairs intervened once again, this time on Foster's side. Given Browder's widespread support within the Party and even within the international movement, the manner and speed of his demise were truly remarkable. This reversal indicates again the strength of Soviet influence in the American movement, but the speed and force of Browder's fall owe something to the domestic history of the Party as well. Browder's new line and the Party's dissolution were fundamental changes, yet neither move was discussed by the membership, as Foster had suggested. Rather, the changes were handed down from Browder to the National Board, from there to the National Committee, and from there to the membership through speeches and articles. Many among the rank and file probably never really understood the changes, and those who apparently resented them had no occasion to discuss any of this. Browder had suppressed debate even at the highest reaches of Party leadership. With the exceptions of Foster and Darcy, anyone who might have had reservations (and many claimed them after Browder's fall) was afraid to speak up—and with good reason. Browder had ruled the Party with a firm hand for a decade. "His word," the National Board later admitted, "virtually became law in the Party." As the story of his reconfiguration of the movement emerged, rank-and-file members were incensed by Browder's systematic repression of Foster's criticisms.[89] There were others besides Foster with resentments against Browder, and when the time came, they welcomed the opportunity to settle scores.

Foster undoubtedly played the key role in Browder's downfall, and when the Party made its reversion to an orthodox version of Marxism-Leninism, it was he who emerged as its spokesman. Yet, as in so many previous turning points in the Party's history, the decisive initiative came from abroad. In this case, what one veteran Communist has called the "thunderbolt" that struck down Browder and transformed the Party line was launched from France, though the inspiration undoubtedly derived from thinking in the Soviet Union.[90]

In April 1945, *Cahiers du communisme,* the theoretical journal of the French Communist Party, published a letter criticizing Browder's Teheran initiatives. The first English translation of the letter appeared in the *New York World Telegram* on May 22, 1945, and it was published in the *Daily Worker* two days later, along with an introduction by Browder. Although published as a letter written by Jacques Duclos, a top French Party leader, and addressed to the members of the French Communist Party, the letter's analysis, timing, and detailed information all suggested that it conveyed the thinking of the Soviet Party leaders. In the context of the expanding cold war, Soviet leaders directed it as much to American policymakers as to the CPUSA. Although Soviet authorship has been established only recently, American Communist leaders interpreted it at the time as Soviet intervention in the dispute between Foster and Browder. They soon swung 180 degrees around to attack Browder for what the Duclos letter called his "notorious revisionism," a phrase that was repeated by Foster and others in attacks on Browder. In Duclos's letter, Isserman pointed out, "Foster found the weapon he needed to bring his hated rival down." The Duclos letter not only attacked Browder but also praised Foster as the lone hold-out against revisionism and quoted at length from Foster's January 1944 letter. The Duclos letter, in effect, signaled a Soviet preference for Foster as the new Party leader.[91]

At first confused, the American Communist leaders soon turned on Browder for what they now suddenly recognized as his opportunism. Browder undoubtedly weakened his own position by refusing to defend himself or even to engage other leaders in discussion of his ideas. His fate may have been preordained by the tone and contents of the Duclos letter, but his haughty stance during the crisis irritated other leaders and facilitated his demise. "I get the impression that most comrades are not thinking," he lectured the National Board, "they are making demonstrations of faith, and when thinking breaks down, perhaps that is the best substitute. But my mind insists upon continuing to work and I ask questions." Foster and several others urged him to reconsider his position and think of what it meant for his leadership. Browder responded, "I am not at all concerned with the question of what is going to be my position in the future." To which Foster responded, "But we are, Earl."[92]

Browder refused to take part in discussions of the crisis at the June 1945 National Committee meetings, which included important trade union leaders as well as the committee members. After a two-hour speech defending virtually all of his positions, Browder retired to his office on the ninth floor of the CPA's headquarters, while the committee met on the fifth floor of the building, debating the Party's future and his own. Steve Nelson, chairing one of the committee's sessions, noted Browder's absence and remarked that the Party should never again give a leader "that much elbow room." "And that includes you too, Bill," said Nelson turning to Foster who responded, "You don't have to worry about me, Steve. I'm not like him." Nelson was not so sure.[93]

The reversal of fortunes was breathtaking. As late as May 1945, the CPA's Central Committee had enthusiastically declared its allegiance to Browder and bitterly criticized Foster. Even Foster was a bit disoriented by the rapid turn of events. At its May 22, 1945, meeting, he urged the National Board to cable the Soviets insisting "that the main line has been correct but we have made serious errors in it"—nineteen of them by Foster's count.[94] But by the end of an emergency national convention in July, Browder was out, the Party was reconstituted, and Foster was reinstated as chairman. Browder finally put up a defense, but this only prolonged the inevitable.

Foster's eventual showdown with Browder at the July emergency convention was framed in rhetoric that captured the strength and weaknesses of the public images each man had long projected within the Party—Foster the mass leader and man of action, Browder the master theoretician. Foster attacked Browder for his "reverence for the spoken word." "He is a talker, not a mass fighter," Foster argued. "He has had very little experience in, or understanding of, the need to back up his word with action. Especially in recent years has this trend become manifest. . . . He eventually got to the point where he seemed to think that all that was necessary . . . was for him to make a speech, for the Party to scatter huge quantities of it throughout the country and all would be well."[95]

In his rebuttal, Browder invoked Foster's oft-noted intellectual and theoretical weakness. "The strangest result of the [draft conference] resolution is to bring forward Comrade Foster as the foremost Marxist. Whatever his qualities in other respects, it is well known to all who have had extended collaboration with Comrade Foster that he has never understood Marxism, that this is not his strong side. Comrade Foster is an eclectic, subject to all sorts of theoretical influences . . . he is by character irresolute and wavering on principle."[96]

Rank-and-file members now attacked the collective leadership that had loyally followed Browder and had kept the conflicts with Foster under wraps. This, the National Board explained, had occurred because of Browder's undemocratic leadership style. It apologized for the "impermissible deluge of adulation" it had regularly bestowed on Browder—and then heaped adulation on Foster. The atmosphere reminded Dorothy Healey, a veteran activist and Los Angeles district leader, of "what happens in a chicken yard when a hen gets hurt and all the other chickens start pecking at it." Browder was finished. The National Committee quickly excluded him from the leadership and then his local branch expelled him in early 1946.[97]

In his speech before the July 1945 emergency convention that reconstituted the Party and elected him chair, Foster announced a decisive break with Browder's "chronic tailism," his "hiding the Party's face and avoidance of mass struggle." The Party "refreshed" its leadership with new faces from the unions and other mass organizations and prepared to assert itself more in the coming postwar conflicts. New delegates also elected a new secretariat, consisting of Foster; Eugene Dennis; John Williamson, the director of trade union activity; and Robert Thompson, a close Foster ally. Foster's reconstitution of the Party on the basis of orthodox Marxism-Leninism was hailed in the Soviet press, and his speeches were recorded and registered in his Comintern file.[98]

Browder's subsequent story is a rather dismal tale. He failed first as an independent political analyst publishing his own newsletter and then as a representative for the official Soviet state publishing house. Nor could he live down his political past and become a professional anti-Communist, a common career path during the Red Scare. For all of his revisionism, in his heart, Browder was still a Communist. While the specter of "Browderism" haunted Foster and other leaders, precipitating a wave of repression within the Party, Browder wished only to return to the fold. He informally pleaded his case in the Soviet Union in the spring of 1946 and received a courteous hearing but no satisfaction. In 1948, at the time of Tito's break with Stalin, Browder formally appealed his expulsion to the CPUSA and was firmly rejected. During the fifties, he served as a paid consultant to the Fund for the Republic's series, *Communism in American Life*.[99] But Browder never recovered from his expulsion, and he died a broken man. How could he have fallen so far so fast?

The most important factor in Browder's demise and Foster's return to power was not new. The Party's history had been shaped over and over not by Soviet dictates alone but by the dynamic between Soviet influence and various "Americanizing" initiatives, based partly on domestic factors. The Popular Front policies and their logical extension in the form of Browder's Teheran theories might be viewed as a manifestation of this dynamic. Soviet influence may have been decisive in the end, but to leave the explanation there ignores important changes in the postwar world that help explain both the direction of this influence and the realignment of the Party itself toward a more confrontational, orthodox form of Marxism-Leninism.

As late as spring 1945, it might still have been possible to sustain Browder's optimistic projections for the postwar world, but over the spring and summer, both the American and Soviet governments took much more aggressive stances so that the promising atmosphere of Teheran and Yalta crystallized rather quickly into the confrontation at Potsdam and eventually into the cold war. The first few months after the end of the war in August 1945 brought economic dislocation and serious industrial conflict that lasted through most of 1946. In the longer term, there was an economic boom, as Browder had predicted, but there was also an employers' counteroffensive and a more general attack on civil liberties and the Left in the form of the Taft-Hatley Act and other antilabor legislation. Various government and private investigations of alleged subversion led to jailings, deportations, and blacklisting. Foster was wrong in assuming that this represented anything like fascism, but in some respects his catastrophic vision of the postwar order was at least as realistic as Browder's prophesy of peaceful coexistence, class harmony, and political enlightenment.[100]

This particular conflict was not simply a struggle against "Browderism," then, but another example of the ongoing tension between the two dynamic elements in the history of the Communist Party and in Foster's own political experience: on the one hand, the genuine radical impulses generated by social conflict in the United States and, on the other, the exigencies of international Communist politics, particularly the policy interests of the Soviet Union. The idea of creating a distinctively American socialist movement did not fade away with Browder. Less than a decade later, a new crisis raised some of the same issues Browder had. The resulting reform movement went considerably beyond Browder's vision for the Communist Party and its future in the United States. It was within this context that Foster fought the last great struggle of his political life.

11 Five Minutes to Midnight, 1945–56

DENIED THE LEADERSHIP he had pursued throughout his life, William Z. Foster achieved it just in time to oversee his movement's destruction. His reemergence as the dominant force in American communism coincided with the Party's decimation in the postwar years. In the spring of 1945, the American Communist Party was still at the zenith of its power and influence. Membership stood in the range of 75,000 to 85,000. During the previous year, recruitment averaged more than 4,000 members each week. In New York City, two Communist councilmen deliberated on municipal affairs, and the Party was an important constituent in successful labor party movements in New York, Minnesota, and California. Communists and their close allies led many unions and cast about one-third of the votes on the executive committee in the new CIO, the most dynamic element of an increasingly powerful labor movement emerging after the war. Communism remained a minority influence in American society, but there was no doubt that the Party was a going concern.[1]

Within a decade, this membership and influence had vanished. In the labor movement, the Party's standing was destroyed, along with many of the unions its activists had painstakingly built throughout the depression and war years. The Left in general had declined, partly because of a concerted attack on the labor movement and the moderate labor leadership's related shift to a more conservative brand of unionism. By the mid-fifties, the Party's membership had fallen to 10,000. Gone were not only the more casual members, recruited through front organizations and then lost through the usual high turnover, but also thousands of lifelong revolutionaries, the cadres that had built the Party into a mass political movement and had sustained it on a day-to-day basis.[2]

The Communist Party's catastrophic decline can be understood only in the context of government and employer repression in the decade following World War II, when the Party itself was virtually proscribed, its programs and activities suppressed, and its leadership harassed and imprisoned. Some newer interpretations of the McCarthy era have minimized its enormous damage not only to thousands of individual lives but also to political and cultural life in the United States. They have embedded the repression of the late forties and early fifties in a larger liberal democratic tradition of anticommunism, and they have stressed what they regarded as a genuine Communist threat. Ellen Schrecker's work has provided a more reliable assessment, stressing both the debilitating effects of the repression on American democracy and the ways in which the character of American communism rendered the Left particularly vulnerable. Whatever its broader effects on life in the United States, there is no mistaking the effects of the McCarthy era on the Communist Party. Schrecker concluded that "McCarthyism destroyed the left. It wiped out the Communist movement."[3] Instead of assuming the valued role in the progressive postwar order that Browder had optimistically prophesied, American communism was largely destroyed in something like the political reaction Foster had envisioned in his criticisms of Browder's rosy postwar forecast.

Given this context, it is difficult to share Edward Johanningsmeier's conclusion that without Foster's "powerful presence in the crucial period after 1945 it is quite possible the Communist Party would have evolved into a different organization than it is today." But the Communist Party's strategy in these years and its own internal crisis undoubtedly facilitated this process of destruction. Stimulated and enhanced by the repressive political atmosphere, this crisis had its own dynamic, and William Z. Foster stood at its very center. He finally achieved leadership of the Communist Party just as it arrived on the precipice of this disaster; indeed, he played a central role in the process. Even as he emerged as the Party's leading spokesperson and his books and articles were translated and read throughout the Communist world, Foster resisted any effort to reform the Party, contributing instead to its increasing isolation and deterioration. The revelations of Communist errors and crimes that produced a search for new organizational forms and strategies among some Party members during the mid-1950s only reinforced Foster's orthodoxy and his dogmatic version of Marxism-Leninism with what Johanningsmeier describes as "a logic of decline, isolation, and helplessness."[4]

There were already signs of trouble by the time the war was drawing to a close in the spring of 1945. Browder's demise was one signal, but the deterioration of Soviet-American relations was another. With the completion of an atomic bomb in the summer of 1945, President Truman took a much harder line in negotiations with the Soviets as they began to consolidate their control in Eastern Europe. A major conflict occurred in July 1945 at the Potsdam Conference when Truman confronted Stalin over his occupation policies, signaling a more aggressive stance on the part of the United States.[5]

Foster had voiced the threat of "a fresh debacle of economic chaos, fascism and war" as early as September 1945. Writing in early 1946, he argued that Lenin's analysis in *Imperialism* still provided the basic explanation for the structure of international monopoly capital and the foreign policy of the United States. "American expansion," Foster argued, "is full of danger to world peace, freedom, and prosperity. . . . Unless checked and eventually defeated by democratic pressure, these imperialist forces would soon plunge the world into a new bloodbath of fascism and war." To neutralize this threat, Foster envisioned a broader cross-class alliance than the Democratic Front of the war years: "the workers should enter into organized cooperation with poorer farmers, the Negro people, with the progressive professionals and middle classes, with the bulk of the veterans against the common enemy, monopoly capital . . . to culminate eventually in a broad third party movement." This new coalition was to be led by class-conscious workers, and for this, it was essential to build a strong Communist Party. "We must carry on Party building as our main political task," Foster concluded, "never losing sight of it in any of our campaigns of mass struggle and mass educational work." At the international level, such a coalition embracing "the organized working class in the capitalist countries, the peoples of the colonial and semi-colonial countries and the new democratic governments" must accept the leadership of the Soviet Union.[6]

While extreme, Foster's apocalyptic postwar vision was shaped by genuine dangers. Even without intervention from the Soviets, American Communists would have been forced to reevaluate Browder's analysis and program for the postwar world; the domestic and international prospects for peaceful coexistence withered with the war's end. The international confrontations between the United States and the USSR, Truman's efforts to justify his new containment policies by emphasizing the Soviet threat, and the GOP's claims that the Democrats had been soft on communism all helped reshape public opinion. In February 1945, in the midst of the Red Army's advance on Germany, 55 percent of Americans answered yes when asked, "Do you think Russia can be trusted to cooperate with us after the war?" By September 1946, the figure had fallen to 32 percent. As Americans began to link the threat of international communism with the activities of domestic radicals, their hostility and fears fixed on the Communist Party in the United States. In the spring of 1947, 61 percent of those polled thought the Party should be outlawed, and the figure rose to 68 percent by November 1949.[7]

In early 1947, in the midst of this gathering storm, Foster left for a long tour through war-torn Europe, his first journey there since 1939—Prague, Sofia, Belgrade, Warsaw, as well as London, Paris, Rome, Geneva, and Trieste. The devastation shocked him. He found the scene in Warsaw, where about 80 percent of the city had been destroyed, and particularly in the city's ghetto, overwhelming. Home to Europe's largest prewar Jewish community, Poles now called this place "the desert." The Germans, having destroyed its population during the Holocaust and a desperate uprising at the end of the war, left few buildings standing. "Never in my life have I looked out upon a more desolate scene," Foster wrote. Everywhere he turned, he found more devastation.[8]

Throughout Europe, Foster saw large Communist parties and new "Peoples' Democracies" based on left-wing coalitions rising from this rubble. Where others perceived an Iron Curtain descending, he found social and economic progress and an extension of the democracy for which the people of Europe had fought. Foster rightly observed that the undisputed popularity of the Soviet Union and left-wing political parties in the mid-forties sprang from the reputation of the Red Army and Communist resistance fighters. The triumph of the Soviet system in Eastern and Central Europe brought Foster confidence. "Many of the leaders of the new governments," he wrote, "I knew personally as old-time workers in the international labor movement."[9]

Enthusiastic about the accomplishments of the new Soviet satellite states, Foster appeared profoundly pessimistic about the role of the United States. Its "atom-bomb diplomacy" brought the threat of war, while domestic policies raised the danger of fascism at home. His European travels seemed to reinforce such fears, and he returned to the hyperbole of the early 1930s. "The United States has indeed become the organizer and leader of reaction all over the world," Foster warned the Party's National Committee in June 1947. "No other nation in history, not even Nazi Germany or militarist Japan, ever set for itself such all-inclusive imperialist goals." Foster labeled the new Truman Doctrine "the 1947 edition of Hitler's Anti-Comintern Pact" and called the Marshall Plan "a scheme to place all of Europe in economic and political bondage to the United States in an attempt to split the world into two armed, hostile camps." In delineating the postwar political economy, Foster identi-fied three groups of capitalists: the "war party" (including the publishers William Randolph Hearst and Robert McCormick), which advocated a "pre-ventive war" against the Soviet Union; a "center group" (including Truman himself, Secretary of State George Marshall, Herbert Hoover, and John Foster Dulles), which saw war with the USSR as possibly inevitable and backed an expansion of the military and various get-tough policies but hesitated to move too aggressively; and an "FDR residue" (including Senator Claude Pep-per and Henry Wallace), which pushed for international peace.[10]

While insisting that a large majority of the population was antiwar and believed in the possibility of cooperation with the Soviets, Foster admitted that anti-Soviet sentiments were common and that the basis for a popular anticommunism was present. The Republican victories in the 1946 congres-sional elections and the passage of the antilabor Taft-Hartley Act in early 1947, Foster warned, meant "there is now a fascist danger in the United States, which means there is also a war danger." The central task for the Communist Party, he argued, was to build a peace movement. Other Party leaders fol-lowed Foster's lead. In early 1946, Eugene Dennis spoke of being "in a race with time" to avoid a new world war, while Alexander Bittelman projected a catastrophic postwar depression, despite all of the government's Keynesian maneuvers. Both the war danger and the depression, the Party leadership believed, were not tendencies but immediate threats.[11] Though Foster occa-sionally wavered on this, the projected depression, the war danger, and the threat of fascism remained central to his views throughout the late forties and early fifties.

At home, the atmosphere of labor-management cooperation that had lasted, at least at the official level, throughout the war, dissipated in fall 1945 into a series of wage disputes, culminating in 1946 in the largest strike wave in the nation's history. The movement revolved around the issue of living stan-dards, with workers fighting for substantial wage increases to make up for inflation and the loss of overtime. President Truman's plan for sustaining the wartime social contract with a labor-management conference collapsed in November at about the same time the UAW began a 113-day strike against General Motors. In early 1946, both Communist and non-Communist labor activists dug in for long strikes against corporations determined to hold the line on wages and to reassert some of the authority they had lost on the shop floor during the war. Textile and meat-packing plants, coal mines, auto, electrical, and steel factories, and New York harbor facilities all shut down. Trains stopped, and general strikes erupted in cities across the country. In all, American corporations lost 116 million workdays.[12] Foster viewed the rise in class conflict as a vindication of his own analysis of the postwar order.

What Foster found particularly invigorating about the 1946 strike wave was not simply its size but also the sophistication with which it was waged. He applauded the coordination and solidarity among unions and their fight for public support, including the UAW's demand that General Motors open its books to prove its argument that it could not afford the large wage increases. Foster advocated a national strategy committee representing all sections of the movement—the railroad brotherhoods and the AFL as well as the CIO unions—to work out joint wage policies and coordinate strike action and support. Greater public relations efforts would allow labor to show Americans how unions were "striving to defend the purchasing power of the masses." Predictably, Foster called for a stronger Communist Party and greater efforts in the 1946 congressional elections.[13] Greater coordination would certainly have strengthened the strikes, and labor's failure to mobilize its ranks in the congressional elections set the stage for major political defeats in the year ahead. Even as Foster turned back to a more sectarian brand of Communist politics, he retained a grasp of effective labor strategy.

This massive strike wave crystallized an "anti-labor movement," shifting middle-class public opinion against unions and mobilizing a political offensive by corporations and conservative groups. The Republicans won control of both houses of Congress in the 1946 elections and, in coalition with a group of conservative Democrats, passed a series of laws, many of them supported by President Truman, that were designed to curb the power unions had obtained during the war. The Taft-Hartley Act, by far the most potent of these weapons, cleared Congress and, overcoming Truman's veto, became law in early 1947. Aimed generally at reversing many of the protections extended to unions under the 1935 Wagner Act, Taft-Hartley targeted the left wing of the labor movement in particular.[14]

Anti-Communist factionalism already existed, particularly in the CIO, but Taft-Hartley intensified such conflict. In one blow, the act delivered a powerful weapon into the hands of right-wing unionists and threatened the left-wing union leadership with annihilation. At the same time, it confronted even liberal centrists with the dilemma of either purging their own ranks of Communists or risking charges of colluding with Communists. As Ellen Schrecker noted, the Party's combination of secrecy and its demands that prominent trade unionists back its positions on foreign as well as domestic policy issues proved fatal.[15] With its labor coalitions jeopardized by the anti-Communist crusade, the Party's specific policies and the nature of the relationship between Party leaders and union "influentials" took on added significance. Particularly damaging were claims by government, employers, and local anti-Communist activists that American Communists were simply foreign agents whose main political object was to advance Soviet foreign policy. Any gesture in the direction of Soviet policy accentuated such charges, rendering left-wing activists even more vulnerable.

Both domestic politics and Soviet influence helped produce a lurch back in the direction of the third-party strategy. In September of 1947, with the cold war storm clouds gathering, representatives from nine major Communist parties met to establish the Communist Information Bureau (Cominform) and to discuss international political strategy. The delegates perceived a grave threat to the Soviet Union and the interests of the international working class in the form of American imperialism and the Marshall Plan and urged all parties to adopt policies to defeat it. Because the Marshall Plan and the Truman Doctrine, which projected a vigorous American campaign to contain the spread of international communism, were cornerstones of the Democratic administration's foreign policy, the next logical step for the CPUSA was to throw all of its energies into Henry Wallace's new third-party movement, with its critique of Truman's aggressive stance against the Soviets. Speaking before an October 1947 conference, Foster said it was time for the Party to "launch a great mass, anti-monopoly, progressive peace party of its own."[16]

Communist discussion of a third-party initiative dated back at least to the fall of 1945, but there was disagreement within the leadership over the nature of the tactic. With the estrangement of Henry Wallace and other liberals from the Democratic Party's cold war foreign policy, many on the Left, in and outside the Communist Party, felt that the time was ripe for such an effort. Eugene Dennis, who had assumed the general secretary's position in the wake of Browder's fall, seemed reticent about a full-fledged effort to defeat the Democrats, preferring to think of the new party as a lever to push the Democrats left. Foster embraced the idea and pushed harder as the third-party initiative assumed greater priority in Soviet strategy.[17] In turn, Foster's strong stand for this political initiative and his demand that left-wing CIO leaders actively oppose the Marshall Plan significantly weakened the Party's position in the CIO and the labor movement generally.

Throughout the Browder regime, left-wing labor leaders, the so-called influentials had enjoyed considerable leeway in their union activities, as Foster had in the early 1920s. Such influentials certainly consulted Foster and other Party leaders, but they generally did what they thought best for their unions, sometimes directly contradicting Party policy. One aspect of the campaign against Browder's revisionism was a Party effort to direct more closely the work of these influentials.

At the end of 1947, the Party began pressuring its trade union leaders. John Williamson, the CPUSA's trade union director, called a large meeting of union notables, announced the third-party policy, and urged their support. Several of the union people had reservations about the effect of such a campaign within the CIO, which strongly supported Truman on the basis of his veto of the Taft-Hartley Act and his generally supportive attitude toward organized labor.

In January of 1948, Mike Quill of the Transport Workers Union appealed directly to Foster. He expressed his fears that supporting a third party "would split the unions, and weaken our position both locally and nationally against the employers." He later testified that Foster said the Communist Party had "decided that all the unions that it can influence within the CIO are to go down the line behind Wallace if it splits the last union down the middle." Quill recalled that Foster was adamant, claiming it might even be necessary to establish a third labor federation "carved out of the AFL and CIO in order to implement the Henry Wallace movement." By the time he testified about this conversation, Quill had broken with the Party and may have been exaggerating the sharpness of Foster's response. But Foster's formulations on labor support for Wallace show that Quill had understood the substance of the message. Foster castigated the AFL and CIO leaders' "labor imperialism" and argued that the rank and file would break with them and support Wallace, a perspective that turned out to be politically naive, at best.[18]

As relations with the CIO centrist leadership became increasingly delicate, Foster reverted to a political language that made it easy for opponents to demonize the Party and much more difficult for allies to come to its defense. Testifying before the Senate Judiciary Committee in the midst of Wallace's 1948 campaign, he answered the inevitable question about a war between the United States and the USSR by declaring, "We are not going to fight against the Soviet Union."[19]

Wallace's massive defeat and Truman's victory in the 1948 election convinced neither Foster nor the Party that their Wallace campaign had been a mistake. Foster later noted "left-sectarian" policies that had helped isolate the Communist Party from the mainstream of the labor movement and undercut whatever political influence it had built by the end of World War II, and he identified the decision to support the establishment of the Progressive Party in 1947 as one of the most serious of these errors. At the time, however, Foster was among the most vociferous supporters of the policy. As late as 1949, he argued that the decision had been fundamentally correct and, far from backing away from the Party's policy in the CIO, he found that the main error was committed by the left-wing unionists, who "fought inadequately against the Marshall Plan, for peace, for friendly relations with U.S.S.R., [and] for independent political action." "This weakness," Foster concluded, "cut into the Wallace vote." Most historians, however, have concluded that it was the Party's inflexible policy, particularly on the Marshall Plan and Wallace candidacy, that cost the Communists their important position in the CIO.[20]

The full extent of Foster's failure in assessing the Wallace campaign can be grasped only by recalling the importance he always attached to extensive labor support in such campaigns—the issue over which he fought Pepper and Lovestone in 1923 and Browder in the 1930s. A premature lurch toward a labor party, Foster often warned, held the danger of cutting Communists off from the mainstream of the labor movement. Increasingly isolated from this movement, with his eye on developments in Europe, Foster actually courted this danger in pressing union influentials to support Wallace in the face of massive opposition from the CIO's center and right. The decision was, of course, not a personal one, but his persistence in this regard undoubtedly cost the Party dearly in the area Foster prized above all—its industrial work.

A second source of conflict between the left and center forces in the CIO involved the Party's position on the Marshall Plan, which Foster labeled a "cold-blooded scheme of American monopolists, to establish their ruthless domination over harassed world humanity . . . a menace to democracy, prosperity, and peace of all mankind." The Party's official position analyzed the plan as an "extension of the notorious Truman Doctrine, a vital part of our Government's reactionary 'cold war' against the Soviet Union, the new democracies of Eastern Europe, and the peoples' movements all over the world, including the United States." In advancing the plan, Wall Street sought to divide the whole world into two hostile camps. Foster warned that in backing the plan, "labor imperialists" were "betraying the working class and the American people as a whole."[21]

Foster's vision of the Progressive Party related directly to this critique of the Marshall Plan. The new party, he argued, would "lay the basis for a long overdue progressive peoples' party." If necessary, Foster believed, rank-and-file labor would split with its leadership to support Wallace.[22]

The Progressive Party campaign and the Communist Party's position on the Marshall Plan provided focal points for the gathering attack on the CIO's left wing and a rationale for purging the Communist and other left-wing activists from the labor movement. The federal government, state and local authorities, and employers launched a massive attack on the Communist Party and the left wing of the labor movement. The FBI and virtually every other branch of the federal government took part, including Congress and its various committees, the State, Justice, and Treasury departments, the Immigration and Naturalization Service, the White House, the Internal Revenue Service, the National Labor Relations Board, the Subversive Activities Control Board, and the Post Office.

In early 1947, President Truman initiated loyalty oaths and a program of internal government investigations, the House Committee on Un-American Activities (HUAC) and state and local investigating committees began new investigations, and Congress passed the Taft-Hartley Act. In June, the entire leadership of the Joint Anti-Fascist Refugee Committee, including several prominent liberals, was convicted of contempt of Congress and jailed for refusing to divulge the names of contributors and refugees. In December, ten important Hollywood writers and directors were indicted and eventually jailed for terms of up to a year for refusing to cooperate with HUAC. The government finally went after the top leadership of the Communist Party itself the following summer.

As early as June 1945, the FBI had been considering a prosecution under the Smith Act, which prohibited teaching or advocating the overthrow of the U.S. government by force and violence. The FBI pressured the attorney general until indictments were finally drawn up against Foster and eleven other Party leaders in June 1948 on the charge of membership in the Communist Party. President Truman kept these indictments secret until after the July 1948 Democratic Party convention, apparently in fear of alienating liberals and civil libertarians in the party's ranks. But on July 20, 1948, FBI agents invaded Communist Party headquarters, arresting Foster; Eugene Dennis, the Party's general secretary; John Williamson, its director of trade union activity; Henry Winston, who directed the Party's work among blacks; and Jack Stachel, the organizational secretary. Within a week, federal agents arrested all the other members of the Party's National Board. That fall, the entire national leadership of the Communist Party was charged with conspiring to advocate the overthrow of the government of the United States and placed on trial at the federal courthouse on Foley Square in lower Manhattan.[23]

While Truman himself never took the domestic Communist threat very seriously, he employed the issue to justify his foreign policy goals. As Ellen Schrecker noted, the government used the Smith Act trials to "create and disseminate a politically useful image of the party as a dangerous conspiracy under the direct control of Moscow." The strategy "deprived the CP of all legitimacy in the eyes of most U.S. citizens."[24]

Foster, the only one of the defendants who seemed to relish the coming fight, missed his day in court and spent his time in planning the defense and in support activities for the others. Party lawyers argued that he was far too ill to stand the strain of a long, intense political trial, and two government appointed physicians agreed. In late August, he experienced a "cerebral spasm," and on September 2, he awoke with a numbness throughout his right side. A November diagnosis noted arteriosclerosis, hypertension, high blood pressure, a rapid heart rate, and an enlarged heart. On January 18, 1949, Judge Harold Medina severed Foster's case from the others and proceeded with the trial without him. This did not mean that Foster was safe. Throughout the early fifties, the government closely documented all of his movements, not simply for the general information this might yield regarding Party activities but also with an eye to placing him on trial as soon as his health allowed. Court-appointed physicians examined Foster repeatedly over the next ten years, and the U.S. district attorney tried to restore the case to the court calendar on three different occasions. Instead, Foster's health continued to deteriorate, and in 1960 the government finally dropped its plans. Until then, Foster lived and worked with the Smith Act indictment hanging over his head.[25]

As the legal historian Stanley Kutler noted, this Smith Act prosecution "marked the most blatant political trial in American history, a trial of the Party's purposes, ideology, and organization, as well as its leaders . . . and signaled a national commitment to destroy domestic Communism." As such, he argued, the trial "threatened long-standing traditions of civil liberties and political dissent."[26] The Party might have fought the case on strictly civil libertarian grounds, appealing to American First Amendment traditions and downplaying Communist politics. (This strategy eventually led to a dismissal of all charges in the only case where it was consistently applied, the trial of the California Party leaders.) Arguing from the outset that their leaders could never get a fair hearing in the current atmosphere, the Communists instead fought the case as a defense of their own political theories and principles, some of which were difficult at best for Americans to grasp. Here Foster played an important role. The strategy, he said, must be to "put the Government, not the Communists . . . on trial," to confront the government at every turn in its argument, and to defend the Party's policies and goals. Once again consistent with his political position since the thirties, Foster argued that the Party should not hide behind social democratic slogans and ideas but should advance its own analysis. The strategy played into the prosecution's hands, as

Ellen Schrecker pointed out: "The defendants inadvertently collaborated with the Justice Department's strategy of making the case a test of the legitimacy of the CP's policies rather than a struggle about Free Speech and the First Amendment."[27]

The "Battle of Foley Square" opened on January 17, 1949, with four hundred uniformed and plainclothes policemen ringing the courthouse. It continued until October 21, making it the longest criminal trial in American history up to that point. The government's strategy was tied closely to the reconstitution of the Party in 1945 and the policies Foster had advocated since then. Prosecutors argued that the Party was reestablished in 1945 with the aim of overthrowing the government "by force and violence," that the classics of Marxism-Leninism and the Party's other literature belied this intent, and that Browder's fall and Foster's rise signaled a repudiation of the Popular Front line. Government agents and paid informers testified that the defendants had advocated, in print and in Party classes, or had conspired to advocate the government's overthrow. Given the government's elaborate campaign against the Communist Party, prosecutors likely would have proceeded against the organization regardless of its precise language. In this sense, it is pointless to blame the political repression of the following decade on the Communists. There is little doubt, however, that the Party's sectarianism and revolutionary hyperbole of the late forties facilitated the government's campaign, and there was no single leader more responsible for the general line in these years than William Z. Foster.

Too ill to testify in court or even to talk for more than half an hour each day, Foster once again summoned up his energy and discipline to produce a well-crafted, 390-page deposition, which the Party considered "the climactic testimony in the trial," a logical refutation of the government's central claims. He laid out and defended the Party's basic policies in clear terms. He flatly denied the "force and violence" argument, challenging the government to cite an instance where the Party had publicly advocated this position, and he argued persuasively for a continuation of the Popular Front orientation into the postwar years. "The Communists in this country as well as in others," Foster testified, "have been going along for the past dozen years with the practical theory that it has become possible, since the rise of fascism in the world, to regularly elect peoples' governments in the capitalist democracies—governments that will possess the capacity and impulse . . . to use their legally constituted powers for the establishment of socialism." The quotations introduced by the government, Foster argued, "do not give any consideration whatsoever to this change in the tactical[,] in some respects the strategical line of the Communist Party." The threat of fascism and war persisted into the postwar era and with it the Popular Front. The result of this line, he concluded, "has been to render obsolete . . . practically all of the literature our party had turned out previously." Foster considered his deposition "the premier presentation of the parliamentary road to socialism in the United States."[28]

Foster consulted often with the defendants and their attorneys and probably shaped the Party's case as much as any other individual did. But the defense was hobbled from the outset by squabbles between the defendants and the lawyers and among the attorneys themselves. One lawyer wanted to model the defense closely on Georgi Dimitrov's 1933 Reichstag fire case, while another complained of defendants' insistence on long-winded Marxist-Leninist statements rather than the impromptu answers he thought would be more understandable to a jury.[29]

Given the political atmosphere in the United States in 1949, the verdict was perhaps a foregone conclusion. All eleven defendants were convicted and sentenced to long prison terms. Judge Medina, clearly irritated by the defense's strategy of continually appealing to public opinion, cited the Communists' lawyers for contempt of court, found them guilty, and sentenced them to prison without even letting them respond to his charges. "Georgi Dimitrov had a much fairer trial before the Nazi tribunal at Leipzig," Foster concluded, "not to speak of getting an acquittal."[30]

Within a year, while the Party was still appealing the Smith Act convictions and the fate of his colleagues hung in the balance, Foster seemed to shift his position entirely on the question of a peaceful transition to socialism. Socialism, he believed, "required the defeat of the capitalist class and the establishment of the dictatorship of the proletariat. . . . One would be naïve to speak of a peaceful election under such circumstances of sharp political struggle."[31]

Foster's analysis and rhetoric set the stage for the Party's underground experience during the 1950s. His later claim that he did not support and was not even present for the vote to go underground was technically correct but grossly misleading. In early spring 1951, George Watt, secretary of the Party's National Cadres and Review Committee, was grappling with the difficult question of how to keep the organization functioning in the face of government repression. He visited Foster, who was vacationing on the West Coast and returned to New York with the chairman's considered opinions on three questions. Foster believed that war between the United States and the Soviet Union and the eventual outlawing of the CPUSA were inevitable. Fascism, he thought, was not inevitable, though the United States was in for a long fascist-like period. In discussions in the National Board, Foster argued that every one of those convicted should skip bail and that the Party should prepare to continue its work in an illegal, clandestine fashion. That he publicly compared the American Party's situation with the historical experience of the Italian and Japanese parties, which had emerged from long periods of extreme repression stronger and more influential than ever, suggests his frame of mind in the early fifties. As on many other issues in these years, the National Board split on this assessment, with Foster, Ben Davis, and Robert Thompson calling for all defendants to jump bail, and Elizabeth Gurley Flynn, Carl Winter, and others insisting that they all report to serve their sentences. A compromise called for most of the defendants to surrender, while several jumped bail. On June 4, 1951, in the midst of the Party's campaign against the Korean Conflict, the U.S. Supreme Court handed down its decision in *Dennis vs. the United States,* upholding the conviction of the Communist Party's National Board under the Smith Act. Foster and other leaders, citing an acceleration in "the process of creeping fascism," prepared the Party for a long period of underground activity.[32]

For a while, Foster's assessment seemed less melodramatic than it might now. In the wake of the Supreme Court decision, the government immediately launched a new round of arrests and trials of 134 of the Party's state and regional "second string" leaders from Hawaii to New England, as well as leaders and supporters in the Party's various front groups. Of those cases where a verdict was reached, nearly 90 percent of the defendants were convicted and sentenced. Successful appeals, beginning in the mid-fifties, saved many of them from prison, but the cases themselves, often lasting several years from the early through the late 1950s, drained the Party and its related organizations of time, energy, money, and ideas. Contacts dried up, members dropped out or went off to jail, and organizations ceased to function.

Joseph Starobin, who himself endured the experience, wrote of the endless government investigations and prosecutions of "subversives" during the early fifties:

> The most repressive aspect of these procedures was . . . the public atmosphere created. Thousands of men and women of left wing views, some having a genuine and others a remote affiliation with Communist organizations, soon found that unless they cooperated abjectly with these committees they faced not only prosecution but also ostracism . . . [and] persons accused of Communist connections were ousted from trade unions, churches, professional societies, neighborhood groups, and were refused rentals and even insurance policies. . . . Near hysteria gripped the nation. . . . In such an atmosphere, many Party members retired from political activity. The tendency was more pronounced on the part of sympathizers.[33]

The oppressive political climate did much of the damage, but the Party's own response to the crisis took its own toll. Foster and other Party leaders took the Supreme Court decision and the political repression surrounding it as signs that the United States had reached "five minutes to midnight" and was now on the verge of war and fascism. Assuming that the Party would be outlawed, they concluded that only a "cadre organization," a smaller Party composed of the most dedicated members, would survive the next several years. The Party announced a formal reregistration of members in early July 1951 and dropped all those who did not or could not comply. Some leaders, such as Foster, remained above ground to keep a shadow organization functioning, but the Party also established several layers of secret leadership. This underground party included all those who had jumped bail or evaded arrest and were "on the run"; a second group of trusted comrades who changed their identities and waited in hiding or abroad to assume leadership in case of a new round of arrests; and an "operative but unavailable" group of individuals who moved about the country, often in disguise, trying to maintain contact between the public Party and the underground.[34] These arrangements claimed a high organizational, financial, and personal cost.

In Foster's view, however, such a threat to the Party's very survival called for a militant defense. In the appeals cases and the second round of Smith Act trials during the early 1950s, Foster insisted on a "thorough-going and full-scale attack upon the capitalist system" and resisted any suggestion of fighting the cases on First Amendment grounds. "We must develop our Party's program as an organic part of the whole question of the eventual establishment of socialism in this country. . . . We must be on guard against tendencies toward American exceptionalism." When some California defendants traveled all the way to the East Coast to discuss strategy with him, they became embroiled in arguments over whether to cross-examine prosecution witnesses and over the political propriety of each defendant's taking the stand. Cross-examination would only lend legitimacy to prosecution testimony, Foster argued, while each defendant's testimony was crucial to making the Party's intended political statement. He concluded, Dorothy Healey recalled, that the California defendants were relying on "bourgeois legalism" to save their own skins.[35] For Foster, it did not pay to place one's faith in the legal process, particularly in the political atmosphere of the early 1950s. Foster's conclusion in the California case was wrong, but it was not irrational. It was several years before any appeals were successful; in the meantime, the Party lost one case after another.

Throughout the postwar era, the government's attacks were paralleled by the Party's own destructive internal dynamic. Foster faced a number of problems at the level of the national Party leadership, which had strongly supported Browder. No one openly defended Browder, and certainly there was no organized opposition to Foster's hard line. But John Gates, a Lincoln Brigade and World War II veteran; Jack Stachel, perhaps the Party's most experienced organizational mind; Elizabeth Gurley Flynn; Irving Potash of the furriers' union; and Steve Nelson, a Lincoln Brigade veteran who ran the Party's foreign-language work, sometimes confronted Foster, Robert Thompson, and Ben Davis. Disputes came over policies that seemed to jeopardize the Party's mass base, particularly among blacks and trade unionists. Foster faced opposition to his Progressive Party initiative, his insistence on an acute war danger, and the decision to go underground. Yet such opposition never jelled and tended to dissipate under the impact of the worsening political atmosphere. Joseph Starobin recalled Foster's waving the "bloody shirt" of Browderism each time such opposition surfaced. Steve Nelson recounted that "it was more hesitation than assertion of an alternative. And when the cold war intensified, we drew the wagons into a circle." Nelson's recollections of his time on the National Board in the late forties suggest a strained atmosphere, fueled in part by Foster's personality and style: "Foster was not the kind of guy you could go to lunch with. He brought his own lunch and ate in his office while he worked. When Bill was through with his work for the day, he grabbed his briefcase and went home."[36]

Particularly in the year following Browder's expulsion, Foster kept up a constant polemical barrage—even though no constituency emerged for what Foster called "the opportunist poison of Browderism." Bella Dodd, a leader in the New York teachers' union, a veteran of New York City coalition politics, and a staunch Browder supporter, was ostracized soon after Browder's demise and was eventually expelled in 1949. She became an important government witness during the McCarthy period. But Dodd's fate was unusual. Other Browder adherents resigned, but few were expelled. Even those National Board members who had been closest to Browder, such as Robert Minor, Jack Stachel, and John Williamson, conformed quickly and were spared. Sam Darcy feared that Foster was not sufficiently purging the Party of reformists. As early as June 1945, in the midst of Browder's demise, he had warned against what he termed a "Centrist Outcome" to the struggle and urged Foster to press the attack against the "Dennis-Williamson-Green-Minor group," but Foster ignored his letters.[37]

Although Foster is known for his left sectarianism, "centrism" seems an appropriate label for some of his actions. It appears that the Party may actually have expelled more members for leftist deviations than for Browderism. When a group of second-tier leaders argued that Foster had not gone far enough with "Browderite" expulsions and that he was soft on revisionism, he began an assault on "left deviationists." Between the fall of 1946 and the fall of 1948, the Party expelled several thousand members, some of whom were old and trusted comrades. Ruth McKenney and Bruce Minton, prominent Party intellectuals; Vern Smith and Harrison George, old-time West Coast Wobblies; and Bill Dunne, a veteran industrial organizer and former *Daily Worker* editor, were all expelled for "ultra-leftism" in the course of 1946 and 1947. Sam Darcy, Foster's only ally on the National Board during his struggle with Browder and the only Party leader to consistently oppose the discredited revisionist policies, now confidently applied for reinstatement. The Party offered to establish a special commission to review Darcy's case, but only if he allowed the commission to read his book manuscript on Party history. Writing to Foster in June 1945, Darcy had called the attack on Browder's revisionism "insufferably tender." His readmission was rejected, probably because of his continuing identification as a leftist. These and others in the Party's leadership and rank and file tried to constitute themselves as a left opposition, first within and then outside the Party but without any notable success.[38]

The left-wing expulsions were only part of a broader pattern of turning inward to solve the Party's problems. "The cause of policy dilemmas came to be sought not in the policies themselves but in the make-up, behavior, and capability of Party members. Unable to evaluate their policies objectively," the Party veteran Joseph Starobin wrote, "Communists began to measure each other for deviations and heresies. Thus, the strange paradox: *in the name of defying the witchhunt against them, the American Communists complemented it by engaging in a witchhunt of their own. Beleaguered from without, they went through agony from within.*" "When attacks came," a New York Communist later wrote, "we could see nothing but enemies on all sides. . . . We began our own type of heresy hunt. In a frenzy of fear and distrust we began to finish the job of decimation begun by the bourgeoisie. We used expulsion and vilification against our own loyal members and friends." Dorothy Healey, a district organizer in Los Angeles at the time, described the effects of such hysteria: "The great irony of the McCarthy period is that we did almost as much damage to ourselves, in the name of purifying our ranks, as Joe McCarthy and J. Edgar Hoover and all the other witch-hunters combined were able to do."[39]

Members might be expelled for any number of political or even personal transgressions (and Party leaders had even more trouble than usual in distinguishing between the two). The Party began dropping homosexuals from its ranks in 1948, less through overt prejudice (though surely there was an element of this) than through paranoia. The FBI did, in fact, place extreme pressure on members to get them to cooperate with investigations. Party leaders held that gay members constituted a security risk because their private sexual lives could be used to blackmail them. This purge of homosexuals paralleled a much larger one launched by the federal government based on precisely the same concern—that gay federal employees were susceptible to blackmail—by Communist agents. The Party also carried on a campaign against psychotherapy as a bourgeois fraud, but the objection was not simply ideological. Though some Party leaders themselves had gathered information on members under treatment, they were concerned that such conversations might be leaked to federal authorities. As David Shannon concluded, "The anti-Freud campaign was at least partly a security measure."[40]

Foster supported one of the most interesting and damaging Party purges—the campaign against white chauvinism, which he called "one of the most important discussions in the entire life of the Party." The campaign began with an article by the African American Communist Pettis Perry in the October 1949 issue of *Political Affairs,* in which he argued for a campaign against racism in the Party. In the wake of the article and the ensuing discussion, Perry toured the country describing the problem to Party branches and explaining how they might cleanse themselves of it.[41]

This fight against white chauvinism has often been regarded as simply a struggle for power and influence in a disintegrating social movement, another symptom of the disease of sectarianism plaguing the Party in the decade after the war. The charge *was* used in this way within the Party, but it was more than a factional tool. Situated in the history of African American thought and the Party's own long-term fight against racism, the campaign appears a bit less peculiar. Since its context and its relation to contemporary events have often been ignored, it is important to distinguish the positive features from its destructive ones.

The Party not only had long emphasized a public struggle against racism but also had made an effort to purify its own ranks of these sentiments. Indeed, it was the example of the Communists and the strength of their commitment to this struggle that largely explain whatever success the Party had in the black community. In the late 1920s, American Communists had employed the Soviets' experiences with their own ethnic minorities and Stalin's writings on the "national question" to develop a theory of self-determination for African Americans, a concept that significantly contributed to later black nationalist thinking. In the late 1940s, American Communists once again emphasized the exploitation of black workers as a result of racism and raised the struggle of minority workers to a special place in their conception of the class struggle.[42]

In 1946, Foster and other Party leaders drew on "that great expert on the national question, Stalin" and once again called for the national self-determination of African Americans. The Party's new emphasis on the struggle for black liberation was undoubtedly related to theoretical developments in the Soviet Union. Internationally, the postwar discussion was framed by widespread anticolonial revolutions throughout Asia and Africa. The late forties and early fifties witnessed a major debate over the relative importance of national liberation and labor activity in the world revolutionary movement. This argument underlay the Sino-Soviet split of the early sixties. But the discussion also represented a genuine difference of opinion on the American Party's National Board, one of several in these years, over strategy and tactics. In Foster's own writing, he drew directly on Stalin, but he was also reacting to a very real increase in confidence, organization, and militancy among African Americans, which he misinterpreted as a rise in black nationalism. "All this signifies," he concluded, "that the Negro people are on the path that leads to national struggle, organization, and consciousness."[43] In emphasizing Stalin's earlier formulation of the question, Foster, ironically, took one step toward Mao and the Chinese Party.

In the trade union world, the new campaign brought an effort to advance black activists to positions of leadership in the Left-led unions, a renewed emphasis on civil rights activities, and radical new seniority plans that prefigured later demands for affirmative action. In the United Electrical Workers and other CIO unions, for example, left-wing activists called for "super seniority," a system to balance seniority rights and the special position for black and other minority workers as "last hired, first fired." Although this particular goal was a genuine innovation, Communist labor activists had long advocated civil rights policies and made special efforts to integrate black workers into not only the rank and file but also the leadership of the movement.[44]

The campaign against "white chauvinism," unfolding from the end of 1949 to the end of 1953, arrived in the Party's moment of greatest crisis, amidst an increasingly repressive political atmosphere and Party factionalism. From the outside, the government used the issue to weaken the Party, while within, factions employed it to attack their opponents. This had a demoralizing effect on the besieged membership and sympathizers in the Left-led unions and progressive organizations, as well as on local leaders, who were expected to root out white chauvinists among their comrades. In the Los Angeles area alone, the hunt resulted in an estimated two hundred expulsions, and the local leadership itself came under severe attack. The Party probably lost thousands of members nationally.[45]

Foster had as much to do with suspending the campaign as he did with sustaining it. His decision to end it may have been prompted by his fears that it threatened the Party's already weakened union efforts.[46] Chicago Party leaders brought charges of white chauvinism against Herb March, certainly the most influential and effective Party activist in the stockyards since the early thirties and a prominent voice for civil rights activity in the United Packinghouse Workers–CIO. Although March played a prominent role in advancing black workers for union office, he was accused of obstructing the development of black women activists. When the Party's Chicago leadership convicted him and demanded that he leave the industry, March appealed to Foster.

Foster promised to write an article attacking contrived charges of white chauvinism and asked March to join him at the Party's next National Board meeting. Here, Pettis Perry sided with the Chicago leadership, but Foster and the rest of the board supported March. March remained in the industry and the Party but was relegated to the sidelines. He never recovered the influence he had once enjoyed in the industry and soon drifted out of the movement.[47]

Foster's article on "left sectarian errors" in the campaign against white chauvinism appeared in the July 1953 issue of *Political Affairs* and was part of a more general campaign for "labor unity." He urged "a more realistic defini-tion of what constitutes white chauvinism than is now the case," warned against "bourgeois nationalism" in the African American community, and noted that "charges of white chauvinism should not be thrown around so recklessly" because of the disruption they caused in trade union work and elsewhere. The second part of a particularly aggressive attack against the leaders of Local 65 of the Distributive, Processing, and Office Workers Union, which had included charges of white chauvinism, Zionism, and "Jewish bourgeois nationalism," was scheduled to appear in the same issue of *Political Affairs* but never surfaced. It seems likely that Foster had called a halt to the campaign in the interests of salvaging what little influence the Party retained in the labor movement. He was clearly supported in his action by a majority of the National Board in an effort to hedge against "left sectarianism."[48]

Foster also pursued a gradual narrowing of intellectual and political life within the Party. In February 1946, the Hollywood writer Albert Maltz ven-tured praise for a number of writers who had broken with the Party and more generally criticized what he perceived as narrow political assessments of art. Over the following two months, a lively debate ensued in the pages of *New Masses,* with some of the best-known writers in or close to the Party, in-cluding John Howard Lawson, Howard Fast, and Alvah Bessie, condemning Maltz, who quickly retreated. (All of these men were jailed over the next few years.) In the Party's new, more sectarian political atmosphere, Foster overcame past insecurities regarding his own intellectual capacities, effectively closing the debate at a public symposium. Outlining a "People's Cultural Policy," which proceeded from the premise that "art is a weapon in the class struggle," he linked Maltz's experimentation with Browder's revisionism and cautioned against the lures of bourgeois culture.[49]

In the wake of Browder's revisionism, Foster called for a general campaign to raise the membership's theoretical level, which had "declined drastically" under Browder. The charge must have seemed ironic to some, given Foster's own reputation for being weak on theory. For him, this meant a return to Marxist-Leninist fundamentals and their application to all aspects of American life. Browder, Foster argued, had "insolently tried to rewrite Marx and Lenin on the back of his bourgeois reformism." He had encouraged the membership to abandon Marxist-Leninist literature, and even the Party's leaders had strayed by losing the link between their political work and the study of the theory that should guide it.[50]

Writing in early 1948, Foster called the Party "back to the books." His elaborate list of "theoretical tasks" included a definition of the U.S. role in the world economy; a serious analysis and refutation of Keynesian economic theory; the application of theory to particular areas of Party work, including the implications of the concept of self-determination for work among blacks and the role of religion in politics; the analysis of reactionary philosophical and scientific theories, particularly John Dewey's "pragmatism" and racially based theories of biological evolution; the writing of Marxist interpretations of American history, including a general history of the nation, the role of black Americans in its development, the experiences of Native Americans, and the development of the labor movement; and, finally, the application of Marxist-Leninist criticism to the Party's own theoretical and intellectual work. Foster also called for much more systematic educational work, regular yearly conferences on Marxist-Leninist theory and its application to current problems, and a special commission to coordinate all of this theoretical work and to review all major publications *before* their release.[51]

Foster shaped each of these discussions during the following decade, though once again his activism was determined by his health. In August 1948, he experienced another stroke, which left him weak and fragile, unable to speak at length or take part in meetings. Even brief walks produced shortness of breath. "I would attend the regular meetings of the NAC [National Administrative Committee], missing more than few," he later recalled. "I would sit in on these meetings for the main report, make a few remarks on it, and then leave . . . about all my shaky health during these years permitted. . . .

Even this very limited regime of work . . . I was often compelled to interrupt for health reasons." Foster later observed that this recovery was even less complete than the one following his 1932 crisis.[52]

In the midst of yet another political and health crisis, Foster immersed himself more than ever in his writing. Between 1948 and 1957, he produced more than two hundred *Daily Worker* columns, about twenty polemical pamphlets, and dozens of articles for *Political Affairs*. He researched and wrote five major historical works between 1951 and 1955: *Outline Political History of the Americas* (1951), *History of the Communist Party of the United States* (1952), *The Negro People in American History* (1954), *History of the Three Internationals: The World Socialist and Communist Movements from 1848 to the Present* (1955), and *Outline History of the World Trade Union Movement* (1957). As late as 1957, Foster was trying to complete a major economic history of the United States, which remained unpublished at the time of his death.

None of these works was widely read in the United States or taken seriously by professional historians. Some of the reasons for this neglect are justifiable; others are not. All of the histories are largely narrative, and they make for rather dreary reading. When Foster did analyze events, his interpretations tended to be simplistic, even formulaic. Written from an orthodox Marxist perspective, the books embody the teleological and deterministic sort of interpretation that many readers would stereotypically associate with Marxist history.

Yet Foster's books reveal much about him as a political person, if not as a great thinker. First, they represented a major personal achievement. As his health deteriorated from the late forties on, it became difficult for him to negotiate the stairs of his apartment building, and his physical stamina would not permit a full research schedule. The Party therefore provided considerable research assistance. His assistant and chauffeur, Arthur Zipser, and other Party members took notes and made photostatic copies for him at the New York Public Library and elsewhere around the city. Foster also collected some of his data from comrades in other countries. Individuals and even editorial committees read and commented on the manuscripts, which Foster then revised accordingly. He also met frequently with Alexander Trachtenberg, director of the Party's International Publishers, which produced all of his major works. This kind of editorial and research support is not at all unusual among academic and popular writers. There is no evidence in archival material or in interviews with Party veterans who were in a position to know that anyone but Foster conceptualized or wrote these books. Given his rather meager educational background, the difficult conditions under which he worked, and the broad range of subjects he grasped, the books must be viewed as a personal intellectual achievement, even if they do not represent good history.[53]

Foster's methodical approach to his writing underscores his disciplined approach to his life and work. "By a system of rigid self discipline and regimentation, consisting of carefully timed alternative periods of rest in bed and writing at his desk," a doctor reported in late 1952, "he apparently gets through a good deal of planned, concerted work. He clocks himself for lying down one hour, then for an hour of work at his desk. . . . He moves at a slow pace and within a restricted area to avoid angina and dysphea." Anyone who has spent hours laboring over a paragraph or two will share Dorothy Healey's envy of Foster's writing facility: "He could sit down at the typewriter and in fifteen minutes have a letter-perfect column which required no further editing and contained not a single typing error."[54]

Foster had sweeping objectives in each of the histories he wrote. His aim in his history of the Americas, he noted, was "to analyze the broad course of economics, political and cultural growth and decay, and to trace the general progress of the class struggle—both in the individual countries and in the hemisphere as a whole." The relative simplicity of Foster's historical analyses represented more than a lack of intellectual rigor. He followed the Soviet prescription that each Communist Party must produce histories of its own party, trade union movement, and society, which were primarily intended not for the academic world but for Party members and for workers. Foster reasoned that they "should deal basically with the main question in hand . . . be written simply, comprising a compilation of the facts and a theoretical explanation of them which will be clear to the inexperienced youth and the broad masses, but which . . . will also contain the deepest Marxist-Leninist conclusions on the subjects." Foster had clearly thought about his potential audience and concluded that "Marxist historians must learn to write briefly and compactly. We are living in the age of radio and television . . . people are economizing on their times for reading."[55] In a word, Foster's histories were explicitly *political* in their function, aimed at interpreting key problems for common readers within the context of the Communist Party's theoretical perspective and program.

Even the more solid European Party histories, written by partisans in the late fifties and early sixties, shared some of the weaknesses of Foster's *History of the Communist Party of the United States*. The finest of these were the products of sophisticated Marxist historians and social scientists who clearly aimed at *both* scholarly and political audiences rather than the self-educated workers Foster had in mind.[56] Foster's Party history more closely resembles the *History of the Communist Party of the Soviet Union*—strictly organizational in structure, narrowly political in subject, and doctrinaire in interpretation.

For good or ill, Foster's histories and some of his other works were important in another way. They interpreted American society—its history, culture, economy, and social relations—to millions of people throughout the world. Translated into Italian, Romanian, Polish, Russian, Japanese, and other languages, they introduced the United States to students in Communist Party schools and even in the state schools of the Soviet Union, the Peoples' Republic of China, the "Peoples' Democracies" throughout Eastern Europe, and in other parts of the world.

The Party undoubtedly modeled its own "turn inward" partly on Soviet policies. More than any other Party leader, Foster kept his eye on the international stage. As the veteran Communist George Charney observed, it was Browder's attempt to "give the party a distinct American image" that Foster and those around him viewed as the "essence of revisionism." Foster labeled Browder "another victim of 'American exceptionalism.'" From the summer of 1945 on, "class and party loyalty were measured, more than ever, in international, Soviet terms."[57]

It was the spectacle of rapidly advancing Communist movements abroad that braced Foster's faith in the international character of the movement. Not only in the "Peoples' Democracies" of Eastern Europe but also in Western European countries, he could point to mass Communist parties that led their nations' labor movements and participated in important broad left coalitions. Increasingly in the early fifties, he was attracted to the Peoples' Republic of China, which he saw as the "outstanding leader in the colonial liberation revolution" of the postwar era. In the midst of repression and decline at home, Foster could still conclude that internationally, at least, history was on his side. "Humanity, especially since World War II, literally comprises two worlds," he wrote in 1952:

> The one is the old, outworn, historically obsolete capitalist world—the world of exploitation, hunger, imperialism, fascism and war, full of confusion, hopelessness, and despair. The other is the great new world of socialism—alive, vibrant, healthy, bearing the mandate of history, and with it a message of hope and security to the oppressed of the earth. . . . The basic development of our times is that the world is advancing from capitalism to socialism, a forward movement that is both irresistible and inevitable. As Molotov has said, "All roads lead to Communism."[58]

Yet there was another facet of postwar international communism, one which Foster embraced with equal enthusiasm. The Soviet Party and then those throughout Eastern Europe and elsewhere launched a series of purges in the late forties to cleanse their own ranks of perceived security threats. When Tito broke with the Soviet Union in 1948 over his vision for Yugoslavia as a nonaligned Communist state, his actions accentuated the siege mentality in the Soviet and other parties. In the United States, Tito's arguments for greater Party autonomy were associated with those of Browder, and a hunt began for American followers of "the renegade Tito," who "treacherously sold out to Wall Street for a share of the Marshall Plan slush funds" in Foster's reckoning. Important fellow travelers, such as the playwright Lillian Hellman and the Slovenian-American writer Louis Adamic, became suspect when they refused to break their ties with the newly independent Yugoslavs.[59] Ironically, the Party attacks did not save such sympathizers from the political repression of the next few years.

While appealing to time-honored international sources of authority, Foster also resorted to an old habit of viewing the Party's internal politics largely in class terms. He tied what he called the "Browder complex" to the influx of middle-class leadership during the Popular Front and Democratic Front years. "These criticisms were vehemently echoed in the ranks," Charney noted, "especially among the seamen, who posed as the most militant, proletarian elements in the party." As in similar crises, a premium was placed on "proletarian leadership," while functionaries from bourgeois backgrounds were more suspect than ever.[60]

As late as the spring of 1956, as the Communist Party faced its own internal problems, repression continued. The Internal Revenue Service launched simultaneous raids on the organization's headquarters in New York, Chicago, San Francisco, and Philadelphia and on *Daily Worker* offices in New York, Chicago, and Detroit, seizing the paper's and the Party's assets. The following month the Social Security Administration cut off payments to Foster and other aged Party leaders. These and other government measures were often reversed in court, but their effects were extremely disruptive. They help explain the Party's inability to pursue much of a program through the mid-fifties.[61]

For all of this repression, Foster's analysis that fascism was growing in the United States was both misguided and costly. It led in the direction of extreme sectarianism, isolating American Communists even further from any potential constituency and depleting the Party of valued members, including some of its most loyal cadres. The underground strategy disrupted what little political and industrial work the Party was able to mount, and it cost those who went underground a great deal in personal as well as political terms. But if Foster's formulation was a misreading of American political reality, it was not irrational. The trajectory of international politics throughout the early fifties was toward ever greater confrontation between the United States and the USSR. Both official and popular anti-Communist paranoia were escalating, and the government's repressive campaign against the Communist Party had reached enormous proportions, with little sign of abatement. In terms of the Party's organizational interests, it would have been far better off remaining above ground and waging an open campaign of self-defense, but the decision to erect an underground structure was predicated on the assumption that the federal government had decided to destroy the Party. In this assumption, Foster and other Party leaders were certainly correct.

Neither the Party's preoccupation with internal security nor its efforts to purify its ranks did much to strengthen or protect it. Paralleling similar events throughout the Soviet Union and Eastern European societies during the late forties and early fifties, the American purges appear somewhat bizarre. Many Communist veterans now agree that they weakened the Party and facilitated its destruction. But the purges appear a bit less peculiar in the context of cold war America's own sort of hysteria and the efforts of voluntary groups of all sorts and government at all levels to systematically root out Communists.

The organization shriveled in the face of this onslaught and its own internal problems. As late as 1950, membership still stood at 43,000, but by 1955, it was down to 22,600. *Daily Worker* circulation, fairly constant at 20,000 to 23,000 from 1945 to 1950, fell to 10,433 by 1953.[62] It is difficult to see how the American Communist Party might have thrived in the postwar era—with or without William Z. Foster. Aside from the widespread government repression that drove Party cadres underground, overseas, and into prison, there were deeper cultural and economic influences reinforcing the official anticommunism of the day. One of the strongest economic booms in the nation's history, together with elaborate union contracts that included a wide range of fringe benefits, raised the living standards of many American workers, though poverty persisted in some parts of the country.[63] American cultural life also took a decisively conservative turn, while ideological conformity dominated the nation's politics. Beyond all this, there was the Party's own internal crisis over the aborted break with Stalinism.

Though Foster did not create the crisis, he responded to it ineptly. Foster's rigidly orthodox version of Marxism-Leninism helped ensure the Party's failure in the crisis it faced. He carried this rigidity, seasoned in a series of personal and political crises, with him into the final conflict of his life.

12 *The Final Conflict, 1956–61*

WATCHING WILLIAM Z. FOSTER at his seventy-fifth birthday celebration on March 9, 1956, no outsider would have guessed that the besieged Communist Party was on the verge of its greatest crisis. In the previous weeks, the pages of the *Daily Worker* had been filled with greetings from around the country and around the world. Ben Davis, perhaps Foster's closest ally, had just emerged from prison to rejoin the rest of the Party's leaders, most of whom had been released two months earlier. Foster's *Outline History of the World Trade Union Movement,* the fifth and last of his major histories, had just appeared. A special "Foster anniversary issue" of *Political Affairs* featured glowing assessments of Foster's career. A foreshadowing of what was to come might be read in the same issue, however. The issue reported on a speech by Nikita Khrushchev, the new Soviet premier and the Soviet Party's general secretary, given at the Soviet Party's Twentieth Congress that warned of the "cult of the individual," which was "alien to the spirit of Marxism-Leninism." The speech's broader implications, however, remained oblique, and the focus of the issue remained on Foster. Eugene Dennis, the American Party's general secretary, introduced Foster at his birthday celebration as "the outstanding leader of our Communist Party, the vanguard of the American working class," and he expressed the Party's great love for the aged warrior. Foster's own remarks were full of optimism. "In this period of capitalist decay and socialist advance," Foster told the overflow crowd, "all roads lead to communism. It gives me the boundless satisfaction of knowing that my life's efforts have been spent on the side of invincible progress, and that the great Socialist cause is marching on rapidly to triumph throughout the world."[1]

The crisis was a long time in coming. Between 1956 and 1958, the recurrent tension between "international proletarian solidarity" and the search for an American road to socialism reached a climax, first offering what appeared to be a promising way forward and then nearly tearing the Party apart. The seeds of this crisis lay at least as far back as the underground era of the early 1950s. Several key Communist leaders who had spent time isolated from the center while in prison or underground emerged with new questions and ideas. Their enforced separation from the closed Party environment had allowed them to think through the experience of the past generation, and this rethinking took them off the path of orthodox Marxism-Leninism, where Foster's own feet were now rather firmly planted. Ironically, Foster's showdown with these "revisionists" might have come even earlier, but government repression and the Party's own security policies precluded a full discussion of differences until 1956.[2]

Two dramatic events, occurring at about the same time, brought this gathering crisis to a head. The first was Nikita Khrushchev's "secret speech" before a closed session of the Soviet Party's Twentieth Congress in February 1956. The second was a speech Eugene Dennis gave at the April 1956 National Committee meeting, where a full translation of Khrushchev's speech first reached American Communists. The Khrushchev speech electrified Communists and others throughout the world because it revealed the full extent of Stalin's crimes against the Soviet people and the international Communist movement. Dennis's speech, based on a reevaluation of recent CPUSA history, seemed to draw out the implications of Khrushchev's words for the American Party's future.

The source of the revelations concerning Stalin explains the explosive effect they had on the Party cadre and the decisive difference between this and earlier crises. Accusations had circulated throughout Stalin's reign—that the so-called Doctors' Plot and other trials were simply political purges, that anti-Semitism was rife, and that Jewish culture, which Stalin referred to as "cosmopolitanism," was being systematically destroyed. In the late 1940s, Stalin consolidated his power in one East European society after another with show trials, imprisonments, and executions of many of the world's leading

Communists—Anna Pauker in Rumania, Rudolf Slansky in Czechoslovakia, Wladislaw Gomulka in Poland, Laszlo Rajk and Janos Kadar in Hungary. By the mid-fifties, as part of a process of de-Stalinization, each of these individuals was rehabilitated. For some, this meant release from prison; for others, the rehabilitation came too late, posthumously. Once again, suspicions and fears surfaced that these were not "mistakes," as the Soviets claimed, but political murders.[3]

Even the Party's dedicated members must have had doubts, but if they did, they had readily dismissed any new accusations as the fabrications of reactionaries and the bourgeois press. When confronted with evidence of political repression, American Communists had told themselves that the Soviets, besieged from without by hostile capitalist states and from within by counterrevolutionaries, had good reason to be on guard, to act vigorously against those seeking to destroy the world's only workers' state. Stalin and other Soviets had told them this, and they had believed it.[4] For these loyal comrades, who had accepted one excuse after another and had sustained their faith even in the face of a mountain of contrary evidence, Khrushchev's speech was devastating.

The critical moment for American Communists came with the arrival of a translation of Khrushchev's speech, smuggled from Russia via England to the United States in early April 1956. It was read aloud at the Party's enlarged National Committee meeting at the end of that month. In the audience sat about 120 people, not only the delegates elected to the National Committee but also dozens of district-level organizers and trade union activists, what one veteran called "the collective backbone of the Party." Steve Nelson, who chaired the meeting, was a proletarian hero among the Party regulars—the sort of person who had built the Communist Party. A veteran organizer of labor and the unemployed, a graduate of the Lenin School, and severely wounded as political commissar of the Abraham Lincoln Battalion in Spain, he was a man who had devoted and very nearly lost his life for the cause. Most recently, he had been sentenced to twenty years in prison for his political beliefs. His detailed recollections of the moment capture the speech's crushing effect on this remarkable collection of American radicals:

> The comrade who brought the speech rose and proceeded to read it in its entirety, which took an hour and a half. For twenty years we'd labeled the stories of Stalin's atrocities as lies and distortions. . . . Now the secretary general of the Communist Party of the Soviet Union confirmed these accusations and added documentation of many more. Of 1,966 delegates to the 1934 Seventeenth Congress of the Soviet Party, 1,108, including many members of the Central Committee, were arrested, and many of them executed by 1936. Sev-

enty percent of the 139 members and candidates for the Party Central Committee elected at the Seventeenth Congress, a group comparable in stature and experience to the comrades sitting before me, were arrested and shot. . . . An entire generation of leadership— . . . the men and women who made the Revolution—wiped out. You might prove that one guy was a rascal. . . . Perhaps you could prove this about two or even a dozen, but 70 percent of the Central Committee? This was a massacre . . . [and] the list of atrocities seemed endless. . . . Tears streamed down the faces of men and women who had spent forty or more years, their whole adult lives, in the movement. I looked into the faces of people who had been beaten up or jailed with me and thought of the hundreds that I had encouraged to join the Party. I thought, "All the questions that were raised along the way now require new answers, and there's no longer one seat of wisdom where we can find them. We're on our own."[5]

This tragedy and the personal and organizational crisis it represented for two generations of American Communists also created a final opportunity to save the movement. The reform impulse, however, was not simply another change of line for the American Party but the culmination of sentiments that had been gathering momentum for several years, sentiments for a thorough reevaluation of its recent history. "The weeks just before and after the publication of Khrushchev's speech," Maurice Isserman wrote, "were the high tide of 'reexaminationist' sentiment in the American Communist Party." *Daily Worker* editor John Gates and his staff opened their columns for the freest discussion the Party had seen. Steve Nelson could "not remember another period in which interest and discussion had been so intense." "The emotion produced by the shock seemed to harden the division that had been growing for some time in the national leadership," Nelson recalled, "and for the first time I feared there might be a split."[6] While rank-and-file readers indicted the collective leadership, Foster and his policies became frequent targets.

Many of these questions and misgivings seemed to fuse in Eugene Dennis's report to the CPUSA's April 1956 National Committee meeting, the committee's first open meeting in six years. Instead of providing the usual perfunctory overview of recent events and the outline of an immediate program, Dennis presented a scathing, self-critical evaluation of Party policy since the fall of Browder. The speech, soon published as *The Communists Take a New Look,* denounced the "left sectarian" quality of the Party's program, which had produced one disaster after another over the past decade. Because of the exaggerated fear of war between the United States and the USSR (a fear Dennis shared and promoted), all other concerns had been subordinated to foreign policy considerations, Dennis declared. All those decisions that had caused the split in the CIO's center-left coalition and led to the expulsion of the left-wing unions—the fight against the Truman Doctrine and Marshall Plan, and the decision to launch the Progressive Party—were related to this faulty reading of world politics. Likewise, for all the political repression of the past decade, the notion that the United States was on the road to fascism was a profound misjudgment that had caused the Party considerable damage during the underground era.[7]

Though Foster's name was never mentioned, it was impossible for him to miss the thrust of Dennis's attack. Dorothy Healey, who observed him during the speech, noted that he was "openly angered." When the committee members voted overwhelmingly to endorse Dennis's analysis, Ben Davis and two others abstained, while Foster stood alone in opposing it. Once again he was on the defensive.[8]

This open repudiation of his leadership and values represented a deep humiliation for Foster. Yet John Gates recalled a conversation he had with him following the National Committee meeting that suggests how Foster weathered such storms. At the meeting, Gates had noted that Foster's monumental books, so often eulogized by Party leaders, were seldom read by anyone outside of the movement. Even within the Party, Gates observed, the books were often simply dumped on lower levels of the organization, not really read or even sold. *Why,* Gates asked, did Americans not read Foster's books? After the meeting, Gates went over to patch things up with Foster but was surprised to find that the old man was not very upset. "Why," Foster said, "my books have been translated all over the world . . . into Russian, into Chinese, and many other languages." Gates was struck by what he termed "Foster's complete divorce from interest in America." "He saw himself a world figure . . . and though more typically 'American' than most party leaders, he was also strangely remote from his own land and people." Gates's conclusion that Foster "lived in a make-believe world of his own" was an exaggeration, but the conversation suggests what sustained Foster throughout the Party's decline and during this last great struggle against what he viewed as revisionism.[9] Even as his views were repudiated in his own party, he could look for and usually find vindication among large and powerful Communist parties abroad.

In the last years of his life, with the American Party in disarray and his own health failing, Foster continued to be considered a great Marxist leader by revolutionaries throughout the world. He consulted regularly with foreign editors and presses and wrote major interpretive articles and reviews of historical and theoretical works for Communist newspapers and journals. As of 1955, Foster's histories, memoirs, and other books had been translated into

Hungarian, Bulgarian, Japanese, Romanian, Polish, Chinese, French, Italian, and, of course, Russian.[10] Academics and dissident intellectuals with wider experience might eschew Foster's works, but if one were to ask a Russian or Rumanian high school student the name of an American historian, one would most likely hear Foster's name. Reviled at home, Foster was often revered abroad.

Dennis's April 1956 speech had the effect of galvanizing reform ideas in the Party. A majority of the dwindling membership, including many of the most talented, those who had led the mass movements of the thirties, began to grope their way toward a new vision of the Party. There was never one coherent "reform group," but certain key ideas began to emerge. Rather than a tightly organized and governed vanguard party, the CPUSA had to become a mass democratic movement for socialism. After analyzing the serious problems facing the United States as a society, it had to propose solutions that made sense to workers and other Americans. In the coming year, these reformers began to break away from deeply ingrained ways of thinking and organizing and to develop a new approach to radical politics, one that might have held the promise of fundamentally reshaping American politics if it had survived.

In the midst of all this reevaluation, Foster emerged as the foremost defender of orthodox Marxism-Leninism against what he later characterized as an "orgy of reckless criticism." "It was 'open season' for assailing the Party and all that it had ever done or stood for. . . . It is doubtful," he asserted, "if ever in the history of the world communist movement a Communist Party stood so passively under such a sea of abuse and misrepresentation." Instead of viewing the reform discussion as constructive criticism of the Party, Foster saw it as the ghost of a sinister force he thought he had purged from the movement. This discussion, Foster feared, was the return of Browderism and a general shift toward revisionism. In discussions of Stalin's "mistakes," Foster tended to explain the whole sordid development in terms of Stalin's own egotism and the threat posed to the USSR by the imperialist powers rather than any flaw in Marxism-Leninism itself. The imperialist threat had required "a high degree of centralization and a strong discipline." Now Communists must confront the efforts of the bourgeois press to use the Stalin revelations to discredit the entire movement. In considering *why* the Soviet leaders and the system had not dealt with Stalin's "cult of personality" before it had done so much damage, Foster invoked the specter of a split in the Party, which would have been "fatal disaster." It was an excuse Foster could understand; his own fear had prevented him from raising principled objections on more than one occasion. Long after the revelations, Foster chose to emphasize the "great share of credit" Stalin deserved for the USSR's many accomplishments rather than the "shortcomings and leadership excesses" during his reign. He showed little inclination to reverse his earlier judgment of Stalin as "one of the greatest fighters ever produced by the world's working class . . . a magnificent organizer" and "the greatest Marxist and the most able political leader of our times."[11]

Foster saw dangers in Stalin's crimes, but he drew no lessons for the functioning of the Party. Rather, he warned readers against hasty judgments and rash criticisms that might fuel right-wing attacks and provide ammunition for the bourgeois press: "This critical discussion will be all to the good, but it will have to be carried out upon a thoroughly responsible basis and in full consciousness of the imperative need for national and international class solidarity. . . . ill-thought-out criticism can do grave injury." In this situation, Foster concluded, what was most important was defense of the Party. "The supreme question confronting us at present," he told the National Committee in the summer of 1956, "is whether we shall give up as a failure our long and heroic efforts to build the Communist Party in the country; whether we will surrender to the ideology of aggressive American imperialism or not?"[12]

For others, the lessons inherent in Stalin's crimes lay far deeper—in the power structure of the Party, its relationship with the Soviet Union, and its policies and strategies over the past three decades. Throughout the spring of 1956, the *Daily Worker* opened its columns to rank-and-file Party members, who raised the most profound questions regarding the organization's history and its implications for future policy, precisely the sort of discussion Foster had hoped to avoid. On September 13, 1956, the National Committee of the CPUSA unanimously adopted a sweeping draft resolution to provide the basis for discussion leading up to the Party's February 1957 national convention. The resolution reiterated Dennis's critique of past practice, emphasized the importance of distinctive American conditions, and called for a new "mass party of Socialism." Foster first cast a "qualified yes," but he soon changed his vote to a no and launched a vigorous counterattack in the October *Political Affairs*. Foster "had been inclined to try to get along with the reform group," Steve Nelson recalled, "but now he went on the offensive, . . . maintaining . . . that the reformers were leading the Party in the direction of revisionism."[13]

In the ensuing discussion, even Foster was forced to face some of the blunders with which he had been associated. Writing in the fall of 1956, he noted three errors that had helped cut the Party off from the "American masses." The insistence that trade union cadres openly support the Wallace campaign isolated Party activists from the CIO's leadership and rank and file, fracturing the organization's center-left coalition. The Party's preoccupation with the Smith Act trials produced an inattention to electoral possibilities. Finally, the exaggerated security measures as a result of the misapprehension about fascist reaction during the McCarthy years slowed the Party's work and demoralized many of its cadres.[14] Foster did not need to emphasize that in each of these cases, he had played a central role. Nor was he prepared to countenance any substantive reforms.

For Foster, the draft resolution weakened the Party's adherence to Marxism-Leninism by asserting its right to interpret the theory in its own way. Many elements of the theory were "universally valid," Foster argued; to remove the words, as some in the leadership urged, from the Party's constitution would be viewed as "a major ideological retreat." By harping on mistakes and stimulating further criticism, the resolution "feeds the plague of pessimism and liquidationism. The idea seems to be that the more 'mistakes' the Party confesses to, the better will be its standing among the masses, which is absurd. . . . It is not constructive criticism, much of it, but a form of self destruction for the Party." Foster distinguished between serious *tactical* errors and the Party line that was and had been basically correct. It was "objective conditions," not the Party's "generally correct" line, that explained its isolation. In naming particular Party leaders and associating them with the threat of revisionism, Foster increased the prospects for a factional conflict, a form of combat he knew well.[15]

Throughout this difficult period in the mid-fifties, Foster remained close to Ben Davis and Robert Thompson, with whom he met regularly at a summer cottage in Crompond, New York, or at his apartment in the Bronx, rather than at the Party's headquarters. With much of the national leadership in jail, on trial, or underground in the early fifties and the headquarters under constant FBI surveillance, substantive discussions and what little organizing occurred beyond defense work tended to take place in such informal settings.

Robert Thompson, wounded while serving with the Lincoln Brigade, had also won a Distinguished Service Cross for bravery as a platoon leader during the war in New Guinea. A man of great courage and "single-minded purpose," he had returned to Party headquarters in 1945 at the age of thirty to become what George Charney called Foster's "ideological muscleman." Extremely dedicated and an agile debater, Thompson was also rigid, intolerant, and often ill-tempered. Formerly a strong Browder supporter, he assumed leadership of the New York state organization, often taking the lead during the postwar anti-Browder campaign. He served as Foster's point man during the confrontations with Mike Quill and other trade union leaders in the late forties and during the campaign against white chauvinism in the early fifties.

According to Carl Dorfman, Foster's personal secretary during the postwar years, the older man "loved Thompson like a son." When reform efforts began, Thompson became Foster's first line of defense.[16]

Foster's relationship with Ben Davis was particularly significant. Davis's star had fallen considerably in the midst of the political repression of the early fifties, but he remained an important political figure in New York, particularly in the city's African American community, where he was well connected and well respected. "Harlem was united behind Davis," George Charney recalled. Within the Party, Foster was deeply respected for his accomplishments in labor organizing, but many saw him as aloof. By contrast, Davis was well liked, and even those who disagreed with him politically admired him personally. Above all, Davis's reputation and contacts shored up Foster's support with the black community, while Foster's own reputation allowed him to maintain the respect of many of the remaining union activists. Davis's biographer, Gerald Horne, described the Davis-Foster relationship as "a walking embodiment of the powerful black-labor alliance."[17] This alliance gave Foster whatever leverage he maintained in Party politics as Party membership declined in the early fifties.

Foster also developed a fairly close relationship with the African American artist and intellectual Paul Robeson, who shared with Foster serious health problems and an orthodox approach to Marxism-Leninism. Robeson called Foster a "master of Marxist theory and practice," while Foster's remarks regarding Robeson in *The Negro People in American History* suggest that the respect was mutual. The details are sketchy, but it seems that this relationship with Robeson bolstered Foster's confidence throughout his own illnesses and the struggles over Soviet policy in Eastern Europe.[18] The most intense of these struggles was yet to come.

If the Khrushchev speech unmasked Stalin to loyal Communists throughout the world, events in Hungary in the late fall of 1956 showed them that the brutal spirit of Stalinism was still very much alive. In June, Polish workers had clashed with Soviet troops in Poznan, and Khrushchev had warned that more trouble would bring a major Soviet military intervention. That fall, Soviet troops clashed once again with workers, this time in Hungary, where a reform-oriented regime with broad popular support was beginning to distance itself from the USSR. The *Daily Worker* noted that Foster was absent when the Party's National Committee adopted a November 1, 1956, resolution expressing mild criticism of Soviet actions in Poland and Hungary. He quickly wrote to the paper, correcting the error and pointing out that he had voted against the resolution.[19] Several others on the National Committee joined Foster in opposition, contending that the resolution went too far and underestimated the threat posed to the Communist government by a revolt that included a strong reactionary element. But few agreed with his contention that the entire episode was a "CIA revolution."[20]

On November 4, 1956, a massive Soviet invasion crushed the Hungarian uprising. Thousands of Russian troops supported by hundreds of tanks shot down workers armed with only light arms and Molotov cocktails.[21] In the United States and elsewhere, the experience further galvanized the Party reformers and their sympathizers. Once again the *Daily Worker* was full of introspective articles and critical letters from rank-and-file members. Once again the Party's leadership was divided. Gates and reform-oriented committee members strongly condemned the invasion, while Foster's own motion called the invasion "a grim necessity and imperatively in the interest of Hungarian Socialism and World Peace." Many others found themselves in between the two positions because the uprising embraced *both* reform-oriented Communist workers and extreme reactionary elements. The committee cobbled together a compromise resolution that satisfied no one and aggravated Foster with its vacillation.[22]

Even this jolt failed to move Foster from his commitment to political orthodoxy and faith in the Soviets. Indeed, as in earlier crises, this one only served to confirm his narrow reading of Marxism-Leninism. He referred to Gates's calls for reform as "a mess of Social-Democratic political and organizational pottage." In the midst of the Hungarian invasion, Foster congratulated Paul Robeson on his "militant stand" in support of Soviet actions. "In view of the wobbling and confusion to be found in our own ranks," Foster wrote, "it is good to see someone showing clarity of understanding and fighting spirit. . . . This is a moment when steadiness is especially necessary in Left ranks. Undoubtedly there has been much confusion and vacillation caused by this Stalin affair, especially the tragedy in Hungary. It is one of those great obstacles that the movement has to overcome in its historic march ahead. It is a crisis of growth."[23] Foster's choice of words here is revealing. Neither Khrushchev's letter nor the Soviet invasion was a fundamental crisis calling for reevaluation of past policies, perhaps even the structure and practice of the Party itself; rather, they were "great obstacles" that the CPUSA had "to overcome."

Foster, often on the defensive on the Party's National Board throughout late 1956 and early 1957, fought every reform impulse as "liquidationist." He criticized the Party's labor activists for class collaboration and demanded continued adherence to Marxism-Leninism and the principles of democratic centralism. As those around him moved to new positions and many left the movement entirely, Foster refused to budge. Long a symbol of the Party's roots in proletarian radical traditions, Foster had become the symbol of its sectarian qualities. As Dorothy Healey recalled, he was "a prisoner of the past who simply kept repeating the old concepts, slogans, and approaches."[24]

Foster's distance from the reform elements in the Party's leadership may be partly explained by his daily experience in the early 1950s. Many of those who pushed the reforms hardest had been cut off from the Party when they went into prison or underground, where they reflected on the policies of the past decade that had isolated the Communists from their previous bases of support. Despite his illnesses, Foster had remained immersed in the daily Party routine, he had been involved with the Party's press, he had been in constant contact with the center in New York, and he had focused more than ever on the Soviet and the Eastern European parties. This immersion in the Party meant that Foster had even less time or inclination for such introspection than he normally had. On the contrary, he saw the Party besieged on all sides, as he had expected it to be, and he concluded that its defense must take top priority.

The political distance between Foster and the reformers was also generational. Part of an older group of functionaries, Foster had entered the Party during its sectarian phase in the twenties and taken part in the factional struggles of that era. Later, he had been largely cut off from direct experience in mass movements as the result of his illness and his political marginalization during Browder's reign. Most of the reformers had entered the Party through the antifascist, unemployed, and industrial union organizing that left them committed to a broad-based and flexible organizing strategy. Union organizing, wartime military service, and work in electoral coalitions brought deep immersion in American cultural and political life and in the process transformed the younger generation's political perspectives. The Popular Front and the Soviet-American wartime alliance allowed Party members to bridge temporarily the seemingly insurmountable gap between being an American and being a Communist. A Communist veteran of these movements recalled beginning to feel "like we were really part of the American Scene. We were looking for some kind of legitimization of our feeling about becoming more American. Browder came along and sort of articulated this."[25] This was an experience largely missing in the lives of the older generation. In a sense, Foster's earlier worries about the dangers of submerging Party identity in Popular Front movements had been realized at the end of a decade of political repression. Though sparked by the Khrushchev revelations, the reform impulse originated in the isolation endured by this Popular Front generation during the McCarthy years.

All of these crises and conflicts converged at the Communist Party's Sixteenth National Convention in February 1957, the first held since 1950, when the Party had virtually been driven underground. The convention was a remarkable event in many respects. Whatever the Party's intentions regarding openness, the McCarthy atmosphere was alive and well. When the Communists tried to find a meeting place, more than sixty New York hotels and restaurants turned them down, and the convention opened in an obscure caterer's hall, a former church on the Lower East Side. An agent photographed each person entering the hall, and uniformed and plainclothes police "swarmed all over the place."[26] Ironically, for the first time in their history, the Communists opened the event to observers and published a full version of the proceedings. Such symbolic gestures were significant for the message they conveyed to the outside world—the intention of many Communists to make this a new, more open and democratic movement. Delegates thoroughly debated the most basic concepts of Marxism-Leninism, including the practice of democratic centralism, and pledged themselves to a new, independent American road to socialism.

Eugene Dennis opened the convention's first afternoon with a keynote speech providing measured support for a reconsideration of Party policy and a reform of Party organization. During the previous year's discussion, he said, "important sections of the Party at *all* levels were temporarily disoriented and demoralized. . . . Some wandered into strange pastures; while others exhibited a hardening of the political arteries." (Foster, diagnosed as suffering from arteriosclerosis, could not have been pleased.) According to Dennis, everyone on the National Committee shared responsibility for this disorientation, though some who "at least until recently clung to inflexible policies and pursued extreme political objectives will perhaps take on themselves more than the common share." Dennis still insisted that the Party's main errors were of a left sectarian nature. "Dogmatism and doctrinairism are still the main danger," he concluded, "and will be the main danger . . . for some time to come." But, hoping for unity, he also struck a conciliatory chord, pleading for patience and understanding.[27]

Foster's speech followed directly after Dennis's. Now seventy-six years old and once again in ill health, Foster was too weak to speak for long. Nevertheless, he was ready for a fight, and he listened intently as Ben Davis read his speech to the delegates. Foster warned that his remarks should not be taken as opposition to Dennis's speech or as the outline for a separate program. Nonetheless, he launched into a bitter attack on the draft resolution and the "revisionists" and "conciliators" he saw behind it. At stake for Foster was the Communist Party itself. "The political demarcation," he argued, "[has been] . . . between those who want to maintain the Communist Party and those who would give it up for a political action association." The association, he said, was "only a resurrection of the discarded Browder Communist Political Association. . . . This convention should let it be known that it is resolved to build the Communist Party and not some futile, opportunistic substitute for it."[28]

The "most vital business before this convention," Foster continued, was to "recognize the universal truth of the vast body of Marxism-Leninism as the science of the world proletariat." To diminish the Party's vanguard role, to reject the notion of democratic centralism, "is Right revisionism, which goes in the direction of Social Democracy," he exclaimed. "If it should prevail, it would cut the heart out of American Communism." Such errors derived from poor leaders, who must be replaced with "proletarians, Negroes, youth, women . . . staunch leaders—who believe in the Party and will fight for its program."[29]

Earlier factional opponents returned to haunt Foster in his address. He argued that the current Right tendency—in its underestimation of American imperialist aggression and the general world capitalist economic crisis, in its overestimation of American imperialism's strength, and in its acceptance of "the bourgeois theory of American exceptionalism" —"is a direct descendent of the Lovestone opportunism of the boom 1920's and the Browder revisionism of the boom 1940's . . . [and] it points in the direction of class collaborationism."[30]

At moments, even Foster reflected the convention's introspective mood and the aim of reimmersing the movement in the mainstream of American life. He acknowledged the negative effects of left sectarianism, "the traditional weakness of the Party," and the need for change, emphasizing what he saw as the two greatest mistakes in the history of the CPUSA. Significantly, both involved disastrous policies that effectively cut the Party off from the labor movement. The first, the break with Fitzpatrick and other labor progressives, had occurred more than thirty years before but had clearly left a deep mark on Foster and the Party. The other was the break with the CIO's center-left coalition in the late forties over foreign policy issues and the Progressive Party campaign. Foster, too, recognized and deeply regretted the damage such policies had done to the Party and to the labor movement. Now in his mid-seventies, he still seemed to be searching for a way to bring his ideas to the great mass of American workers. But in reaching for a new path into the mainstream, he was certainly not prepared to stray as far as most delegates from the fundamental precepts of Marxism-Leninism and was still far more inclined to look toward the Soviets for direction. In the only mention of Hungary at the convention, Foster again supported the Soviet invasion and condemned the Party's compromise November 20, 1956, resolution as "impermissible yielding before aggressive American imperialism." Far from distancing themselves from the Soviet and other parties, the Americans needed to strengthen proletarian internationalism.[31]

The discussion of the past year had been useful, Foster concluded, but it had gone on too long, bringing with it the danger of a split. Now was the time to close ranks. He moved for a resolution for the continuation of the Communist Party. Even though the Party was continuing to shrink and the political space was continuing to narrow, he ended on a note of optimism, some might say naïveté: "objective conditions are growing more and more favorable for our Party."[32]

Despite the factional character of Foster's speech, the convention was notable for a new unity and enthusiasm among the leadership—at least on the surface. Al Richmond, one of the participants, recalled, "All the conflicting crosscurrents had the freest play . . . and the outcome was an apparent reconciliation of irreconcilables." At the end of the proceedings, Foster and Ben Davis joined hands onstage with Eugene Dennis, by this time a centrist of sorts, and John Gates, who represented the most aggressive reform elements. The assembled delegates cheered what appeared to be a united leadership and then rose to close the convention not with the "Internationale" but with the "Star-Spangled Banner." For a moment, it seemed that the Popular Front had reemerged amidst the rubble of McCarthyism and that a "New Left" might indeed be born.[33]

The Party came out of its 1957 convention with a resolution to move away from Foster's orthodoxy and toward a broader, more democratic form of organization. Looking only at the general tenor of the discussion and at the resolutions passed, one might conclude that it was Gates and the other reformers who had carried the day, not Foster. Yet the Party made none of the major changes prescribed, Foster remained, and in little more than a year Gates and most of the other reform-minded Communists were gone. What happened?

With all the fraternal expressions of solidarity at the convention, factional conflict resumed almost immediately. Foster was still operating with the model of a small cadre party. As Dorothy Healey walked out of the convention, she heard Foster remark, "Well, we may have lost this convention, but we'll win the next one." Angry at his apparent disregard for the Party's obvious catastrophic decline, she confronted him afterward, pointing out that they were losing many of their most valued cadres. "Let them go, who cares?" Foster said. "You must understand, Dorothy, that even if the Party goes down to only fifty members, if they are true Marxist-Leninists, staunch people, it doesn't matter. It is better to have fifty true members than fifty thousand who are not genuine Communists."[34]

In the spring of 1957, Dennis wrote to John Williamson, "Bill has become very rigid and inflexible on tactical and personnel questions." At a National Committee meeting on March 13, 1957, Foster, Ben Davis, and Charles Loman, a Foster supporter from Brooklyn, advanced a motion to remove Gates as editor of the *Daily Worker*. It lost by a seven-to-three vote, and for the moment Gates retained his position, but Foster and the Party's other fundamentalists continued to view the newspaper as a target.[35] In late April, Foster was humiliated when his own call for new leadership nearly swept him out of office. The Party's National Committee failed to elect him to the National Board, an action that would have removed him from the Party's top leadership for the first time since he joined the organization in the early twenties. A hasty motion to expand the National Board from seventeen to twenty allowed Foster to rejoin the Party's executive body, and the National Committee also elected him chairman emeritus, an honorary title with no real authority. At the same time, however, Foster's faction made sweeping gains in elections to county committees around New York City. Here, where the reform forces had enjoyed some of their greatest strength during the previous year, many activists had dropped out, and hard-liners took over.[36]

In late 1957 and early 1958, Foster published "The Party Crisis and the Way Out," a two-part article that mainly restated his earlier arguments. In the postconvention context, however, the article represented a serious counterattack on the reform program.[37]

By early 1958, it was clear that Foster had survived a major factional struggle to retain control, though there was little left to control. "First it was Lovestone," Gerald Horne wrote, "then Browder, and now Gates; in the eyes of many comrades they embodied a triangle or trinity." In each case, Foster had faced what appeared to be an overwhelming drive to revise substantially the Party's traditional Marxism-Leninism. In each case, often with the help of Soviet intervention, Foster survived by clinging to a political orthodoxy that appeared to be out of step with the times. "It was like Pascal's wager on God; it was best not to bet against him," Horne observed.[38]

Yet Foster won his struggle with the reform elements less with spectacular confrontations than through a steady evaporation of the Party's membership and perhaps also through failures on the part of the reformers themselves. No clear leader emerged from the reform group, less a unified faction with a clear vision for a new kind of party than a collection of people backing discrete reforms. Most strongly supported a departure from past policy, but few were able to project a logical path forward. John Gates lacked the sort of backing that would have been required to defeat Foster, and no other candidate emerged. "The most depressing moments were when we caucused," Steve Nelson recalled, "searching for someone of the stature to replace Foster." Here, Dennis played a key role. With what Nelson called "an unlimited capacity for vacillation," Dennis started out aggressively in his 1956 "Take a New Look" manifesto, wavered at the convention, and then, in its wake, retreated slowly but surely to more secure ground closer to Foster's orthodoxy. "He was a great man for moving 'resolutely' in one direction," George Charney wrote, "and then changing course." "The longer Gates temporized by waiting on Dennis," Isserman observed, "the more his own potential support within the Party eroded." Even the most ardent reformers lacked the stomach for a long faction fight with Foster, who continued, at an advanced age and in ill health, to show a real zest for intraparty combat. Repeatedly frustrated in their every effort to implement what they took to be a convention mandate to revamp the Party, more and more activists, including many who had been important leaders in the reform effort, simply dropped out. Many of these men and women had undergone long court battles, years in prison and underground away from their friends and families, and the loss of jobs and leadership positions that meant a great deal to them, but they had still clung to their belief in the Party. Now the Communist Party itself achieved what government repression and popular harassment had failed to accomplish. "Whoever won the struggle," Steve Nelson concluded, "would have inherited a tiny sect with a bankrupt newspaper."[39]

In the wake of the reformers' failure, Foster began to represent the 1957 convention as a "rejection of revisionism."[40] With Soviet support and in control of Party funds, he and his supporters consolidated their hold as the Party continued to shrivel up. Invoking the conclusion of a late 1958 international Communist conference that the greatest threat came from revisionism and not sectarianism, Foster pursued his factional aims throughout 1958 and 1959. He analyzed the 1956–57 reform movement as a conscious, international conspiracy "to divide the parties and to disorientate them." Acknowledging "left sectarian" mistakes, including some of his own, Foster nevertheless concluded that throughout the postwar period, "the basic political line of the CPUSA was fundamentally correct."[41]

Foster soon got the opportunity to test his theory of fewer but better Communists. Over the next year, Party schools closed, the *Daily Worker* was reduced to a one-page weekly, and membership continued to plummet. By the end of the 1950s, the Party had been reduced to about 3,000 hard-core members. In effect, this meant that Foster was also right about losing the battle at the 1957 convention but winning the war for control of the Party. As

disgusted reformers "voted with their feet" during 1957 and 1958, he consolidated his hold and returned the organization to much more orthodox ideas
and policies. "Essentially, what took place in these recent months," Foster
wrote in May 1958, "was important moves on the part of the National Committee to unify the Party and to strengthen the line . . . in a Marxist-Leninist
sense."[42] Yet in winning power, Foster was losing the Communist Party.

In the midst of the Party's decline, Foster's own health deteriorated further. In late 1955, a court-appointed physician had found that his arteriosclerosis had "affected not only his heart and circulatory apparatus but also cerebral circulation." The illness, Dr. Henry Riley reported, would "continue to
progress." On October 16, 1957, Foster suffered another severe stroke, which
left him in a semicomatose state. When he emerged, it was to find that he had
lost much of his speech and his ability to move the extremities on his right
side. "Isn't this a hell of a way to be?" Foster asked Elizabeth Gurley Flynn
when she visited his bedside in January 1958. "He is amazingly forthright and
impersonal about his own condition," Flynn observed, "viewing its problems
with a scientific detachment."[43]

During this severe illness and his partial recovery over the next three
years, he stayed in touch with the Party's National Executive through a series
of more than a dozen long letters that he dictated to a secretary. These simply
restated his position that the main threat since the 1956 crisis had been right
opportunism, that the Party must reassert its pride and prestige through adherence to Marxism-Leninism, and that American Communists must defend
the Soviet Union. Throughout this period, Foster remained staunchly left-
wing, applauding forthright identification with Marxist-Leninist principles,
criticizing any equation of left sectarianism with the more serious "right revisionist" danger, and condemning any tendency away from Lenin's vanguard
model and toward a "united party of socialism."[44]

With the same grim determination with which he had faced earlier challenges, Foster went through extensive rehabilitation, gradually recovering
most of his speech and some of his motor skills by the spring of 1959. That
summer, a visitor found that he had taught himself to type with his left hand
and was once again working several hours each day on a pamphlet. But Foster
suffered recurrent anginal attacks and mild strokes as a result of generalized
arteriosclerosis, and he remained confined to bed for the rest of his life, except for a brief period in the spring and summer of 1958. He described his
condition in a December 1958 letter addressed to Mao Tse Tung to mark the
tenth anniversary of the Chinese Revolution, a political achievement with
which Foster was coming to identify more closely. "I am 78 years old," Foster
wrote. "I have been confined to my room for the past 14 months with a para-

lytic stroke; and I am held under two police indictments, each of them carrying penalties of from five to ten years in prison—so my chances of getting to revolutionary China are pretty slim, although I have not given up on my efforts to get a passport."[45]

Again, it was the international movement that seemed to sustain Foster. "For years they have been trying here to destroy our party, but in this they will never be able to succeed," he told a young Hungarian journalist. "The party cannot be killed when the forces of communism triumph all over the world." Mao's message to him must have bolstered Foster: "Allow me, on behalf of the Communist Party of China and the Chinese people, to extend hearty greetings to you, glorious fighter and leader of the American working class, and to wish you an early recovery." The strength of the "reactionary forces" in the United States was "entirely a temporary phenomenon," Mao assured Foster, and "they will not have too many days to live."[46]

As Foster's health deteriorated, his physician, Dr. Harry Epstein, appealed to the government to allow him to go abroad for the sort of rehabilitation therapy he could not receive in his home. Foster received offers of medical treatment and travel expenses from Czechoslovakian, Rumanian, Hungarian, Soviet, and other authorities, but he was not allowed to leave the country because of the still-pending federal indictments. Esther Foster, suffering from an advanced case of osteoarthritis as well as arteriosclerosis, was also in need of medical treatment, the cost of which, Foster's lawyers argued, was prohibitive. As late November 1960, however, government authorities apparently still had hopes that a minimal recovery would allow them to place Foster on trial. His appeals for permission to seek medical treatment abroad were repeatedly denied until December 3, 1960, when Foster finally was granted a one-year leave to travel to Moscow.[47]

In his final letter to the CPUSA before his departure, Foster thanked members for their legal and financial support. He remained optimistic and showed uncharacteristic emotion in urging loyalty to the Party. "Our Party is part of the great worldwide Communist movement," he wrote. "Time has shown that it is indestructible, and is part of the movement which will eventually dominate the world. . . . We must actually *love* our Party."[48]

In January 1961, William Z. Foster left for his final trip to the Soviet Union, accompanied by two Soviet officials, his son-in-law Emmanuel Kolko, and his physician, Dr. Harry Epstein. His daughter Sylvia, his great-grandson Joey, and Esther, quite ill herself at the time of his departure, joined Foster in June. The journey had the practical object of securing medical care that Foster felt he could not receive in the United States. He was weak enough at this point that attendants carried him from the plane on a stretcher during a brief stop at Amsterdam. When he arrived in Moscow, the noted Russian cardio-vascular surgeon Anatoli Vasilyevich Alekseyev, who assumed direction of Foster's treatment, examined him and confirmed the effects of a recent stroke as well as heart problems. Within a week of his arrival, Epstein reported that Foster was responding to treatment, that his speech impairment had cleared up, and that he looked bright and alert.[49]

In February, Foster celebrated his eightieth birthday with greetings from throughout the world and a surprise visit from several members of the Central Committee of the Soviet Communist Party, including Premier Nikita Khrushchev and his wife. Left-wing newspapers around the world honored Foster for his contributions to the Communist movement and hailed him as one of the world's greatest "Marxist theoreticians." Soviet newspapers and journals published excerpts from his works and the Institute for Marxism-Leninism displayed a large collection of his books. Foster appeared on television, thanking the Soviet people and others throughout the world for their gifts and expressions of support. "On his eightieth birthday, the jubilarian is far from his home . . . in a Soviet sanatorium," the American *Morning Freiheit* noted. "However, he remains close to the hearts of the masses."[50]

One of Foster's proudest moments came on March 25, 1961, when the president of Moscow State University awarded him an honorary professorship in recognition of his contributions to Marxist history and theory. "This is the most wonderful single letter that I ever wrote . . . this is a splendid and exclusive honor," he told Esther, Sylvia, and Joey. In a subsequent letter, he asked Esther to distribute several copies of the certificate. Gus Hall, the Party's general secretary, should hang one of these in the CPUSA's headquarters, he instructed, and Ben Davis should follow up, lest Hall forget. The old Wobbly and worker-intellectual took obvious pride in his elevation to the highest ranks of Soviet academia.[51]

Bedridden at eighty, Foster continued to work. Visitors found his bedside table crowded with newspapers, books, and documents. An aide spent three hours each day reading to him, and Foster listened to radio news programs and Russian folk music in the evenings. In the last stage of his life, Foster still craved the discipline and order the Soviet system seemed to offer. Viewing a television broadcast of Soviet May Day celebrations, he was excited by cosmonaut Yuri Gagarin's role but was most thrilled by the Red Army's precision marching. "There is not a single man who is out of step or even half out of step," he wrote Esther.[52]

Not surprisingly, Foster attributed whatever recovery he experienced to the superiority of Soviet medicine. "The thing that strikes me here," he wrote to his American physician, "is the intensity and the effectiveness of the treatment that is only to be expected in the greatest socialist country." Although he had some setbacks, Foster believed that his condition was generally improving in the spring and summer of 1961, and he was convinced that the trip to Moscow had saved his life. "I will have to leave it to you to look into the matter medically if you are so inclined," he wrote to Dr. Epstein. "To me it appears as a sort of a miracle."[53]

But Foster and those around him could not have missed the symbolic importance of this final Russian journey. His correspondence shows a rare introspection and a deep affection for his family. When Dorothy Healey visited him at Barvicha sanitarium outside Moscow shortly before his death in 1961, she found Foster predictably concerned with Communist politics, but she also noted some mellowing in his attitude about the Party's decline. When she had confronted him at the 1957 convention with the fact that the Party was losing many of its most valuable cadres, he seemed genuinely unconcerned. This time, his mood was very different. "How's the party in Los Angeles?" Foster asked. Healey mentioned some of the people who were leaving. "Well, we are losing some very wonderful people, irreplaceable people," Foster said sadly.[54]

William Z. Foster died in a Moscow sanitarium on September 1, 1961, far from the industrial battlegrounds where he had earned his reputation as a brilliant organizer and strike leader. About a thousand people gathered for a memorial service at Carnegie Hall, including members of a Nazi group with signs reading "One Less Red Pest" and "Dead Red Rat." From a flower-bedecked stage where Foster's ashes rested, Ben Davis and other American Party leaders spoke of Foster's contributions and read eulogies from thirty-one Communist parties around the world. General Secretary Gus Hall called him the "Tom Paine of the working class." A young black activist from Philadelphia sang "Beloved Comrade" and "Joe Hill." An old miner recalled Foster's coalfield exploits, and an aging garment worker recounted his organizing in the needle trades. A *Daily Worker* headline captured the American Party's image of Foster: "He Was, Above All, a Fighter."[55]

The Moscow memorial at the time of Foster's death dwarfed the New York affair. Otto Kuusinen, a veteran Comintern leader, organized the memorial, and important leaders served as pallbearers. Foster's body lay in state in the Hall of Columns at the historic House of Trade Unions, where Premier Nikita Khrushchev and a small group of dignitaries attended an early private ceremony. After the cremation, top Soviet Party functionaries and other international Communist leaders attended a solemn state funeral at the Lenin Mausoleum on Red Square. Foster's old Wobbly friend Elizabeth Gurley Flynn, representing the American Communist Party; the legendary Spanish leader

Delores Ibarurri; Chinese ambassador Liu Hsiao Chi; and other dignitaries eulogized Foster. Red Square was also filled with thousands of common Russian citizens, who apparently still viewed Foster as the leading figure in the history of American labor and radicalism. The pallbearers—including Leonid Brezhnev, head of state and future premier; Alexei Kosygin, first deputy premier; and Nicolai Ignatov, deputy premier—paused at the Kremlin Wall to pay respects to other American radicals buried there—the Communists John Reed and Charles Ruthenberg and the Wobbly leader "Big Bill" Haywood. The Russians placed the ashes temporarily there, alongside those of other revolutionaries from around the world.[56]

Foster's final resting place was not in the Kremlin Wall on Red Square but in Waldheim Cemetery, just west of the Chicago city limits. His remains lay near the monument to the Haymarket anarchists, close to those of other American radicals. The distance, the symbolic juxtaposition, between Foster's grave and the location of his deathbed and funeral ceremony suggests the two great influences in his life as well as the trajectory of his career. At Waldheim, on the outskirts of the city he had always considered the heart of America's radical labor movement, Foster was surrounded by those who had built that movement and those with whom he had worked for so long—the Haymarket anarchists, Lucy Parsons, Emma Goldman, Sam Hammersmark, Jack Johnstone, and other, more obscure figures.

Like most of these radicals, William Z. Foster was undeniably a product of industrial America and the conflicts engendered in the course of its development. His radicalism and his remarkable organizational talents found their roots in his experience as an industrial worker and "practical" trade unionist. Yet he also became a loyal soldier of the international Communist movement. These loyalties—to the tradition of American labor radicalism and to international Marxism-Leninism—sustained him throughout his life, but in the end they clashed. Foster and his American Communist movement were born in the heart of the American working class, but they were fundamentally shaped by the influence of Soviet communism. Having contributed so much to the growth of the working-class movement in the United States, Foster and his Party perished far from home, isolated from the lives and concerns of most American workers.

Conclusion

ULTIMATELY, the story of William Z. Foster and the Communist Party of the United States of America is one of failure. The American organization, like most old style Communist parties, is all but gone now; even many of the revamped parties appear to be in disarray and decline or to have reinvented themselves as moderate social democratic electoral machines. Some perceive in this crisis the end not only of socialist politics but of history itself. For them, the apparent victory of free enterprise capitalism and pluralist democracy has resolved the ideological conflicts that have always appeared inherent in the system and have provided the rationale for Communist and other radical politics.[1]

Yet such thinking appears rather presumptuous in an age when poverty and homelessness persist in the wealthiest nations on earth, organized racism and other forms of intolerance appear to be on the rise, and millions throughout the world cling to a frail existence amidst famine and war. The old struggle between Soviet communism and American capitalism is dead, and few will mourn its passing. But inequality and oppression, the sources for Foster's communism and other varieties of American radicalism, are still with us, even if there are few among us with the will to address such problems. American Communists failed in their efforts to remake the United States; most American workers rejected their particular model for social change. There is, however, still need for a radical advocacy of the poor and disfranchised and a need for organization and strategy, even if it is difficult at the moment to see a clear path forward. Instead of congratulating ourselves, we might end Foster's story by returning to the biggest question of all. What do his failure and his party's tell us about the United States as a society and the place of such radicalism within it?

In this context, Foster's talents and the depth of his commitment to radical change make his story all the more tragic. Emerging from a more or less typical working-class background, he developed a remarkable talent for mass organization and leadership, devoting himself selflessly to this pursuit. His instincts in this regard were far more reliable than those of most of his comrades in the Party leadership. Never a charismatic speaker, he nevertheless succeeded in conveying his own vision of a radical labor movement to a generation of activists in the twenties and thirties. What little success the Party enjoyed in these years derived largely from Foster and the group around him, indigenous radicals who hitched their wagon to the Soviet star. Never an intellectual, Foster educated himself and wrote widely from the twenties on, assuming a perspective that was rare in American society.

What became of this talent and dedication? What explains this tragedy of a remarkably talented working-class radical ending his life in political oblivion? Such questions return us to the historical debates that have preoccupied historians of American communism over the past twenty years, but Foster's story provides us a different perspective on this familiar debate.

Quickly rising to Party leadership shortly after he joined, Foster carried his syndicalist lessons and values with him. Long after he became a Communist, he continued to understand revolutionary change largely in terms of industrial struggles and resisted policies that threatened this agenda. In this sense, the New Left historians' conception of American communism as a legitimate heir of earlier radical movements, a product of indigenous economic and political conflicts shaped by experiences in particular industries and communities, makes a good deal of sense.

But it is impossible to comprehend the *transformation* of Foster's politics without considering the unique character of the Communist Party as an organization and particularly the role of Soviet influence in American Party policy. Time after time during his early years in the Party, the exigencies of "international proletarian solidarity," which too often amounted to Soviet policy concerns, collided with Foster's instincts and experience: in the labor party fight and the split with Fitzpatrick; during his factional struggles with Lovestone; most decisively in the 1928 decision to launch dual revolutionary unions. Likewise, Foster's reemergence as the dominant influence in the Party following World War II was conditioned by Soviet influence. He was not the first or last Communist to bend his own will to that of the Party, though his decision to do so deeply influenced the prospects for a radical labor movement in the United States.

The older historians of American communism may have assigned too much weight to specific Comintern policy formulations and little if any to domestic and personal considerations, but the international dimension of the Party's life has certainly been slighted in some of the newer histories. As Geoff Eley noted, "The pull towards social history can sometimes diminish the significance of formal communist affiliations, leading in extreme cases (mainly in the literature of the CPUSA) to a history of communism with the Communism left out."[2] The nature of democratic centralism in the American Party and the dominant position of the Soviet Party in the international movement meant that Soviet policy did shape the American Communist experience—in the world of "practical" organizing as well as in the realm of theory.

So far, the divergent interpretations of American communism have led largely to hostile confrontations among scholars who disagree not only about Communist history but also about contemporary politics. As Harvey Klehr and his collaborators noted, the issues involved "go beyond arcane academic interpretations to questions about basic American values and our understanding of our own political culture."[3] What is needed now is an *integration* of the international and indigenous elements of American communism. There was, in fact, a constant tension between these two dimensions of the movement: communism as a genuine reflection of social inequalities and oppression and communism as the product of Comintern directives, Soviet policy initiatives, and the Soviet Party politics that shaped both.

Foster's life exemplifies this tension. His constant preoccupation with detailed industrial organizing emphasizes the significance of domestic and even local conditions for the daily work of the Party. This was a reality Foster never tired of pressing upon his more theoretically minded comrades. Yet his position as a Party leader made it impossible for Foster to ignore, even when he wanted to, the influence of Soviet policies and politics on the American organization's fate. Personal considerations were also undoubtedly at work in this equation. Entering the Party at the age of forty with a wealth of work, organizing, and strike experience as well as an enormous ambition to transform the labor movement, Foster continued to focus his own efforts on industrial work and fought for what he perceived to be effective policies. Yet he functioned in a party full of factional conflict and found that his success in promoting his ideas depended on the outcome of these conflicts and on those in the Comintern.

Throughout the twenties, the exigencies of Communist *theory,* as developed by the Comintern and implemented by the American Party, repeatedly conflicted with Foster's Communist *practice* in the unions, the labor party movement, and elsewhere. His commitment to Party discipline, the principles of democratic centralism, and his own ambition had overwhelmed the more creative elements of his perspective by the early years of the Great Depression. Yet even during the Popular Front and war years, he resisted those policies with which he disagreed, often finding himself marginalized as a result. He shifted his positions on a variety of questions over time, but his opposition to Browder's Popular Front policies tended to come from a more or less coherent left-wing critique of social democratic tendencies. He regained a position of power at the end of World War II, just as the Party went into decline. Indeed, his own dogmatic version of Marxism-Leninism in the postwar period—the product of both the repressive political atmosphere in the United States and Foster's perception of the international line—contributed mightily to the organization's deterioration.

Yet Foster's story suggests not the inevitability of radicalism's failure but the significance of historical contingency and even personal experience for a particular political outcome. Here biography remains important even in the midst of sweeping social and political change. Foster's original commitment to communism was based not only on the apparent lack of radical alternatives but also on strong attractions inherent in Marxism-Leninism in general and the Soviet model in particular. The revolutionary elitism Foster embraced in his early syndicalist days proved remarkably compatible with Lenin's notion of a vanguard party. For Foster, who had always valued discipline and hard work, the Party represented the most viable militant minority. In official Soviet representations of communism, he found a systematic model and a scientific language, both of which resonated with his own deeply held values. Foster's physical and psychological breakdown in the mid-thirties, products of rather brutal Third Period conflicts, removed him from active Party leadership and from those activities that had formed his political perspective, his personal identity, and his most durable contacts with American workers. Largely detached from the social and ideological transformation represented by the Popular Front, Foster never accommodated himself to the reformist language or the expanded social base of the Party in these years. He defined his political identity in opposition to Earl Browder's and kept the

Marxist-Leninist flame alive during the Party's World War II drift toward social democracy.

It is difficult to see any way in which American communism might have thrived in the postwar political atmosphere. It was virtually proscribed by law, it was under siege by employers and the state, and its leadership was in jail or in hiding. Much of the Party's decline can be explained, as Foster argued, by this repression. Newer interpretations of the McCarthy era that excuse its excesses by arguing that American communism posed a real threat tend to rationalize an enormous amount of damage to thousands of individual lives and to the fabric of American politics and culture.[4] There is no doubt that political repression during the decade following World War II remains the single most important explanation for the destruction of the American Left. Yet Foster's personal situation and the influence of the international movement were important in sealing the organization's fate. Browder's decline and Foster own reemergence were both shaped by the Soviets, while the Party's postwar perspective, emphasizing the threat of war and fascism, clearly reflected Soviet perspectives more than American political realities and left the Party peculiarly vulnerable to this repression. Foster reasserted himself on the strength of Marxist-Leninist orthodoxy, a political position that not only served Soviet interests but also squared with his own political experiences—even as it led the Party toward political destruction.

The lesson to be taken from William Z. Foster's life concerns not the futility or irrelevance of radical politics in the American context but the importance of rooting such politics in the reality of everyday life, in the political and cultural traditions of our own society, and in the democratic aspirations shared by most Americans. The tragedy of Foster's political life was to suppress his own initiatives and instincts and those of two generations of other political activists in the name of Communist discipline. But it would be a greater tragedy, an act of inexcusable historical condescension, to abandon the vision of a more just and democratic American society because the Communist prescription failed. If William Z. Foster's life story can be seen as a tragedy, then we might ask ourselves if it is not an American tragedy as well as a personal one. Many of the problems that moved Foster in sometimes erratic political directions are still with us. It is in the struggle to find solutions to them that we continually create our own history.

Notes

INTRODUCTION

1. Bert Cochran, *Labor and Communism: The Conflict that Shaped American Unions* (Princeton, N.J., 1977), 92; Theodore Draper, *The Roots of American Communism* (New York, 1957), 62.

2. David Montgomery, *The Fall of the House of Labor: The Workplace, the State, and American Labor Activism, 1865–1925* (New York, 1987), 2.

3. Harvey Klehr, *Communist Cadre: The Social Background of the American Party Elite* (Stanford, Calif., 1978), 10.

4. Nick Salvatore, *Eugene V. Debs: Citizen and Socialist* (Urbana, Ill., 1982).

5. See, for example, James Weinstein, *Ambiguous Legacy: The Left in American Politics* (New York, 1975); John P. Diggins, *The American Left in the Twentieth Century* (New York, 1973); and Milton Cantor, *The Divided Left: American Radicalism, 1900–1975* (New York, 1978). Paul Buhle, *Marxism in the USA from 1870 to the Present Day* (London, 1987), appears to be an exception in this regard.

6. Edward P. Johanningsmeier, *Forging American Communism: The Life of William Z. Foster* (Princeton, N.J., 1994), 4. The theme of Foster's persistent syndicalism is developed in Weinstein, *Ambiguous Legacy,* 49–54, 77–78; and James Oneal, *American Communism* (New York, 1947), 31.

7. Johanningsmeier, *Forging American Communism,* 5.

8. Ibid., 8–9.

9. Theodore Draper, *American Communism and Soviet Russia* (New York, 1960), 5; Harvey Klehr, *The Heyday of American Communism: The Depression Decade* (New York, 1984), xi, 415; Irving Howe and Lewis Coser, *The American Communist Party: A Critical History* (Boston, 1957), 506. See also Daniel Bell, *Marxian Socialism in the United States* (Princeton, N.J., 1967). For a more recent interpretive history that follows this line of argument, see Harvey Klehr and John Earl Haynes, *The American Communist Movement: Storming Heaven Itself* (New York, 1992).

10. Maurice Isserman, *Which Side Were You On? The American Communist Party during the Second World War* (Middletown, Conn., 1982); Fraser M. Ottanelli, *The Communist Party of the United States from the Depression to World War II* (New Brunswick, N.J., 1991); Buhle, *Marxism in the USA,* 121–220. Local or industrial studies reflecting this perspective include Roger Keeran, *The Communist Party and the Auto Workers Unions* (Bloomington, Ind., 1980); Joshua Freeman, *In Transit: The Transport Workers Union in New York City, 1933–1966* (New York, 1986); Paul Lyons, *Philadelphia Communists, 1936–1956* (Philadelphia, 1982); Mark Naison, *Communists in Harlem during the Depression* (Urbana, Ill., 1983); Paul Buhle, "Jews and American Communism: The Cultural Question," *Radical History Review* 23 (December 1980): 9–33; and Randi Jill Storch, "Shades of Red: The Communist Party and Chicago's Workers, 1929–1939" (Ph.D. diss., University of Illinois at Urbana-Champaign, 1998). Memoirs, narratives, and oral biographies that tend to reinforce this interpretation include Al Richmond, *A Long View from the Left: Memoirs of an American Revolutionist* (Boston, 1972); George Charney, *A Long Journey* (Chicago, 1968); Nell Irvin Painter, *The Narrative of Hosea Hudson* (Cambridge, Mass., 1979); Steve Nelson, James R. Barrett, and Rob Ruck, *Steve Nelson: American Radical* (Pittsburgh, 1981); Kenneth Kann, *Joe Rappaport: The Life of a Jewish Radical* (Philadelphia, 1981); Junius Scales and Richard Nickson, *Cause at Heart: A Former Communist Remembers* (Athens, Ga., 1987); and Dorothy Healey and Maurice Isserman, *Dorothy Healey Remembers: A Life in the Communist Party* (New York, 1990). For a critical review of much of this literature, see Theodore Draper, "American Communism Revisited," *New York Review of Books,* May 9, 1985, 32–37; and Theodore Draper, "The Popular Front Revisited," *New York Review of Books,* May 30, 1985, 79–81. For a review more sympathetic to the new approach and interpretations, see Maurice Isserman, "Three Generations: Historians View American Communism," *Labor History* 26 (Fall 1985): 517–45.

11. E. J. Hobsbawm, *Revolutionaries: Contemporary Essays* (New York, 1973), 3. On the reception of the Bolshevik Revolution by left-wingers in the United States, see Philip S. Foner, ed., *The Bolshevik Revolution: Its Impact on American Radicals, Liberals, and Labor* (New York, 1967); and Christopher Lasch, *The American Liberals and the Russian Revolution* (New York, 1962).

12. *Voice of Labor,* August 26, 1921, 11.

13. Hobsbawm, *Revolutionaries,* 6–7.

14. Steve Nelson, for example, was often quite open about painful and embarrassing political experiences but found it more difficult to deal with the personal side of his

story. Judging from other memoirs and narratives, this has been a general problem. See Nelson, Barrett, and Ruck, *Steve Nelson;* and Painter, *Narrative of Hosea Hudson,* 36–37, 39–40. For other representative memoirs and narratives, see John Williamson, *Dangerous Scot: The Life and Work of an American "Undesirable"* (New York, 1969); Elizabeth Gurley Flynn, *I Speak My Own Piece: Autobiography of the Rebel Girl* (New York, 1955); Hosea Hudson, *Black Worker in the Deep South* (New York, 1972); Ben Davis, *Communist Councilman from Harlem* (New York, 1969); Harry Haywood, *Black Bolshevik: Autobiography of an Afro-American Communist* (Chicago, 1978); William L. Patterson, *The Man Who Cried Genocide* (New York, 1971); Ben Gold, *Memoirs* (New York, 1985); Jack Kling, *Where the Action Is: Memoirs of a U.S. Communist* (New York, 1986); and Vera Buch Weisbord, *A Radical Life* (Bloomington, Ind., 1977). Interestingly, women veterans have been somewhat more open about their personal lives, but even in these stories, the political overwhelms the personal. See Ellen Kay Trimberger, "Women in the Old and New Left: The Evolution of a Politics of Personal Life," *Feminist Studies* 5 (Fall 1979): 432–50; Peggy Dennis, *The Autobiography of an American Communist: A Personal View of Political Life* (Westport, Conn., 1977); Healey and Isserman, *Dorothy Healey Remembers;* Jessica Mitford, *A Fine Old Conflict* (New York, 1977); Richmond, *Long View from the Left;* and Scales and Nickson, *Cause at Heart.* For two of the most successful biographies in this regard, see Martin B. Duberman, *Paul Robeson: A Biography* (New York, 1988); and Rosalyn Baxandall, *Words on Fire: The Life and Writings of Elizabeth Gurley Flynn* (New Brunswick, N.J., 1987). Vivian Gornick, *The Romance of American Communism* (New York, 1977), which is based on interviews with veterans of the movement, demonstrates that it is possible to trivialize the political by *overemphasizing* the personal. I have addressed the relationship between personal development and crisis and political activism in "Revolution and Personal Crisis: Communist Politics and Changing Identity in the Life of William Z. Foster" (1997 manuscript).

CHAPTER 1: SKITTEREEN AND THE OPEN ROAD, 1881–1904

1. William Z. Foster, *Pages from a Worker's Life* (New York, 1939), 15; Sam Bass Warner, *The Private City: Philadelphia in Three Periods of Its Growth* (Philadelphia, 1971), 137–57; Dale B. Light Jr., "Class, Ethnicity and the Urban Ecology in a Nineteenth Century City: Philadelphia's Irish, 1840–1890" (Ph.D. diss., University of Pennsylvania, 1979), 26–27, 46, 47, 50–51; Dennis Clark, *The Irish in Philadelphia* (Philadelphia, 1973); Bruce Laurie, Theodore Hershberg, and George Alter, "Immigrants and Industry: The Philadelphia Experience, 1850–1880," in *Philadelphia: Work, Space, Family and Group Experience in the Nineteenth Century,* ed. Theodore Hershberg (New York, 1981), 93–119; Theodore Hershberg, Dale B. Light Jr., Harold E. Cox, and Richard Greenfield, "The 'Journey to Work': An Empirical Investigation of Work, Residence, and Transportation, 1850–1880," in *Philadelphia,* ed. Hershberg, 128–73; Bruce Laurie, *The Working People of Philadelphia, 1800–1850* (Philadelphia, 1980), 151–54; David Montgomery, "The Shuttle and the Cross: Weavers and Artisans in the Kensington of 1844," *Journal of Social History* 5 (Summer 1972): 411–47; Bruce Laurie, "Fire Companies and Gangs in South-

wark: The 1840's," in *The Peoples of Philadelphia: A History of Ethnic Groups and Lower-Class Life, 1790–1940,* ed. Allen F. Davis and Mark H. Haller (Philadelphia, 1973), 71–88; Dennis Clark, "The Philadelphia Irish: Persistent Presence," in *Peoples of Philadelphia,* ed. Davis and Haller, 141; Susan G. Davis, *Parades and Power: Street Theatre in Nineteenth-Century Philadelphia* (Philadelphia, 1986), 115, 143–47. The word *Skittereen* may have been a corruption of Skibbereen, the name of a town in County Cork that fared badly during the great famine of the 1840s. See Cecil Woodham-Smith, *The Great Hunger: Ireland, 1845–1849* (New York, 1962), 141–44. My thanks to Jim Hurt and Seamus Reilly for insight here.

2. William Z. Foster, *From Bryan to Stalin* (New York, 1937), 11–12 (first quote); Paul Douglas, *Six upon the World: Toward an American Culture for an Industrial Change* (Boston, 1954), 61, 62 (second quote). See also Joseph North, *William Z. Foster: An Appreciation* (New York, 1955), 7–8. Sources suggest that Foster himself was unclear on the details of his parents' lives. In different places, he noted his father immigrated in 1866 and 1868. Unless otherwise noted, biographical details are drawn from Foster's *From Bryan to Stalin* and from Foster's Comintern personnel file, fond 495, opis 261, delo 15, listki 1–121, plus several volumes of press clippings, Archives of the Communist International, Russian Center for the Preservation and Study of Documents of Recent History, Moscow (hereafter Comintern Archives). The Molly Maguires, descended from the secret societies of rural Ireland, were a group of militant miners who had practiced terrorism against their coal employers in Pennsylvania's anthracite fields during the late 1870s. Foster might have been referring to veterans of the movement or to radical Irish miners more generally. On reactions to the Molly Maguires in Philadelphia's Irish community, see Light, "Class, Ethnicity and the Urban Ecology," 197–99.

3. On the relationship between the Land League's Irish nationalism and Irish American labor radicalism, see Eric Foner, "Class, Ethnicity, and Radicalism in the Gilded Age: The Land League and Irish America," in his *Politics and Ideology in the Age of the Civil War* (New York, 1980), 150–200; and David Brundage, "Irish Land and American Workers: Class and Ethnicity in Denver, Colorado," in *"Struggle a Hard Battle": Essays on Working-Class Immigrants,* ed. Dirk Hoerder (DeKalb, Ill., 1986), 55–58, 60–63. On Irish nationalism in Philadelphia in this era, see Ken Fones-Wolf, *Trade Union Gospel: Christianity and Labor in Industrial Philadelphia, 1865–1915* (Philadelphia, 1989), 71–73; Dennis J. Clark, *The Irish Relations: Trials of an Immigrant Tradition* (Rutherford, N.J., 1982), 70, 103–13, 117–19; Dale B. Light Jr., "The Role of Irish-American Organizations in Assimilation and Community Formation," in *The Irish in America: Emigration, Assimilation, and Impact,* ed. P. J. Drudy (Cambridge, 1985), 131–32; and Light, "Class, Ethnicity and the Urban Ecology," 52, 99–110, 204–9.

4. Edward Johanningsmeier, "Philadelphia, 'Skittereen,' and William Z. Foster: The Childhood of an American Communist," *Pennsylvania Magazine of History and Biography* 117 (October 1993): 290–91; Foster, *From Bryan to Stalin,* 12 (quote). On the decline of the English handloom trade and its social consequences, see E. P. Thompson, *The Making of the English Working Class* (New York, 1963). On infant mortality in the late

nineteenth century, see Samuel H. Preston and Michael R. Haines, *Fatal Years: Child Mortality in Late Nineteenth-Century America* (Princeton, N.J., 1991), 91–92.

5. Douglas, *Six upon the World,* 62.

6. Foster, *From Bryan to Stalin,* 16, 18. On the significance of the 1890s upsurge in the broader pattern of nineteenth-century strikes, see David Montgomery, "Strikes in Nineteenth Century America," *Social Science History* 4 (February 1980): 81–102; and J. Amsden and S. Brier, "Coal Miners on Strike: The Transformation of Strike Demands and the Formation of a National Union," *Journal of Interdisciplinary History* 7 (Spring 1977): 583–616. On Coxey's Army, see Carlos Schwantes, *Coxey's Army, 1860–1910* (Berkeley, Calif., 1979).

7. Lorin Blodget, *The Social Condition of the Industrial Classes of Philadelphia* (Philadelphia, 1884).

8. Michael R. Haines, "Poverty, Economic Stress, and the Family in a Late Nineteenth-Century City: Whites in Philadelphia, 1880," in *Philadelphia,* ed. Hershberg, 240–73, especially 245–57, tables 2, 3; John F. Sutherland, "Housing the Poor in the City of Homes: Philadelphia at the Turn of the Century," in *Philadelphia,* ed. Hershberg, 182–87; Light, "Class, Ethnicity and the Urban Ecology," 55–62; Light, "Role of Irish-American Organizations in Assimilation and Community Formation," 117–20; Johanningsmeier, "Philadelphia, 'Skittereen,' and William Z. Foster," 296–97; Daniel Nelson, *Managers and Workers: Origins of the New Factory System in the United States, 1880–1920* (Madison, Wis., 1975), 6, 7; Walter Licht, *Getting Work: Philadelphia, 1840–1950* (Cambridge, Mass., 1992); Bruce Laurie and Mark Schmitz, "Manufacture and Productivity: The Making of an Industrial Base, 1850–1880," in *Philadelphia,* ed. Hershberg, 43–92; Laurie, Hershberg, and Alter, "Immigrants and Industry," in *Philadelphia,* ed. Hershberg, 93–119.

9. Warner, *Private City,* 169–79; Caroline Golab, "The Immigrant and the City: Poles, Italians, and Jews in Philadelphia, 1870–1920," in *Peoples of Philadelphia,* ed. Davis and Haller, 203; Light, "Class, Ethnicity and the Urban Ecology," 26–28.

10. W. E. B. Du Bois, *The Philadelphia Negro* (1899; reprint, New York, 1967), 61; see also the maps on the preceding four pages. On the transformation of the neighborhood by the turn of the century, see Johanningsmeier, "Philadelphia, 'Skittereen,' and William Foster," 294–95; and John T. Emlen, "The Movement for the Betterment of the Negro in Philadelphia," *Annals of the Academy of Political and Social Science* (September 1913), reprinted in *Black Politics in Philadelphia,* ed. Miriam Ershkowitz and Joseph Zikmund (New York, 1973), 40–52.

11. Douglas, *Six upon the World,* 63 (first quote); Foster, *Pages from a Worker's Life,* 17 (second quote), 18 (third, fourth, and fifth quotes). On Philadelphia street crime and racial violence, see also Peter McCaffery, *When Bosses Ruled Philadelphia: The Emergence of the Republican Machine, 1867–1933* (University Park, Pa., 1993), 11–14; David R. Johnson, "Crime Patterns in Philadelphia, 1840–1870," in *Peoples of Philadelphia,* ed. Davis and Haller, 89–110; Light, "Class, Ethnicity and the Urban Ecology," 162–63; and Warner, *Private City,* 140–41. On the relations between Jews and Irish in Philadelphia,

see Clark, *Irish Relations,* 178–81. The racial confrontation in Philadelphia was not un-usual. On the troubled relationship between Irish Americans and African Americans who shared many characteristics and experiences, see David Roediger, *The Wages of Whiteness: Race and the Making of the American Working Class* (London, 1991), 133–84; and Kerby A. Miller, "Green over Black: The Origins of Irish-American Racism," 1965 paper in author's possession.

12. Mary Jo Maynes, *Taking the Hard Road: Life Course in French and German Workers' Autobiographies in the Era of Industrialization* (Chapel Hill, N.C., 1995).

13. Foster, *Pages from a Worker's Life,* 17, 15, 18.

14. William Z. Foster, *The Twilight of World Capitalism* (New York, 1949), 158–59. There is considerable evidence that Foster's attitude toward religion softened toward the end of his life. See, for example, Johanningsmeier, *Forging American Communism,* 353; and Douglas, *Six upon the World,* 89.

15. William Z. Foster, *The Great Steel Strike and Its Lessons* (New York, 1920), 151 (first quote); Henry Steele Commager, ed., *Lester Ward and the Welfare State* (Indianapolis, Ind., 1967), xxvii (second quote).

16. Foster, *From Bryan to Stalin,* 14, 22 (first quote); Foster, *Twilight of World Capital-ism,* 157 (second quote). On Ward, see also James Quayle Dealey, "Lester Frank Ward," in *Dictionary of American Biography,* vol. 19, ed. Dumas Malone (New York, 1936), 430–31; and Clifford H. Scott, *Lester Frank Ward* (Boston, 1976). In *Social Darwinism in Ameri-can Thought* (Philadelphia, 1945), Richard Hofstadter contrasts Ward with William Graham Sumner, the American apostle of Social Darwinism. Although Foster never mentioned any particular work, he likely had encountered Ward's *Dynamic Sociology* (New York, 1883).

17. William Z. Foster, "Unemployment," *Daily World Magazine,* September 28, 1974, M4. On the function of the family economy and the significance of children's earnings to the standard of living among Philadelphia's laboring poor at the end of the nine-teenth century, see Haines, "Poverty, Economic Stress, and the Family," 257–61, tables, 4, 5, 6; Claudia Goldin, "Family Strategies and the Family Economy in the Late Nine-teenth Century: The Role of Secondary Workers," in *Philadelphia,* ed. Hershberg, 277–310, especially, 281–96; Fones-Wolf, *Trade Union Gospel,* 10–11; and Light, "Class, Eth-nicity and the Urban Ecology," 60–61. On the severity of the depression of the 1890s, see David M. Gordon, Richard Edwards, and Michael Reich, *Segmented Work, Divided Workers: The Historical Transformation of Labor in the United States* (Cambridge, 1982), 94–106; and Licht, *Getting Work,* 10.

18. Foster, *From Bryan to Stalin,* 12. Clearly confused about his father's age at death, Foster told Paul Douglas that his father lived to sixty, while in documents submitted to the Comintern, he estimated that he was only about fifty at the time of his death. See Foster, Comintern personnel file, fond 495, opis 261, listok 20, Comintern Archives. See also Johanningsmeier, *Forging American Communism,* 360–61.

19. Foster, *From Bryan to Stalin,* 21; Foster, *Pages from a Worker's Life,* 20–23 (quote on 21).

20. The Socialist Labor Party (SLP) was established in 1877 and grew out of the Work-ingmen's Party, the original Marxist organization in the United States. It played a ma-

jor role in the labor upsurge of the late 1870s. Its activists helped lead the 1877 railroad strike and unemployed demonstrations in various cities, and several were elected to local office in Illinois and elsewhere. Having declined in the course of the 1880s, the SLP enjoyed a resurgence during the depression and labor strikes of the mid-1890s. The SLP drew its strength from radical immigrant subcultures and, to a lesser extent, native nineteenth-century radical traditions. The organization declined in the early twentieth century amidst ideological divisions on the left and the rise of the Socialist Party of America, but it provided an important base for the new Communist movement when it emerged in 1919. The Knights of Labor was secretly established by a group of tailors at Philadelphia in 1869 and developed into a major political and industrial force during the labor upheavals of the mid-1880s. The organization was in decline in Philadelphia and elsewhere by the time Foster was growing up. On the Knights, see Leon Fink, *Workingmen's Democracy: The Knights of Labor and American Politics* (Urbana, Ill., 1983); and Judith Goldberg, "Strikes, Organizing, and Change: The Knights of Labor in Philadelphia, 1869–1890" (Ph.D. diss., New York University, 1985). On the Socialist Labor Party, see L. Glen Seratan, *Daniel DeLeon: The Odyssey of an American Marxist* (Cambridge, Mass., 1979); and Paul Buhle, "The Socialist Labor Party," in *Encyclopedia of the American Left*, ed. Mari Jo Buhle, Paul Buhle, and Dan Georgakas (New York, 1990), 711–16.

21. On the formation of a working-class movement in Philadelphia during the early nineteenth century, see Laurie, *Working People of Philadelphia*, 85–104; and Ronald Schultz, *The Republic of Labor* (New York, 1993). On the strength of the Knights in the city during the mid-1880s, see Goldberg, "Strikes, Organizing, and Change"; and Light, "Class, Ethnicity and the Urban Ecology," 200–209.

22. Paul Krause, *The Battle for Homestead: Politics, Culture, and Steel, 1880–1892* (Pittsburgh, 1992); Salvatore, *Eugene V. Debs*, 127–37; Almont Lindsey, *The Pullman Strike* (Chicago, 1942).

23. Foster, *From Bryan to Stalin*, 15; Foster, *Pages from a Worker's Life*, 18 (quotes); *Philadelphia Evening Bulletin*, December 19, 21, 1895, 1, 2; *Philadelphia Enquirer*, December 18, 1895, 2, 3.

24. *Philadelphia Evening Bulletin*, December 10, 1895, 1; *Philadelphia Enquirer*, December 18, 1895, 2; Foster, *From Bryan to Stalin*, 15.

25. Foster, *From Bryan to Stalin*, 15.

26. Ibid., 14 (first and third quotes), 19 (fifth quote), 21 (sixth quote), 23 (seventh quote); Foster, *Twilight of World Capitalism*, 157 (second quote); Douglas, *Six upon the World*, 123 (fourth quote).

27. Foster, *From Bryan to Stalin*, 23 (quotes); Maynes, *Taking the Hard Road*, 154.

28. Foster, *Twilight of World Capitalism*, 160.

29. Foster, *Pages from a Worker's Life*, 25 (first quote), 26 (second quote). On the peonage system, see Pete Daniel, *The Shadow of Peonage* (Urbana, Ill., 1972); and C. Vann Woodward, *Origins of the New South, 1877–1913* (Baton Rouge, 1951).

30. Foster, *Pages from a Worker's Life*, 28.

31. Hutchins Hapgood, *The Spirit of Labor* (New York, 1907), 41–44, 48–49; Frank T.

Higbie, "Indispensable Outcasts: Seasonal Laborers and Community in the Upper Midwest" (Ph.D. diss., University of Illinois at Urbana-Champaign, 1999).

32. John C. Schneider, "Tramping Workers, 1880–1920: A Subcultural View," in *Walking to Work: Tramps in America, 1790–1935,* ed. Eric Monkonen (Lincoln, Nebr., 1984), 219. For more on the life of hobos, see Roger Bruns, *Knights of the Road: A Hobo History* (New York, 1980); Nels Anderson, *The Hobo: The Sociology of the Homeless Man* (Chicago, 1923), 137–49; and Carlton H. Parker, *The Casual Laborer and Other Essays* (New York, 1920), 70–72. There were female hobos, but they represented a very small minority of the transient population. See Lynn Weiner, "Sisters of the Road: Women Transients and Tramps," in *Walking to Work,* ed. Monkonen, 171–88.

33. Schneider, "Tramping Workers," 224; Foster, *Pages from a Worker's Life,* 115–30 (quotes on 116 and 123).

34. Anderson, *Hobo,* 171–249; Melvyn Dubofsky, "The Radicalism of the Dispossessed: William D. Haywood and the IWW," in *Dissent: Explorations in the History of American Radicalism,* ed. Alfred Young (DeKalb, Ill., 1968), 175–213.

35. Foster, *Pages from a Worker's Life,* 44 (quote); William Z. Foster, "Pages from a Worker's Life," unpublished manuscript, fond 615, opis 1, delo 22, listki 17–20, William Z. Foster Papers, Russian Center for the Preservation and Study of Documents of Recent History, Moscow (hereafter Foster Papers). On varieties of railroad work at the end of the nineteenth century, see Shelton Stromquist, *A Generation of Boomers: The Pattern of Railroad Conflict in Nineteenth-Century America* (Urbana, Ill., 1987), 104–15.

36. Foster, *From Bryan to Stalin,* 25.

37. Foster, *Pages from a Worker's Life,* 55–56, 67–72, 75–77; W. E. Home, *Merchant Seamen: Their Diseases and Their Welfare Needs* (New York, 1922), 83, 84–85. As late as the 1930s, the rate for fatal accidents was still much higher among merchant seamen than for any other class of British worker except miners, and the death rate from all causes was higher among seamen than any other occupational group. See James C. Healey, *Foc's'le and Glory-Hole: A Study of the Merchant Seaman and His Occupation* (New York, 1936), 105–9.

38. Dr. D. W. Wright, medical officer of the Glasgow Port Authority, quoted in Home, *Merchant Seamen,* 39. See also ibid., 40, 82–97.

39. Foster, *Pages from a Worker's Life,* 80.

40. Ibid., 82.

41. Ibid., 76–77.

42. North, *William Z. Foster,* 12; Foster, *Pages from a Worker's Life,* 76.

43. Foster, *Pages from a Worker's Life,* 85–89. See also Home, *Merchant Seamen,* 3–4.

44. Foster, *Pages from a Worker's Life,* 69.

45. William Z. Foster to "Brothers and Sisters," November 18, 1904, Joseph Manley Kolko's private papers, quoted in Johanningsmeier, *Forging American Communism,* 29.

46. Foster, *From Bryan to Stalin,* 27.

47. Foster, *Pages from a Worker's Life,* 33.

48. Douglas, *Six upon the World,* 71.

49. U.S. Senate, Committee on Labor and Education, *Investigation of Strike in the Steel Industry,* 66th Cong., 1st sess. (Washington, D.C., 1919), 388.

CHAPTER 2: FROM SOCIALISM TO SYNDICALISM, 1904–12

1. North, *William Z. Foster,* 16; Seratan, *Daniel DeLeon;* Foster, *From Bryan to Stalin,* 43 (quote).

2. Ira Kipnis, *The American Socialist Movement, 1897–1912* (New York, 1952); James Weinstein, *The Decline of Socialism in America, 1912–1925* (New York, 1967); Paul Buhle, "Socialist Party," in *Encyclopedia of the American Left,* ed. Buhle, Buhle, and Georgakas, 716–23.

3. Foster, *From Bryan to Stalin,* 30.

4. *Socialist* (Seattle), December 17, 1907, 1, January 18, 1908, 1, February 8, 1908, 1, June 27, 1908, 2.

5. Thomas Sladden, "The Working Class," *Socialist,* April 11, 1908, 6; Thomas Sladden, "The Revolutionist," *International Socialist Review* 8 (December 1908): 423–30 (quotes on 423 and 430).

6. Foster, *From Bryan to Stalin,* 28.

7. Jault P. I. Reiff, "Urbanization and the Social Structure: Seattle, Washington, 1852–1910" (Ph.D. diss., University of Washington, 1981); Dana Frank, *Purchasing Power: Consumer Organizing, Gender, and the Seattle Labor Movement, 1919–1929* (Cambridge, 1993), 15–21.

8. *Socialist,* March 21, 1908, 1, December 26, 1908, 3, January 4, 1908, 3, January 9, 1909, 4; Foster, *From Bryan to Stalin,* 30 (quotes). For the general context of Seattle's factional politics, see Carlos Schwantes, *Radical Heritage: Labor, Socialism, and Reform in Washington and British Columbia, 1885–1917* (Seattle, 1979), 168–78; and Jonathan Dembo, *Unions and Politics in Washington State, 1885–1935* (New York, 1983), 30–40, 45–46.

9. "Proletarianizing the Party" (editorial), *Socialist,* July 3, 1909, 4; "The Attitude of *The Socialist*" (editorial), October 23, 1909, 4

10. Foster, *From Bryan to Stalin,* 31 (quote); Schwantes, *Radical Heritage,* 95–96.

11. Hermon Titus, "Revolutionary Socialism and Reform Socialism," *Socialist,* September 15, 1906, quoted in Johanningsmeier, *Forging American Communism,* 34

12. William Z. Foster, *History of the Communist Party of the United States of America* (New York, 1952), 121–22.

13. *Solidarity,* September 17, 1919, quoted in Philip S. Foner, *The Industrial Workers of the World,* vol. 4 of *History of the Labor Movement in the United States* (hereafter, *IWW*) (New York, 1965), 119–20; Foster, *History of the Communist Party of the United States of America,* 199–200.

14. Quoted in Foner, *IWW,* 151. Melvyn Dubofsky, *We Shall Be All: A History of the IWW* (Chicago, 1969) remains the definitive study. For Joe Hill's songs, the Mr. Block cartoons, and other forms of IWW propaganda, see Joyce Kornbluh, ed., *Rebel Voices: An IWW Anthology* (Ann Arbor, Mich., 1964).

15. Ava Baron, *Work Engendered: Toward a New History of American Labor* (Ithaca, N.Y., 1991), 1–46; Ann Schofield, "Rebel Girls and Union Maids: The Woman Question in the Journals of the AFL and IWW, 1905–1920," *Feminist Studies* 9 (Summer 1983): 335–58; Foner, *IWW,* 128–29; Philip S. Foner, *Women and the Labor Movement: From Colonial*

Times to the Eve of World War One (New York, 1979), 250–52; Alice Kessler-Harris, *Out to Work: A History of Wage Earning Women in the United States* (New York, 1982), 153–59; Melvyn Dubofsky, "The Origins of Western Working-Class Radicalism, 1890–1905," *Labor History* 7 (Spring 1977): 131–54.

16. For the significance of masculine experiences and values for labor activists, see Montgomery, *Fall of the House of Labor*, 58–111, especially 88–90; David Montgomery, *Workers' Control in America: Studies in the History of Work, Technology, and Labor Struggles* (London, 1979), 11–15; and Salvatore, *Eugene Debs*, passim.

17. Foner, *IWW*, 173 (first quote); *Solidarity*, July 25, 1914, quoted in ibid., 174.

18. The following account is based largely on Foner, *IWW*, 177–85; Dubofsky, *We Shall Be All*, 175–84; Robert L. Tyler, *Rebels of the Woods: The I.W.W. in the Pacific Northwest* (Eugene, Oreg., 1967), 33–39; and John B. Clutterbuck's splendid undergraduate thesis, "From Spokane to Moscow: William Z. Foster, 1909–1921" (Wesleyan University, 1985), 13–28. (My thanks to Ron Schatz and John Clutterbuck for sharing the thesis.) See also Foster, *Pages from a Worker's Life*, 143–46; and Dembo, *Unions and Politics in Washington State*, 72–74.

19. *Industrial Worker*, October 28, 1909, 1.

20. Quoted in Dubofsky, *We Shall Be All*, 180–81. For Flynn's own version of her arrest and trial, see Elizabeth Gurley Flynn, "Story of My Arrest and Imprisonment," *Workingman's Paper* (Seattle), November 20, 1909, 1.

21. William Z. Foster, "Special Spokane Dispatches," *Workingman's Paper*, November 20, 1909, 1; William Z. Foster, "Special Spokane Dispatches," ibid., November 27, 1909, 1; William Z. Foster, "Three Spokane Mushrooms," ibid., December 25, 1909, 1, 4; William Z. Foster, "The Sweat Box," ibid., December 11, 1909, 3; Clutterbuck, "From Spokane to Moscow," 17–18.

22. William Z. Foster, "Forty Seven Days in the Spokane City Jail," *Workingman's Paper*, February 12, 1910, 1 (quote); Foster, *From Bryan to Stalin*, 41; Foster, *Pages from a Worker's Life*, 144–45.

23. Beulah Hyde, "Foster in Jail," *Workingman's Paper*, January 15, 1910, 4; "Foster's Letter from Rockpile," *Workingman's Paper*, January 8, 1910, 1. See also *Workingman's Paper*, January 29, 1910, 4.

24. "From Foster in Jail," *Workingman's Paper*, January 22, 1910, 1 (first quote); Foster, "Forty Seven Days in the Spokane City Jail," 1 (remaining quotes).

25. Central Executive Committee, Spokane Local, IWW, "Treaty Negotiations," *Workingman's Paper*, March 19, 1910, 3; Glen J. Broyles, "The Spokane Free Speech Fight, 1909–1910: A Study in IWW Tactics," *Labor History* 19 (Spring 1978): 238–52, argues that the Spokane fight was a failure on both the particular issue of the labor agencies and the more general health of the IWW. I rely more on Foner and Dubofsky regarding the generally positive effects of the fight. For Foster's own assessment, see Foster, *Pages from a Worker's Life*, 145.

26. Montgomery, *Workers' Control in America*, 91–112; Maxine Schwartz Seller, "The Uprising of the Twenty Thousand: Sex, Class, and Ethnicity in the Shirtwaist Makers' Strike of 1909," in *"Struggle a Hard Battle,"* ed. Hoerder, 254–79; Steve Fraser, *Labor Will*

Rule: Sidney Hillman and the Rise of American Labor (New York, 1991), 40–76; Dubofsky, *We Shall Be All,* 198–209; Foner, *IWW,* 281–95; Paul Kellogg, "The McKees Rocks Strike," *Survey* 22 (August 7, 1909): 656–65; Philip S. Foner, *The AF of L in the Progressive Era, 1910–1915,* vol. 5 of *History of the Labor Movement in the United States* (New York, 1980), 143–63, 164–81; Carl Person, *The Lizard's Tail: A Story of the Illinois Central and Harriman Lines Strike of 1911–1915* (Chicago, 1918).

27. Clutterbuck, "From Spokane to Moscow," 32–33; William Z. Foster and Herman F. Titus, *Insurgency or the Economic Power of the Middle Class* (Seattle, 1910), 14 (quote).

28. Foster, *From Bryan to Stalin,* 48–49.

29. Roger Magraw, "Socialism, Syndicalism, and French Labor Before 1914," in *Labor and Socialist Movements in Europe before 1914,* ed. Dick Geary (Oxford, 1989), 87 (first two quotes); William Z. Foster, "Sabotage," *Solidarity,* January 7, 1911, 3 (third quote); William Z. Foster, "Stirring Events in France," *Solidarity,* December 31, 1910, 4 (fourth quote). On French syndicalist theory and practice, see F. F. Ridley, *Revolutionary Syndicalism in France: The Direct Action of Its Time* (Cambridge, 1970), esp. 83–187. On instances of sabotage in the railroad strike, see Peter N. Stearns, *Revolutionary Syndicalism in France: A Cause without Rebels* (New Brunswick, N.J., 1971), 69–70.

30. Quoted in Foster and Titus, *Insurgency or the Economic Power of the Middle Class,* 11.

31. William Z. Foster, "C.G.T. and S.P.," *Solidarity,* March 25, 1911, 1 (first quote); William Z. Foster, "First Days of Strike," *Solidarity,* November 5, 1910, 4 (second quote); William Z. Foster, "Railway Strike," *Solidarity,* November 12, 1910, 3, 4; Max Nomad, *Rebels and Renegades* (New York, 1932), 48–82.

32. Foster, *From Bryan to Stalin,* 48.

33. Foster, "Stirring Events in France," 4 (quote); Stearns, *Revolutionary Syndicalism in France,* 69–70, 75; Clutterbuck, "From Spokane to Moscow," 38–39.

34. William Z. Foster, "Note—William Haywood," *La vie ouvriere,* December 5, 1910, 797–99; William Z. Foster, "La lutte pour la liberte de parole a Spokane," *La vie ouvriere,* January 20, 1911, 91–100, and February 5, 1911, 167–80; Clutterbuck, "From Spokane to Moscow," 40–41.

35. Gary Steenson, *Not One Man, Not One Penny: German Social Democracy, 1863–1914* (Pittsburgh, 1981), 94; Dick Geary, "Socialism and the German Labor Movement before 1914," in *Labor and Socialist Movements in Europe before 1914,* ed. Geary, 101–2.

36. William Z. Foster, "L'enterrement de Singer," *La vie ouvriere,* February 20, 1911, 220–21 (quotes); Foster, *Pages from a Worker's Life,* 286–89.

37. Foster, *Pages from a Worker's Life,* 289–91 (quote on 290); Foster, *From Bryan to Stalin,* 50.

38. William Z. Foster, "May Day in Berlin," *Solidarity,* June 3, 1911, 2; William Z. Foster, "Le VIIIe Congress des Syndicats Allemands," *La vie ouvriere,* August 20–September 5, 1911, 264–70; William Z. Foster, "German Socialist Unions—Hold Tame Convention without a Breath of Revolutionary Spirit," *Solidarity,* September 2, 1911, 2 (quotes).

39. Foster, *From Bryan to Stalin,* 50–51. On Karl Legien (1861–1920), see Steenson, *Not One Man, Not One Penny,* 96–97.

40. William Z. Foster, "The Socialist Labor Movement in Germany," *Solidarity,* September 30, 1911, 2, quoted in Foner, *IWW,* 418.

41. Foster, *From Bryan to Stalin,* 49.

42. "Tom Mann in Paris," *Solidarity,* June 25, 1910, 4; Tom Mann, *Tom Mann's Memoirs* (1923; reprint, London, 1967), 203–6; Chushichi Tsuzuki, *Tom Mann, 1856–1941* (Oxford, 1991), 143, 146, 148–49; Joseph White, *Tom Mann* (Manchester, England, 1991), 158–59, 160–65; Rob Holton, *British Syndicalism, 1900–1914* (London, 1976), 55; Foner, *IWW,* 417–18.

43. William Z. Foster, "Tom Mann," in *More Pages from a Worker's Life,* ed. Arthur Zipser (New York, 1979), 7–8. Mann held Foster in equally high regard. See Mann, *Tom Mann's Memoirs,* 268.

44. Melvyn Dubofsky, *Big Bill Haywood* (Manchester, England, 1987), 53–54, 62; Dubofsky, *We Shall Be All,* 224; William D. Haywood, *Bill Haywood's Book: The Autobiography of William D. Haywood* (New York, 1929), 27.

45. William Z. Foster, "Civic Federation at Budapest Conference," *Solidarity,* September 16, 1911, 1, 4; Foster, *Pages from a Worker's Life,* 291; "Budapest Conference, International Secretariat," *American Federationist,* October 1911, 827; "Delegate Duncan's Splendid Work at Budapest," *American Federationist,* November 1911, 901; "International Secretariat," *American Federationist,* December 1911, 978; Susan Milner, *The Dilemmas of Internationalism: French Syndicalism and the International Labour Movement, 1900–1914* (New York, 1990), 113–14; James Weinstein, *The Corporate Ideal in the Liberal State, 1900–1918* (Boston, 1968). Foster's actions also caused him problems with some IWW leaders, who were embarrassed by his performance. See Joseph Conlin, *Bread and Roses Too: Studies of the Wobblies* (Westport, Conn., 1969), 11–12.

46. Foster, *From Bryan to Stalin,* 51; William Z. Foster, "Budapest," in *More Pages from a Worker's Life,* 19–21.

47. William Z. Foster, *The Bankruptcy of the American Labor Movement* (New York, 1922), 47; John Laslett, *Labor and the Left: A Study of Socialist and Radical Influences in the American Labor Movement, 1881–1924* (New York, 1970); James R. Barrett, "Dual Unionism," in *Encyclopedia of the American Left,* ed. Buhle, Buhle, and Georgakas, 200–202; David Saposs, *Left Wing Unionism: A Study of Radical Policies and Tactics* (New York, 1926), 9–47.

48. Karl Rathje, "Boring from Within," *Solidarity,* June 11, 1910, 4.

49. William Z. Foster, "Labor Day in New York," *Solidarity,* September 9, 1911, 1; Dubofsky, *We Shall Be All,* 221–23; Foner, *IWW,* 418–19; Foster, *From Bryan to Stalin,* 55–56.

50. William Z. Foster, "As to My Candidacy," *Industrial Worker,* November 2, 1911, 3. See also *Solidarity,* November 4, 1911, 2. Foster's articles and most, if not all, of the responses were printed in both papers.

51. J. S. Biscay, "Building from Without," *Industrial Worker,* November 16, 1911, 2. See also J. J. Ettor's comments in *Industrial Worker,* December 2, 1911, 2. Philip Foner summarizes the arguments in Foner, *IWW,* 420–22.

52. William Z. Foster, "Have We Been Kicked Out of the IWW?" typescript of an article rejected by *Solidarity,* n.d. [1911], fond 615, opis 1, delo 5, listki 2–6, Foster Papers.

53. Jack W. Johnstone, "This One Wants Fusion," *Solidarity,* December 2, 1911, 3–4 (quote); "Discussion Closed," *Solidarity,* December 16, 1911, 2; Dubofsky, *We Shall Be All,* 223–25.

CHAPTER 3: THE MILITANT MINORITY, 1912–16

1. Frank Pease, "Boring from Within," *Agitator,* February 15, 1912, 2 (quote); Foster, *From Bryan to Stalin,* 58; Foner, *IWW,* 427.

2. Foster, *Pages from a Worker's Life,* 128–30, 139 (quote).

3. Foster, *From Bryan to Stalin,* 58; William Z. Foster, "Revolutionary Tactics," *Agitator,* April 15, 1912, 2–3, May 1, 1912, 2, 4, May 15, 1912, 2, 4, June 1, 1912, 2 (quote), June 15, 1912, 2, July 1, 1912, 2. Another series, "Syndicalism in France," ran in July and August.

4. Foster, *Pages from a Worker's Life,* 42–43.

5. Ibid., 48 (first quote); Earl C. Ford and William Z. Foster, *Syndicalism* (Chicago, 1912; reprint, London, 1978), 3 (remaining quotes), 4. Although Ford was listed as an author of the pamphlet, the claim seems dubious. In the late thirties, Foster claimed that he had written the pamphlet "in consultation" with Ford (Foster, *Pages from a Worker's Life,* 43), but he later confided that he had written the work himself and that Ford had simply provided the money for printing (Arthur Zipser, *Working Class Giant: The Life of William Z. Foster* [New York, 1981], 38).

6. Ford and Foster, *Syndicalism,* 6, 7, 8; Peter A. Kropotkin, *The Conquest of Bread* (New York, 1907); Ridley, *Revolutionary Syndicalism in France,* 43–44. Compare Foster's formulations with those of V. I. Lenin in *State and Revolution* (New York, 1932).

7. Johanningsmeier, *Forging American Communism,* 60–62, 367–68; Ford and Foster, *Syndicalism,* 8 (quotes). Foster's scientific language is even more pronounced in William Z. Foster [and Jack Jones, "collaborator"], "Is Government Necessary to the Operation of Industry," fond 615, opis 1, delo 86, listki 26–35, Foster Papers, which was produced around the same time and included an elaborate diagram of the copper industry's market system designed to demonstrate the automatic quality of production and distribution in large, monopolized industries. Foster was influenced by Jones's ideas regarding "automatic" production and distribution.

8. Ford and Foster, *Syndicalism,* 14–18, 9, 10 (first quote); "Preamble—SL of NA," fond 615, opis 1, delo 86, listok 21 (second and third quotes), Foster Papers.

9. Ford and Foster, *Syndicalism,* 9.

10. Ibid., 9, 13.

11. On the intellectual and rhetorical relationship between the Blanquist tradition and twentieth-century French syndicalism, see Ridley, *Revolutionary Syndicalism in France,* 33–37; and Stearns, *Revolutionary Syndicalism in France,* 11.

12. William Z. Foster wrote the following articles for *La vie ouvriere:* "L'affaire Mac-Namara," February 5, 1912, 184–89; "La deuxieme affaire MacNamara," February 20,

1913, 239–42; "La grève de la confection de New-York," March 20, 1913, 366–69; "L'affaire Haywood," April 5, 1913, 435–37; "La duperie, de l'arbitrage," April 20, 1913, 192–95; "Une renaissance de 'AF of L,' " May 20, 1913, 640–42; "Une association capitaliste de corruption parlementaire: Chicago, 10 juillet, 1913," August 5, 1913, 177–79; "Grèves et poursuite," November 20, 1913, 623–25; "Le congres de l'AFL," January 5, 1914, 52–54; and "La crise industrielle; La catastrophe de Calumet," January 20, 1914, 102–4. See also Larry Portis, *IWW et syndicalisme révolutionnaire aux Etats Unis* (Paris, 1985), 199–200.

13. William Z. Foster and W. A. Jones, "The Future Society," *Toiler,* March 1914, 7–8. See also Foster [and Jones], "Is Government Necessary?" James R. Barrett, "Syndicalist League of North America," in *Encyclopedia of the American Left,* ed. Buhle, Buhle, and Georgakas, 764–65; Foner, *IWW,* 427–30; Edward Johanningsmeier, "William Z. Foster and the Syndicalist League of North America," *Labor History* 30 (Summer 1989): 329–53; Charlton Brandt, "William Z. Foster and the Syndicalist League of North America" (M.A. thesis, Sangamon State University, Springfield, Ill., 1985); and Foster's own characterization of the organization in Foster, *From Bryan to Stalin,* 58–72.

14. Foster, *From Bryan to Stalin,* 63.

15. Ibid., 65; Mann, *Tom Mann's Memoirs,* 267–68; Tsuzuki, *Tom Mann,* 168; White, *Tom Mann,* 185–87; Dubofsky, *We Shall Be All,* 289–90; Foner, *IWW,* 430–34.

16. Foner, *IWW,* 430–34; Paul Avrich, *The Haymarket Tragedy* (Princeton, N.J., 1984), 451–54; Carolyn Ashbaugh, *Lucy Parsons, American Revolutionary* (Chicago, 1976), 230–31.

17. Foster, *From Bryan to Stalin,* 63.

18. Ashbaugh, *Lucy Parsons,* 206–16, 219–21; Charles P. LeWarne, *Utopias on Puget Sound, 1885–1917* (Seattle, 1975), 206–11; Lucy Robins Lang, *Tomorrow Is Beautiful* (New York, 1948), 48–52; E. A. Slosson, "An Experiment in Anarchy," *Independent* 55 (April 2, 1903): 779–85; "Editorial," *Agitator,* November 15, 1911, 2. For Foster's recollections of Fox, see Foster, "Pages from a Worker's Life," especially 139.

19. Foster, "Pages from a Worker's Life," 139; Ashbaugh, *Lucy Parsons,* 230; Melvyn Dubofsky, "*The Agitator* and *The Syndicalist,*" in *The American Radical Press, 1880–1960,* ed. Joseph Conlin (Westport, Conn., 1974), 113–16; Mary M. Carr, "Anarchist of Home: Jay Fox," *Columbia* 3 (Spring 1980): 3–10.

20. Hapgood, *Spirit of Labor,* 290 (Hapgood quotes); Hutchins Hapgood, *A Victorian in the Modern World* (New York, 1939), 196–207; Lang, *Tomorrow Is Beautiful,* 27–31 (Lang quote on 31); Foster and Ford, *Syndicalism,* 17 (Foster quote on "new supply of slaves"). My thanks to Steve Sapolsky for calling these works to my attention. My approximation of the children's ages is based on reports from a Burns Detective Agency operative who spied on Fox and his family at the Home Colony. See William J. Burns, *The Masked War* (New York, 1913), 75. See also Johanningsmeier, *Forging American Communism,* 520. The character of anarchist free love has been wildly misinterpreted and exaggerated. The expression could refer to a variety of lifestyles, but it appears that some degree of sexual liberation and multiple sexual partners, or what anarchists called "varietism," was part of the lifestyle at the Home Colony and in Chicago's anar-

chist subculture. See Margaret S. Marsh, *Anarchist Women, 1870–1920* (Philadelphia, 1981), 39–41, 69–94, 117–18; and Hutchins Hapgood, *An Anarchist Woman* (New York, 1909), 153–54, passim. For rare personal information on Esther Abramowitz Foster, see Hapgood, *Spirit of Labor,* 290–91; Lang, *Tomorrow Is Beautiful,* 49, 78; Douglas, *Six upon the World,* 119; William Z. Foster, Comintern personnel questionnaire, December 26, 1931, fond 495, opis 261, delo 15, listki 19–20, Comintern Archives; Nisov, biographical memo on Foster, fond 495, opis 261, delo 15, listki 72–74, Comintern Archives; and Carl Dorfman to James R. Barrett, taped responses to written questions, July 6, 1997, in author's possession; Carl Dorfman to James R. Barrett, May 2, 1997, letter in author's possession.

21. Foster, *From Bryan to Stalin,* 59.

22. Ibid., 64. On the "Labor Forward" movement, see William Z. Foster, "Lettre des Etats-Unis," *La vie ouvrier,* May 20, 1913, 641; C. F. Steckham, "The Labor Forward Movement of Greater Kansas City," *Toiler,* April–May 1914, 5–6; Elizabeth Fones-Wolf and Kenneth Fones-Wolf, "Trade Union Evangelism: Religion and the AF of L in the Labor Forward Movement, 1912–1916," in *Working-Class America: Essays in Labor, Community, and American Society,* ed. Michael H. Frisch and Daniel Walkowitz (Urbana, Ill., 1983), 153–84; and Philip S. Foner, *The TUEL to the End of the Gompers Era,* vol. 9 of *History of the Labor Movement in the United States* (New York, 1991), 87–91.

23. Foster, *From Bryan to Stalin,* 64.

24. Ibid., 66; Johanningsmeier, *Forging American Communism,* 78; Charlotte Todes, *Labor and Lumber* (New York, 1931), 155–58.

25. David Emmons, *The Butte Irish: Class and Ethnicity in an American Mining Town, 1875–1925* (Urbana, Ill., 1989), 277–84. Compare Dubofsky, *We Shall Be All,* 302–3.

26. Dubofsky, *We Shall Be All,* 304–7; Foster, *From Bryan to Stalin,* 66–67; William Chance, interview by James P. Cannon, March 10, 1962, 50–64 (quotes on 62 and 64), Section I: "Biographical and Background Material," James P. Cannon Papers, State Historical Society of Wisconsin, Madison (hereafter Cannon Papers). For Foster's own accounts, see William Z. Foster, "The Miners' Revolt in Butte," *Toiler,* August 1914, 8–10; and Foster, "Pages from a Worker's Life," 22–27.

27. Foster, *IWW,* 133–190; Dubofsky, *We Shall Be All,* 198–200, 207–9; Ann Huber Tripp, *The I.W.W. and the Paterson Silk Strike of 1913* (Urbana, Ill., 1987); James R. Green, "The Brotherhood of Timber Workers, 1910–1913," *Past and Present* 60 (August 1973): 161–200; James D. Osborne, "Paterson: Immigrant Strikers and the War of 1913," and Roy Wortman, "The IWW and the Akron Rubber Strike of 1913," both in *At the Point of Production: The Local History of the IWW,* ed. Joseph Conlin (Westport, Conn., 1981), 61–78, 49–60.

28. Foster, *From Bryan to Stalin,* 73–85; Foner, *TUEL to the End of the Gompers Era,* 92–97.

29. William Z. Foster, *Trade Unionism: The Road to Freedom* (Chicago, 1916); Foster, *From Bryan to Stalin,* 74 (quote).

30. Foster, *Trade Unionism,* 18, 28.

31. Ibid., 26, 27, 28, 25.

32. Ibid., 22, 23–24, 25. See also Foster and Jones, "Future Society," 7–8.

33. Foster, *Trade Unionism,* 28–29.

34. Ibid.; Foster, *From Bryan to Stalin,* 74. It seems that Foster had some success distributing this and later pamphlets through trade union channels. See his circular "To All Lodges of the Brotherhood of Carmen," December 1917, with an endorsement from a district official of the union, fond 615, opis 1, delo 86, Foster Papers.

35. Montgomery, *Workers' Control in America,* 91–112; Foster, *From Bryan to Stalin,* 74–75. Foster told Chicago Federation of Labor delegates that the 1911 Illinois Central strike, often thought of as a catastrophic defeat for railroad shop craftworkers, was "actually a great victory" (Chicago Federation of Labor Minutes, May 7, 1916, Chicago Historical Society). He was referring not only to a recent wage advance on the Chicago and Northwestern Railroad but also to the spread of the federation system.

36. Foster, *From Bryan to Stalin,* 81–82.

37. Montgomery, *Workers' Control in America,* 57–58; Ray Stannard Baker, *The New Industrial Unrest* (Garden City, N.Y., 1920), 112; Elizabeth McKillen, *Chicago Labor and the Quest for a Democratic Diplomacy* (Ithaca, N.Y., 1995); James R. Barrett, *Work and Community in the Jungle: Chicago's Packinghouse Workers, 1894–1922* (Urbana, Ill., 1987), 142–43, 191–92.

38. Foster, *From Bryan to Stalin,* 82–83; Foster, *Trade Unionism,* 14 (quote). Foster had little success with his council plan in the short run, but something like it emerged in the course of the 1919–20 railway switchmen's strike led by L. M. Hawver, who had been a member of the ITUEL. See Edward P. Johanningsmeier, "William Z. Foster: Labor Organizer and Communist" (Ph.D. diss., University of Pennsylvania, 1988), 243–44; Selig Perlman and Philip Taft, *History of Labor in the United States,* vol. 4 (New York, 1935), 454–56; and Foster, *From Bryan to Stalin,* 84.

CHAPTER 4: THE CHICAGO STOCKYARDS, 1917–18

1. Foster, *Great Steel Strike and Its Lessons,* 17.

2. Montgomery, *Workers' Control in America,* 91–138; Montgomery, *Fall of the House of Labor,* 330–410; David Montgomery, "New Tendencies in Union Struggles in Europe and the United States, 1916–1922," in *Work, Community, and Power: The Experience of Labor in Europe and America, 1900–1925,* ed. James E. Cronin and Carmen Siriani (Philadelphia, 1983), 89–110; James Cronin, "Labor Insurgency and Class Formation," in *Work, Community, and Power,* ed. Cronin and Siriani, 20–48; Stanley Shapiro, " 'Hand and Brain': The Farmer-Labor Party of 1920," *Labor History* 26 (Summer 1985): 405–22; Philip S. Foner, *Labor and World War I, 1914–1918,* vol. 7 of *History of the Labor Movement in the United States* (New York, 1987); Philip S. Foner, *Postwar Struggles, 1918–1920,* vol. 8 of *History of the Labor Movement in the United States* (New York, 1988); Alan Dawley, *Struggles for Justice: Social Responsibility and the Liberal State* (Cambridge, Mass., 1991), 196–203, 219–28.

3. Foster, *From Bryan to Stalin,* 88. The situation brought Foster's earliest conflict with

Earl Browder, who opposed the war, resisted the draft, and went to prison. For an early statement of Foster's syndicalist position on the war, see William Z. Foster, "The Syndicalist and the War," *Toiler,* January 1914, 5–6.

4. Roger A. Bruns, *The Damndest Radical: The Life and World of Ben Reitman, Chicago's Celebrated Social Reformer, Hobo King, and Whorehouse Physician* (Urbana, Ill., 1987), 230–45; Ashbaugh, *Lucy Parsons,* 258–59; Ralph Chaplin, *Wobbly: The Rough and Tumble Story of an American Radical* (Chicago, 1948), 171; Ray L. White, ed., *Sherwood Anderson's Memoirs* (Chapel Hill, N.C., 1942), 357, quoted in Bruns, *Damndest Radical,* 231.

5. Dil Pickle Club Scrapbooks, Newberry Library, Chicago; Dr. Ben Reitman, manuscript autobiography, 375–76, Special Collections, University of Illinois Library, Chicago; W. F. Hoxie to Bill Foster, Chicago, March 29, 1916, fond 615, opis 1, delo 5, listok 1, Foster Papers.

6. William Z. Foster, *American Trade Unionism* (New York, 1947), 20; William Z. Foster, "The Chicago Federation of Labor," *Labor Herald* 1 (December 1922): 8, 9 (quotes); John H. Keiser, "John Fitzpatrick and Progressive Labor" (Ph.D. diss., Northwestern University, 1965); David Brody, "John Fitzpatrick," in *Dictionary of American Biography,* supp. 4, ed. John A. Garraty (New York, 1974), 279–80.

7. Foster, *From Bryan to Stalin,* 82.

8. Ibid., Richard H. Frost, *The Mooney Case* (Stanford, Calif., 1968), 269–70; Lang, *Tomorrow Is Beautiful,* 105–6. The Chicago Federation of Labor estimated attendance at the March meeting at 17,000, and Foster estimated 20,000 (Chicago Federation of Labor Minutes, April 1, 1917; Foster, "Chicago Federation of Labor," 9).

9. McKillen, *Chicago Labor and the Quest for a Democratic Diplomacy;* Elizabeth McKillen, "American Labor, the Irish Revolution, and the Campaign for a Boycott of British Goods: 1916–1924," *Radical History Review* 61 (Winter 1995): 35–61; Baker, *New Industrial Unrest,* 112.

10. William Z. Foster, "An Open Letter to John Fitzpatrick," *Labor Herald* 2 (January 1924): 6; Foster, *From Bryan to Stalin,* 83.

11. Foster, *From Bryan to Stalin,* 124. See also Foster, "Open Letter to John Fitzpatrick."

12. Upton Sinclair, *The Jungle,* edited with an introduction and notes by James R. Barrett (Urbana, Ill., 1988), 36. Writing to Upton Sinclair in November 1920, Foster vividly remembered his first encounter with the novel, which he read in French while living in Paris in 1910. See William Z. Foster to Upton Sinclair, November 28, 1920, Upton Sinclair Papers, Lilly Library, Indiana University.

13. Foster, *Pages from a Worker's Life,* 152–53.

14. Barrett, *Work and Community in the Jungle,* 64–117; Robert Slayton, *Back of the Yards: The Making of a Local Democracy* (Chicago, 1986), 15–38; Thomas J. Jablonksy, *Pride in the Jungle: Community and Everyday Life in Back of the Yards Chicago* (Baltimore, 1993).

15. David Brody, *The Butcher Workmen: A Study in Unionization* (Cambridge, Mass., 1964), 13–58; Barrett, *Work and Community in the Jungle,* 118–87.

16. Barrett, *Work and Community in the Jungle,* 192–94; Chicago Federation of Labor

Minutes, July 15, August 5, November 4, and December 2, 1917; *Butcher Workman* 5 (November 1919); *Butcher Workman* 8 (April 1922).

17. Foster, *American Trade Unionism*, 22.

18. Barrett, *Work and Community in the Jungle*, 192–93; Foster, *From Bryan to Stalin*, 90–91 (quotes).

19. Foster, *From Bryan to Stalin*, 91–92.

20. Chicago Federation of Labor Minutes, September 2, 1917 (first quote); "Americanization Study," typescript notes of interview with Dennis Lane, president, Amalgamated Meat Cutters and Butcher Workmen of North America (second quote), box 26, folder 2, David J. Saposs Papers, State Historical Society of Wisconsin, Madison (hereafter Saposs Papers); Barrett, *Work and Community in the Jungle*, 195–96.

21. Chicago Federation of Labor Minutes, August 19, 1917 (Foster quote); Barrett, *Work and Community in the Jungle*, 194–95, 204–14; Rick Halpern, "Race, Ethnicity, and Union in the Chicago Stockyards, 1917–1922," in *Racism and the Labour Market: Historical Studies*, ed. Marcel van der Linden and Jan Lucassen (Bern, 1995), 186–96; Sterling Spero and Abram L. Harris, *The Black Worker* (1931; reprint, New York, 1974), 270, 271–74, 279–82; James R. Grossman, *Land of Hope: Chicago, Black Southerners, and the Great Migration* (Chicago, 1989), 208–33 (discussion of the "white man's movement").

22. William Z. Foster, "How Life Has Been Brought into the Stockyards," *Life and Labor* 7 (April 1918): 64.

23. Quoted in Chicago Commission on Race Relations, *The Negro in Chicago* (Chicago, 1922), 428–29; Foster, *From Bryan to Stalin*, 92–93. The black middle class and the community's major institutions were actually divided over the issue of unionism, but Foster's observation of considerable opposition is consistent with the most careful analyses of the matter. See Grossman, *Land of Hope*, 225–33; and Barrett, *Work and Community in the Jungle*, 204–14.

24. Quoted in Chicago Commission on Race Relations, *Negro in Chicago*, 429.

25. Barrett, *Work and Community in the Jungle*, 197–98.

26. Joseph A. McCartin, *Labor's Great War: The Struggle for Industrial Democracy and the Origins of Modern American Labor Relations, 1912–1921* (Chapel Hill, N.C., 1998), 24–37 (quote on 24), 66–68, 90–93, 197, 224; *Chicago Herald*, quoted in Valerie Jean Conner, *The National War Labor Board: Stability, Social Justice, and the Voluntary State in World War I* (Chapel Hill, N.C., 1983), 52. On Walsh, see also Leon Fink, *Progressive Intellectuals and Dilemmas of Democratic Commitment* (Cambridge, Mass., 1998).

27. *Report of the President's Mediation Commission* (Washington, D.C., 1918); U.S. Department of Labor, Mediation and Conciliation Service, Record Group 280, Case 33/864, boxes 40, 41, National Archives, Washington, D.C.; Foster, "How Life Has Been Brought into the Stockyards," 64 (first quote), 65 (second quote). See also Frank Walsh's closing arguments before Judge Alschuler, which were published as a pamphlet, *Over the Top at the Yards* (Chicago, 1918), a bestseller in English and Polish (microfilm copy, Chicago Historical Society).

28. Mary McDowell, "Easter Day after the Decision," *Survey* 40 (April 13, 1918): 38; Fitzpatrick quoted in Barrett, *Work and Community in the Jungle*, 200.

29. William Z. Foster to Frank Walsh, July 6, 1918, Frank Walsh Papers, New York Public Library, quoted in Brody, *Butcher Workmen,* 83.

30. Philip Taft, *The AF of L in the Time of Gompers* (New York, 1957), 386.

CHAPTER 5: THE GREAT STEEL STRIKE, 1918–19

1. *New York Times,* August 27, 1919, quoted in David Brody, *Labor in Crisis: The Steel Strike of 1919* (Philadelphia, 1965), 101–2.

2. Foster, *Great Steel Strike and Its Lessons,* 5.

3. Ibid., 21.

4. Foster, "Open Letter to John Fitzpatrick," 6.

5. Ibid., 6–7. George P. West, a writer for the *Nation,* saw this sort of scenario as the main significance behind the great campaign in steel. His article on the subject embarrassed Foster and Fitzpatrick and clearly worried Gompers, who demanded and received a reply from Fitzpatrick denying such ambitions. George P. West, "Will Labor Lead?" *Nation,* April 9, 1919; John Fitzpatrick to Oswald Garrison Villard, editor of the *Nation,* May 6, 1919 [copy], fond 615, opis 1, delo 84, listki 18–21, Foster Papers.

6. William Z. Foster to Mary Heaton Vorse, New York, March 10, 1938, box 64, correspondence "1938–March," Mary Heaton Vorse Papers, Archives of Labor History and Urban Affairs, Walter Reuther Library, Wayne State University (hereafter Vorse Papers); William Z. Foster to John Fitzpatrick, Chicago, June 22, 1918 (quote), Foster correspondence file, John Fitzpatrick Papers, Chicago Historical Society (hereafter Fitzpatrick Papers). Except where noted, the description of the organizing campaign is based on Foster, *Great Steel Strike and Its Lessons;* Brody, *Labor in Crisis;* and David Brody, *Steelworkers in America: The Nonunion Era* (New York, 1969). Foster's resolution to organize steel is in *Report of the Proceedings of the Thirty-eighth Annual Convention of the American Federation of Labor, St. Paul, Minnesota, June 1918* (Washington, D.C., 1918), 163.

7. "Minutes of Conference of Organizations in the Steel Industries, St. Paul, June 17–20, 1918," fond 615, opis 1, delo 83, listki 2–9, Foster Papers; "Minutes of Iron and Steel Industry Organizations, Held in the New Morrison Hotel, Chicago, August 1 and 2, 1918," ibid., listok 12.

8. Quoted in Brody, *Steelworkers in America,* 218. See also Foster, *From Bryan to Stalin,* 112.

9. Quoted in Zipser, *Working Class Giant,* 50 (Vorse), 51 (Steffens), Foster, *Great Steel Strike and Its Lessons,* 29.

10. E.N., "The Steel Strike and the Bill of Rights," *Socialist Review* 8 (January 1920): 94; Mary Heaton Vorse, *Men and Steel* (New York, 1920), 68 (quote).

11. Vorse, *Men and Steel,* 60–61.

12. Quoted in ibid., 60.

13. Foster, *Great Steel Strike and Its Lessons,* 39.

14. Ibid., 34–38 (quote on 38); "Financial Report of the Steel Workers' Strike Fund, Being a True Account of All Moneys Received and to Whom Paid," October 22, 1919, to February 18, 1920, fond 615, opis 1, delo 85, listki 54–77; William Z. Foster, "General

Report on the Steel Strike Fund," January 31, 1920, fond 615, opis 1, delo 85, listki 31–42, all in Foster Papers. See also audits, receipts, reports, and books, in fond 615, opis 1, delo 85, listki 3–48, Foster Papers.

15. U.S. Senate, *Investigation of Strike in the Steel Industry,* 382.

16. Cochran, *Labor and Communism,* 93; George Soule, "William Z. Foster: A Henry Ford of the Labor Movement," *New Republic,* October 5, 1932, 197; Vorse, *Men and Steel,* 48.

17. Foster, *Great Steel Strike and Its Lessons,* 40.

18. Ibid., 50–64 (flying squadron quote on 52), 97 (western Pennsylvania quote); Vorse, *Men and Steel,* 48.

19. Foster, "Pages from a Worker's Life," 129–31.

20. E. H. Gary, chairman, United States Steel, to John Fitzpatrick, David J. Davis, William Hannon, William Z. Foster, and Edwin J. Evans, Committee, telegram, August 27, 1919, fond 615, opis 1, delo 84, listok 29, Foster Papers; Samuel Gompers to John Fitzpatrick, telegram, September 11, 1919, ibid., listok 46; John Fitzpatrick to Samuel Gompers, telegram (copy), September 12, 1919, ibid., listok 47; union officials' telegrams, ibid., listki 50–56.

21. For field organizers' demands for action, dated September 5–26, 1919, see fond 615, opis 1, delo 84, listki 31–44, Foster Papers.

22. E.N., "Steel Strike and the Bill of Rights," 94–95; Foster, *Great Steel Strike and Its Lessons,* 97 (quote).

23. *New York Times,* September 23, 1919, 1, 2; numerous affidavits, box 120, Vorse Papers; Brody, *Labor in Crisis,* 148 (quote).

24. Brody, *Labor in Crisis,* 149 (first quote); Interchurch World Movement, Commission of Inquiry, *Report on the Steel Strike of 1919* (New York, 1920), 236–38; U.S. Senate, *Investigation of Strike in the Steel Industry,* 427–28; Foster, *Great Steel Strike and Its Lessons,* 96–97 (second quote on 97).

25. Foster, *Great Steel Strike and Its Lessons,* 146–48; *New York Times,* August 27, 1919, 2. Foster was particularly affected by Sellins's death, mentioning it often in his public writings and statements. The National Committee's staff created a recruitment poster featuring enlarged photographs of her battered corpse, which Foster placed on the wall of the National Committee's office, as the organizing continued (Vorse, *Men and Steel,* 68). For a copy of the Sellins poster, see fond 615, opis 1, delo 84, listok 30, Foster Papers.

26. T. J. Conboy to Foster, Johnstown, Pennsylvania, March 25, March 27, 1920, fond 615, opis 1, delo 5, listki 7–8, 9–16, Foster Papers; Foster, *Great Steel Strike and Its Lessons,* 188–89; *New York Times,* November 8, 1919, 1.

27. *Labor World,* April 19, 1919, 1, 7; "The Red Disorganizer Is Unwelcome in the Legitimate Assemblies of Labor," large broadside, fond 615, opis 1, delo 83, listki 21, 22, 44, Foster Papers; *New York Times,* September 26, 1919, 5 (first quote), September 29, 1919; *Wall Street Journal,* quoted in Robert K. Murray, "Communism and the Great Steel Strike of 1919," *Mississippi Valley Historical Review* 38 (December 1951): 458 (second quote); Interchurch World Movement, *Report on the Steel Strike of 1919,* 20–43 (on re-

production of the pamphlet, 34–35). Compare Marshall Olds, *Analysis of the Interchurch World Movement Report on the Steel Strike* (New York, 1923), 189–209.

28. U.S. Senate, *Investigation of Strike in the Steel Industry*, 388 (first quote), 419 (second quote), 399 (third quote); Elizabeth Gurley Flynn, *Memories of the Industrial Workers of the World (IWW)* (New York, 1977), 20–21.

29. U.S. Senate, *Investigation of Strike in the Steel Industry*, 77 (first quote), 78 (second quote), 77–78 (third quote).

30. Ibid., 112. See also *New York Times*, September 27, 1919, 2, September 29, 1919, 2.

31. U.S. Senate, *Investigation of Strike in the Steel Industry*, 17 (both quotes).

32. *Current Opinion* 67 (December 1919): 292, 293; *New York Evening World*, quoted in Brody, *Labor in Crisis*, 142.

33. U.S. Senate, *Investigation of Strike in the Steel Industry*, 826 (Margolis quote); Draper, *Roots of American Communism*, 66 (second and third quotes); *New York Times*, October 21, 1919, 1; Earl Browder, interview, 118, Columbia University Oral History Collection, microfilm edition (Sanford, N.C., 1979); *Communist*, September 27, 1919, 2.

34. Interchurch World Movement, *Report on the Steel Strike of 1919*, 161–64; Foster, *Great Steel Strike and Its Lessons*, 200–201 (quote).

35. James R. Barrett, "Americanization from the Bottom Up: Immigration and the Remaking of the Working Class in the United States, 1880–1930," *Journal of American History* 79 (December 1992): 1008–15; *Iron and Steel Workers Bulletin*, no. 5, 1 (quotes), and no. 16, box 120, Vorse Papers.

36. Brody, *Labor in Crisis*, 73; Foster, *Great Steel Strike and Its Lessons*, 204.

37. Robert Asher, "Painful Memories: The Historical Consciousness of Steelworkers and the Steel Strike of 1919," *Pennsylvania History* 45 (1978): 61–86; Peter Gottlieb, *Making Their Own Way: Southern Blacks' Migration to Pittsburgh, 1916–1930* (Urbana, Ill., 1987), 172.

38. Foster, *Great Steel Strike and Its Lessons*, 205, 206. See also Brody, *Labor in Crisis*, 162.

39. Foster testimony, quoted in Chicago Commission on Race Relations, *Negro in Chicago*, 429. See also agent's report, Los Angeles, October 11, 1924, 4, document 61-330-176, FOIA file 270, 224, FBI Headquarters, Washington, D.C. (hereafter Foster FOIA file).

40. Elliott Rudwick, *Race Riot at East St. Louis, July 2, 1917* (1964; reprint, Urbana, Ill., 1982); William M. Tuttle Jr., *Race Riot: Chicago in the Red Summer of 1919* (1970; reprint, Urbana, Ill., 1998).

41. Interchurch World Movement, *Report on the Steel Strike of 1919*, 177–78, quoted in Philip S. Foner, *Organized Labor and the Black Worker, 1619–1973* (New York, 1976), 144; Chicago Commission on Race Relations, *Negro in Chicago*, 429.

42. Foster, *Great Steel Strike and Its Lessons*, 213–33; Vorse, *Men and Steel*, 60–61, 68; Brody, *Labor in Crisis*, 157 (quote).

43. Strike bulletins and other publicity material in various languages, boxes 120 and 121, Vorse Papers.

44. Wood quoted in Foner, *Postwar Struggles*, 163; Raymond A. Mohl and Neil Betten, *Steel City: Urban and Ethnic Patterns in Gary, Indiana, 1906–1950* (New York, 1986), 32,

38–41 (quote on 41). On the use of federal troops, see also Interchurch World Movement, *Report on the Steel Strike of 1919,* 240–42; and Foster, *Great Steel Strike and Its Lessons,* 170–73.

45. Barrett, *Work and Community in the Jungle,* 204–6; Alma Herbst, *The Negro in the Slaughtering and Meat Packing Industry of Chicago* (Boston, 1932), 42 (Johnstone quote).

46. Tuttle, *Race Riot;* Grossman, *Land of Hope,* 178–80, 222–23, 259–60; Carl Sandburg, *The Chicago Race Riots* (1919; reprint, New York, 1969); Barrett, *Work and Community in the Jungle,* 202–24.

47. Barrett, *Work and Community in the Jungle,* 224–30.

48. Ibid., 255–62.

49. William Z. Foster, "The Next Step," [1920], fond 615, opis 1, delo 83, listok 42, Foster Papers.

50. *New Majority,* September 18, 1920, 5, July 31, 1920, 5.

51. Johanningsmeier, *Forging American Communism,* 152, 159.

52. Foster repeatedly used his wartime experiences in his later writings to instruct Party activists and other left-wingers on organization and strategy. See William Z. Foster, *Strike Strategy* (Chicago, 1926); and Foster, *American Trade Unionism,* 219–44.

53. Foster, *From Bryan to Stalin,* 138; Soule, "William Z. Foster," 197.

54. Foster, *Great Steel Strike and Its Lessons,* 225 (first quote); Foster, "Open Letter to John Fitzpatrick," 7 (subsequent quotes).

CHAPTER 6: FROM SYNDICALISM TO COMMUNISM, 1920–22

1. William Z. Foster, "A Statement of the Aims of the Trade Union Educational League," fond 615, opis 1, delo 86, listki 5–6, Foster Papers.

2. Foner, *TUEL to the End of the Gompers Era,* 107; Charles Ruthenberg, *Liberator,* February 1923, 13, quoted in Draper, *Roots of American Communism,* 198.

3. Draper, *Roots of American Communism,* 316. Draper's list of names came from Browder's own recollections of the trip. This group joined a small IWW delegation led by "Big Bill" Haywood and a few delegates from small independent unions in New York City. See Foster, *From Bryan to Stalin,* 138.

4. William Z. Foster, *The Railroader's Next Step—Amalgamation* (Chicago, 1921). The pamphlet's title probably was inspired by an early British syndicalist pamphlet, *The Miner's Next Step* (Tonypandy, U.K., 1912).

5. Draper, *Roots of American Communism,* 314.

6. Quoted in Chaplin, *Wobbly,* 347. See also Foster, *From Bryan to Stalin,* 157–58.

7. "Communist Party of America, Program," September 5, 1919, 6, quoted in Johanningsmeier, *Forging American Communism,* 158; *Communist,* October 18, 1919, 2, quoted in Draper, *Roots of American Communism,* 199 (see also 186, 198–200).

8. Draper, *American Communism and Soviet Russia,* 70; Foster, *From Bryan to Stalin,* 138 (quote); Zipser, *Working Class Giant,* 64. On the importance of Lenin's arguments for the Party's trade union work, see also Earl Browder, interviews by Daniel Bell, June 14, 1955, 1–2, 10, (with William Goldsmith), June 22, 1955, 22, July 12, 1955, 9, all in box 1,

folder 20, Addendum (1982), Daniel Bell Papers, Tamiment Institute Library, New York University (hereafter Bell Papers).

9. Holton, *British Syndicalism;* Allen Hutt, *The Postwar History of the British Working Class* (Wakefield, U.K., 1972), 59–64; Foster, *From Bryan to Stalin*, 74–75, 79 (quote).

10. William Z. Foster, *The Revolutionary Crisis in 1918–1921 in Germany, England, Italy and France* (Chicago, December 1921), 21–31 (quotes on 29 and 30).

11. Alfred Rosmer, *Moscow under Lenin* (New York, 1971), 139; William Z. Foster, *The Russian Revolution* (Chicago, 1921), 5.

12.Foster, *From Bryan to Stalin*, 158 (first quote); *Voice of Labor*, August 26, 1921, 11 (second quote).

13. Foster, *Russian Revolution*, 7 (first and second quotes); "Typescript Report of Speech at Detroit Armory, Dec. 4, 1921," in letter from W. D. Mahon, Detroit, to Samuel Gompers, December 14, 1921, in *American Federation of Labor Records: The Samuel Gompers Era, 1877–1924* (Sanford, N.C.: Microfilming Corporation of America, 1982), reel 105 (third and fourth quotes). See also William Z. Foster, "Russia in 1924," *Labor Herald* 3 (July 1924): 67.

14. Foster, *From Bryan to Stalin*, 156.

15. Ibid., 160; Foster, *Revolutionary Crisis*.

16. Foster, *Russian Revolution*, 7–8.

17. Tom Mann, "Roots of the British Minority Movement," *Workers Monthly* 4 (December 1924): 678; White, *Tom Mann*, 200–202; Roderick Martin, *Communism and the British Trade Unions* (Oxford, 1969). On the syndicalists at the first RILU congress, see Rosmer, *Moscow under Lenin*, 135–40. On the official IWW version of the congress, see George Williams, *The First Congress of the Red Trade Union International at Moscow, 1921* (Chicago, 1922).

18. Draper, *American Communism and Soviet Russia*, 70 (first quote); Draper, *Roots of American Communism*, 321 (second quote).

19. Earl Browder, interview by Theodore Draper, October 22, 1954, 2, box 1, folder 3, Theodore Draper Papers, Woodruff Library, Emory University (hereafter Draper Papers). Having worked as a blacksmith and tailor, Solomon Abramovich Lozovsky (1878–1952) shared with Foster a trade union background. He directed the Red International of Labor Unions, or Profintern, from its establishment in 1921 to its dissolution in 1937. Arrested in 1949, he died in prison. See Branko Lazitch, in collaboration with Milorad M. Drachkovitch, *Biographical Dictionary of the Comintern*, new, revised, and expanded ed. (Stanford, Calif., 1986), 279–81.

20. Foster, *From Bryan to Stalin*, 157; Foster, *Russian Revolution*, chaps. 11, 20; Foster, "Pages from a Worker's Life," 2; William J. Chase, *Workers, Society, and the Soviet State: Labor and Life in Moscow, 1918–1929* (Urbana, Ill., 1987), 173–213.

21. Foster, *Pages from a Worker's Life*, 309 (first quote); William Z. Foster, "Emma Goldman," in *More Pages from a Worker's Life*, quoted in Zipser, *Working Class Giant*, 36–37 (second quote). See also Browder, interview, 133–35, Columbia University Oral History Project. On rationing and the diet in Moscow in this period, see Chase, *Workers, Society, and the Soviet State*, 178–80.

22. Foster, *Pages from a Worker's Life,* 294–95.

23. Klehr, *Heyday of American Communism,* 5–7; Workers (Communist) Party, *The Party Organization* (Chicago, 1925). Storch, "Shades of Red," emphasizes the weaknesses of this structure and the importance of local initiative.

24. James G. Ryan, *Earl Browder: The Failure of American Communism* (Tuscaloosa, Ala., 1997), 4–21; Browder, interview, 22–112, Columbia University Oral History Project; Earl Browder, interviews by Theodore Draper, May 4, 1954, 1, October 22, 1954, 2, box 1, folder 3, Draper Papers, Woodruff Library; Obituary, *New York Times,* June 28, 1973; Draper, *Roots of American Communism,* 307–11. On the *Appeal to Reason* and the radical midwestern culture from which it sprang, see Elliot Shore, *Talkin' Socialism* (Lawrence, Kans., 1988).

25. James P. Cannon, interview by Theodore Draper, New York City, September 23, 1955, 1–2, Section I: "Biographical and Background Material," Cannon Papers; James P. Cannon, interviews by Harry Ring, Los Angeles, April 4, 1973, April 11, 1973, April 18, 1973, May 10, 1973, ibid.; James P. Cannon, *James P. Cannon and the Early Years of American Communism: Selected Writings and Speeches* (New York, 1992), xiii–xiv, 3–9; Draper, *Roots of American Communism,* 305–7. Cannon was most closely associated with the International Labor Defense, a united front legal organization, from its founding until his expulsion from the Workers (Communist) Party in 1928. He established the Trotskyist movement in the United States later that year and remained the central figure in the Socialist Workers Party until his death in 1974.

26. Johnstone (1880–1942) visited Russia soon after the Revolution and later traveled throughout the world as a Comintern representative, including to India where he worked with Ghandi. He served most of the period from 1927 to 1942 on the Party's Central Committee. See Solon DeLeon, ed., *American Labor Who's Who* (New York, 1925), 147; and Bernard K. Johnpoll and Harvey Klehr, eds., *Biographical Dictionary of the American Left,* 225–26.

27. On Sam Hammersmark (1878–1957), see *Daily Worker,* June 7, 1938, 6, September 23, 1937, 3, September 30, 1957, 5, 7; DeLeon, *American Labor Who's Who,* 95; Ashbaugh, *Lucy Parsons,* 234; and Nelson, Barrett, and Ruck, *Steve Nelson,* 72.

28. Arne Swabeck (1890–1986) was expelled from the Communist Party as a Trotskyist in 1928 and from the Socialist Workers Party as a Maoist in 1967. See Arne Swabeck, "From Gene Debs to Mao Tse-Tung," autobiography, box 8, Charles H. Kerr Papers, Newberry Library, Chicago. Joe Manley later led the Party's Federated Farmer-Labor Party. See Foster, *From Bryan to Stalin,* 38, 59, 82, 174, 179; and DeLeon, *American Labor Who's Who,* 147. Charles Krumbein (1889–1947) served as the Party's district organizer in New York from 1924 to 1925, studied at the Lenin School in 1926–27, and worked as a Comintern representative, mostly in China, from 1927 to 1934. He was the Party's treasurer from 1938 to 1947. See *Daily Worker,* August 2, 1935, 7; and Johnpoll and Klehr, *Biographical Dictionary of the American Left,* 233–34.

29. William F. Dunne, document 61-130-79, FOIA file 72,685/190-7276, box 3, Harvey Klehr Papers, Woodruff Library, Emory University (hereafter Klehr Papers); DeLeon,

American Labor's Who's Who, 64; Draper, *Roots of American Communism,* 316–17; Aaron Gutfield, "The Murder of Frank Little: Radical Agitator in Butte, 1917," *Labor History* 10 (January 1969): 177–92; Emmons, *Butte Irish,* 364–83; Foner, *Labor and World War I,* 281–91; Joseph Freeman, *An American Testament: A Narrative of Rebels and Romantics* (New York, 1936), 292–93.

30. Freeman, *American Testament,* 293–94 (quote); biographical data and manuscripts, box 2, William F. Dunne Papers, Tamiment Institute Library, New York University (hereafter Dunne Papers). One of the Communist Party's more tragic figures, Dunne seems never to have recovered from his young son's death in an auto accident. He developed a serious drinking problem in the wake of the tragedy. As the problem worsened, he was removed from the leadership in 1934 and expelled from the Party in 1946.

31. Alexander Bittelman, manuscript autobiography, Bittelman Papers, Tamiment Institute Library, New York University (hereafter Bittelman Papers); Draper, *American Communism and Soviet Russia,* 88–89; Melech Epstein, *The Jew and Communism: The Story of Early Communist Victories and Ultimate Defeats in the Jewish Community, USA, 1919–1941* (New York, 1959), 398–403.

32. Arne Swabeck to Theodore Draper, June 25, 1957, copy, box 30, Draper Papers, Hoover Institution, Stanford University.

33. Draper, *Roots of American Communism,* 324.

34. Hoxie to Foster, March 29, 1916; John R. Commons, *Myself: The Autobiography of John R. Commons* (Madison, Wis., 1964), 149 (quote). My thanks to Steve Sapolsky for bringing this passage to my attention.

35. James P. Cannon, "The Workers Party Today—And Tomorrow," *Worker,* August 25 to September 22, 1923, reprinted in Cannon, *James P. Cannon and the Early Years of American Communism,* 134 (Cannon quote); Bittelman, manuscript autobiography, 357; Alexander Bittelman, interview by Theodore Draper, January 20, 1969, 1 (Bittelman quotes), box 10, folder 22, Draper Papers, Woodruff Library; Gil Green, interview by Sidney Lens, December 28, 1973, notes, 5–7, box 66, folder 9, Sidney Lens Papers, Chicago Historical Society (hereafter Lens Papers)

36. Weisbord, *Radical Life,* 95. Compare Myra Page's recollection of Foster in Christina Looper Baker, *In a Generous Spirit: A First-Person Biography of Myra Page* (Urbana, Ill., 1996), 84–85.

37. Sam Darcy, interview by Theodore Draper, May 14–15, 1957, microfilm series 2.3, roll 8, Draper Papers, Woodruff Library; Benjamin Gitlow, *I Confess* (New York, 1939), 191.

38. Weisbord, *Radical Life,* 95, 98–99 (quotes); Bittelman, manuscript autobiography, 398–99 (quotes), 407–8, 434–35. See also Gitlow, *I Confess,* 106, 313; and Oliver Carlson, interview by Harvey Klehr, March 20–March 22, 1978, Klehr Papers.

39. Earl Browder to Charlie [Lozovsky], November 24, 1924, fond 534, opis 7, delo 464, Profintern Papers, Russian Center for the Preservation and Study of Documents of Recent History, Moscow (hereafter Profintern Papers).

CHAPTER 7: BORING FROM WITHIN, 1922–25

1.Earl Beckner, "The Trade Union Educational League and the American Labor Movement," *Journal of Political Economy* 33 (August 1925): 410.

2. See, for example, Cochran, *Labor and Communism;* Draper, *American Communism and Soviet Russia;* and Howe and Coser, *American Communist Party.*

3. For Foster's relative autonomy in his trade union work, see Daniel Bell and William Goldsmith, interview with Earl Browder, June 22, 1955, 28–29, box 1, folder 20, Bell Papers.

4. William Z. Foster to Solomon Lozovsky, Chicago, April 10, 1923, fond 534, opis 7, delo 459, listok 3, Profintern Papers.

5. William Z. Foster to Solomon Lozovsky, Chicago, May 31, 1923, ibid., listok 46 (first quote); *New Majority,* December 24, 1921, 8 (second and third quotes). Foster, Browder, and other TUEL organizers regularly requested funds in letters to Lozovsky. See, for example, William Z. Foster to "Comrade" [Lozovsky], Chicago, December 16, 1922, fond 534, opis 7, delo 457, listok 141, Profintern Papers; and William Z. Foster to Profintern Executive, May 9, 1923, fond 534, opis 7, delo 459, listok 18, Profintern Papers. For confirmation that at least some funds were received, see Johanningsmeier, *Forging American Communism,* 179, 187; John Haynes and Harvey Klehr, "Communication," *Labor History* 33 (1992): 557; and Browder, interview by Bell, June 22, 1955, 27.

6. Jack Johnstone, "The League in Chicago," *Labor Herald* 1 (April 1922): 29; Browder, interview by Bell, June 22, 1955; "Questions Asked of Borden [Foster] regarding Trade Union Work and His Answers," [August, 1922], photostat, box 16, folder 20, Klehr Papers. Toward the end of 1924, the Labor Research Department of the Rand School of Social Science, with close links to the Workers Party, estimated the TUEL's national membership at about 1,700. This figure would not include sympathizers who did not subscribe to the *Labor Herald.* See Rand School of Social Science, Labor Research Department, *The American Labor Year Book, 1923–1924* (New York, 1924), 88.

7. Foster to Lozovsky, April 10, 1923, 3 (first quote); Foster, *Bankruptcy of the American Labor Movement,* 24 (second and third quotes); David Saposs, "What's Back of Foster?" *Nation,* January 17, 1923, 70; "Foster's Reply to Scott Nearing," *Daily Worker,* May 10, 1924, quoted in Draper, *American Communism and Soviet Russia,* 123. For similar rhetoric, see the series of articles Foster did for the *Worker* in February and March 1922, quoted in Foner, *TUEL to the End of the Gompers Era,* 121.

8. The description of the TUEL and its program is based on Foster, *Bankruptcy of the American Labor Movement;* William Z. Foster, "The Principles and Program of the Trade Union Educational League," *Labor Herald* 1 (March 1922), 3–7; and Rand School of Social Science, *American Labor Year Book,* 86–92. See also David M. Schneider, *The Workers' (Communist) Party and American Trade Unions* (Baltimore, 1928), 1–7.

9. The following description of the Farmer-Labor Party's evolution is based largely on Nathan Fine, *Labor and Farmer Parties in the United States, 1828–1928* (New York, 1928), 377–97; Weinstein, *Decline of Socialism in America,* 222–29, 274; Keiser, "John Fitzpatrick and Progressive Labor," 106–33; and Foner, *Postwar Struggles,* 256–74. The

Farmer-Labor Party program is quoted in David Thelen, *Robert M. La Follette and the Insurgent Spirit* (Boston, 1976), 162.

10. Foster, *From Bryan to Stalin*, 160–61 (quote on 140); Johanningsmeier, *Forging American Communism*, 156. John Fitzpatrick was attracted to the labor party idea for similar reasons, as a hedge against injunctions and as a political arm of the trade union movement on the British model. See Keiser, "John Fitzpatrick and Progressive Labor," 113.

11. On the international context for the united front and its application worldwide, see Franz Borkenau, *World Communism: A History of the Communist International* (New York, 1939), 221–37; and Edward Hallett Carr, *The Bolshevik Revolution, 1917–1923*, vol. 3 (New York, 1953), 383–425. For the effects of Lenin's formulation on the thinking of Foster and other American Communists regarding the labor party idea, see Foster, *From Bryan to Stalin*, 137–38; and James P. Cannon, *The First Ten Years of American Communism: Report of a Participant* (New York, 1962), 59–61.

12. Central Executive Committee, Workers Party, "The Present Political Situation and the Immediate Tasks of the Party," [1923], fond 515, opis 1, delo 283, listki 1–4, CPUSA Papers, Russian Center for the Preservation and Study of Documents of Recent History, Moscow (hereafter CPUSA Papers); Weinstein, *Decline of Socialism in America*, 275–78; Foner, *TUEL to the End of the Gompers Era*, 340–43; Foster, *History of the Communist Party of the United States of America*, 214–18; William Z. Foster to A. Kalinin, Chicago, April 24, 1923, fond 534, opis 7, delo 59, listok 26 (quote), Profintern Papers.

13. Draper, *American Communism and Soviet Russia*, 39 (Draper quote), 41; Swabeck to Draper, June 25, 1957 (Swabeck quote); Swabeck, "From Gene Debs to Mao Tse-Tung." Browder recalled Fitzpatrick's using different words but making the same point. Browder's recollection is quoted in Draper, *American Communism and Soviet Russia*, 487.

14. Foster to Profintern Executive, May 9, 1923 (quote); William Z. Foster, "A Political Party for Labor," *Labor Herald* 1 (December 1922): 3–6; Earl Browder, "The League's Labor Party Referendum," *Labor Herald* 2 (June 1923): 12–13. For the referendum itself, see "To All Local Unions of All Trades in the US," March 10, 1923, fond 615, opis 1, delo 86, listok 4, Foster Papers, reprinted in *Labor Herald* 2 (March 1923): 12.

15. Eugene Staley, *History of the Illinois State Federation of Labor* (Chicago, 1930); Earl Browder, "Gompers Attacks the League," *Labor Herald* 1 (May 1922): 16; Draper, *American Communism and Soviet Russia*, 71. The resolution itself, which became a model for the efforts in other unions and federations, is in "Chicago Federation for Amalgamation," *Labor Herald* 1 (April 1922): 12; *Voice of Labor*, March 24, 1922, 11.

16. *Voice of Labor*, April 21, 1922, 1 (first quote), 2 (second quote); Israel Amter, "Report of the American Party to the Profintern, March 12, 1923," fond 534, opis 7, delo 458, listki 8–9, Profintern Papers; Taft, *AF of L in the Time of Gompers*, 453–54; Samuel Gompers, "The Soviet Camouflage," *American Federationist* 29 (April 1922): 276–85; editorial, "Another Attempt at Soviet Dictatorship Unmasked," *American Federationist* 29 (May 1922): 337–45; Jay Fox, *Amalgamation* (Chicago, 1923); Earl Browder, "Gompers Attacks the League," *Labor Herald* 1 (May 1922): 16–17, 31; Earl Browder, "Progress of the Amalgamation Movement," *Labor Herald* 1 (October 1922): 1–6; "Amalgamation

Movement Sweeps Onward," *Labor Herald* I (November 1922): 11; Earl Browder, "Eleven States Demand Amalgamation," *Labor Herald* I (December 1922): 7; Edward B. Mittelman, "Basis for American Federation of Labor Opposition to Amalgamation and Politics at Portland," *Journal of Political Economy* 32 (February 1924): 90; William Z. Foster to Samuel Gompers, Washington, D.C., April 20, 1922, reprinted in *Labor Herald* I (May 1922): 14; William Z. Foster to "Comrade" [Lozovsky], Chicago, December 12, 1922, fond 534, opis 7, delo 457, listok 140, Profintern Papers (third quote). See also Samuel Gompers, *Seventy Years of Life and Labor,* vol. 2 (New York, 1925), 518.

17. On the roots of needle trades unionism and the radical Jewish subculture from which it sprang, see Irving Howe, *World of Our Fathers: The Journey of the East European Jews to America and the World They Found and Made* (New York, 1976), 295–304; and Moses Rischin, *The Promised City: New York's Jews, 1870–1914* (New York, 1970), 175–83. On early left-wing activity in the ILGWU, see Charles S. Zimmerman, interview by Theodore Draper, May 21, 1957, notes, 1, box 18, folder 25, Draper Papers, Woodruff Library; Lewis L. Lorwin (Louis Levine), *The Women's Garment Workers* (New York, 1924); David Gurowsky, "Factional Disputes within the ILGWU, 1919–1928" (Ph.D. diss., SUNY–Binghamton, 1978), vi–xiii, xxiv–xxvii, 49–59, 94–106; Rose Wortis, "The Shop Delegate League in the Needle Trades," *Labor Herald* I (May 1922): 24–25; Cochran, *Labor and Communism,* 38–39; and Schneider, *Workers'(Communist) Party and American Trade Unions,* 87–90. On the fur workers union, see Schneider, *Workers' (Communist) Party and American Trade Unions,* 72–77; and Philip S. Foner, *The Fur and Leather Workers Union* (Newark, N.J., 1950), 179–312. On the TUEL in the needle trades generally, see Foner, *TUEL to the End of the Gompers Era,* 269–310; and Johanningsmeier, "William Z. Foster: Labor Organizer and Communist," 628–30.

18. National Committee, Needle Trades Section, Report, May 13, 1925, 6 (quote), Party History Section: "AF of L Convention Resolutions and Other Trade Union Materials," Cannon Papers; J. B. Salutsky, "Constructive Radicalism in the Needle Industry," *Labor Herald* I (May 1922): 10–13, 19; Fraser, *Labor Will Rule,* 178–83; Foner, *TUEL to the End of the Gompers Era,* 302–7; Stanley Nadel, "The Communists and the Needle Trades, 1920–1928" (M.A. thesis, Columbia University, 1973), 47–51.

19. Montgomery, *Fall of the House of Labor,* 338–41 (Montgomery quote on 338–39); Melvyn Dubofsky and Warren Van Tine, *John L. Lewis: A Biography* (New York, 1977), 47–52, 61–62, 74–75, 91–94; William Goldsmith, "Notes on Interview with John Brophy, November 11, 1955, CIO Headquarters, Washington, D.C.," box 1, folder 20, Addendum, Bell Papers (Brophy quote). See also Alan Singer, "Communists and Coal Miners: Rank and File Organizing in the United Mine Workers of America during the 1920's," *Science and Society* 55 (Summer 1991): 135–39.

20. On the TUEL's work in the UMWA, see Schneider, *Workers' (Communist) Party and American Trade Unions,* 38–59; Cochran, *Labor and Communism,* 47–49; Dubofsky and Van Tine, *John L. Lewis,* 99–100, 122–24; Foner, *TUEL to the End of the Gompers Era,* 208–68; Johanningsmeier, *Forging American Communism,* 185–86; and Foster, *From Bryan to Stalin,* 196–200.

21. Foner, *TUEL to the End of the Gompers Era,* 259–65; Singer, "Communists and Coal Miners," 139–43; notes in box 1, vol. 3, New Series, Bell Papers. On Howat, see Dubofsky and Van Tine, *John L. Lewis,* 118–22; John Dorsey, "How the Machine Got Howat," *Labor Herald* 1 (June 1922): 14–15, 23, 31; and John Dorsey, "Alexander Howat," *Labor Herald* 2 (April 1923): 5–6. Dorsey was one of at least two aliases Foster employed in the early 1920s.

22. J. W. Johnstone, "Workers Party in Action at Local Miners Convention," *Daily Worker,* February 12, 1924, 1; T. J. O'Flaherty, "The Miners' Convention," *Daily Worker,* February 9, 1924, 5, 8. On the Progressive International Committee of the UMWA, see Selig Perlman and Philip Taft, *History of Labor in the United States,* vol. 4 (New York, 1935), 562–71; Gitlow, *I Confess,* 377–89; William Z. Foster, "The Left Wing and the Trade Union Elections," *Workers Monthly* 4 (February 1925): 147–48; John Dorsey [Foster], "Progressive International Committee of the United Mine Workers of America," *Labor Herald* 2 (March 1923): 10–11; and William Z. Foster, "The Progressive Miners' Conference," *Labor Herald* 2 (July 1923): 3–6.

23. Colin J. Davis, *Power at Odds: The 1922 Railroad Shopmen's Strike* (Urbana, Ill., 1998), 67–68; William Z. Foster, *Misleaders of Labor* (New York, 1927), 142–44 (quote on 143); William Z. Foster, "Railroad Workers, Amalgamate!" *Labor Herald* 1 (November 1922): 3–5; William Z. Foster, "The National Railroad Amalgamation Conference," *Labor Herald* 2 (January 1923): 3–5, 26–27.

24. Foster, *Misleaders of Labor,* 143; Schneider, *Workers' (Communist) Party and American Trade Unions,* 9–25, 29–35; Mark Perlman, *The Machinists* (Cambridge, Mass., 1961), 16–17; Johanningsmeier, *Forging American Communism,* 182, 184; Robert Christie, *Empire in Wood: A History of the Carpenters' Union* (Ithaca, N.Y., 1956), 256, 245–48, 260; Richard Schneirov and Thomas J. Suhrbur, *Union Brotherhood, Union Town: The History of the Carpenters' Union of Chicago, 1863–1987* (Carbondale, Ill., 1988), 94–108; Foner, *TUEL to the End of the Gompers Era,* 170–207; Morris Rosen, manuscript autobiography, 25–27, 130–31, 89–90, 104–10, 118–21, 183–84, Tamiment Institute Library, New York University; William Z. Foster, "Five Vital Conferences," *Labor Herald* 2 (January 1923): 11–15; Joseph Manley, "The League Booming," *Labor Herald* 2 (March 1923): 20.

25. James P. Cannon to Theodore Draper, Los Angeles, August 4, 1954, 2, box 31, Draper Papers, Hoover Institution; William Z. Foster, *Worker,* April 22, 1922, 2, quoted in Draper, *American Communism and Soviet Russia,* 72–73 (Draper quote on 73). See also S. T. Hammersmark, "How To Win Support in Your Union," *Labor Herald* 1 (December 1922), 21. On the group of labor progressives on whom Foster based this strategy, see Montgomery, *Fall of the House of Labor,* 399–410.

26. *New York Times,* August 21, 1922, 1 (first quote); Eugene V. Debs, "A Letter from Eugene V. Debs," *Labor Herald* 1 (October 1922): 14; "William Foster Kidnapped," *Voice of Labor,* August 18, 1922, 11; *New Majority,* September 16, 1922, 3 (second quote); Johanningsmeier, *Forging American Communism,* 192.

27. *New Majority,* August 9, 1922, 4, 5; Foster, *From Bryan to Stalin,* 75–76; Foster, *Pages from a Worker's Life,* 217–18, 224–28; *New York Times,* August 8, 1922, 2, August 23, 1922,

1, August 24, 1921, 1; *Voice of Labor,* August 18, 1922, 8, 11; Benjamin Gitlow, *The Whole of Their Lives* (New York, 1948), 92–94 (quote on 93); Foster quoted in Ted Morgan, *A Covert Life, Jay Lovestone: Communist, Anti-Communist, and Spymaster* (New York, 1999), 28; Browder, interview, 206–8, Columbia University Oral History Project; Moritz Loeb, "The Gary Frame-Up," *Labor Herald* 1 (October 1922): 21–22, 23.

28. Eugene V. Debs, "Getting Together," *Labor Herald* 3 (April 1923): 14, 16; *New Majority,* September 16, 1922, 3, September 23, 1922, 1, 6 (first two quotes); *Chicago Tribune,* March 29, 1923, 5; Lillian Herstein, interview by Elizabeth Balanoff, 60, 67, transcripts, Labor Oral History Project, Roosevelt University, Chicago; Labor Defense Council, Chicago, *Nine Questions and Eight Answers about the Michigan "Red Raid" Cases* (Chicago, [1922]) (third quote); Richard Merrill Whitney, *Reds in America* (New York, 1924), 171–76. On the defense work, see Foner, *TUEL to the End of the Gompers Era,* 142–46; *Story of Assault on Liberty in Michigan "Red" Case* (Chicago, [1923]), leaflet, box 1, Dunne Papers; *"This Christmas Give for Liberty and Freedom," "Help Repel This Attack upon Labor,"* and other Labor Defense Council flyers in box 30, clippings file, Saposs Papers, and in fond 534, opis 7, delo 457, listki 223–26, Profintern Papers.

29. *Chicago Tribune,* March 13, 1923, 2, March 16, 1923, 3, March 28, 1923, 1, 12, April 4, 1923, 16, April 5, 1923, 1, April 6, 1923, 12; *New York Herald,* December 4, 1922, 1 (first quote); *New York Times,* April 15, 1923, 5; Robert Minor to [Workers Party?], telegram, March 15, 1923, fond 515, opis 1, delo 237, listki 1–2, CPUSA Papers; Robert Minor, "The Trial of William Z. Foster," *Liberator* 6 (April 1923): 8–11 (second quote on 10); William Z. Foster, "On Trial in Michigan," *Labor Herald* 2 (May 1923): 3–6, 25–27 (third quote on 26). The Frank Walsh Papers at the New York Public Library contain some correspondence and extensive newspaper clippings on the trial in volume 16 of Walsh's scrapbooks. Foster's FBI file also includes extensive clippings assembled by agents assigned to the case. See the clippings following document 61-330-185, Foster FOIA file.

30. Browder, interview by Bell, June 22, 1955, 45–48; James P. Cannon to Theodore Draper, Los Angeles, March 22, 1955, 1, box 31, Draper Papers, Hoover Institution; Sam Darcy, interview by Theodore Draper, April 30–May 1, 1957, microfilm series 2.3, reel 8, Draper Papers, Woodruff Library.

31. Quoted in U.S. Senate, *Recognition of Russia: Hearings before a Subcommittee of the Committee on Foreign Relations,* 68th Cong., 1st sess. (Washington, D.C., 1924), 369.

32. Workers Party Trade Union Committee Minutes, box 2, New Series, Bell Papers; TUEL National Committee Minutes, box 3, New Series, Bell Papers.

33. Political Committee Meeting Minutes, June 13, 14, 1928, box 1, folder 1, Bell Papers, Woodruff Library; Max Bedacht to Theodore Draper, Lake Grove, N.Y., June 13, 1957, box 10, folder 15, Woodruff Library; Max Bedacht, interview by Theodore Draper, June 1, 1954, 3, box 10, folder 16, Draper Papers, Woodruff Library; Baker, *In a Generous Spirit,* 63.

34. Jay Lovestone to Ella [Wolfe], January 8, 1923 [1924], box 9, folder 74, Bertram Wolfe Papers, Hoover Institution, Stanford University (hereafter Wolfe Papers); [Jay Lovestone?] to Solomon Lozovsky, March 15, 1923, fond 534, opis 7, delo 461, listki 1–2

(first two quotes), Profintern Papers; William Z. Foster to Solomon Lozovsky, August 9, 1923, fond 534, opis 7, delo 459, listok 102 (Foster quote), Profintern Papers.

35. Samuel Gompers to John Fitzpatrick, Chicago, April 25, 1923, "Correspondence, 1918–1922," Addendum, Fitzpatrick Papers; McKillen, *Chicago Labor and the Quest for a Democratic Diplomacy,* 204; "Statement of the Seattle Central Labor Council Relative to Its Controversy with the Executive Council of the American Federation of Labor," n.d. [June 1923], quoted in Frank, *Purchasing Power,* 186 (AFL quote). See also Dembo, *Unions and Politics in Washington State,* 338–40; Harvey O'Conner, *Revolution Seattle* (New York, 1964), 213–14; "The Seattle Central Labor Council, Statement by the National Committee of the Trade Union Educational League," *Labor Herald* 2 (June 1923): 16; and Hulet Wells, "Gompers Shows Seattle Where to Head In," *Labor Herald* 2 (December 1923): 6–7, 31–32.

36. Swabeck to Draper, June 25, 1957, 1.

37. James P. Cannon et al. to C. E. Ruthenberg, New York City, May 25, 1923, reprinted in Cannon, *James P. Cannon and the Early Years of American Communism,* 124–26; Lowell K. Dyson, *Red Harvest: The Communist Party and American Farmers* (Lincoln, Nebr., 1982), 11–19; Charles Shipman, *It Had to Be Revolution: Memoirs of an American Radical* (Ithaca, N.Y., 1993), 149–51.

38. C. E. Ruthenberg to the Executive Committee of the Comintern, Chicago, April 11, 1924, copy inserted in Earl Browder to Theodore Draper, Yonkers, March 1, 1956, box 31, Draper Papers, Hoover Institution; Earl Browder, interview by Theodore Draper, September 29, 1953, 2, box 1, folder 3, Draper Papers, Woodruff Library; Darcy, interview by Draper, April 30–May 1, 1957, 2–3; Lovestone to [Wolfe], January 8, 1923 [1924]; Jay Lovestone to Bert and Ella [Wolfe], October 11, 1923, box 9, folder 73, Wolfe Papers; Cannon, *First Ten Years of American Communism,* 80, 81 (Cannon quotes). On Pepper's career, see Malcolm Sylvers, "Pogany/Pepper: Un representative du Komintern apres du Parti Communiste des Etats Unis," *Cahiers d'histoire de l'Institut de Re cherche Marxiste* 28 (Summer 1987): 119–31.

39. Swabeck, "From Gene Debs to Mao Tse Tung," 149–50; Bedacht, interview by Draper; Browder, interview by Bell, July 12, 1955.

40. Swabeck to Draper, June 25, 1957, 2–3; Keiser, "John Fitzpatrick and Progressive Labor," 133–35; William Z. Foster to Solomon Lozovsky, July 9, 1924, fond 534, opis 7, delo 459, listok 92 (quote), Profintern Papers. See also John Pepper, "The Workers Party and the Federated Farmer-Labor Party," *Liberator* 6 (August 1923): 10–14; J. B. S. Hardman, "The World We Live In," *American Labor Monthly* 1 (August 1923): 3–15; and Weinstein, *Decline of Socialism in America,* 282–83.

41. William Z. Foster, "The Federated Farmer-Labor Party," *Labor Herald* 2 (August 1923): 3 (first quote), 7; James P. Cannon to Theodore Draper, May 28, 1954 (second Foster quote), box 31, Draper Papers, Hoover Institution. See also Cannon, *First Ten Years of American Communism,* 87.

42. Jay G. Brown, "The Farmer-Labor Side," *American Labor Monthly* 1 (September 1923): 33–37 (quote on 33).

43. Foster, *History of the Communist Party of the United States of America,* 217. See also Swabeck, "From Gene Debs to Mao Tse-Tung," 150–51; and Weinstein, *Decline of Socialism in America,* 284–88.

44. *New Majority,* July 14, 1923, 2, quoted in Keiser, "John Fitzpatrick and Progressive Labor," 145.

45. Ibid., passim; Herstein, interview by Balanoff, 63–67; Weinstein, *Decline of Socialism in America,* 288–89.

46. William Z. Foster to Solomon Lozovsky, September 10, 1923, fond 534, opis 7, delo 460, listki 13, 14 (first two quotes); William Z. Foster, "The Battle of Decatur," *Labor Herald* 2 (November 1923): 6.

47. Quoted in Staley, *History of the Illinois Federation of Labor,* 398.

48. Ibid., 398–405; Foster, "Battle of Decatur," 6–8.

49. Illinois State Federation of Labor, *Proceedings,* 41st Annual Convention, September 10–15, 1923, Decatur, Illinois (Springfield, Ill., 1923), 337, 338–39.

50. Foster, *History of the Communist Party of the United States of America,* 221 (Foster quote); American Federation of Labor, *Proceedings of the American Federation of Labor, 1923* (Washington, D.C., 1923), 256–59; "Labor Federation Ousts Communists 27,838 Votes to 130," *New York Times,* October 9, 1923, 1, 7; William F. Dunne, "Labor's Chamber of Commerce," *Labor Herald* 2 (November 1923): 3–5; Mittelman, "Basis for American Federation of Labor Opposition to Amalgamation and Politics at Portland"; Montgomery, *Fall of the House of Labor,* 433 (Gompers observation), 434 (Montgomery quote); Taft, *AF of L in the Time of Gompers,* 476–86; Staley, *History of the Illinois State Federation of Labor,* 396–97. See also Browder, interview, 158, Columbia University Oral History Project; and *William F. Dunne's Speech at the AF of L Convention, Portland, 1923* (Chicago, 1923). For evidence of the Chicago Communists' isolation in the CFL, see the debate over the federation's decisive turn away from independent labor politics and back toward the two-party system in minutes for the November meeting, *New Majority,* November 10, 1923, 4. See also McKillen, *Chicago Labor and the Quest for a Democratic Diplomacy,* 211.

51. Earl Browder to CEP of WP, September 18, 1923, fond 534, opis 7, delo 458, listki 118–19, Profintern Papers.

52. William Z. Foster, "Next Task of the Left Wing," *Labor Herald* 3 (September 1924): 200.

53. On early expulsions of left-wing activists in the Chicago ILGWU, where the league had a strong foothold, see Earl Browder, "Reactionaries Smashing Ladies Garment Workers," *Labor Herald* 2 (November 1923): 13–16. Because most of the ILGWU leaders were members of the Socialist Party, Foster tried to enlist Eugene V. Debs, who had shown considerable sympathy for the TUEL, in his efforts to end the warfare between the union's right and left wings. Foster did succeed in arranging a meeting between Debs and the TUEL leadership, but the ILGWU leaders refused to have anything to do with the Communists. See William Z. Foster to Eugene V. Debs, September 5, 1923; Eugene V. Debs to William Z. Foster, September 12, 1923; William Z. Foster to Eugene V. Debs, September 22, 1923; Eugene V. Debs to William Z. Foster, October 8,

1923; William Z. Foster to Eugene V. Debs, October 25, 1923, November 7, 1923; and Eugene V. Debs to William Z. Foster, November 8, 1923, in *Letters of Eugene V. Debs,* vol. 3, *1919–1926* (Urbana, Ill., 1990), ed. J. Robert Constantine, 393–94, 397–99, 402–4, 406–8, 408–9, 411, 415–16.

54. Fraser, *Labor Will Rule,* 202–5; Steve Fraser, "Dress Rehearsal for the New Deal: Shopfloor Insurgents, Political Elites, and Industrial Democracy in the Amalgamated Clothing Workers," in *Working-Class America,* ed. Frisch and Walkowitz, 212–55.

55. Beckner, "Trade Union Educational League and the American Labor Movement," 425–26; Perlman, *Machinists,* 64–65; Saposs, *Left Wing Unionism,* 56 (quote).

56. William Z. Foster, "Party Industrial Methods and Structure," *Workers Monthly* 4 (June 1925): 351.

57. William Z. Foster, "The Coming Struggle," *Labor Herald* 3 (February 1924): 3–5. Foster developed this theme at length in his *Misleaders of Labor,* especially 21–47.

58. Foster, "Open Letter to John Fitzpatrick," 6, 8, 26–27.

59. Joseph Manley, "Statement of the Federated Farmer-Labor Party," [February 5, 1924], "Farmer-Labor Party," Addendum, Fitzpatrick Papers; "Report of the National Farmer-Labor Progressive Convention, St. Paul, Minnesota, June 17, 1924," Party History Section: "C.P. History, 1924," Cannon Papers; Weinstein, *Decline of Socialism in America,* 290–313; William Z. Foster, "La Follette vs. the Farmer-Labor Party," *Daily Worker,* June 28, 1924, 4; Harvey Klehr, John Earl Haynes, and Kyrill M. Anderson, *The Soviet World of American Communism* (New Haven, Conn., 1998), 21–23, 27–29 (Comintern telegram).

60. William Z. Foster, "Farmer-Labor Opportunism," *Daily Worker,* magazine supplement, December 13, 1924, quoted in Weinstein, *Decline of Socialism in America,* 320 (first quote); William Z. Foster to Gregory Zinoviev, chairman, Communist International, Moscow, March 8, 1924, 2 (remaining quotes), and William Z. Foster, James P. Cannon, Fahls Burman, Earl Browder, W. F. Dunne, Alex Bittelman, and Martin Abern to Executive Committee of the Communist International, March 27, 1924, copies of both enclosed with Arthur Bliss Lane to J. E. Hoover, Washington D.C., March 5, 1925, document 61-330-178, U.S. Department of State, Washington, D.C., Foster FOIA file; Browder, interview, 151–56, Columbia Oral History Project.

61. Theodore Draper analyzes Foster's behavior in terms of opportunism (*American Communism and Soviet Russia,* 116–18), while Edward Johanningsmeier argues for some continuity between Foster's rejection of La Follette and his longtime position on the need for a union and working class based labor party (*Forging American Communism,* 209–11). Though documenting motivation is always difficult, it is reasonable to assume that it was a mixture of these influences. Once the Comintern took a firm position on the question, however, it is unlikely that Foster would have rejected this lead.

62. *New York Times,* June 19, 1924, 3; *Daily Worker,* June 19, 1924, 1 (quote). Foster's remarks, made in a public speech, echoed a similar statement for which Clarence Hathaway, a Minnesota Communist leader, had been criticized by the Communist International. Foster's factional opponents, who argued for Communist leadership of any labor party movement, used the Comintern's criticism of Hathaway against Foster.

See "Report of the National Farmer-Labor-Progressive Convention, St. Paul, Minnesota, June 17, 1924," 5; and "Comrades," memo to the Central Executive Committee, [1924], box 4, Robert Minor Papers, Rare Book and Manuscript Library, Columbia University (hereafter Minor Papers).

63. John Earl Haynes, *Dubious Alliance: The Making of Minnesota's DFL Party* (Minneapolis, 1984).

64. William Z. Foster to Eugene V. Debs, July 15, 1924, and Eugene V. Debs to William Z. Foster, July 23, 1924, Debs Clipping Book Number 2, Eugene V. Debs Papers, Tamiment Institute Library, New York University, quoted in David Shannon, *The Socialist Party of America* (New York, 1955), 178. For Foster's contemporary assessment of the La Follette movement and the decision to discard the farmer-labor party idea, see William Z. Foster, "The Significance of the Elections: Three Stages of Our Labor Party Policy," *Workers Monthly* 4 (December 1924): 51–54.

65. That Foster clearly intended a break with Debs is suggested by the fact that he made his second letter an open one, which appeared in the *Daily Worker* on July 31, 1924. I am quoting here from the manuscript letter published in *Letters of Eugene V. Debs,* 431. The second and third quotes are from William Z. Foster, "La Follette, Gompers, and Debs," *Labor Herald* 3 (October 1924): 231, 232.

66. Foster, "La Follette, Gompers, and Debs," 230–32; Weinstein, *Decline of Socialism in America,* 313–23.

67. Foster, *History of the Communist Party of the United States of America,* 219, 220 (quote).

68. *American Labor Monthly* 4 (December 1926): 13.

69. Buhle, *Marxism in the USA,* 131 (first quote), 132 (second quote).

70. James P. Cannon to Theodore Draper, March 28, 1954, 4, box 31, Draper Papers, Hoover Institution.

71. Ibid.

CHAPTER 8: FACTIONALISM, 1925–29

1. Pepper, "Workers Party and the Federated Farmer-Labor Party," 10–14; John Pepper, "Facing the Third American Revolution," *Liberator* 6 (September 1923): 9–12; John Pepper, "Shall We Assume Leadership?" *Liberator* 6 (October 1923): 9–11, 28.

2. James Cannon and William Z. Foster, "Statement on Our Labor Party Policy," November 1923, in "Farmer-Labor Party Maneuvers," Addendum, Bell Papers; I. Amter, "Decision of the CEC in the Farmer-Labor Party," December 15, 1923, fond 534, opis 7, delo 458, listki 215–24, Profintern Papers.

3. Earl [Browder] to Charlie [Lozovsky], November 24, 1924, fond 534, opis 7, delo 464, listok 43. On the 1925 American Commission, see Edward Hallett Carr, *Socialism in One Country, 1924–1926,* vol. 3, part 1 (New York, 1964), 408. For the Foster and Ruthenberg positions on the labor party issue, see Rand School of Social Science, *American Labor Year Book,* 161–65; Foster, "Significance of the Elections"; C. E. Ruthenberg, "Is the Movement towards Class Political Action Dead?" *Workers Monthly* 4 (December

1924): 77–79; and Alexander Bittelman, "In Retrospect," *Workers Monthly* 4 (December 1924): 85–90.

4. The following account of the Comintern's intervention is based on E. H. Carr, *Socialism in One Country*, 406–13; Draper, *American Communism and Soviet Russia*, 127–52; Cannon, *First Ten Years of American Communism*, 131–38; and Howe and Coser, *American Communist Party*, 152–61. Foster's official Party account is brief and unhelpful. See Foster, *History of the Communist Party of the United States of America*, 223.

5. Cable quote in *Workers Monthly*, October 1925, 237, quoted in Draper, *American Communism and Soviet Russia*, 144. See also Browder, interview, 164–66, Columbia Oral History Project; William Z. Foster and Alexander Bittelman, "Report to the Executive Committee of the Communist International, January 18, 1926," research files, microfilm series 2.3, reel 12, Draper Papers, Woodruff Library; E. H. Carr, *Socialism in One Country*, 410; and Howe and Coser, *American Communist Party*, 159.

6. Foster, *Daily Worker*, September 1, 1925, 1, quoted in Draper, *American Communism and Soviet Russia*, 147 (first quote); William Z. Foster to S. Lozovsky, Chicago, September 4, 1925, fond 534, opis 7, delo 468, listki 98, 105 (second quote), Profintern Papers. It was at this point that Foster parted ways with Bill Dunne, though he had never had much patience for Dunne's drinking habits.

7. Foster, *Daily Worker*, October 8, 1925, quoted in Draper, *American Communism and Soviet Russia*, 149. See also Howe and Coser, *American Communist Party*, 159–60; and C. E. Ruthenberg, "The Tasks of the Party in the Light of the Comintern," *Workers Monthly* 4 (July 1926): 401–5.

8. "Minutes of the Anglo-American Secretariat, June 5, 1927," fond 495, opis 72, delo 32, listok 32, Comintern Archives.

9. For Foster's argument for a separate TUEL with its own identity independent of the Party's, see Foster, "Party Industrial Methods and Structure."

10. "Dear Comrade," letter to Foster faction adherents, enclosed with Herbert Benjamin to Jay Lovestone, Chicago, November 28, 1925, Party History Section, Cannon Papers; Mary Heaton Vorse, *The Passaic Strike* (New York, 1927); Martha Stone Asher, "Recollections of the Passaic Textile Strike of 1926," *Labor's Heritage* 2 (April 1990): 4–23; Morton Siegel, "The Passaic Textile Strike of 1926" (Ph.D. diss., Columbia University, 1953), Cochran, *Labor and Communism*, 30–33; William Z. Foster to Solomon Lozovsky, August 6, 1926, fond 534, opis 7, delo 473, listok 3, Profintern Papers.

11. C. Ruthenberg, W. Z. Foster, and C. W. Kuusinen, "Letter to All District, City, Section Committees and Language Propaganda Bureaus, April 15, 1926," enclosing resolution adopted by the Executive Committee of the Communist International, entitled "The Situation in Our Party and the Main Tasks of the Party," research files, microfilm series 2.3, reel 12, Draper Papers, Woodruff Library; "Resolution on the Broadening of the TUEL and the Building of an Oppositional Bloc in Conformity with the CI Decision," May 24, 1926, fond 534, opis 7, delo 470, listki 1–13 (quotes on 13), Profintern Papers.

12. Cannon and Foster, "Statement on Our Labor Party Policy"; Draper, *American Communism and Soviet Russia*, 75–95.

13. Laslett, *Labor and the Left,* 127–31; Browder, interview, 167, Columbia Oral History Project; Cochran, *Labor and Communism,* 38–42; Joel Seidman, *The Needle Trades* (New York, 1942), 164–67; Schneider, *Workers' (Communist) Party and American Trade Unions,* 100–104.

14. Powers Hapgood to Mother and Father, July 10, 1926 (quote), and July 26, 1926, box 4, Powers Hapgood Papers, Lilly Library, Indiana University, Bloomington (hereafter Hapgood Papers); William Z. Foster to Solomon Lozovsky, February 14, 1927, fond 534, opis 7, delo 476, listok 30 (first Foster quote), Profintern Papers; William Z. Foster to Solomon Lozovsky, May 3, 1928, fond 534, opis 7, delo 481, listki 169–70 (second Foster quote), Profintern Papers. Though the Party worked closely with Hapgood and Brophy, the initiative for the Save the Union campaign clearly came from Foster. See "Confidential Report, WP(C) of S, September 12, 1926," fond 534, opis 7, delo 470, listki 61–65, Profintern Papers.

15. William Z. Foster to Solomon Lozovsky, March 16, 1928, fond 534, opis 7, delo 481, listki 183–87; William F. Dunne, "The Crisis in the United Mine Workers," *Communist* 7 (February 1928): 105–9; John Brophy, Pat Toohey, and Powers Hapgood, "Save-the-Miners' Union Call," *Communist* 7 (March 1928): 175–80; William Z. Foster, "The Tasks and Lessons of the Miners' Struggle," *Communist* 7 (April 1928): 195–200; William Z. Foster, "Two Mine Strike Strategies," *Communist* 7 (May 1928): 279–83; William Z. Foster, "The Mining Crisis Deepens," *Communist* 7 (June 1928): 323–26. See also William Z. Foster, "Proposals for Work in the Coal Mining Industry, n.d., spring, 1927(?)," box 2, "Miners," Closed Series, Bell Papers; [William Z. Foster], "Proposals on Mining Situation, April 30, 1928," box 1, folder 1, Open Series, Bell Papers; "Draft of Plan for Work in Miners Union and Agenda for National Miners Conference, Chicago, May 8–9, 1928 (Submitted by Foster to the T[rade] U[nion] Committee, May 6, 1928)," box 1, vol. 5, Closed Series, Bell Papers; "Proposals for Policy in the Mining Industry, Submitted by William Z. Foster, May 16, 1928," box 1, folder 2, Open Series, Bell Papers; and "Foster Replies to Distortion of Communist Party History," *Daily Worker,* December 14, 1958, 11. For details on the relief work and Communist press releases on the strike, see box 4, Hapgood Papers.

16. Political Committee Minutes, March 2, 1927, box 28, Draper Papers, Hoover Institution; [CEC Majority] to Solomon Lozovsky, [May] 1928, fond 534, opis 7, delo 481, listki 252–55; William Z. Foster to V. F. Calverton, September 8, 1925 (Foster quote), box 5, V. F. Calverton Papers, New York Public Library; Draper, *American Communism and Soviet Russia,* 357–76; E. H. Carr, *Socialism in One Country,* 52–122; Foster, *History of the Communist Party of the United States of America,* 269–70; Philip J. Jaffe, *The Rise and Fall of American Communism* (New York, 1975), 31 (Stalin quote); Cannon, *First Ten Years of American Communism,* 222–26. For an early attack on Foster for being "soft" on Trotsky, see C. E. Ruthenberg, "From the Third through the Fourth Convention of the Workers (Communist) Party," *Workers Monthly* 4 (October 1925): 531–38.

17. Foster, *History of the Communist Party of the United States,* 271 (quotes). On Lovestone, see Morgan, *Covert Life.* See also "Memorandum for Mr. Ladd Re: Jay Lovestone," September 9, 1942, document 61-1292-65, Lovestone FOIA file, FBI Headquarters, Washington, D.C. My thanks to David Montgomery for providing a copy of this source.

18. On Foster's arguments regarding the peculiar weakness of the American labor movement, see Foster, *Bankruptcy of the American Labor Movement.* Browder's notions of "communism as twentieth century Americanism" and the progressive character of finance capital in the United States during World War II are discussed in chapter 10, and the postwar efforts to create a distinctively American "mass party of socialism" in chapter 12. See also Ryan, *Earl Browder.*

19. Nelson, Barrett, and Ruck, *Steve Nelson,* 66–67; Howe and Coser, *American Communist Party,* 175–76; William Z. Foster, "The Workers (Communist) Party in the South," *Communist* 7 (November 1928): 676–81; "Statistical Report of William Z. Foster during Presidential Campaign, Sept. 9 to Nov. 7, 1928," fond 515, opis 1, delo 1487, listok 53, CPUSA Papers.

20. On the Third Period, Stalin's campaign against Bukharin, and the rise of Stalinism in the Soviet Party and the Comintern, see Stephen F. Cohen, *Bukharin and the Bolshevik Revolution: A Political Biography, 1888–1938* (New York, 1973), 277–336; Borkenau, *World Communism,* 436–37, 439; and Draper, *American Communism and Soviet Russia,* 278–81, 286–94. For Foster's own application of the Third Period line to the American situation, see William Z. Foster, "The Growing World Offensive against Capitalism," *Communist* 9 (March 1930): 199–203.

21. "Transcripts of the Anglo-American Secretariat, April 12, 1929," fond 495, opis 72, delo 61, listki 33–53, 93, Comintern Archives; H. M. Wicks to Louis [Weinstock], Helsingfors, Finland, May 29, 1929 (quotes), box 6, folder 8, Draper Papers, Woodruff Library.

22. "Speech of William Z. Foster before the American Commission of the Communist International, May 6, 1929," transcript, fond 495, opis 72, delo 66, listki 1–97 (quote on 89), Comintern Archives.

23. Ibid., 96–97.

24. "The Significance of the Comintern Address," *Communist* 8 (June 1929): 291–302; Draper, *American Communism and Soviet Russia,* 405–30; Cannon, *First Ten Years of American Communism,* 201–9; Earl Browder to Philip Jaffe, August 31, 1954, box 1, folder 3, Philip Jaffe Papers, Woodruff Library, Emory University (hereafter Jaffe Papers); Cohen, *Bukharin and the Bolshevik Revolution,* 277. In his own analysis of Lovestone's revisionism and its significance, Foster quotes at length from Joseph Stalin, *Speeches on the American Communist Party* (New York, 1929), but not from those sections of the speeches that criticized Foster for his factionalism. See Foster, *History of the Communist Party of the United States of America,* 273–74. On Lovestone's opposition party, see Robert Alexander, *The Right Opposition* (Westport, Conn., 1981), 13–112; and "Memorandum for Mr. Ladd Re: Jay Lovestone." On Lovestone's later ties with the CIA, see Ronald Radosh, *Labor and United States Foreign Policy* (New York, 1969), 438–39.

25. William Z. Foster to Solomon Lozovsky, December 19, 1927, fond 534, opis 7, delo 476, listok 184, Profintern Papers.

26. William Z. Foster to Solomon Lozovsky, April 14, 1928, fond 534, opis 7, delo 481, listki 182–84, Profintern Papers; Foster to Lozovsky, May 9, 1928, ibid., listki 197–200.

27. Howe and Coser, *American Communist Party,* 253–55; A. Lozovsky, "Results and Prospects of the United Front," *Communist International* 5 (March 1928): 142–48; Fos-

ter, "Tasks and Lessons of the Miners' Struggle," 198–99; "Proposals for Policy in the Mining Industry, Submitted by William Z. Foster, May 16, 1928"; William Z. Foster, "Old Unions and New Unions," *Communist* 7 (July 1928): 404, 405 (quotes). Compare James P. Cannon, "Trade-Union Questions," *Communist* 7 (July 1928): 406–12. An early draft of Foster's general resolution on trade union work is in box 28, Draper Papers, Hoover Institution. On Foster's discussions with figures in the UMWA and IWW about the new miners' union, see David Roediger and Fred Thompson, *Fellow Worker* (Chicago, 1994), 62.

28. William Z. Foster, "The Decline of the American Federation of Labor," *Communist* 8 (January–February 1929): 47–58; Max Bedacht, "The Decline of the American Federation of Labor: Some Serious Errors in Comrade Foster's Article on the American Federation of Labor," *Communist* 8 (January–February 1929): 44, 46 (Bedacht quotes); "The Opposition Declaration against Comrade Foster," *Daily Worker*, February 11, 1929, 3; Earl Browder, interview by William Goldsmith, July 6, 1955, 17–18, box 1, folder 20, Addendum, Bell Papers; William Z. Foster, "Right Tendencies at the Trade Union Unity Congress," *Communist* 8 (July 1929): 369–74; William Z. Foster, "The Party Trade Union Work during Ten Years," *Communist* 8 (November 1929): 609–18. See also Weisbord, *Radical Life*, 283.

29. James R. Barrett, "Trade Union Unity League," in *Encyclopedia of the American Left*, ed. Buhle, Buhle, and Georgakas, 779–80; Foster, *From Bryan to Stalin*, 209–13.

30. Hapgood and Foster quoted in Saul Alinsky, *John L. Lewis: An Unauthorized Biography* (New York, 1949), 58; *Daily Worker*, June 4, 1930, 1 (second Foster quote). See also Cannon, *First Ten Years of American Communism*, 198–99. Joseph Zack, a charter Party member and trade union activist, later claimed, after he had left the Party, that Foster confided he never believed in the new dual union line and had accepted it only to avoid expulsion (Cannon to Draper, August 4, 1954, 4).

31. Foster, *From Bryan to Stalin*, 299–300.

32. Peggy Dennis, *Autobiography of an American Communist*, 32 (first quote); Buhle, *Marxism in the USA*, 133–34 (second quote). See also Nelson, Barrett, and Ruck, *Steve Nelson*, 62–65; and Earl Browder to Philip Jaffe, March 27, 1959, box 1, folder 3, Jaffe Papers.

CHAPTER 9: CLASS AGAINST CLASS, 1929–35

1. Irving Bernstein, *The Lean Years: A History of the American Worker, 1920–1933* (New York, 1966), 291–302, 316–32; Joseph R. Starobin, *American Communism in Crisis, 1943–1957* (Cambridge, Mass., 1972), 27 (Wilson quote). On the human experience of unemployment, see Robert S. McElvaine, *The Great Depression: America, 1929–1941* (New York, 1993), 170–95.

2. Howe and Coser, *American Communist Party*, 181–82.

3. Originally, the demonstration was set for February 24. When local organizers complained that this date left little time for organizing, it was pushed back. See Franklin Folsom, *Impatient Armies of the Poor: The Story of Collective Action of the Unemployed*

(Boulder, Colo., 1991), 242–44, 251. The charge regarding Soviet funds for organizing the unemployed was first made by the Department of Justice. Woll's letter about the charge appeared on the front page of the *New York Times* on the eve of the demonstration, but I am quoting from Richmond, *Long View from the Left*, 78.

4. Richmond, *Long View of the Left*, 83–84; *New York Times*, March 7, 1930, 1, 2; *New Republic*, March 19, 1930, 110. See also J. Louis Engdahl, "Wall Street's Bloody Feast," *Equal Justice*, May 1930, 84; Klehr, *Heyday of American Communism*, 33–34; Roy Rosenzweig, "Organizing the Unemployed: The Early Years of the Great Depression, 1929–1933," *Radical America* 10 (July–August 1976): 40–41; Foster, *Pages from a Worker's Life*, 84–86; and Folsom, *Impatient Armies of the Poor*, 255–60. Estimates of the crowd's size range from the 110,000 in the *Daily Worker*, March 7, 1930, 1, to 35,000 in the *New York Times*, March 7, 1930, 7.

5. Earl Browder, "The American Communist Party," in *As We Saw the Thirties: Essays on Social and Political Movements of a Decade*, ed. Rita James Simon (Urbana, Ill., 1967), 219 (quotes); Bernstein, *Lean Years*, 427.

6. *Daily Worker*, March 11, 1930, 1, March 12, 1930, 1, March 15, 1930, 5 (quotes); *New York Times*, March 15, 1930, 1; "Foster Said," *Equal Justice*, June 1930, 119.

7. *Daily Worker*, April 12, 1930, 1; Foster, *Pages from a Worker's Life*, 243–68 (first quote on 249, remaining quotes on 256, 260); William Z. Foster, "Prisoners," *Daily World Magazine*, May 3, 1975, M11.

8. Foster, "Prisoners"; Israel Amter, manuscript autobiography, 28–32, Tamiment Institute Library, New York University.

9. Foster, "Prisoners"; William Z. Foster and Israel Amter to Max [Bedacht], New York, May 15, 1930, May 24, 1930, July 4, 1930, August 29, 1930, September 2, 1930, October ?, 1930, fond 515, opis 1, delo 1952, listki 2, 3, 9, 39, 40–42, 77, CPUSA Papers; William Z. Foster to Earl Browder, New York, July 6, 1930, ibid., listki 11–12; William Z. Foster to Secretariat, New York, August 26, 1930, ibid., listok 34. Robert Minor's health was badly weakened during his prison term, and he spent considerable time recovering from its effects. See Foster and Amter to Max, October 8, 1930, ibid., listki 70–71, and *Daily Worker*, September 15, 1933, 5.

10. "Stalin of America, William Z. Foster," informant report, International Labor Defense, 1941, 2, microfilm edition, reel 28, U.S. Military Intelligence Reports, Series 2664, Fourth Corps Area–Atlanta Headquarters.

11. On the TUUL's structure for organizing the unemployed and its significance in the endeavor, see Folsom, *Impatient Armies of the Poor*, 115; Rosenzweig, "Organizing the Unemployed," 37–60; and Frances Fox Piven and Richard Cloward, *Poor Peoples' Movements* (New York, 1977). For the typical experiences of Communist organizers of the unemployed in Birmingham, Chicago, and the anthracite region of Pennsylvania, see Painter, *Narrative of Hosea Hudson*, 123–24, 138–45; and Nelson, Barrett, and Ruck, *Steve Nelson*, 74–87, 96–117, 153–60, 176–79.

12. Foster, *Pages from a Worker's Life*, 188 (quote); William Z. Foster, "The Workers' Power—The National Hunger March Showed It!" *Labor Unity* 7 (January 1932): 3–6; *Daily Worker*, December 8, 1931, 1, 3; *New York Times*, December 9, 1931, 2; Klehr, *Heyday*

of American Communism, 56–58; Sam Darcy to Central Committee, CPUSA, February 24, 1931, box 1, folder 12, Samuel A. Darcy Papers, Tamiment Institute Library, New York University (hereafter Darcy Papers); Folsom, *Impatient Armies of the Poor,* 284–300. See also papers on the organization of the Hunger March in fond 515, opis 1, delo 2570, CPUSA Papers.

13. B. J. Widdick, memo on the Communist Party and the auto workers, n.d. [1955], 7–9, box 3, folder 86, Nat Ganley Papers, Archives of Labor and Urban Affairs, Wayne State University (hereafter Ganley Papers); Alex Baskin, "The Ford Hunger March—1932," *Labor History* 13 (Summer 1972): 331–60; Bernstein, *Lean Years,* 255, 432–34; James R. Green, *The World of the Worker: Labor in Twentieth-Century America* (New York, 1980), 135; McElvaine, *Great Depression,* 92–93; Foster, *Pages from a Worker's Life,* 191–93. That summer the U.S. Army, under General Douglas MacArthur, employed tanks, tear gas, and bayonets to drive unarmed veterans and their families from the nation's capital. For Foster, the destruction of the veterans' "Bonus March," unrelated to Communist organizing, seemed to validate his vision of class war.

14. William Z. Foster, "Unity of the Employed and the Unemployed," *Labor Unity* 7 (April 1932): 6; William Z. Foster, Report on Unemployed Work, 1930, fond 515, opis 1, delo 1930, CPUSA Papers.

15. Trade Union Unity League, *The Trade Union Unity League, Affiliated to R.I.L.U.: Its Program, Structure, Methods and History* (New York, n.d. [1929]); Foster, *From Bryan to Stalin,* 216–20 (quote on 217); Barrett, "Trade Union Unity League," 779–80.

16. TUUL membership estimates are based on comparing Foster's estimates in *Toward Soviet America* (New York, 1932), 103, and *From Bryan to Stalin,* 257–58, with those in Klehr, *Heyday of American Communism,* 421, 433; Cochran, *Labor and Communism,* 357–58; and Jack Stachel, "Recent Developments in the Trade Union Movement," *Communist* 12 (December 1933): 1155–68.

17. Labor Research Association, *Labor Fact Book, I* (New York, 1934), 116–20; *Daily Worker,* September 14, 1931, 4; Cochran, *Labor and Communism,* 43–81; Klehr, *Heyday of American Communism,* 38–48; Ottanelli, *Communist Party of the United States,* 49–55; Foster, *From Bryan to Stalin,* 224–44, 251–64.

18. Bernstein, *Lean Years,* 262–333, 334–90; Ottanelli, *Communist Party of the United States,* 28; Howe and Coser, *American Communist Party,* 257 (quote).

19. Ottanelli, *Communist Party of the United States,* 24–26.

20. Bernstein, *Lean Years,* 255, 360.

21. Fred Erwin [Beal] to Al Weisbord, February 1929 [excerpt], fond 515, opis 1, delo 1660, listok 2 (first Beal quote), CPUSA Papers; Erwin [Beal] to Weisbord, n.d. [March 1929], ibid., listok 58 (second Beal quote); Vera Buch to Robert Minor, June 2, 1929, ibid., listki 23–24; Bernstein, *Lean Years,* 20–28; William Z. Foster, "Organize the Negro Workers, Fight Inequality," *Labor Unity* 3 (May 11, 1929): 5; *New York Times,* October 13, 1929, 21; *Gastonia Daily Gazette,* quoted in Cochran, *Labor and Communism,* 35.

22. "Gastonia," *Labor Unity* 3 (October 12, 1929), 3; Fred Beal, *Proletarian Journey* (New York, 1937); William J. Dunne, *Gastonia: Citadel of the Class Struggle in the New South* (New York, 1929); Foster, *Pages from a Worker's Life,* 281 (quote). On Foster's involve-

ment in the strike, see "Stalin of America," 1. See also Theodore Draper, "Gastonia Revisited," *Social Research* 37 (Spring 1971): 3-29.

23. "Minutes of the National Textile Workers Union, Providence, Rhode Island, February 1931," fond 515, opis 1, delo 2355, listki 3-6, CPUSA Papers; "Report on Lawrence Situation by Pat Devine: Summary of day to day events," n.d., 1931, ibid., listki 70-75; Foster, *From Bryan to Stalin*, 235-36; Klehr, *Heyday of American Communism*, 43-44.

24. William Z. Foster, "The Coal Strike," *Communist* 10 (July 1931): 595 (quotes); William Z. Foster, "Next Steps in the Coal Strike," *Communist* 10 (September 1931): 703-5; Tony Bubka, "The Harlan County Coal Strike of 1931," *Labor History* 11 (Winter 1970): 43; Johanningsmeier, *Forging American Communism*, 259-60.

25. Baker, *In a Generous Spirit*, 104 (first quote); Bernstein, *Lean Years*, 385-88; Theodore Draper, "Communists and Miners—1928-1933," *Dissent* 19 (Spring 1972), 377-80; Foster, *Pages From a Worker's Life*, 180-82; William Z. Foster, "War in the Coal Fields," *Equal Justice*, July 1931, 127; Linda Nyden, "Black Miners in Pennsylvania, 1925-1931: The NMU and the United Mine Workers of America," *Science and Society* 41 (Spring 1977): 69-101; Harvey O'Connor, "Official Report Reveals How Miners Live," January 14, 1932 (second quote), press release, Federated Press Pittsburgh Bureau, box 29, Harvey O'Connor Papers, Archives of Labor History and Urban Affairs, Reuther Library, Wayne State University; Haywood, *Black Bolshevik*, 371-72 (last quote). See also Browder, interview by Goldsmith, 24-26.

26. Bernstein, *Lean Years*, 387. On Lewis's strategy of employing the Communist threat to secure contracts, see Dubofsky and Van Tine, *John L. Lewis*, 174-78. On the resurgence of the UMWA in 1933, see Irving Bernstein, *The Turbulent Years: A History of the American Worker, 1933-1941* (Boston, 1971), 40-66.

27. Baker, *In a Generous Spirit*, 104 (Page quotes), 124; "Transcripts of Speeches before the Anglo-American Secretariat of the ECCI," January 3, 1932, fond 495, opis 72, delo 164, listki 3-86 (Browder quote on 38), Comintern Archives; Sam Darcy, interview by Theodore Draper, May 14-15, 1957, 2 (close friend quote), microfilm series 2.3, reel 8, Draper Papers, Woodruff Library; William Weinstone quoted in Ryan, *Earl Browder*, 47. My thanks to Theodore Draper for permission to quote the Darcy interview.

28. Foster, *From Bryan to Stalin*, 231 (first quote); Foster, *Pages from a Worker's Life*, 180 (second quote); Foster, "Next Steps in the Coal Strike," 703-5. See also Darcy, interview by Draper, May 14-15, 1957, 3; and "Minutes of the Central Committee Bureau on the Western Pennsylvania Coal Strike, June 5, 8, 9, 1931," fond 515, opis 1, delo 2355, listki 1-6, CPUSA Papers. For a Communist field organizer's assessment of the strike's failure, see S. Willner, "Some Lessons of the Last Miners' Strike," *Communist* 11 (January 1932): 27-45.

29. Military intelligence reports for 1931-32 provide some feel for how Foster was organizing simultaneously for both the TUUL unions and the unemployed councils at this point. See "Stalin of America," 4-5.

30. *Daily Worker*, February 19, 1932, 1 (Foster quote); William Z. Foster, "The Kentucky-Tennessee Strike," *Labor Unity* 7 (February 1932): 10-11; Bubka, "Harlan County Strike," 41-57; John Hevener, *Which Side Are You On? The Harlan County Coal Miners,*

1931-1939 (Urbana, Ill., 1978), 56-71; Klehr, *Heyday of American Communism,* 46-47; Draper, "Communists and Miners," 380-89; Earl Browder to ECCI, memo, September 12, 1932, fond 515, opis 1, 2693, listki 1-8 (Browder quote on 6), CPUSA Papers. On the role of intellectuals in the strike, see Daniel Aaron, *Writers on the Left* (New York, 1961), 194-96. Dreiser's committee produced *Harlan Miners Speak* (New York, 1932).

31. Foster, *From Bryan to Stalin,* 231-32; Tom Johnson, "The Fight against Sectarianism in the N.M.U.," *Communist* 11 (August 1932): 697-704 (field organizer quote on 701); William Z. Foster, "Our Work in the Reformist Trade Unions," *Labor Unity* 7 (March 1932): 5 (second quote). For an eyewitness account of the competition between the NMU and the other organizations in West Virginia, see Edmund Wilson, "Frank Keeney's Coal Diggers," reprinted in *The American Earthquake: A Documentary of the Twenties and Thirties* (New York, 1958), 310-27.

32. Foster, "Our Work in the Reformist Trade Unions," 5 (first and second quotes), 4 (third quote). See also William Z. Foster, "Some Elementary Phases of the Work in the Reformist Trade Unions," *Communist* 11 (June 1932): 509-18. For Foster's persistent reservations regarding the dual union line, see Sam Darcy, interviews by Theodore Draper, May 1, 1957, May 15, 1957, microfilm series 2.3, reel 8, Draper Papers, Woodruff Library.

33. Walter Goodman, *The Committee: The Extraordinary Career of the House Committee on Un-American Activities* (Baltimore, 1968), 5-9; House of Representatives, *Investigation of Communist Propaganda: Hearings before a Special Committee to Investigate Communist Activities in the United States,* 71st Cong., 2d Sess., part 4, vol. 1 (Washington, D.C., 1930), 18-70; Klehr, *Heyday of American Communism,* 37-38 (Coughlin testimony, membership estimate).

34. House of Representatives, *Investigation of Communist Propaganda,* part 1, vol. 4, 342-95 (quotes on 352, 359, and 384).

35. Edmund Wilson, "Foster and Fish," reprinted in Wilson, *American Earthquake,* 179, 180. The writer Joseph Freeman also observed a quiet confidence come over Foster when he spoke in the name of his movement: "Within the party, Foster had an engaging modesty," Freeman recalled, but "in contact with the enemy class there emerged a powerful pride in which his person and his class were identical" (Freeman, *American Testament,* 295).

36. Foster, *Toward Soviet America,* vi, 69, 70.

37. Ibid., 177, 256, 225, 228, 254.

38. Ibid., 213-14.

39. Ibid., 282. Since the Soviet biologist Trofim Lysenko's theories on genetics and evolution were not known in the United States at this time, Foster's discussion of changing social conditions and social planning facilitating healthier human evolution most likely drew, once again, on the work of the American sociologist Lester Frank Ward. See, for example, Ward's *Glimpses of the Cosmos,* vol. 3 (New York, 1913), 563-73; and *Glimpses of the Cosmos,* vol. 6 (New York, 1918), 58-63. On Lysenko's theories, see

David Joravsky, *The Lysenko Affair* (Cambridge, Mass., 1970). On the American Party's efforts to promote them, see Starobin, *American Communism in Crisis,* 203, 300.

40. William Z. Foster, *Russia in 1924* (Chicago, 1924); William Z. Foster, *Russian Workers and Workshops in 1926* (Chicago, 1926). See also William Z. Foster, *Victorious Socialist Reconstruction* (New York, 1930), a pamphlet based on Foster's observations during an extended trip to the Soviet Union in 1930.

41. Foster, *Toward Soviet America,* 134, 138.

42. Quoted in *Daily Worker,* magazine section, May 28, 1932, 8.

43. For Foster's correspondence on planning for the election, which betrays a certain reluctance to withdraw from union activity in the interests of the electoral campaign, see fond 515, opis 3, delo 2707, listki 1–57, esp. 40, 42–43, CPUSA Papers.

44. "Resolution on the Struggle against White Chauvinism," fond 515, opis 1, delo 3356, listok 67, CPUSA Papers; Robin D. G. Kelley, *Race Rebels: Culture, Politics, and the Black Working Class* (New York, 1994), 105–9, 114, 115; Robin D. G. Kelley, "A New War in Dixie: Communists and the Unemployed in Birmingham, Alabama, 1930–1933," *Labor History* 30 (Summer 1989): 367–84; Robin D. G. Kelley, *Hammer and Hoe: Alabama Communists during the Great Depression* (Chapel Hill, N.C., 1990); Klehr, *Heyday of American Communism,* 324 48; Isaac Deutscher, *Stalin: A Political Biography* (New York, 1960), 182–85; Haywood, *Black Bolshevik,* 5–175; Roger Kanet, "The Comintern and the 'Negro Question': Communist Policy in the United States and Africa, 1921–1941," *Survey* 19 (Autumn 1973): 86–122; Harvey Klehr and William Thompson, "Self-Determination in the Black Belt: Origins of a Communist Policy," *Labor History* 30 (Summer 1980): 354–66; Dan Carter, *Scottsboro: A Tragedy of the American South* (New York, 1971); Painter, *Narrative of Hosea Hudson,* 83–88, 100–101, 138–45.

45. Nathan Glazer, *The Social Basis of American Communism* (New York, 1961), 169–92; Horace Cayton and St. Clair Drake, *Black Metropolis* (New York, 1945; reprint, 1962), 85–88, 734–36; Naison, *Communists in Harlem during the Depression;* Richard Wright, *American Hunger* (New York, 1977).

46. *Daily Worker,* July 15, 1930, 4, quoted in Klehr, *Heyday of American Communism,* 69

47. Ibid., 80–81; Aaron, *Writers on the Left,* 211 15; North, *William Z. Foster,* 17 (Dreiser quote); James Gilbert, *Writers and Partisans* (New York, 1968), passim; Mathew Josephson, *Infidel in the Temple* (New York, 1967), 125–26 (Foster's continuing suspicion of intellectuals in this period), 149–66; League of Professional Groups for Foster and Ford, *Culture and Crisis* (New York, 1932). The League of Professional Writers, which emerged from the National Committee for the Defense of Political Prisoners' work in Harlan County, became a focus for broader organizing among professionals, resulting in the League of Professional Groups. On the Party's efforts to recruit intellectuals and produce a viable radical culture, see Klehr, *Heyday of American Communism,* 69–84; Howe and Coser, *American Communist Party,* 273–318; and fond 515, opis 3, delo 2969, CPUSA Papers. Stalin's purge trials in the late thirties and the 1939 Hitler-Stalin Pact took their heaviest tolls on intellectual members and fellow travelers. For the

disillusionment of the intellectuals and the development of an anti-Stalinist critique, see William L. O'Neill, *A Better World, the Great Schism: Stalinism and the American Intellectuals* (New York, 1982); and Judy Kutulas, *The Long War: The Intellectual Peoples' Front and Anti-Stalinism, 1930–1940* (Durham, N.C., 1995). For a personal reflection on this experience, see Granville Hicks, *Where We Came Out* (New York, 1954).

48. Foster's correspondence with Party headquarters on the 1932 campaign is in fond 515, opis 2, delo 2707, listki 1–57, CPUSA Papers. For Foster's attacks on FDR, see William Z. Foster, *The Words and Deeds of Franklin D. Roosevelt* (New York, 1932); and William Z. Foster, "Who Is Roosevelt" (text of campaign speech in Columbus, Ohio), *Daily Worker,* August 29–30, 1932, 1.

49. *Los Angeles Times,* June 26, 1932, 1.

50. Ibid., June 29, 1932, 1; *Daily Worker,* June 29, 1932, 1–2 (quote on 1); *New York Times,* June 29, 1932, 3, August 9, 1932, 31, September 15, 1932, 12. Foster's own account of his arrest and beating in Los Angeles is in Foster, *Pages from a Worker's Life,* 228–31.

51. William Z. Foster to Earl Browder, June 1, 1932, fond 515, opis 2, delo 2707, listok 2, CPUSA Papers; William Z. Foster to Clarence Hathaway, ibid., June 1, 1932, listok 3, June 30, 1932, listki 15–19, August, n.d., 1932, 57 (quote). Foster's campaign can most easily be followed in the *Daily Worker,* but I have tried to corroborate events by referring to local papers.

52. Solon Bernstein to Dr. Saltzman, September 8, 1932, fond 515, opis 1, delo 2710, listki 67–68 (first quote), CPUSA Papers; Solon Bernstein, M.D., to Earl Browder, New York, September 17, 1932, ibid., listok 75 (second quote). For descriptions of Foster's physical collapse, see *Daily Worker,* September 13, 1932, 1, September 15, 1932, 1; and Douglas, *Six upon the World,* 93–94.

53. Cary Eggelston to U.S. Attorney, Southern District of New York, attention Judge Medina, November 4, 1948, from the files of the Executive Office for U.S. Attorneys, document 61-330-485, Foster FOIA file; *Daily Worker,* September 15, 22, 1932, 1. Foster, *Pages from a Worker's Life,* 284 (Foster quote). As late as the spring of 1934, Foster was still unable to attend the Party's Eighth Convention because of his illness. See Haywood, *Black Bolshevik,* 418.

54. Sam Darcy to James R. Barrett, November 6, 1986, letter in possession of author (first quote); "Pre-Plenum Meeting of the National Committee, March 23, 1939," original typed stenogram, 3 (Foster quote), box 35, folder 4, Jaffe Papers; unnamed physician to Judge Harold Medina, November 11, 1948, from the files of the Executive Office for U.S. Attorneys, document 61-330-485, Foster FOIA file. For correspondence between Browder and other Party leaders regarding the severity of Foster's illness and its implications for Party leadership, see fond 515, opis 1, delo 2710, listki 1–75, CPUSA Papers.

55. William Z. Foster to William Weinstone, June 20, 1933, personnel file, fond 495, opis 261, delo 15, listki 25–29, Comintern Archives.

56. Sylvia Manley Kolko to William Weinstone, Kislovodsk, USSR, August 16, 1933, Foster personnel file, fond 495, opis 261, delo 15, listki 34–35, Comintern Archives; William Z. Foster to Comrade Lozovsky, Sochi, USSR, October 19, 1933, ibid., listki 40–44. My thanks to Dasha Lotoreva for her translation.

57. Foster to Lozovsky, October 19, 1933, 41–44.

58. William Z. Foster to "Bill" [Weinstone], Paris, January 5, 1934, Foster personnel file, fond 495, opis 261, delo 15, listok 49, Comintern Archives; Darcy to Barrett, November 6, 1986. See also William Z. Foster to Earl Browder, San Francisco, March 7, 1934, microfilm, reel 1, section 29, Earl Browder Papers, 1891–1975 (Microfilming Corporation of America, Glen Rock, N.Y., 1976) (hereafter Browder Papers); Foster, *From Bryan to Stalin*, 254; Foster, *Pages from a Worker's Life*, 194; and *Daily Worker*, August 23, 1933, 1.

59. William Z. Foster to Earl Browder, April 17, 1934, April 18, 1934, n.d. [May] 1934, May 27, 1934, June 26, 1934, fond 515, opis 1, delo 3442, listki 4–5 (first quote), 6 (second and third quotes), 18–19 (fourth quote), 29–30, CPUSA Papers.

60. Foster to Browder, May 30, 1934, 22; Foster to Browder, May 15, 1934, 17.

61. Henry Alsop, physician, to Judge Harold R. Medina, New York City, November 11, 1948, fond 615, opis 1, delo 1, listki 30–34, Foster Papers.

62. Earl Browder to Executive Committee, Communist International, "Memorandum regarding Party Leadership Situation," 1932, fond 515, opis 1, delo 2693, listki 1–8, CPUSA Papers; J. Peters's 1931 report quoted at length in Comrade Belov, "secret" memo, January 15, 1938, Foster personnel file, fond 495, opis 261, delo 15, listki 69–70, Comintern Archives; Stalin's speech before the Anglo-American Secretariat of the ECCI, May 6, 1929, quoted in Spravka signed by Comrade Nisov, July 4, 1938, fond 495, opis 261, delo 15, listok 73, Comintern Archives.

63. Browder, interview by Draper, May 4, 1954, 2; Earl Browder, "Relations between the American Communist Party and the Communist International," memo to Daniel Bell, 22–23, box 1, folder 23, Addendum, Bell Papers; Darcy, interview by Draper, May 14, 1957; Ryan, *Earl Browder*, 46–47, 50–55; Klehr, *Heyday of American Communism*, 87.

64. Ryan, *Earl Browder*, 47; Cannon, *First Ten Years of American Communism*, 114 (quotes). See also Starobin, *American Communism in Crisis*, 52, 258; Gitlow, *I Confess*, 173; and Gil Green, interview by Lens.

CHAPTER 10: ON THE MARGINS OF THE POPULAR FRONT, 1935–45

1. Michael Denning, *The Cultural Front: The Laboring of American Culture in the Twentieth Century* (New York, 1996), 3–7 (quote on 4).

2. Starobin, *American Communism in Crisis*, 53, 263. Foster's return to active Party service was not announced in the *Daily Worker* until November 11, 1934.

3. Ottanelli, *Communist Party of the United States*, 70–75; "Speech of William Z. Foster, 7th Congress of the Communist International, July 28, 1935," fond 495, opis 72, delo 286, listki 32–50 (quote on 49), Comintern Archives.

4. "Speech of William Z. Foster, 7th Congress of the Communist International, July 28, 1935"; "Interview of William Z. Foster with Comrade Manuilsky, May 11, 1935," fond 495, opis 72, delo 287, listki 21–40, Comintern Archives; Ryan, *Earl Browder*, 82–87.

5. Mark Naison, "Remaking America: Communists and Liberals in the Popular

Front," in *New Studies in the Politics and Culture of U.S. Communism,* ed. Michael E. Brown, Randy Martin, Frank Rosengarten, and George Snedeker (New York, 1993), 47.

6. Howe and Coser, *American Communist Party,* 325.

7. Isserman, *Which Side Were You On?* 10–11; Maurice Isserman, "The Generation of 1956: An Alternative Approach to the History of American Communism," *Radical America* 14 (March–April 1980): 43–51; Nelson, Barrett, and Ruck, *Steve Nelson,* xiv–xv; Healey and Isserman, *Dorothy Healey Remembers,* 3, 27–41; Paolo Spriano, *Stalin and the European Communists* (London, 1985), 36, quoted in Geoff Eley, "International Communism in the Heyday of Stalin," *New Left* 157 (January–February 1986): 95. Both Harvey Klehr and Theodore Draper take a more critical view of the Popular Front; they see more continuity with the earlier, more sectarian period, fewer generational differences among the Party cadres, and the continuing decisive importance of Soviet intervention. See Klehr, *Heyday of American Communism,* 185, 305–90; and Draper, "Popular Front Revisited," 79–81.

8. Starobin, *American Communism in Crisis,* 268 (Dimitrov quote), 54 (Starobin quote); Naison, "Remaking America," 47; Anders Stephenson, "Interview with Gil Green," in *New Studies in the Politics and Culture of U.S. Communism,* ed. Brown et al., 310.

9. Foster, "Some Elementary Phases of Our Work in the Reformist Trade Unions," 509–18; Jack Stachel, "Our Trade Union Policy," *Communist* 13 (November 1934): 1103–4; "Report by Jack Stachel, National Secretary, TUUL, on Communist Fraction in AF of L, September 9, 1933," fond 534, opis 7, delo 515, listki 1–23, Profintern Papers; "For a Powerful United AF of L, Statement by Central Committee, Communist Party, USA," *Daily Worker,* February 12, 1936, 1. On the 1933–34 strike wave and the formation of the CIO, see Robert H. Zieger, *The CIO, 1935–1955* (Chapel Hill, N.C., 1995), 18, 30, 73, 79–80; and Bernstein, *Turbulent Years,* 217–317. For Foster's position at the time Lewis resigned and on the eve of the Congress of Industrial Organizations, see William Z. Foster, "The Meaning of Lewis's Resignation and the Industrial Union Fight," *Daily Worker,* November 28, 1935, 1.

10. Browder, interview by Draper, September 29, 1953, 1.

11. Isserman, *Which Side Were You On?* 4.

12. William Z. Foster, Alexander Bittelman, James W. Ford, and Charles Krumbein, *Party Building and Political Leadership* (New York, 1937), 22–27, 33 (first quote), 34 (second quote), 66–67 (third quote), 69 (fourth quote). See also Klehr, *Heyday of American Communism,* 186–206; and Ottanelli, *Communist Party of the United States,* 87–89.

13. William Z. Foster, "The Communist Party and the Professionals," *Communist* 17 (September 1938), 805, 806, quoted in Howe and Coser, *American Communist Party,* 344.

14. Communist Party membership figures are notoriously hard to estimate. These are based on the Party's own official report before the Comintern at the beginning of 1939, which declared 88,186 members enrolled and approximately 66,000 registered and paying dues ("Organizational Status and Organizational Problems of the CPUSA," fond 495, opis 14, listki 151–72, Comintern Archives). See also Klehr, *Heyday of American Communism,* 366.

15. Howe and Coser, *American Communist Party,* 226.

16. Isserman, *Which Side Were You On?* 15, 16 (Bittelman quote); Ryan, *Earl Browder,* 94.

17. Johanningsmeier, *Forging American Communism,* 272–73 (quote on 273); William Z. Foster to Sam Darcy, Los Angeles, 1937–38(?), box 1, folder 23, Darcy Papers; "Pre-Plenum Meeting of the National Committee, March 23, 1939" (Foster quote); Alsop to Medina, November 11, 1948.

18. Johanningsmeier, *Forging American Communism,* 268; Nelson, Barrett, and Ruck, *Steve Nelson,* 291; Steve Nelson, interview by James R. Barrett, November 12, 1986, in author's possession; Gil Green, interview by James R. Barrett, March 10, 1994, in author's possession; Gil Green, interview by Lens; Arthur Zipser to James R. Barrett, taped responses to written questions, November 28, 1986, in author's possession; Dorfman to Barrett, taped responses to written questions; North, *William Z. Foster,* 36. On Foster's apartment, see Harry Epstein, "William Z. Foster," 1961 manuscript, in possession of Sandra Epstein, Brookline, Mass. Foster's FOIA file suggests that he held to this work regimen throughout most of his remaining years except when serious illness prevented him from working at all. He did receive occasional visitors, usually other Party leaders.

19. Gil Green, interview by Barrett; Arthur Zipser to James R. Barrett, taped responses to written questions, March 1991, in author's possession; Douglas, *Six upon the World,* 118–19; Alsop to Medina, November 11, 1948; *Saturday Evening Post,* July 9, 1938, 5.

20. David Ramsey, interview by Theodore Draper, New York City, March 27, 1957, box 15, folder 27, Draper Papers, Woodruff Library; Earl Browder, interview by Theodore Draper, October 10, 1955, 25–27, box 1, folder 8, Draper Papers, Woodruff Library; Klehr, *Heyday of American Communism.*

21. William Z. Foster, "Fascist Tendencies in the United States," *Communist* 14 (October 1935): 883–902.

22. William Z. Foster, "Syndicalism in the United States," *Communist* 14 (November 1935): 1044.

23. Browder, interview by Draper, October 10, 1955.

24. Ramsey, interview by Draper, quoted in Ryan, *Earl Browder,* 81; Howe and Coser, *American Communist Party,* 345 (lion quote).

25. Zieger, *CIO,* 254; Harvey A. Levenstein, *Communism, Anti-Communism, and the CIO* (Westport, Conn., 1981), 37.

26. "For a Powerful United AF of L"; Ottanelli, *Communist Party of the United States,* 137–42; Foster, *From Bryan to Stalin,* 275 (quote).

27. William Z. Foster, *Industrial Unionism* (New York, [April] 1936); William Z. Foster, "Regarding Trade Union Unity," *Daily Worker,* October 20, 1937, 3; William Z. Foster, "The American Federation of Labor and Trade Union Progress," *Communist* 17 (August 1938): 689–98; Klehr, *Heyday of American Communism,* 223–29; Levenstein, *Communism, Anti-Communism, and the CIO,* 37–38. Some historians have argued that the Party failed to support early CIO initiatives. Max Kampelman dates the Party's shift to the CIO from a statement by Foster in late 1937. But Cochran points to Foster's *Industrial*

Unionism pamphlet and other evidence that the Party encouraged such movements, while trying to avoid an open split within the AFL. See Max Kampelman, *The Communist Party vs. the CIO: A Study in Power Politics* (New York, 1957), 15; Howe and Coser, *American Communist Party,* 369–70; and Cochran, *Labor and Communism,* 345–47.

28. Ottanelli, *Communist Party of the United States,* 140.

29. Goldsmith, "Notes on Interview with John Brophy, November 11, 1955, CIO Headquarters, Washington, D.C."; Len DeCaux, interview by William A. Sullivan, Archives of Labor and Urban Affairs, Walter P. Reuther Library, Wayne State University; Levenstein, *Communism, Anti-Communism, and the CIO,* 46–48.

30. Levenstein, *Communism, Anti-Communism, and the CIO,* 48; Bernstein, *Turbulent Years,* 451–55; Max Gordon, "The Communist Party and the Drive to Organize Steel, 1936," *Labor History* 23 (Spring 1982): 254, 257–59; Cochran, *Labor and Communism,* 96–97; Williamson, *Dangerous Scot,* 125–26; Klehr, *Heyday of American Communism,* 229–32.

31. Healey and Isserman, *Dorothy Healey Remembers,* 74–75. See also Steve Nelson, interview by Barrett.

32. Lizabeth Cohen, *Making a New Deal: Industrial Workers in Chicago, 1919–1939* (New York, 1990), 314, 502 (Foster quote); Goldsmith, "Notes on Interview with John Brophy, November 11, 1955, CIO Headquarters, Washington, D.C."; William Z. Foster, *Unionizing Steel* (New York, 1936); William Z. Foster, *Organizing Methods in the Steel Industry* (New York, 1936); William Z. Foster, *What Means a Strike in Steel* (New York, 1937); William Z. Foster, *A Manual of Industrial Unionism, Organizational Structure and Policies* (New York, 1937). In 1937 and 1938, Foster published a comparable series of pamphlets aimed at railroad workers: *Railroad Workers, Forward!* (New York, 1937); *Halt the Railroad Wage Cut* (New York, 1938); and *Stop the Wage-Cuts and Layoffs on the Railroads: A Reply to President T. C. Cashen of the Switchmen's Union of North America* (New York, 1938).

33. Herbert March, interview, October 21, 1986, 17–18 (Foster quote), 27, United Packinghouse Workers of America Oral History Project, State Historical Society of Wisconsin, Madison; Vicky Starr, interview, August 4, 1986, 915, 921, ibid; Stella Nowicki [Vicky Starr], interview, in *Rank and File: Personal Histories by Working-Class Organizers,* ed. Alice and Staughton Lynd (Princeton, N.J., 1981), 74–75; Art Shields, *On the Battle Lines, 1919–1939* (New York, 1986), 217.

34. Ryan, *Earl Browder,* 146.

35. Phillipe LeJeune, *On Autobiography,* ed. Paul John Eakin, trans. Katherine Leary (Minneapolis, 1989), xi.

36. Foster, *Pages from a Worker's Life,* 11.

37. Foster, *History of the Communist Party of the United States of America.*

38. Elizabeth Gurley Flynn, "The Life of a Great American Working Class Leader," *Communist* 18 (May 1939): 476.

39. Foster, *Pages from a Worker's Life,* 11.

40. Flynn, "Life of a Great American Working Class Leader," 476–77; Freeman, *American Testament,* 295.

41. Foster, *From Bryan to Stalin,* 59. On Esther's health and habits, see agent's report, New York, May 6, 1942, document number 61-330-227, Foster FOIA file.

42. Klehr, *Communist Cadre,* 72. On the male-gendered quality of the Party's propaganda and line during the Third Period, when Foster was in his element, see Van Gosse, " 'To Organize in Every Neighborhood, in Every Home': The Gender Politics of American Communists between the Wars," *Radical History Review* 50 (Spring 1991): 109–42. On the proportion of women on the Central Committee, see Klehr, *Communist Cadre,* 70–82.

43. Browder, interview, Columbia University Oral History, quoted in James Ryan, "Earl Browder and Americanism at High Tide: 1934–1945" (Ph.D. diss, University of Notre Dame, 1981), 454.

44. Klehr, *Heyday of American Communism,* 213–16; Ottanelli, *Communist Party of the United States,* 130–32. For the Soviet intervention, see Klehr, Haynes, and Anderson, *Soviet World of American Communism,* 37–39. Foster's speech before the Party convention that summer emphasized the need for a farmer-labor party under Communist leadership. See *Daily Worker,* June 26, 1936, 1.

45. William Z. Foster, "Congress of the Communist Party of France," *Communist* 17 (February 1938): 113–21.

46. "Draft Resolution of the Secretariat of the ECCI on the American Question," [1937], fond 495, opis 1, delo 4064, Comintern Archives; "Additional Memorandum of Problems of the CPUSA," March 23, 1937, fond 495, opis 1, delo 4065, Comintern Archives; Ryan, *Earl Browder,* 130, 131 (quotes); "Decision of the Secretariat of the ECCI," February 2, 1938, fond 495, opis 20, delo 509, reprinted in Klehr, Haynes, and Anderson, *Soviet World of American Communism,* 37–38 (Comintern quotes). See also Browder, "Relations between the American Communist Party and the Communist International," 23–24; and Ryan, *Earl Browder,* 108–9, 127–29, 312–33.

47. Ryan, *Earl Browder,* 148–54, 157; Earl Browder, interview by Theodore Draper, May 19, 1953, 3, box 1, folder 3, Draper Papers, Woodruff Library; Peter Carroll, *The Odyssey of the Abraham Lincoln Brigade: Americans in the Spanish Civil War* (Stanford, Calif., 1994), 176–81

48. Browder, "Relations between the American Communist Party and the Communist International" (all Browder quotes); Browder, interview by Draper, October 10, 1955; Ryan, *Earl Browder,* 157–58.

49. Klehr, *Heyday of American Communism,* 213. Documents in Foster's Comintern personnel file suggest that, while the Comintern leaders retained a firm belief in his commitment, they questioned his judgment. See, for example, A. Volkov, assistant, Cadres Commission, memo, April 25, 1941, Foster personnel file, fond 495, opis 261, delo 15, listki 82–85, Comintern Archives, which notes that Foster "often undervalues and underestimates the role and achievements of the Party" (85); and Comrade Belov, memo, January 15, 1938, ibid., listki 69–70. These lingering doubts about Foster, as well as his high public profile, may explain why there is no evidence of his involvement in espionage activity.

50. Stephenson, "Interview with Gil Green," 310–11.

51. Foster et al., *Party Building and Political Leadership,* Foster statement, 57. James P. Cannon shared Browder's assessment of Foster as an opportunist. See James P. Cannon, interview by Sidney Lens, July 16, 1974, 14, box 66, folder 8, Lens Papers. On Foster's support for and the Party's repudiation of Weinstone's UAW policies, see Harvey Klehr, "American Communism and the United Auto Workers: New Evidence on an Old Controversy," *Labor History* 24 (Summer 1983): 404–13; and "Politburo Minutes," March 23, 1939, box 1, folder 60, Draper Papers, Woodruff Library. See also Foster, "Congress of the Communist Party of France." Foster's clearest statement concerning the dangers of following reformist policies in the Popular Front is in William Z. Foster, "Political Leadership and Party Building," *Communist* 16 (July 1937): 628–46. That Foster's remarks were republished in pamphlet form seems to suggest some support for his position as late as the summer of 1937. See also Foster, "American Origins of the People's Front," *Communist* 16 (December 1937): 1103–7.

52. See, for example, Klehr, *Heyday of American Communism,* 415–16; Klehr and Haynes, *American Communist Movement,* 59–95, 179–80; and Draper, "Popular Front Revisited," 79–81.

53. Levenstein, *Communism, Anti-Communism, and the CIO,* 40–46 (quote on 40); Starobin, *American Communism in Crisis;* Ottanelli, *Communist Party of the United States,* 146–48; Cochran, *Labor and Communism,* 18–19, 74–75.

54. This and the subsequent two paragraphs are drawn from "Pre-Plenum Meeting of the National Committee, March 23, 1939," 1 (first quote), 2 (second and third quotes), 3 (fourth and fifth quotes). Foster had apparently written Browder a number of letters expressing his suggestions or reservations regarding policy. For one example, written a few weeks prior to this meeting that refers to earlier letters, see William Z. Foster to Earl Browder, February 21, 1939, microfilm, reel 1, Browder Papers.

55. "Pre-Plenum Meeting of the National Committee, March 23, 1939," 7.

56. Ibid., 9, 22 (Hudson quote); Jaffe, *Rise and Fall of American Communism,* 58–59.

57. "Pre-Plenum Meeting of the National Committee, March 23, 1939." 39–40, 42.

58. Comrade Ryan, memo to the ECCI, April 11, 1941, Foster personnel file, fond 495, opis 261, delo 15, listok 81, Comintern Archives; Starobin, *American Communism in Crisis,* 54.

59. Isserman, *Which Side Were You On?* 32–53, 67–73; Levenstein, *Communism, Anti-Communism, and the CIO,* 85–90, 102–20, 140–46, 150.

60. "Discussion by National Committee on International Situation, September 14, 16, 1939," stenographic minutes, box 35, folder 5a, Jaffe Papers; Starobin, *American Communism in Crisis,* 54, 263; "Keep America out of Imperialist War," declaration of the National Committee, CPUSA, William Z. Foster, national chairman, Earl Browder, general secretary, *Communist* 17 (October 1939): 899–904; Isserman, *Which Side Were You On?* 40–43.

61. "William Z. Foster Celebration, Madison Square Garden, Monday, March 17," program, box 5, Minor Papers; *Daily Worker,* March 16, 1941, sec. 1, 6, sec. 2, 4, March 18, 1941, 1, 3 (Dreiser quote), 7; Earl Browder, "Speech at Foster's 60th Birthday, March 17, 1941," microfilm, reel 9, Browder Papers; Duberman, *Paul Robeson,* 652.

62. Gil Green, interview by Barrett; William Z. Foster, "Seven Years of Roosevelt," *Communist* 19 (May 1940): 232–58; Isserman, *Which Side Were You On?* 85; Klehr, *Heyday of American Communism,* 398; Johanningsmeier, *Forging American Communism,* 288; Ryan, memo to ECCI, April 11, 1941, 81.

63. William Z. Foster, *The War Crisis: Questions and Answers* (New York, January 1940), 6, 39 (quotes), 10; William Z. Foster, "On the State," *New Masses* 39 (March 1941): 17–18; William Z. Foster, *Roosevelt Heads for War* (New York, February 1940), 3, 15.

64. Isserman, *Which Side Were You On?* 87–100 (Isserman quote on 95; Foster quote from *Daily Worker,* December 25, 1940, on 81); See also William Z. Foster, "Lessons of the Inglewood Strike," *Daily Worker,* June 17, 1941, 1, 4; Nelson Lichtenstein, *Labor's War at Home: The CIO In World War II* (Cambridge, 1982), 46–47, 57–63; and James Green, *World of the Worker,* 176–77.

65. William Z. Foster, *Capitalism, Socialism, and the War* (New York, [June] 1940), 23 (quotes); William Z. Foster, "Earl Browder and the Fight for Peace," *Communist* 20 (June 1941): 498.

66. William Z. Foster, *Defend America by Smashing Hitlerism* (New York, [September] 1941), 6 (this was a speech Foster delivered on August 20, 1941, at the Chicago Stadium); "Memorandum of Comrade Aerova on the CPUSA," August 24, 1941, fond 515, opis 3, delo 4093, listki 1–7, CPUSA Papers, and [Aerova], "Memorandum on the CPUSA II," August 24, 1941, ibid., listki 15–20.

67. Georgi Dimitrov to [Earl Browder], New York, June 26, 1941, fond 495, opis 184, delo 3, quoted in Klehr, Haynes, and Anderson, *Soviet World of American Communism,* 85; Perry Anderson, *Arguments within English Marxism* (London, 1980), 142, quoted in Eley, "International Communism in the Heyday of Stalin," 96; William Z. Foster, "The New World Situation and Our Tasks" (abridged report to National Committee of the CPUSA, June 28, 1941), in William Z. Foster and Robert Minor, *The Fight against Hitlerism* (New York, [July] 1941), 3–12 (quotes on 3 and 4).

68. *Sunday Worker,* September 25, 1949, sec. 3, 10; William Z. Foster, *The Trade Unions and the War* (New York, 1942); Foster quoted in agent's report, April 19, 1943, document 61-330-242, Foster FOIA file. Foster produced a whole series of pamphlets during the early war years, most of which, presented in a question and answer formula reminiscent of the Catholic Church's Baltimore Catechism, were culled from the *Daily Worker* columns and highlighted labor questions: *The Soviet Union—Friend and Ally of the American People* (New York, 1941); *The Trade Unions and the War* (New York, 1942); *Communism versus Fascism; Labor and the War* (New York, 1942), *From Defense to Attack* (New York, 1942); *The Steelworkers and the War* (New York, 1942); and *The Railroad Workers and the War* (New York, 1942). For an example of Foster's ill will toward Lewis, see *The Coal Miners: Their Problems in War and Peace* (New York, February 1945).

69. Earl Browder, *Victory and After* (New York, 1942); Isserman, *Which Side Were You On?* 145; Earl Browder, *Teheran and America* (New York, 1944).

70. Browder's speech at Bridgeport, Connecticut, on December 12, 1943, quoted in Ryan, *Earl Browder,* 218 (first phrase); Browder's January 7, 1944, National Committee report, quoted in Starobin, *American Communism in Crisis,* 55 (second quote); Browder

quoted in Gerald Horne, *Black Liberation/Red Scare: Ben Davis and the Communist Party* (Newark, Del., 1993), 134–35 (third quote).

71. Johanningsmeier, *Forging American Communism,* 196; Isserman, *Which Side Were You On?* 184–86 (quote on 185). See also Ottanelli, *Communist Party of the United States,* 208–9.

72. Barrington Moore Jr., "The Communist Party of the USA; An Analysis of a Social Movement," *American Political Science Review* 39 (February 1945): 33.

73. Foster, *Trade Unions and the War;* Foster quoted in agent's report, March 7, 1942, document 61-330-225, Foster FOIA file (first quote); William Z. Foster, "President Roosevelt and the Congressional Opposition," *Daily Worker,* April 9, 1943, 8; William Z. Foster, "Reaction's Attack against Organized Labor," *Daily Worker,* April 15, 1943, 8; William Z. Foster, "Problems of the Postwar World," *Daily Worker,* November 16, 1943, 2; William Z. Foster, "War and Postwar: Planning for the Era after Victory," *New Masses* 49 (December 14, 1943): 11–13 (remaining quotes on 12); Johanningsmeier, *Forging American Communism,* 296–97, 411; Lichtenstein, *Labor's War at Home,* 167–68, 207–8. During the Smith Act trial in 1949, Foster cited these early formulations as evidence of the continuity of his own thinking since the declaration of the Popular Front. See Starobin, *American Communism in Crisis,* 66, 266.

74. Starobin, *American Communism in Crisis,* 74–76; Eley, "International Communism in the Heyday of Stalin," 96–97 (Eley quote); Spriano, *Stalin and the European Communists;* Jaffe, *Rise and Fall of American Communism,* 62–63; Ryan, "Earl Browder and Americanism at High Tide," 215–35; Ottanelli, *Communist Party of the United States,* 209–10 (Browder quote on 210), 400–401, 276; Isserman, *Which Side Were You On?* 174–79.

75. Moore, "Communist Party of the USA," 32; "Constitution of the Communist Political Association, Adopted by National Convention in N.Y.C., on Sunday May 21, 1944," 1 (CPA aims quote), microfilm, reel 4, Browder Papers; Isserman, *Which Side Were You On?* 190; Starobin, *American Communism in Crisis,* 55–61; "Stenogram of CPUSA Plenum, 8 January 1944," box 36, folders 1a–1b, Jaffe Papers.

76. "Foster Says Teheran Guide to Postwar," *Daily Worker,* January 10, 1944, 6; Samuel Adams Darcy, "Autobiography," 588 (quote), box 11, folder 21, Draper Papers, Woodruff Library.

77. William Z. Foster, "To the Members of the National Committee, CPUSA," January 20, 1944, box 5, Minor Papers.

78. Ibid.

79. "National Board Meeting, 8 February 1944," stenogram, box 36, folders 2a–2b, Jaffe Papers.

80. Ibid. (Foster quotes); "Excerpts from Remarks of S. A. Darcy at Polbureau Meeting, February 8, 1944," box 1, folder 9, Darcy Papers.

81. "National Board Meeting, 8 February 1944," quoted in Jaffe, *Rise and Fall of American Communism,* 62.

82. Ibid. See also "Excerpt from Remarks of S. A. Darcy at Polbureau Meeting, February 8, 1944."

83. Agent's report, August 25, 1944, 6, document 61-330-284, Foster FOIA file; *New York World Telegram,* March 9, 1944, 1; *Daily Worker,* March 10, 1944, 1 (Foster's denial).

84. Jaffe, *Rise and Fall of American Communism,* 62–63; Starobin, *American Communism in Crisis,* 74–75. The Russian translations for these documents are in fond 515, opis 1, delo 4096, CPUSA Papers. For an English translation of Foster's appeal and Dimitrov's letter to Browder, see Georgi Dimitrov to Vyacheslav Molotov, March 8, 1944, fond 495, opis 74, delo 482, Comintern Archives, in Klehr, Haynes, and Anderson, *Soviet World of American Communism,* 105.

85. Klehr, Haynes, and Anderson, *Soviet World of American Communism,* 98 (quote), 106; Gil Green, interview by Barrett.

86. William Z. Foster, *In Defense of the Communist Party and Its Indicted Leaders* (New York, 1949), 13; Isserman, *Which Side Were You On?* 196; Foster, *History of the Communist Party of the United States of America,* 428–30. Foster's letter was eventually published in *Political Affairs* (formerly the *Communist*) 24 (July 1945): 640–54.

87. Isserman, *Which Side Were You On?* 196–97; Starobin, *American Communism in Crisis,* 73, 52 (quote). William and Esther Foster developed a close personal friendship with Darcy and his wife in California during 1933–34, while Foster was recuperating from his heart attack and stroke. The two men corresponded often over the following decade. See Darcy's correspondence with Foster in box 1, folder 23, Darcy Papers. For Darcy's description of Foster's emotional state during the ordeal, see Darcy, "Autobiography," 591. Regarding the likely prospect of Foster's expulsion if he had pursued his criticism publicly, see Johanningsmeier, *Forging American Communism,* 411. Foster later claimed that Browder had *already* laid plans at this point for Foster's own expulsion. See Foster, *History of the Communist Party of the United States of America,* 434.

88. William Z. Foster, "New Features of American Economic and Political Life," [1945], 29, box 37, folder 3, Jaffe Papers. Jaffe, *Rise and Fall of American Communism,* 64–66, contains excerpts from Foster's article and Browder's marginal comments.

89. "The Present Situation and the Next Tasks, Draft Resolution of the National Board, Amended and Approved June 20, 1945," *Daily Worker,* July 2, 1945, 8. For evidence of some rank-and-file opposition to Browder at the time of the Party dissolution, see Isserman, *Which Side Were You On?* 197. For anger over Browder's suppression of Foster's criticisms, see Isserman, *Which Side Were You On?* 203.

90. Nelson, Barrett, and Ruck, *Steve Nelson,* 273–74.

91. A translation of the Duclos letter was first published in the May 25, 1945, edition of the *Daily Worker,* then in the July 1945 edition of *Political Affairs,* 656–72, and later in a Party pamphlet, *Marxism-Leninism vs. Revisionism* (New York, 1946). For the remarks regarding Foster, see *Marxism-Leninism vs. Revisionism,* 25–27. That Duclos quoted at length from Foster's letter and other internal Party documents, which the Soviets held as a result of Browder's February 1944 exchange with Dimitrov, was one of several indications at the time that his letter reflected the official Soviet perspective. Recent research in the Russian archives proves that the Soviets not only instigated but actually composed the Duclos document. See Klehr, Haynes, and Anderson, *Soviet World of American Communism,* 95–98, 101, 104. The following description of the Party crisis

precipitated by the Duclos letter is based largely on Starobin, *American Communism in Crisis,* 83–106; Isserman, *Which Side Were You On?* 221–43; Howe and Coser, *American Communist Party,* 437–53; Gabriel Kolko, *The Politics of War* (New York, 1968), 440–42, 447; and David Shannon, *The Decline of American Communism: A History of the Communist Party of the United States since 1945* (New York, 1959), 9–15, as well as on coverage in the *New York Times* and the *Daily Worker* for June and July 1945. For Foster's own interpretation of events, see Foster, *History of the Communist Party of the United States of America,* 434–38.

92. "Earl Browder's First Speech on the Duclos Article, May 22, 1945, in National Board, CPA," 3, 22, box 36, folders 3a–3d, Jaffe Papers.

93. Ryan, *Earl Browder,* 257–58; Nelson, Barrett, and Ruck, *Steve Nelson,* 274 (quotes).

94. Foster quoted in "Earl Browder's First Speech on the Duclos Article," 1.

95. William Z. Foster, "The Struggle against Revisionism," *Political Affairs* 23 (September 1945): 794, quoted in Starobin, *American Communism in Crisis,* 264.

96. Browder quoted in Starobin, *American Communism in Crisis,* 264.

97. "The Present Situation," *Daily Worker,* July 2, 1945, 7 (first quote), 8; Healey and Isserman, *Dorothy Healey Remembers,* 94 (Healey quote). See also Isserman, *Which Side Were You On?* 221–35; and Starobin, *American Communism in Crisis,* 83–106.

98. *Daily Worker,* July 27, 1945, 3, July 30, 1945, 2 (first quote); Healey and Isserman, *Dorothy Healey Remembers,* 94 (second quote); TASS clippings, Foster personnel file, fond 495, opis 26, delo 15, listki 125–36, Comintern Archives. The new National Board did include several trade unionists, such as Louis Weinstock of the painters' union, Josh Lawrence of the National Maritime Union, and Irving Potash of the furriers' union, as well as Steve Nelson, who was recruited for his "proletarian viewpoint."

99. Shannon, *Decline of American Communism,* 18–20; Starobin, *American Communism in Crisis,* 278–79, 297; Howe and Coser, *American Communist Party,* 452–53; Jaffe, *Rise and Fall of American Communism,* 137–44, 163–65, 10. The well-financed Fund for the Republic research project produced almost a dozen major studies of the Party in various settings. Browder's most direct involvement came in connection with Theodore Draper's two histories of the Party, *Roots of American Communism* and *American Communism and Soviet Russia,* which analyzed the Party's development up to the Great Depression. Through his interviews, letters, and memos, Browder affected Draper's analysis, which, interestingly, placed far more emphasis on Soviet influence than Browder did. "What I miss in Draper," Browder wrote to Clinton Rossiter, the project's director, "is the understanding that he is writing about an organic part of *American* history, and not merely a study of the American section of the *Communist International*" (Browder to Rossiter, November 22, 1957, quoted in Isserman, *Which Side Were You On?* ix).

100. The literature on the origins of the cold war is enormous. I have relied on Walter LaFeber, *America, Russia, and the Cold War* (New York, 1993); and Stephen Ambrose, *Rise to Globalism* (New York, 1988). For the postwar economic dislocation and the strike wave, see Lichtenstein, *Labor's War at Home,* 222–30; and George Lipsitz, *Rainbow at Midnight: Labor and Culture in the 1940s* (Urbana, Ill., 1994), 99–154. The postwar political reaction is dealt with in the following chapter.

CHAPTER 11: FIVE MINUTES TO MIDNIGHT, 1945–56

1. Klehr, *Heyday of American Communism,* 238–39, 257–73, 411; Shannon, *Decline of American Communism,* 3.

2. Starobin, *American Communism in Crisis,* 224–30; Shannon, *Decline of American Communism,* 362–63.

3. Ellen Schrecker, *Many Are the Crimes: McCarthyism in America* (Boston, 1998), 369. See also David Caute, *The Great Fear: The Anti-Communist Purge under Truman and Eisenhower* (New York, 1978); Michal R. Belknap, *Cold War Political Justice: The Smith Act, the Communist Party, and American Civil Liberties* (Westport, Conn., 1977); and Robert W. Griffith and Athan Theoharis, eds., *The Specter: Original Essays on the Cold War and the Origins of McCarthyism* (New York, 1974), especially the essays by Mary McAuliffe, David Oshinsky, and Norman Markowitz. For the revisionist interpretation, see John Earl Haynes, *Red Scare or Red Menace? American Communism and Anticommunism in the Cold War Era* (Chicago, 1996). For a more developed and nuanced version of the same argument, see Richard Gid Powers, *Not without Honor: The History of American Anticommunism* (New York, 1995).

4. Johanningsmeier, *Forging American Communism,* 8–9.

5. Ambrose, *Rise to Globalism,* 67–70; LaFeber, *America, Russia, and the Cold War,* 24–25; Kolko, *Politics of War,* 568–93.

6. Foster, *Daily Worker,* September 19, 1945, quoted in Starobin, *American Communism in Crisis,* 122 (first quote); William Z. Foster, "Leninism and Some Practical Problems of the Postwar Period," *Political Affairs* 25 (February 1946): 99–109 (second quote on 101, third on 103, fourth on 102, and fifth on 108). See also William Z. Foster, "American Imperialism, Leader of World Reaction," *Political Affairs* 25 (August 1946): 686–95; and William Z. Foster, *The Menace of a New World War* (New York, March 1946) and FBI coverage of Foster's speech at the Party's twenty-seventh anniversary rally at Madison Square Garden on September 19, 1946, where he insisted that "the war danger is acute" and urged a "vast mobilization for peace" (field agent's report, November 2, 1946, document 61-330-347, Foster FOIA file).

7. Hadley Cantril, ed., *Public Opinion* (Princeton, N.J., 1951), 370–71; Michal R. Belknap, "Cold War in the Courtroom: The Foley Square Trial," in *American Political Trials,* ed. Michal Belknap (Westport, Conn., 1981), 237.

8. William Z. Foster, *The New Europe* (New York, 1947), 8 (quote). Foster's travels were covered extensively in both FBI reports and the European Communist press. See documents 61-330-356, 61-330-372, 61-330-373, Foster FOIA file.

9. Foster, *New Europe,* passim; Foster, *Twilight of World Capitalism,* 22 (quote). Foster's close surveillance by State Department officials throughout Europe provides details on his various movements and conveys his stature among Communists in various parts of the world. See documents 61-330-412, 61-330-413, and 61-330-415, Foster FOIA file.

10. William Z. Foster, "American Imperialism and the War Danger," *Political Affairs* 26 (August 1947): 676, 679, 680, 681, 683.

11. Ibid., 685 (Foster quote); Starobin, *American Communism in Crisis,* 125–30 (Dennis quoted on 125). See also Foster, *New Europe,* 12, 107, 108.

12. Zieger, *CIO*, 212–27; Lichtenstein, *Labor's War at Home*, 216–30.

13. William Z. Foster, "The Wage and Strike Movement," *Political Affairs* 25 (February 1946): 121–28 (quote on 127).

14. Ibid.; Christopher Tomlins, *The State and the Unions: Labor Relations, Law, and the Organized Labor Movement in America, 1880–1960* (Cambridge, 1985); Melvyn Dubofsky, *The State and Labor in Modern America* (Chapel Hill, N.C., 1994), 206–9; Zieger, *CIO*; Ellen W. Schrecker, "McCarthyism and the Labor Movement," in *The Left-Led Unions*, ed. Steven Rosswurm (New Brunswick, N.J., 1992), 139–58.

15. Schrecker, *Many Are the Crimes*, 25–26.

16. "Nine Nation Communist Meeting Not Anti-US, Foster Declares," *Daily Worker*, October 21, 1947, 10. Resolutions from the Nine Party Conference appeared in *Political Affairs* 26 (November 1947): 1051–56, but they were also published in the *Daily Worker* shortly before Foster's speech.

17. Shannon, *Decline of American Communism*, 113–14, 121, 133–34.

18. Congress of Industrial Organizations, "Hearings before the Committee to Investigate Charges against ILWU," May 17, 1950, AFL-CIO Headquarters, Washington, D.C., mimeographed, 71–72, quoted in Shannon, *Decline of American Communism*, 155–56. The details of Quill's testimony were questioned at the time and since, but there is no doubt that Foster and other Party leaders pressured union leaders to support Wallace. See Levenstein, *Communism, Anti-Communism, and the CIO*, 223–24, 232; and Starobin, *American Communism in Crisis*, 167–69. For Foster's perspective, see William Z. Foster, "Organized Labor and the Marshall Plan," *Political Affairs* 27 (February 1948): 104–8. See also Shannon, *Decline of American Communism*, 393.

19. Quoted in *Time Magazine*, June 7, 1948, 22.

20. Foster's assessment in the wake of the 1948 defeat is in *History of the Communist Party of the United States of America*, 471–72 (quotes on 472). For his later regrets over the policy in the CIO (with no recognition that he bore responsibility for it), see ibid., 491–94. On the importance of the Communist Party's support of Wallace and its opposition to the Marshall Plan in splitting the CIO's center-left coalition, see Levenstein, *Communism, Anti-Communism and the CIO*, 220–27; David Brody, *Workers in Industrial America: Essays on the Twentieth Century Struggle* (New York, 1980), 222–28; and Lichtenstein, *Labor's War at Home*, 235–36.

21. Foster, "Organized Labor and the Marshall Plan," 99–109 (Foster quotes on 99); "Communist Position on the Marshall Plan," statement of the Communist Party, USA, to the Foreign Affairs Committee, House of Representatives, on the proposed European Recovery Program, *Political Affairs* 27 (April 1948): 304–10 (Party quote on 304).

22. Foster, "Organized Labor and the Marshall Plan," 107 (quote), 108.

23. Stanley I. Kutler, *The American Inquisition: Justice and Injustice in the Cold War* (New York, 1982), 153; Belknap, *Cold War Political Justice*; Belknap, "Cold War in the Courtroom," 238–39; Schrecker, *Many Are the Crimes*, 190–96.

24. Ellen Schrecker, "McCarthyism and the Decline, 1945–1950," in *New Studies in the Politics and Culture of U.S. Communism*, ed. Brown et al., 128 (first quote); Schrecker, *Many Are the Crimes*, 237 (second quote).

25. Mary M. Kaufman to William Rogers, U.S. Attorney General, February 29, 1959, fond 615, opis 1, delo 111, listok 2, Foster Papers; Alsop to Medina, November 11, 1948; Eggelston to Medina, November 4, 1948, 28–29, 30–34; Shannon, *Decline of American Communism*, 197.

26. Kutler, *American Inquisition*, 152.

27. Schrecker, *Many Are the Crimes*, 197 (both Foster and Schrecker quotes). On the successful California defense in opposition to Foster's plan, see Healey and Isserman, *Dorothy Healey Remembers*, 133–49.

28. "Speech of William Z. Foster, National Committee Meeting, August 26, 1956," fond 615, opis 1, delo 65, listok 46, Foster Papers; *Sunday Worker*, September 25, 1949, sec. 3 (quotes on 1, 3, 4). Selections from the deposition were published as a pamphlet designed to lay out the Party's position and raise funds for the defense. See Foster, *In Defense of the Communist Party and Its Indicted Leaders*. For discussion of Foster's testimony and his role in the trial, see Johanningsmeier, *Forging American Communism*, 324–28; and Healey and Isserman, *Dorothy Healey Remembers*, 142–43.

29. Kutler, *American Inquisition*, 156–57.

30. Caute, *Great Fear*, 196; Foster, *History of the Communist Party of the United States of America*, 511 (quote).

31. William Z. Foster, "Peoples' Front and Peoples' Democracy," *Political Affairs* 29 (June 1950): 14–31, quoted in Starobin, *American Communism in Crisis*, 207.

32. William Z. Foster, "The Revisionist Crisis in the Communist Party USA, 1945–1948 [1958]," fond 615, opis 1, delo 71, listki 118–20, Foster Papers; Starobin, 219–20, 106–7; Schrecker, *Many Are the Crimes*, 200.

33. Starobin, *American Communism in Crisis*, 196–97.

34. Ibid., 220–22; Healey and Isserman, *Dorothy Healey Remembers*, 129. Foster continued to believe to the end of his life that "during the middle 1950s, for a time it looked as though the United States would go fascist" (William Z. Foster, "The USSR and the USA," *Pravda*, December 2, 1958, fond 615, opis 1, delo 21, listok 8, Foster Papers).

35. Foster quoted in Horne, *Black Liberation/Red Scare*, 252; Healey and Isserman, *Dorothy Healey Remembers*, 142, 143 (last quote).

36. Joseph Starobin to David A. Shannon, January 27, 1959, 7 (first quote), box 2, folder 4, Joseph Starobin Papers, State Historical Society of Wisconsin, Madison; Nelson, Barrett, and Ruck, *Steve Nelson*, 277–97 (remaining quotes on 291 and 288).

37. William Z. Foster, "On the Expulsion of Earl Browder," *Political Affairs* 25 (April 1946): 339–48; William Z. Foster, "One Year of Struggle against Browderism," *Political Affairs*, 25 (September 1946): 771–77 (Foster quote on 771); Bella Dodd, *School for Darkness* (New York, 1954); Samuel A. Darcy to William Z. Foster, June 13, 1945, June 29, 1945 (quotes), box 1, folder 23, Darcy Papers.

38. "Statement of the National Board of the Communist Party on the Recent Expulsions of Vern Smith, Ruth McKenney, Bruce Minton, and William F. Dunne," *Political Affairs* 25 (November 1946): 1011–15; Foster, "On the Expulsion of Earl Browder," 339–48; Foster, "One Year of Struggle against Browderism," 771–77; "San Francisco Memorandum, October 12, 1946," box 1, Dunne Papers; "Statement by Vern Smith to Califor-

nia State Control Commission, C.P., August 15, 1946," box 1, Dunne Papers; Darcy to Foster, June 29, 1945; Harrison George, *The Crisis in the CPUSA* (San Francisco, 1947); "Vern Smith Expelled from the Communist Party," *Daily Worker,* September 20, 1946, 9; "William Dunne Expelled from the Communist Party," *Daily Worker,* September 27, 1946, 4; Shannon, *Decline of American Communism,* 20–23; Starobin, *American Communism in Crisis,* 114–15, 279–80; Foster, *History of the Communist Party of the United States of America,* 484; Scales and Nickson, *Cause at Heart,* 178–80. Several of the left-wingers who were expelled set up opposition groups and published their own papers. On the postexpulsion histories of these leftists, see Shannon, *Decline of American Communism,* 20–22.

39. Starobin, *American Communism in Crisis,* 197–98; Chick Mason, "Sources of the Present Dilemma," *Party Voice,* September 1956, quoted in Howe and Coser, *American Communist Party,* 449; Healey and Isserman, *Dorothy Healey Remembers,* 125.

40. Healey and Isserman, *Dorothy Healey Remembers,* 129–30; John D'Emilio, *Sexual Politics, Sexual Communities: The Making of a Homosexual Minority in America* (Chicago, 1983), 58–70; Shannon, *Decline of American Communism,* 241 (quote). There was some cause for concern about therapy. Some therapists did cooperate with government investigators and academic researchers. See Gabriel Almond, *The Appeals of Communism* (Princeton, N.J., 1954); and Isserman and Healey, *Dorothy Healey Remembers,* 130. Notes and recording disks from Almond's interviews are in the Bell Papers.

41. Foster, *History of the Communist Party of the United States of America,* 478 (quote); Robert Thompson, "Strengthen the Struggle against White Chauvinism," *Political Affairs* 28 (June 1949): 14–28; Pettis Perry, "Destroy the Virus of White Chauvinism," *Political Affairs* 28 (June 1949): 1–14; Pettis Perry, "Next Stage in the Struggle against White Chauvinism," *Political Affairs* 28 (October 1949): 33–46; Pettis Perry, "Press forward the Struggle against White Chauvinism," *Political Affairs* 29 (May 1950): 138–50.

42. William Z. Foster et al., *The Communist Position on the Negro Question* (New York, 1947); Harold Cruse, *The Crisis of the Negro Intellectual* (New York, 1967), 140–44.

43. Foster et al., *Communist Position on the Negro Question,* 14 (first quote); William Z. Foster, "On Self-Determination for the Negro People," *Political Affairs* 25 (June 1946): 549–54 (second quote on 553); William Z. Foster, "On the Question of Negro Self-Determination," *Political Affairs* 26 (January 1947): 54–58. See also Benjamin J. Davis, "Foster's Contributions to the Cause of National and Colonial Liberation," *Political Affairs* 30 (March 1951): 36–50. On the National Board's conflicts over the issue, see Nelson, Barrett, and Ruck, *Steve Nelson,* 288–89.

44. Robert Korstad and Nelson Lichtenstein, "Opportunities Found and Lost: Labor, Radicals, and the Early Civil Rights Movement," *Journal of American History* 75 (December 1988): 786–811; Michael Goldfield, "Race and the CIO: The Possibilities for Racial Egalitarianism during the 1930's and 1940's," *International Labor and Working-Class History* 44 (Fall 1993): 13–32; Montgomery, *Workers' Control in America,* 149–50; John Williamson, "Defend and Extend the Rights of Negro Workers," *Political Affairs* 28 (June 1949): 28–37; Hal Simon, "The Struggle for Jobs and for Negro Rights in the Trade Unions," *Political Affairs* 29 (February 1950): 33–48.

45. Shannon, *Decline of American Communism,* 58–67; Scales and Nickson, *Cause at Heart,* 209–11; Gerald Zahavi, "Passionate Commitments: Race, Sex, and Communism at Schenectady General Electric, 1932–1954," *Journal of American History* 83 (September 1996): 515–48; Healey and Isserman, *Dorothy Healey Remembers,* 126–28.

46. Healey and Isserman, *Dorothy Healey Remembers,* 129; Gil Green, interview by Barrett.

47. March, interview, 20–21; Roger Horowitz, *Black and White, Unite and Fight: A Social History of Industrial Unionism in the Packinghouse Industry* (Urbana, Ill., 1997), 203, 223–27.

48. William Z. Foster, "Left Sectarianism in the Fight for Negro Rights and against White Chauvinism," *Political Affairs* 32 (July 1953): 24 (first quote), 29 (second quote), 25 (third quote); Alex H. Kendrick and Jerome Golden, "Lessons of the Struggle against Opportunism in District 65," *Political Affairs* 32 (June 1953): 26–37; Shannon, *Decline of American Communism,* 260–61; Starobin, *American Communism in Crisis,* 299–300. Foster later revealed that his article was written at the direction of and discussed extensively by the Party's National Board. See "Excerpts from Foster Speech at April NC Meeting, 1956, (Not Delivered)," fond 615, opis 1, delo 65, listok 14, Foster Papers.

49. Aaron, *Writers on the Left,* 397–402; Albert Maltz, "What Shall We Ask of Writers?" *New Masses* 59 (February 12, 1946): 19–22; Albert Maltz, "Moving Forward," *New Masses* 59 (April 9, 1946): 8–10; William Z. Foster, "Elements of a People's Cultural Policy," *New Masses* 59 (April 23, 1946): 6–9.

50. William Z. Foster, "On the Theoretical Work of the Party," *Political Affairs* 27 (April 1948): 319–26 (quotes on 320).

51. Ibid., 321, 322. Betty Gannett's papers at the State Historical Society of Wisconsin, Madison, suggest the effects of Foster's arguments on the organization's program for political education. Foster's own works, as well as Lenin's and Stalin's, loom large.

52. Foster, "Revisionist Crisis in the Communist Party USA, 1945–1948 [1958]," 118; Louis Finger, M.D., to Carl Dorfman, December 14, 1951, fond 615, opis 1, delo 1, listok 38, Foster Papers.

53. Arthur Zipser to James R. Barrett, March 1989, taped responses to taped questions, in author's possession; Gil Green, interview by Barrett; Dorfman to Barrett, taped responses to written questions; Foster memo to Alex Bittelman, Gil Green, and Bob Thompson, box 2, folder 20B, Bittelman Papers; Irving [Potash] to Foster, June 3, 1956, fond 615, opis 1, delo 6, listki 13–15, Foster Papers.

54. Louis Finger to Carl Dorfman, October 28, 1952, fond 615, opis 1, delo 1, listok 40, Foster Papers; Healey and Isserman, *Dorothy Healey Remembers,* 159.

55. William Z. Foster, *Outline Political History of the Americas* (New York, 1951), 12 (first quote); William Z. Foster, "Soviet Stress on History Writing," *Political Affairs* 33 (December 1954): 55–56 (remaining quotes).

56. Central Committee of the C.P.S.U., *History of the Communist Party of the Soviet Union* (Bolsheviks) (Moscow, 1939); Hobsbawm, *Revolutionaries,* 3–10, 11.

57. Charney, *Long Journey,* 137 (first quote), 138 (last quote); Foster, *Twilight of World Capitalism,* 106 (first Foster quote), 107 (second Foster quote). See Foster's contrast be-

tween Browder's appeals to American nationalism in the Party's 1938 constitution and the reassertion of "sound Marxist-Leninist" principles at the emergency convention of July 1945 (Foster, *History of the Communist Party of the United States of America,* 338–39).

58. Foster, *History of the Communist Party of the United States of America,* 439–51 (quotes on 442 and 451).

59. Ibid., 441 (quotes); Starobin, *American Communism in Crisis,* 198, 299.

60. Charney, *Long Journey,* 139.

61. Caute, *Great Fear,* 182, 206.

62. Ibid., 185–86.

63. Brody, *Workers in Industrial America,* 188–98; Nelson Lichtenstein, "From Corporatism to Collective Bargaining: Organized Labor and the Eclipse of Social Democracy in the Postwar Era," in *The Rise and Fall of the New Deal Order, 1930–1980,* ed. Steve Fraser and Gary Gerstle (Princeton, N.J., 1980), 122–52; Montgomery, *Workers' Control in America,* 161–80.

CHAPTER 12: THE FINAL CONFLICT, 1956–61

1. *Daily Worker,* March 1, 1956, 5, March 6, 1956, 5, March 8, 1956, 5, March 9, 1956, 1, March 11, 1956, 10, March 12, 1956, 1 (Dennis quote); Zipser, *Working Class Giant,* 189; N. S. Khrushchev, "Report of the XXth Congress, CPSU," *Political Affairs* 35 (March 1956): 64; William Z. Foster, "Birthday Speech, March 9, 1956," fond 615, opis 1, delo 65, listok 7, Foster Papers.

2. Starobin, *American Communism in Crisis,* 225–28; Nelson, Barrett, and Ruck, *Steve Nelson,* 380–98; Peggy Dennis, *Autobiography of an American Communist,* 220–24.

3. Vojtech Mastny, *The Cold War and Soviet Insecurity: The Stalin Years* (New York, 1996).

4. Foster himself played a role in defusing concerns about the 1930s purge trials. See William Z. Foster, *Questions and Answers on the Piatakov-Radek Trial* (New York, 1937); and Emelian Yaroslavsky, *The Meaning of the Moscow Trials,* introduction by William Z. Foster (New York, 1937).

5. Nelson, Barrett, and Ruck, *Steve Nelson,* 386 (first quote), 386–87 (long quote). For another veteran's recollection of the moment, see Healey and Isserman, *Dorothy Healey Remembers,* 152–55.

6. Isserman, *If I Had a Hammer,* 23 (first quote); Nelson, Barrett, and Ruck, *Steve Nelson,* 391 (second quote), 388 (third quote); Johanningsmeier, *Forging American Communism,* 339.

7. Eugene Dennis, *The Communists Take a New Look* (New York, 1956); Starobin, *American Communism in Crisis,* 3–4.

8. Starobin, *American Communism in Crisis,* 3–4; Healey and Isserman, *Dorothy Healey Remembers,* 152 (quote); John Gates, *Story of an American Communist* (New York, 1958), 165.

9. Gates, *Story of an American Communist,* 166.

10. For examples of Foster's writing for various international journals and for state

radio in Czechoslovakia, Bulgaria, and elsewhere, see Foster to S. Sanakoev, November 18, 1959, fond 615, opis 1, delo 6, listok 49, Foster Papers; V. Ivanov to William Z. Foster, March 30, 1960, ibid., listok 55; and William Z. Foster to Feder Orekov, November 15, 1960, ibid., listok 81. On the translations, see correspondence in ibid., listki 5–19.

11. Foster, "Revisionist Crisis in the Communist Party USA, 1945–1948 [1958]," 35 (first two quotes); William Z. Foster, "The Reevaluation of Stalin's Work," *Daily Worker,* March 16, 1956, 2 (third, sixth, and seventh quotes); "What Was Done to Check Stalin?" *Daily Worker,* April 2, 1956, 4 (fourth and fifth quotes); William Z. Foster, *History of the Three Internationals: The World Socialist Movements from 1848 to the Present* (New York, 1955), 524–25 (final quote). See also William Z. Foster, "How the Stalin Cult Developed," *Daily Worker,* April 4, 1956, 4; William Z. Foster, "Why the Stalin Revaluation Takes Place at this Time," *Daily Worker,* April 10, 1956, 5; and Foster, *Twilight of World Capitalism,* 21. All *Daily Worker* citations are from clippings, box 32, folder 26, Ganley Papers.

12. William Z. Foster, "Lessons from the Stalin Question," *Daily Worker,* March 28, 1956, 4 (first quote); "Speech of William Z. Foster, National Committee Meeting, August 23, 1956," fond 615, opis 1, delo 65, listok 60 (second quote), Foster Papers.

13. Isserman, *If I Had a Hammer,* 14–22; Starobin, *American Communism in Crisis,* 226; Shannon, *Decline of American Communism,* 303–8; *Draft Resolution for the 16th National Convention of the Communist Party, USA* (New York, 1956); Nelson, Barrett, and Ruck, *Steve Nelson,* 392 (Nelson quote).

14. William Z. Foster, "The Situation in the Communist Party," *Political Affairs* 35 (October 1956): 15–45.

15. William Z. Foster, "On the Party Situation," *Political Affairs* 35 (October 1956): 15, 16, 17.

16. Charney, *Long Journey,* 131, 136–37 (first two quotes on 137); Shannon, *Decline of American Communism,* 12; Starobin, *American Communism In Crisis,* 280 (Dortman quote).

17. Charney, *Long Journey,* 282–83 (quote on 282); Horne, *Black Liberation/Red Scare,* 144–45, 275–78 (quote on 278). Foster's FOIA file shows frequent meetings with Davis throughout the 1950s.

18. Duberman, *Paul Robeson,* 419–22, 444, 454, 712 (quote); William Z. Foster, *The Negro People in American History* (New York, 1954), 515, 524, 525, 563. Foster's FOIA file documents several visits with Robeson in the mid-fifties.

19. *Daily Worker,* November 6, 1956, 3.

20. Quoted in Scales and Nickson, *Cause at Heart,* 313.

21. For the Hungarian Revolution and the Soviet invasion, see Charles Gati, *Hungary and the Soviet Bloc* (Durham, N.C., 1986).

22. *Daily Worker,* November 21, 1956; Foster's resolution, fond 615, opis 1, delo 65, listok 72 (quote), Foster Papers; Nelson, Barrett, and Ruck, *Steve Nelson,* 189–90; Healey and Isserman, *Dorothy Healey Remembers,* 161; National Committee, CPUSA, "On the Events in Hungary," *Political Affairs* 35 (December 1956): 1–5; Shannon, *Decline of*

American Communism, 309–17. See also Foster's glowing review of Herbert Aptheker, *The Truth about Hungary* (New York, 1957), a justification of the Soviet invasion, in *Daily Worker,* July 9, 1957, 6.

23. William Z. Foster, "For Marxism-Leninism in a Changing World," *Political Affairs* 35 (November–December 1956), 62, quoted in Shannon, *Decline of American Communism,* 323; Foster to Paul Robeson, November 27, 1956, quoted in Duberman, *Paul Robeson,* 444.

24. Nemmy Sparks, "National Secretariat Discussion, 1956–1957," notes, box 6, folder 10, Nemmy Sparks Papers, Archives of Labor and Urban Affairs, Walter P. Reuther Library, Wayne State University, Detroit; Healey and Isserman, *Dorothy Healey Remembers,* 160.

25. Maurice Isserman, "1956 Generation: An Alternative Approach to the History of American Communism," *Radical America* 14 (March–April 1980): 43–51; Nelson, Barrett, and Ruck, *Steve Nelson,* xiv, xvi; Ottanelli, *Communist Party of the United States,* 83–105; Klehr, *Heyday of American Communism,* 167–206; George Watt, interview by Maurice Isserman, January 7, 1978, in Maurice Isserman's possession, quoted in Barrett, "Americanization from the Bottom Up," 1007–8. The typical Communist leader of the mid-1950s had entered the Party early in life, usually as a teenager or young adult, in the early 1930s and came of age during the Popular Front era. Foster's trajectory was quite different. See Robert T. Holt, "Age as a Factor in the Recruitment of Communist Leadership," *American Political Science Review* 48 (June 1954): 486–99.

26. Typescript report of Bernard Rosenberg, Fund for the Republic, quoted in Shannon, *Decline of American Communism,* 324.

27. *Proceedings (Abridged) of the Sixteenth National Convention, Communist Party, U.S.A.,* New York, February 9–12, 1957 (New York, 1957), 47–57 (quotes on 47 and 55).

28. Ibid, 58, 59.

29. Ibid, 60–61, 62.

30. Ibid, 64.

31. Ibid, 66.

32. Ibid, 66, 67 (quote).

33. Richmond, *Long View from the Left,* 380 (quote); Roy Finch, "An Observer Reports on the Communist Convention," *Liberation,* March 1957, 4–6. Compare Bert Cochran, "The Communist Convention," *American Socialist,* March 1957, 5–7; A. J. Muste, "The Convention and Democratic Socialism," *Liberation,* March 1957, 7–10.

34. Healey and Isserman, *Dorothy Healey Remembers,* 164.

35. Dennis quoted in Peggy Dennis, *Autobiography of an American Communist,* 232; Ben Davis, William Z. Foster, and Charles Loman to National Administrative Committee, Moscow, March 26, 1957, fond 615, opis 1, delo 7, listki 1–5, Foster Papers; *New York Post,* March 15, 1957, 2; agent's report, June 3, 1957, 27, document 61-330-986, Foster FOIA file.

36. Agent's report to the Director, May 17, 1957, document 61-330-978, Foster FOIA file; *Daily Worker,* May 6, 1957, 3; *New York Times,* May 11, 1957, 12.

37. William Z. Foster, "The Party Crisis and the Way Out, I," *Political Affairs* 36 (De-

cember 1957): 47–61; William Z. Foster, "On the Party Situation and the Way Out, II," *Political Affairs* 37 (January 1958): 49–65.

38. Horne, *Black Liberation/Red Scare,* 278.

39. Nelson, Barrett, and Ruck, *Steve Nelson,* 385 (first and second quotes), 393 (last quote); Charney, *Long Journey,* 301; Isserman, *If I Had a Hammer,* 25–30 (quote on 26); Healey and Isserman, *Dorothy Healey Remembers,* 164–66.

40. William Z. Foster, "Differing Estimates of the US Communists' Convention," *Daily Worker,* June 12, 1957, 4.

41. Foster, "USSR and the USA," 18 (first quote); Foster, "Revisionist Crisis in the Communist Party USA, 1945–1948 [1958]," 109 (second quote).

42. Shannon, *Decline of American Communism,* 359–60; William Z. Foster to National Committee, CPUSA, May 26, 1958, fond 615, opis 1, delo 7, listok 15, Foster Papers.

43. Dr. Riley's reports are quoted in Kaufman to Rogers, February 29, 1959; Elizabeth Gurley Flynn, "A Visit with William Z. Foster," *Worker,* January 18, 1958, 5.

44. William Z. Foster to National Committee, CPUSA, May 26, 1958, fond 615, opis 1, delo 7, listki 7–25, Foster Papers; ibid., December 12, 1958, listki 27–31; ibid., September 21, 1959, listki 25–27; ibid., November 1, 1959, listok 28; William Z. Foster to Secretariat and Gus Hall, general secretary, February 15, 1960, ibid., listki 58–64.

45. Foster to National Committee, CPUSA, May 26, 1958, 7; deposition of Harry Epstein before United States District Court of the Southern District of New York, September 8, 1959, in possession of Sandra Epstein, Brookline, Mass.; Harry Epstein, M.D., to Whom It May Concern, January 26, 1959, in possession of Sandra Epstein; William Z. Foster, "A Letter to Mao Tse Tung," *Political Affairs* 38 (March 1959): 22 (quote).

46. Anna Bebrits, "A Visit to the Sickbed of Comrade Foster," enclosed in memo to Pratt Byrd, second secretary of legation, Budapest, to State Department, October 30, 1959, document 61–330–NR, Foster FOIA file. Foster's correspondence with Mao was published in Chinese and distributed as a pamphlet throughout China by the Peoples' Publishing House, *Letter from Comrade William Z. Foster to Comrade Mao Tse-Tung* (Peking, 1959), 4 (quotes). Foster had shown an increasingly strong affinity for the Chinese Revolution and for Mao throughout the postwar era. His own party leadership "had many essentially Maoist features," Joseph Starobin wrote. "Death had spared him the excruciating choice between Moscow and Peking." Joseph R. Starobin, "North America," in *International Communism after Khrushchev,* ed. Leopold Labedz (Cambridge, Mass., 1965), 148, 149.

47. W. Z. Foster to V. Pasek, Prague, Czechoslovakia, October 2, 1959, box 1, folder 3, Arnold Johnson Papers, Tamiment Institute Library, New York University; Dr. V. Kharitonovich to W. Z. Foster, October 1, 1959, fond 615, opis 1, delo 8, listok 6, Foster Papers; Trade Union of Hungarian Physicians and Health Care Workers to W. Z. Foster, telegram, October 18, 1959, fond 615, opis 1, delo 8, listok 20, Foster Papers; Dr. A. Aslan to W. Z. Foster, November 6, 1959, fond 615, opis 1, delo 8, listok 52, Foster Papers; deposition of Epstein; Tiffany Lawyer, M.D., to Harry Epstein, M.D., New York, October 21, 1960, in the possession of Sandra Epstein, Brookline, Mass.; *New York Times,* July 9, 1959, 20, October 22, 1959, 16, October 11, 1960, 48, December 3, 1960, 6.

48. William Z. Foster to CPUSA, Gus Hall, General Secretary, December 5, 1960, fond 615, opis 1, delo 7, listki 86–88 (quote on 87; emphasis added), Foster Papers.

49. U.S. Embassy, Moscow, to U.S. Department of State, telegram, January 17, 1961, document 61-330-?, Foster FOIA file; U.S. Embassy, the Hague, to U.S. Department of State, telegram, January 18, 1961, document 61-330-1711, Foster FOIA file.

50. U.S. Embassy, Moscow, to U.S. Department of State, telegram, February 28, 1961, document 61-330-1740, Foster FOIA file; *New York Times,* January 11, 1961, 6, March 12, 1961, 70; excerpts from *Tass, World Marxist Review, l'Humanite,* and other papers with honors and birthday greetings in agent's report, May 12, 1961, 1–11, document 61-330-1723, Foster FOIA file; *Morning Freiheit,* 6 (quote), document 61-330-1723, Foster FOIA file.

51. William Z. Foster to Esther, Sylvia, and Joe, Moscow, March 25, 1961 (quote), fond 615, opis 1, delo 5, listok 85, Foster Papers; Foster to "My Dearest Esther," Moscow, April 4, 1961, ibid., listok 87.

52. Bill to Esther, May 1, 1961, fond 615, opis 1, delo 5, listok 88, Foster Papers. For Foster's work routine, see *Peoples' World,* March 11, 1961, in ibid.; and interview, *Pravda,* February 17, 1961, reproduced in U.S. Department of State, memo, March 1, 1961, document 61-330-1717, Foster FOIA file.

53. William Z. Foster to Harry Epstein, February 2, 1961, July 6, 1961, in possession of Sandra Epstein, Brookline, Mass.

54. Healey and Isserman, *Dorothy Healey Remembers,* 174–75.

55. Agent's report, September 19, 1961, document 61-330-1742, Foster FOIA file; agent's report, October 19, 1961, document 61-330-1745, Foster FOIA file; *Daily Worker,* September 24, 1961, 3 (quotes); *New York Times,* September 19, 1961, 39. Estimates for attendance at the service range from the *New York Times'* 900 to the *Daily Worker's* 1,200.

56. *Pravda,* September 3, 4, 1961, excerpted in U.S. Embassy, Moscow, to U.S. Department of State, memo, September 5, 1961, document 61-330-1740, Foster FOIA file; *New York Times,* September 2, 1961, 15, September 4, 1961, 15, September 7, 1961, 35.

CONCLUSION

1. Francis Fukuyama, "The End of History?" *National Interest* 16 (Summer 1989): 3–18.

2. Eley, "International Communism in the Heyday of Stalin," 92. On the failure of much of the research on American Communism to appreciate fully the international dimension, see Ottanelli, *Communist Party of the United States,* 3–4 and passim; Draper, "Popular Front Revisited," 79–81; and Malcolm Sylvers, "The Communist International and the CPUSA: Channels of Influence, Political Consequences, Historiographical Discussion," 1991, paper in author's possession. Some of the newer studies interpreting particular periods of the Party's history do document relations with the Comintern and the Soviet Communist Party, but even these tend to focus primarily on domestic influences, aim for a more detailed picture of everyday Party life, and ascribe

less influence to these international forces than is probably due. See, for example, Isserman, *Which Side Were You On?* Ottanelli, *Communist Party of the United States;* and Buhle, *Marxism in the USA.*

3. Klehr, Haynes, and Anderson, *Soviet World of American Communism,* 3. An exchange of letters in the *New York Review of Books,* August 15, 1985, suggests the tenor of the debate.

4. See, for example, Haynes, *Red Scare or Red Menace?* and Powers, *Not Without Honor.* Ellen Schrecker documents the political devastation wrought by the repression in *Many Are the Crimes.*

Index

JAMES R. BARRETT is a professor of history and the chair of the Department of History at the University of Illinois at Urbana-Champaign. He is the coauthor of *Steve Nelson, American Radical* (1981) and the author of *Work and Community in the Jungle: Chicago's Packinghouse Workers, 1894–1922* (1987) and numerous articles and essays.

Typeset in 9/13 Stone Serif
with Palatino display
Designed by Paula Newcomb
Composed by Keystone Typesetting, Inc.
Manufactured by Thomson-Shore, Inc.

University of Illinois Press
1325 South Oak Street
Champaign, IL 61820–6903
www.press.uillinois.edu